William Shakespeare and 21st-Century Culture, Politics, and Leadership

NEW HORIZONS IN LEADERSHIP STUDIES

Series Editor: Joanne B. Ciulla, *Academic Director, Institute for Ethical Leadership and Professor of Leadership Ethics, Department of Management and Global Business, Rutgers Business School, USA*

This important series is designed to make a significant contribution to the development of leadership studies. This field has expanded dramatically in recent years and the series provides an invaluable forum for the publication of high-quality works of scholarship and shows the diversity of leadership issues and practices around the world.

The main emphasis of the series is on the development and application of new and original ideas in leadership studies. It pays particular attention to leadership in business, economics and public policy and incorporates the wide range of disciplines which are now part of the field. Global in its approach, it includes some of the best theoretical and empirical work with contributions to fundamental principles, rigorous evaluations of existing concepts and competing theories, historical surveys and future visions.

Titles in the series include:

William Shakespeare and 21st-Century Culture, Politics, and Leadership

Bard Bites

Edited by

Kristin M. S. Bezio

Associate Professor of Leadership Studies, University of Richmond, USA

Anthony Presti Russell

Associate Professor of English and Comparative Literature, University of Richmond, USA

NEW HORIZONS IN LEADERSHIP STUDIES

 Edward Elgar
PUBLISHING

Cheltenham, UK • Northampton, MA, USA

Published by
Edward Elgar Publishing Limited
The Lypiatts
15 Lansdown Road
Cheltenham
Glos GL50 2JA
UK

Edward Elgar Publishing, Inc.
William Pratt House
9 Dewey Court
Northampton
Massachusetts 01060
USA

A catalogue record for this book
is available from the British Library

Library of Congress Control Number: 2021932423

This book is available electronically in the **Elgar**online
Political Science and Public Policy subject collection
http://dx.doi.org/10.4337/9781839106422

ISBN 978 1 83910 641 5 (cased)
ISBN 978 1 83910 642 2 (eBook)

Printed and bound by CPI Group (UK) Ltd, Croydon, CR0 4YY

Contents

Figures

Contributors

Kristin M. S. Bezio is Associate Professor of Leadership Studies at the Jepson School of Leadership Studies, University of Richmond. Her publications include *Staging Power in Tudor and Stuart English History Plays: History, Political Thought, and the Redefinition of Sovereignty*; "From Rome to Tyre to London: Shakespeare's *Pericles*, Leadership, Anti-Absolutism, and English Exceptionalism"; and "Muslims Are the New Jesuits: What We Can Learn about Leadership and Modern Islamophobia from Shakespeare's England" in *Leadership, Populism, and Resistance*, a volume she co-edited with George R. Goethals.

Melissa Caldwell is Professor of English at Eastern Illinois University. Her work has appeared in *Studies in Philology* and *The Seventeenth Century*. Her first monograph, *Skepticism and Belief in Early Modern England* (Routledge, 2016), focuses on the intersections between religious discourse and the history of skepticism in sixteenth- and seventeenth-century England.

Maria Carrig is Professor Emerita of English and Theater at Carthage College. Her work focuses on Shakespeare and Renaissance drama, as well as magic and witchcraft beliefs of the early modern period. She also writes about contemporary theater and culture for publications in the Chicago area.

Samantha Dressel is Instructional Assistant Professor at Chapman University, where she teaches courses ranging from an early-world-literature survey course through post-colonial speculative fiction, and everything in between. She has been published in *Quidditas* and *Early Modern Literary Studies.*

Ryan Farrar is Professor of English at Collin College in Frisco, Texas. He has taught across the Southern United States, including Texas, Louisiana, Arizona, and Florida. He completed a PhD in English literature in 2014 at the University of Louisiana at Lafayette and has research interests in English Renaissance drama and utopian literature. He has published an article exploring the relationship between utopia and *As You Like It* in the *Journal of Utopian Studies* and most recently contributed a chapter to the book *Utopia and Dystopia in the Age of Trump*, drawing analogies between Katherine Burdekin's novel *Swastika Night* (1937) and Trumpism.

Peter Iver Kaufman is Professor Emeritus at the University of North

Carolina, Chapel Hill and Professor of Leadership Studies at the University of Richmond. In 2013, he published *Religion Around Shakespeare*. His most recent book (2020) is *Agamben, Arendt, Christianity, and the Dark Arts of Civilization*. An earlier version of the chapter on *Coriolanus* presented here was delivered at the United States Military Academy at West Point.

Kayode Gboyega Kofoworola is a freelance editor, poet, critic, and teacher. He holds a PhD degree in literature from Ahmadu Bello University, Zaria, Nigeria and is presently a member of the teaching faculty at the Department of English, University of Lagos, Nigeria. Some of his published works include "The Court Jester in Nigerian Drama" in David Robb (ed.), *Clowns, Fools and Picaros: Popular Forms in Theatre, Fiction and Film* (2007) and "Landmines and Booby-traps: Multilingualism and Translation in Nigeria" in Micheala Wolf (ed.), *Übersetzen–Translating–Traduire: Towards a "Social Turn"?* (2006). He is a fellow of the Institute for Critical Social Inquiry and a member of the American Comparative Literature Association and Lagos Studies Association. His areas of interest include African and African American literature, translation and publishing studies, children's literature, and cultural, media, and film studies.

Fumiaki Konno is Senior Assistant Professor at Meiji University (Tokyo) in the Faculty of Commerce. Publications on Shakespeare include "Charles Kean's Edition of *Henry VIII*: A Study of its Base Text," *The Bulletin of Arts and Sciences, Meiji University* no. 524 (2017); "*King Richard II* (1857) and Chronicles," *The Bulletin of Arts and Sciences, Meiji University* no. 533 (2018); and co-edited with Tetsuhito Motoyama and Rosalind Fielding, *Re-imagining Shakespeare in Contemporary Japan: A Selection of Japanese Theatrical Adaptations of Shakespeare* (Bloomsbury, 2021).

Jess Landis is Associate Professor in the College of Liberal Arts and Social Sciences at Franklin Pierce University in Rindge, NH. She teaches in the English, Composition, and Women in Leadership programs. Her research focuses on subversive representations of gender and sexuality in early modern English drama. Her work has appeared in *Medieval and Renaissance Drama in England* and the *Journal of the Wooden O*, among other outlets.

Tetsuhito Motoyama is Professor at Waseda University (Tokyo) in the Faculty of Law. Publications on Shakespeare include: co-edited with Hiromi Fuyuki, *The Text Made Visible: Shakespeare on the Page, Stage, and Screen* (Sairyūsha, 2011); co-authored with Kaoru Edo, "Strange Oeillades No More: *The Three Daughters of Lear* from the Tokyo Shakespeare Company's 'Shakespeare through the Looking-glass'," *Shakespeare* 9 no. 4 (2013); and co-edited with Rosalind Fielding and Fumiaki Konno, *Re-imagining*

Shakespeare in Contemporary Japan: A Selection of Japanese Theatrical Adaptations of Shakespeare (Bloomsbury, 2021).

Debaditya Mukhopadhyay is Assistant Professor of English at Manikchak College, affiliated with the University of Gourbanga, India. He is pursuing his PhD on spy fiction from Rabindra Bharati University. His primary areas of interest are popular literature and films, myths, adaptations, and theater. His chapters "What Is Beauty, What Is Beast? The Edutainment Value of Bill Condon's *Beauty and the Beast*" and "The Temple of Orientalism" have been published, respectively, in *Parenting Through Pop Culture*, edited by J. L. Schatz, and *Excavating Indiana Jones*, edited by Randy Laist.

Katey Roden is Assistant Professor of English at Gonzaga University, where she also teaches in Women's and Gender Studies and serves as the director of an interdisciplinary digital humanities initiative. Her book project, *Supplement to the Soul: Disability, Devotion, and the Prosthetic Text in Early Modern England*, traces how somatic expressions in poetry, drama, pamphlet prose, and sermons reveal culturally constructed stigmas attached to non-normative bodies as well as sustained interest in traversing contemporary constructions of embodied states, like disability and gender, within socially acceptable reformation frameworks. A portion of this project will appear in the article "A Fruitless, Female Body: Disability and Devotion in An Collins's *Divine Songs and Meditacions* (1653)," forthcoming in the fall 2020 issue of *Early Modern Women: An Interdisciplinary Journal*.

Anthony Presti Russell is Associate Professor of English and Comparative Literature at the School of Arts and Sciences, University of Richmond. His comparative and interdisciplinary research in early modern studies focuses on the relationship between magic, literature, and philosophy; the construction of authenticity in lyric poetry; Italian art criticism; and Shakespeare and adaptation. Among his publications are "Spirits, Vitality, and Creation in the Poetics of Tommaso Campanella and John Donne" in *The Invention of Discovery, 1500–1700*; "'Sans artifice est ma simplicité': Sincérité et Vertu dans les *Regrets* et *Astrophil and Stella*" in *La Valeur des Lettres à la Renaissance. Débats et Réflexions autour de la Vertu de la Littérature*; "Portia Goes to Washington: Shakespeare and Judge Kavanaugh," in *Forum Italicum*; and "'La forza della virtù': Vasari on Skill and Holiness in the Lives of Fra Angelico and Fra Filippo Lippi" in *I Tatti Studies in the Italian Renaissance*. He is currently working on a monograph entitled *Performing Life: Grace, Vitality, and the Miracle of Art in Vasari's Vite*.

Raphael Seligmann is an independent scholar in Richmond, Virginia, where he works in the financial services industry and creates a lot of business proposals in PowerPoint. He has published scholarly articles on music in the plays of Thomas Middleton and on Middleton's *The Roaring Girl*. He is also a musician and founder of an early music ensemble, which in 2019 performed an original opera, *MINERVA: Times Change*, for which he wrote the libretto. He earned his PhD in Renaissance literature from Brandeis University in 1997.

Acknowledgments

We would like to thank all the scholars who participated in this volume for their contributions, as well as for their patience and dedication to this project in the midst of the COVID-19 pandemic. In addition, we wish to thank the editors and editorial team at Edward Elgar (including Alan Sturmer), and the New Horizons in Leadership Series Editor, Joanne Ciulla, for accepting the volume. We are grateful to Cassie Price for her careful eye for detail, and to Dean Sandra Peart and the Jepson School of Leadership Studies and Dean Patrice Rankin and the University of Richmond College of Arts and Sciences for their professional support. Anthony Russell would like to express a particular debt of gratitude to his always remarkable wife, friend, and colleague, Lidia Radi. Kristin Bezio is especially grateful to her husband, Kirk, for his support. Finally, we would like to thank the rest of our friends and family for their patience and understanding as we put together this volume during a time of global, political, and social crises.

Introduction. "I that please some, try all": Shakespeare this time

Anthony Presti Russell and Kristin M. S. Bezio

Triumph, my *Britain*, thou hast one to show,
To whom all scenes of *Europe* homage owe.
He was not of an age but for all time!
(Ben Jonson, "To the Memory of My beloved, the Author, Mr. *William Shakespear*")[1]

When Ben Jonson celebrated Shakespeare's timeless appeal in the prefatory materials to the *First Folio* edition of the Bard's works, he used the language of conquest. Because Shakespeare's plays had managed to break free from the limitations of his "age," Britain had triumphed over the rest of Europe. There's a bit of a paradox here. The British Shakespeare prevailed over his rivals by creating works that transcended the specific time and place of their making. In creating art that represents the universal essence and experience of humankind, Shakespeare had scored a victory for Britain by erasing Britishness in his works.

In the ensuing four centuries, Shakespeare has become an almost ubiquitous presence in the cultures not just of England, America, and the West, but of the world. Given the historical fact that Shakespeare's theater (from 1599 until its unfortunate conflagration in 1613) was presciently named the Globe, it seems particularly appropriate for us to consider the global and trans-historical reach of Shakespeare's works not only with respect to the creation and study of theater, literature, and art, but also in relation to our changing perspectives on leadership, politics, and social justice.

Shakespeare criticism of the past 50 years or so has insistently challenged Jonson's kind of praise. In the first place, it has questioned the very idea that any work of art can be disassociated from the specific historical circumstances—political, economic, cultural—out of which it emerges. Moreover, twentieth- and twenty-first-century thinkers have also critiqued the very notion of a universal humanity that transcends cultural or linguistic differences. The reality, many have claimed, is that universalizing notions of "man" or of the "human" experience have reflected the values and ideologies of Western white patriarchy. As a correlate to this, critics have also argued that claims for the "greatest" art (Shakespeare, Dante, Michelangelo, etc.) as timeless have in reality served to canonize a narrow range of works, usually by Western white men. From this perspective, the idea of "timelessness" has functioned to reinforce the dominance in the world of patriarchal and Western values. Shakespeare, after all, was a required part of the curriculum in colonial schools in both India and South Africa. "Tri'umph, my Britain," indeed.

It is worth pointing out, however, that at the very moment that Shakespeare scholars were rightly demystifying facile assumptions about the Bard's supremacy, they were also reaping the professional benefits of their particular appropriations of his work. They themselves helped to inflate the Shakespeare name and industry. Indeed, whatever one may think about Jonsonian celebrations of Shakespearean exceptionalism, since Shakespeare's death his works have continued to be performed, imitated, consulted, referenced, adapted, and appropriated across a remarkable range of disciplinary and artistic practices across the globe. In the United States, for example, Shakespeare was the intellectual backbone for the development of theater and culture from the Republic's very inception. As James Shapiro has noted, Shakespeare was performed and referenced across the centuries in defense of a wide variety of political standpoints: Ulysses S. Grant was cast as Desdemona in a Union camp rendition of *Othello*; *Othello* was used by both abolitionists and anti-miscegenation activists (including John Quincy Adams) to support their viewpoints; and both Abraham Lincoln and John Wilkes Booth made explicit reference to Shakespeare's works (*Macbeth* and *Julius Caesar*, in particular) defending their positions on secession.[2] In the past 50 years, the Shakespeare phenomenon has only grown. The "Globe to Globe" festival, created in tandem with the 2012 Olympics in Britain, was one sensational manifestation of his ubiquity, as theater companies across the world staged, in their native languages, their particular visions of Shakespeare's plays, including a Maori *Troilus and Cressida*, a Hindi *Twelfth Night*, and a Japanese *Coriolanus*. From Hollywood to the BBC to Bollywood, film and television adaptations of Shakespeare's plays have also proliferated in recent years, as have adult, young adult, and graphic novels more or less loosely based on his stories and characters. In this context, one might be tempted to sympathize with Terence Hawkes's assessment of contemporary Shakespeare as an

International Superstar: an undeniably 'modern dress', shape-shifting, boundary-blurring Bard who, anchored strategically in his home town, nonetheless readily breaks those bonds, to float vacuously up and away as a force for a nebulous and undefined freedom: his stock-in trade the dispensation of gaudy pop-star favours; peace, tolerance, and love, to be pinned promiscuously to the chests of the self-applauding. This Shakespeare somehow comes to be equated, less with a firmly grounded Englishness, than with a cloudy, portable, one-size-fits-all, transatlantic Goodness.[3]

An International Superstar he has indeed become, and in many cases this stardom is closely linked to corporate profit. And yet, one should hesitate before acceding to this deflating skepticism. In a now notorious statement, Harold Bloom claimed some years ago that "he [Shakespeare] has become the first universal author, replacing the Bible in the secularized consciousness."[4] We may wish to resist Bloom's affirmation of Shakespeare's universality, echoing Jonson's, and yet the comparison of his collected works to the Bible is worthy of further consideration. The "Old" and "New" Testaments have permeated and continue to permeate Western and non-Western cultures, regardless of what one thinks of these works. They have been interpreted, reinterpreted, and overinterpreted in different times and different places; they have been historicized and de-historicized; some affirm that these texts reveal universal truths, some that they do not; but they have penetrated the language(s) of believer, agnostic, and unbeliever across the globe. It is difficult, in other words, to speak and think apart from these texts, whatever inherent value we choose to assign to them.

From this perspective, Bloom's analogy—absent his vision of one set of texts agonistically replacing another—may indeed be of use. Shakespeare's ascent to global stardom is due to any number of factors, including the undeniable success of his plays in Elizabethan and Jacobean England; his canonization in the English literary tradition; the hegemonic drive of Western white culture manifested most clearly in British colonialism; the identification of Shakespeare with high-brow culture in the United States and other English-speaking countries; the integration of his works—to this day—in secondary schooling; the appropriation of his works by Hollywood and Broadway; and, of course, ongoing affirmations of his unique excellence as poet and playwright. But whatever the reasons, it cannot be denied that Shakespeare and his plays—the stories and especially his characters—have become a part of the "language" that increasing numbers of "us" across the globe speak, even if we've never read a word of his. Hamlet's "to be or not to be"; Romeo's and Juliet's yearnings; Macbeth's nihilism; Lear's sorrows; Othello's self-doubt; Richard III's gleeful dastardliness. From South Africa, to Japan, to Italy, to India, to the United States, they have become shared reference points frequently accessed to define, interpret, re-interpret, or gain perspective on our own experiences. This is neither good nor bad, nor does it imply that the experiences in question are universally shared. Indeed, perhaps the very openness of Shakespeare's plays to a multiplicity of readings and meanings may have something to do with their susceptibility to appropriation. Like the Scriptures, Shakespeare's works have traveled through time not because they are timeless, but because they so often seem timely to particular groups at particular moments. Whatever inherent value an individual may wish to assign to these texts, people across the globe have chosen and continue to choose to appropriate Shakespeare as part of the language they speak.

This anthology, too, is a kind of appropriation of Shakespeare, insofar as his works serve as a springboard for analyses, reflections, and critiques of contemporary leadership, politics, and culture across the globe. While not advocating Jonson's or Bloom's claims about Shakespeare's timelessness or universality, we believe that there is a heuristic value in participating in the ongoing investigations and conversations that his plays continue to stimulate. Huang and Rivlin remind us that the work of appropriation "is valuable—not for reinstating Shakespeare as some kind of universal translator—but for generating sites of discussion between otherwise strongly divergent frameworks of understanding."[5] In this anthology, those diverse frameworks include currently polarizing debates about authoritarianism, populism, and democracy; immigration, national boundaries, and local identities; gender and race; and sexual aggression against women. All of these, in different ways, deal with the extreme pressure placed recently upon the very ideas of truth and facts. Of course, we should not look to Shakespeare's works for answers to our questions or problems. "It is precisely in revealing the limits of our truth claims," writes one critic, "that Shakespeare remains significant."[6] But if his works can provoke constructive dialogue about the problems that haunt us today, then they can perhaps help us achieve a greater and more empathic awareness of the desires, motives, and prejudices that lead us and others to construct competing truths. This kind of awareness, of course, is fundamental to good leadership.

"THOU CAM'ST TO BITE THE WORLD": SHAKESPEARE AS PROVOCATEUR

In recent decades, it has become almost a truism in leadership studies that leadership requires—and thrives upon—storytelling.[7] The creation of narratives is an inherently human impulse, one which defines and is defined by the civilizations out of which those narratives arise. It can hardly be surprising, then, to find that master storytellers occupy prominent positions in society, helping to further define and even transform the ways we think about ourselves, our cultures, and our leaders. Since Shakespeare has been anointed as one such master, scholars of leadership, history, and politics have frequently turned to his works, just as have creative artists and literary scholars. Our word "leader," in fact, derives from the Old English *liðan*, or "to travel." In its original meaning, a leader is a traveler who guides his followers along a shared journey. If Shakespeare is a kind of time traveler, then we may perhaps also view him as a leader who, for a host of complex and sometimes contradictory reasons, has become one important point of reference in our progress toward an always uncertain future. Albeit in vastly different contexts, we continue to choose his stories and characters as conduits to meaning, as provocations to read ourselves. A provocation is literally a "calling forth"; it is what the best leaders do when they manage to stimulate in their followers a new or renewed sense of purpose and identity, and in so doing, to stimulate them to action that can change the world for the better. This anthology responds to Shakespeare's provocations as calls to know ourselves and our diverse social, political, and cultural contexts more fully (though always imperfectly) and to consider what kinds of people we need as leaders to enact that knowledge constructively.

There is much more nuance that we might derive from the complexity of Shakespeare's works than simple character studies of fictional (or fictionalized) leaders. The plays also offer critiques of social movements and policy decisions and lay claim to arguments for social justice, toleration, and citizen participation. Further, the afterlives of those works—modern films, television series, and stage productions—convey political and social perspectives that seek to reorient Shakespeare's original language and ideas within a contemporary framework, often reshaping words and values to reflect more critically on the global contexts of the twenty-first century.

It therefore behooves scholars of leadership to take a broader approach to the vastness and heterogeneity of the Shakespearean canon; in this volume, we advocate for the many "Shakespeares" that lay claim to political and social relevance across the globe, from Japan, Kashmir, and Nigeria, to England and the United States. The "Shakespeares" we engage here may require us to consider the original contexts of Shakespeare's England, drawing connections between the historical milieu of the sixteenth and early seventeenth centuries and our own; other "Shakespeares" will include looser modern appropriations into film, stage, and television of the original plays and translations and modifications of text and performance into different languages and cultures. In our approach to Shakespeare's works, we not only examine the examples offered to us by the central figures of the plays, but we also engage with the multiple discourses and meanings encoded in the texts and productions of the plays. We make use of literary analysis and historical context in order to suggest how the ideas and perspectives articulated in these works are still relevant to contemporary socio-political debates, and we use the evidence of these "Shakespeares" to provoke reflection on the nature of politics and leadership that might be undertaken by both leaders themselves and those who choose—or refuse—to follow them. In his introduction to *Presentist Shakespeares*, Terence Hawkes urges scholars not to neglect the principal reason for our engagement with compelling works of literature from the past:

> We can never, finally, evade the present. And if it's always and only the present that makes the past speak, it speaks always and only to – and about – ourselves. It follows that the first duty of a credible presentist criticism must be to acknowledge

that the questions we ask of any literary text will inevitably be shaped by our own concerns, even when those include what we call 'the past'.[8]

In this spirit, our anthology aims—perhaps with somewhat unorthodox transparency—to engage Shakespeare with questions that reflect our urgent concerns. That said, this volume is not a manual or guide for using Shakespeare to conduct leadership training nor a key to unlock a mysterious "Shakespearean style" of leadership. Rather, we appropriate Shakespeare in order to carry on his commitment to holding, "as 'twere, the mirror up to nature" (*Ham.* 3.2.21–2), to seeing ourselves more clearly.[9] It is never easy to do so, and in this sense, the Bard can "bite" as he pricks us into a sometimes-painful consciousness.

We have arranged this anthology into four sections—"Performance," "Truth," "Resistance," and "Freedom"—intended to highlight problems or issues of topical relevance that Shakespeare's plays and their adaptations can help us reflect on. In the first section ("Performance"), our authors interrogate the relations between politics, rhetoric, performance, and power. Is power always "performed," and in what ways might such performances be evaluated as constructive or toxic? In Caldwell's reading, *Richard II* provokes us to think about the relationship between performance, leadership, and civic activism, while Farrar examines *Macbeth*'s evocation of linguistic equivocation or dissembling as relevant to our understanding of political "theater" today. Kaufman also addresses the problem of politics and performance in *Coriolanus* (and a recent film adaptation) by considering what role personal sincerity and integrity should have in establishing an affective and effective relationship with one's followers.

In the second section ("Truth"), the chapters share a concern with the knowability and value of truth or facts in the public arena. Russell examines *Macbeth* and two recent adaptations of the play (the film *Scotland, PA* and the television series *Breaking Bad*) in the context of the often false prophecies about the American Dream promulgated by politicians, while Roden examines the truth-telling "wise fools" in *King Lear* in order to question our contemporary readiness to receive facts. Dressel develops this theme in her readings of *Othello*, Boyle's scientific writings, and current political discourse by reminding us that truth is always mediated by language and rhetoric.

In the third section ("Resistance"), the focus will be on strategies for resisting abuses of power. For Landis, *Much Ado About Nothing* sheds light on the problem of belief posed by women's claims of sexual aggression in the #MeToo movement. Mukhopadhyay traces how Shakespeare has been appropriated by the film *Haider* (an adaptation of *Hamlet*) to call attention to the oppression of Kashmiris by India and Pakistan, while Motoyama and Konno explain how the founding of a Shakespeare theater in provincial Japan has served to affirm local cultural identity against the hegemonic pressures of the central government.

The chapters in the fourth section ("Freedom") explore some ways in which Shakespeare's works can be explicitly or implicitly associated with the dismantling of physical, mental, or cultural boundaries. The collaboratively composed *Sir Thomas More*, according to Bezio, resonates with our times in appealing to the common humanity of immigrants to England and to freedom of conscience in the face of ego-centered leadership, while Carrig calls attention to *Twelfth Night*'s interrogation of traditionally defined and restrictive conceptions of gender. Kofoworola, finally, traces translations and adaptations of Shakespeare in Nigeria as instances of liberating forms of appropriation in a post-colonial context.

There is, inevitably, significant overlap among these groupings of chapters, since none of these sections' topics or themes can be fully considered apart from each other. However, it is our hope that they can serve as a reminder of the central and urgent questions Shakespeare's works might inspire us to address. "Teeth hadst thou in thy head when thou wast born / To signify thou cam'st to bite the world" (*3H6* 5.6.53–4), claims King Henry to the future Richard III shortly before the latter stabs him.[10] The line, spoken by the titular king to the future tyrant Richard III, is particularly relevant in an age when despotism and tyranny—the hallmarks of Richard III—are on the rise. We may understandably resist identifying Richard with Shakespeare, but this anthology implicitly argues that we engage with Shakespeare most productively if we imagine him as a "biting Bard" whose incisive and inciting works continue to provoke a globally diverse community of creative artists, readers, thinkers, scholars, and theater-goers who believe in making the world a better place. In this spirit, we conclude our anthology with a light-hearted, biting "dramatic epilogue" that revisits many of the collection's principal concerns, while reminding us that Shakespeare always also meant to entertain.

NOTES

1. Ben Jonson, "To the Memory of My beloved, the Author, Mr. *William Shakespear*," in *Comedies, Histories, and Tragedies. Published According to the True Original Copies. Unto which is Added, Seven Plays, Never Before Printed in Folio. The 4. Edition*, by William Shakespeare (London: H. Herringman, E. Brewster, and R. Bentley, 1685). Introduction title quotation taken from Shakespeare's *The Winter's Tale* (4.1.1), ed. J. H. P. Pafford (London: Arden Shakespeare, 1963).
2. James Shapiro, *Shakespeare in a Divided America: What His Plays Tell Us about Our Past and Future* (New York: Penguin Press, 2020).
3. Hugh Grady and Terence Hawkes, eds., *Presentist Shakespeares* (London: Routledge, 2006), 19.
4. Harold Bloom, *Shakespeare: The Invention of the Human* (New York: Riverhead Books, 1999), 2.

5.   Alexa Huang and Elizabeth Rivlin, eds., *Shakespeare and the Ethics of Appropriation* (New York: Palgrave, 2014), 10.
6.   John J. Joughin, ed., *Philosophical Shakespeares* (New York, Routledge, 2000), 3.
7.   See Kristin M. S. Bezio and Kimberly Yost, eds., *Leadership, Popular Culture and Social Change* (Cheltenham, UK and Northampton, MA, USA: Edward Elgar, 2018); Michael Harvey, "Leadership and the Human Condition," in *The Quest for a General Theory of Leadership*, ed. George R. Goethals and Georgia L. J. Sorenson, New Horizons in Leadership Studies (Cheltenham, UK and Northampton, MA, USA: Edward Elgar, 2006), 39–45; Bert Alan Spector, "Carlyle, Freud, and the Great Man Theory More Fully Considered," *Leadership* 12, no. 2 (2016): 250–60; Kim Nehls, "Leadership Education: The Power of Storytelling," in *Leading in Complex Worlds*, ed. JoAnn Danelo Barbour, Gloria J. Burgess, Lena Lid-Falkman, and Robert M. McManus (San Francisco: Jossey-Bass, 2012), 63–77; Frank Shushok Jr. and Scott H. Moore, "Reading, Study, and Discussion of the 'Great Texts' of Literature, Philosophy, and Politics as a Complement to Contemporary Leadership Education Literature," *Journal of Leadership Studies* 3, no. 4 (2010): 71–80.
8.   Grady and Hawkes, *Presentist Shakespeares*, 3.
9.   Edition cited: William Shakespeare, *Hamlet: The Texts of 1603 and 1623*, eds. Ann Thompson and Neil Taylor, The Arden Shakespeare (London: Arden Shakespeare, 2006).
10. Edition cited: William Shakespeare, *King Henry VI Part 3*, eds. John D. Cox and Eric Rasmussen, The Arden Shakespeare, Third Series (London: Thomson Learning, 2001).

REFERENCES

Bezio, Kristin M. S., and Kimberly Yost, eds. *Leadership, Popular Culture and Social Change*. Cheltenham, UK and Northampton, MA, USA: Edward Elgar, 2018.

Bloom, Harold. *Shakespeare: The Invention of the Human*. New York: Riverhead Books, 1999.

Grady, Hugh, and Terence Hawkes, eds. *Presentist Shakespeares*. London: Routledge, 2006.

Harvey, Michael. "Leadership and the Human Condition." In *The Quest for a General Theory of Leadership*, edited by George R. Goethals and Georgia L. J. Sorenson, 39–45. New Horizons in Leadership Studies. Cheltenham, UK and Northampton, MA, USA: Edward Elgar, 2006.

Huang, Alexa, and Elizabeth Rivlin, eds. *Shakespeare and the Ethics of Appropriation*. New York: Palgrave, 2014.

Jonson, Ben. "To the Memory of My beloved, the Author, Mr. *William Shakespear*." In *Comedies, Histories, and Tragedies. Published According to the True Original Copies. Unto Which Is Added, Seven Plays, Never Before Printed in Folio. The 4. Edition*, by William Shakespeare. London: H. Herringman, E. Brewster, and R. Bentley, 1685.

Joughin, John J., ed. *Philosophical Shakespeares*. New York: Routledge, 2000.

Nehls, Kim. "Leadership Education: The Power of Storytelling." In *Leading in Complex Worlds*, edited by JoAnn Danelo Barbour, Gloria J. Burgess, Lena Lid-Falkman, and Robert M. McManus, 63–77. San Francisco: Jossey-Bass, 2012.

Shakespeare, William. *Hamlet: The Texts of 1603 and 1623*. Edited by Ann Thompson and Neil Taylor. The Arden Shakespeare. London: Arden Shakespeare, 2006.

Shakespeare, William. *King Henry VI Part 3*. Edited by John D. Cox and Eric Rasmussen. The Arden Shakespeare, Third Series. London: Thomson Learning, 2001.

Shakespeare, William. *The Winter's Tale*. Edited by J. H. P. Pafford. The Arden Shakespeare. London: Arden Shakespeare, 1963.

Shapiro, James. *Shakespeare in a Divided America: What His Plays Tell Us about Our Past and Future*. New York: Penguin Press, 2020.

Shushok, Frank, Jr., and Scott H. Moore. "Reading, Study, and Discussion of the 'Great Texts' of Literature, Philosophy, and Politics as a Complement to Contemporary Leadership Education Literature." *Journal of Leadership Studies* 3, no. 4 (2010): 71–80.

Spector, Bert Alan. "Carlyle, Freud, and the Great Man Theory More Fully Considered." *Leadership* 12, no. 2 (2016): 250–60.

PART I

Performance

1. Performance and the political subject in *Richard II*

Melissa Caldwell

INTRODUCTION: THE AUDIENCE AS POLITICAL SUBJECT

For its unflinching examination of the dangers of incompetent and weak political leadership, *Richard II* is among the most politically resonant of all of William Shakespeare's plays for a twenty-first-century audience. At first glance, its medieval setting and formal versification style might suggest that Shakespeare's intent was to work within the inflexible outcomes of morality plays or the *de casibus* tradition, which invariably trace the undoing of a leader back to their moral weakness. However, Shakespeare takes this historical tragedy in a different direction, as what is at issue in this play is not a leader's moral strength, but rather his skill and ability to perform as a leader. Dramatizing a monarch who lacks the expertise, maturity, and decision-making abilities of England's more accomplished kings, Shakespeare places the audience in the difficult position of having to decide how intolerable Richard really is as a king and to imagine what, if anything, they could do if such a monarch were to rule on England's throne again. The audience's position in this play is all the more striking since Richard II is unquestionably an anointed king with an uncontested claim to the throne.[1] Henry Bolingbroke, Richard's cousin, and ultimately his rival, emerges as one possible, though imperfect, response to Richard's weak political leadership.

Through both Richard II and Bolingbroke, Shakespeare makes clear that a crucial component of leadership is performance itself, as both characters use political performance as a means to shore up their power. From the first to the last scenes of the play, Shakespeare draws our attention to their political performances in a way that demands judgment. As Shakespeare takes up the task of dramatizing the individual motivations of both Richard II and Bolingbroke, their performativity becomes the evidence upon which the audience must evaluate their success as political leaders. Nevertheless, the play stubbornly resists providing comforting conclusions to the audience about either of these characters. As Charles R. Forker writes in his introduction to the Arden Shakespeare edition, "Depending on one's perspective ... Richard is either a tyrant or a martyr, Bolingbroke either a patriot or a ruthless opportunist."[2] The words and actions of both Richard and Bolingbroke seem to make a case for their versions of leadership, yet Shakespeare never fully validates either character's claims. Hence, the play stages an unresolved clash between the prerogatives of absolute rule and the reality of human fallibility, for *Richard II* is invested in the idea of sacred kingship even as it grapples with the consequences of that investment.

Written during the mid-1590s not long after England's defeat of the Spanish Armada, *Richard II* is the first installment of Shakespeare's second tetralogy that includes the two plays dramatizing the reign of Henry IV and culminates in the triumphant rise of the great English king Henry V. The play narrowly focuses on the end of the historic Richard II's reign, centering on the deposition of the king by his rebel cousin, the aristocrat Henry Bolingbroke. Although Richard banishes Bolingbroke from England early in the play, Bolingbroke quickly returns to England after his father dies and the king attempts to steal his lands. Having both popular support and that of a number of the English aristocracy, Bolingbroke ascends the throne when Richard abdicates his power. The play stages a dialectic between conformity to the status quo and radical reform that takes the form of treason and rebellion, but it is hardly clear-cut in endorsing either response as the correct one for a citizen to take.[3] Like many of Shakespeare's other plays written during the late sixteenth century, it is difficult to read *Richard II* without considering how it reflects on Queen Elizabeth and the looming uncertainty of the succession crisis. With an aging monarch on the throne and the next monarch still in question, the play unearths England's anxieties about monarchy at a pivotal point in English history.[4] While the tetralogy as a whole can be read as political propaganda in support of Elizabeth, taken alone *Richard II* is a much edgier play. During the reign of Elizabeth I, the first three quartos were printed only in censored format without Richard's deposition scene.[5] In the 1640s, the play must also chillingly have suggested a precedent for the deposition of Charles I, who identified with Richard.[6] Seeking to distance himself from deposed monarchs altogether, Charles II banned the play during the Restoration. This pattern of censorship suggests the degree to which the play made England's monarchs nervous about its potential message about civic activism and monarchical reform.

Shakespeare's portrait of Richard emphasizes the monarch's lack of leadership in a way that makes Richard's performativity an index of his weakness. It also illustrates what happens when a monarch is profoundly indifferent to his audience's judgment. As Kristin Bezio argues, Richard has very little respect for his subjects, "believing them unworthy and himself above the need for performative negotiation."[7] Richard can be so cavalier toward his political subjects because he believes his power is divinely sanctioned and therefore absolute. "Not all the water in the rough rude sea," Richard confidently affirms, "can wash the balm from an anointed king. / The breath of worldly men cannot depose / The deputy elected by the Lord" (3.2.50–3).[8] The fact that the play reveals his arrogance and his error calls in question both his leadership abilities and the theory of divinely sanctioned monarchy. As a political counterpoint, Bolingbroke does not operate from such a presumption of power, and consequently, he never loses sight of his audience. The role Bolingbroke plays as a legitimate alternative to the monarch shows Shakespeare staging not just resistance to leadership, but resistance *as* leadership. But if Bolingbroke's performance is a more effective leadership strategy, it is not a more earnest or a morally superior one.[9]

While it is difficult not to read *Richard II* in light of the larger historic-tragic narrative of Shakespeare's tetralogy, considering Richard II and Bolingbroke solely within the world that Shakespeare creates for them is the most instructive approach to interpreting the play in a twenty-first-century context.[10] If we read this play simply as the prologue to a narrative that will lead to Henry V's successful career as a monarch who seamlessly reunites legitimacy and political performance, then it is more difficult to recognize the critical perspectives on leadership that Shakespeare explores here. If instead we assess these political opponents on their own merits as leaders within the context of this work, the complexity of Shakespeare's attitudes toward political leadership and performance becomes more apparent. This framing in a sense replicates the imperfect process by which we formulate our own political judgments in the twenty-first century, which necessarily are made with the uncertainty of partial knowledge.[11]

At the same time that the play asks us to choose between Richard and Bolingbroke, it also offers a highly skeptical view of political leadership altogether. Recognizing the way that this play breaks ranks with the sixteenth-century trend of dramatists casting the usurper as the unequivocally evil tyrant, Doyeeta Majumder argues, "In the figure of Bolingbroke Shakespeare presents to us the new prince *par excellence*, a man who astutely understands the pulse of the nation as well as the shifting political discourses around him."[12] Yet even if Bolingbroke is a more skilled performer, the play does not readily allow for such a reading. *Richard II* presents both Bolingbroke and Richard as viable and less-than-ideal candidates for the throne, while placing the theatrical audience in the seat of political judgment. Political pamphleteers at the turn of the century read Richard's deposition as "a kind of test case confirming or denying the rights of subjects to judge their rulers."[13] As Louise Cowan argues, the play does not question "whether the king can do no wrong"; rather, it asks the audience to consider "what to do with a monarch who has committed serious and habitual offenses."[14] Shakespeare is not shy about documenting Richard's offenses: he replaces common law with kingly prerogative; seizes Bolingbroke's land; assassinates his political enemies; taxes his people excessively and without legitimate purpose; and disregards wise counsel, preferring the opinion of flatterers. Yet even with all these flaws, he is more a foolish than an evil king. But the reform of Richard and his court is complicated by the way in which Richard's performativity creates a culture of performance among his subjects. This is especially true for Bolingbroke, whose leadership at times seems more reactive than proactive, as he finds himself in the position of playing a role the king has created for him. If Bolingbroke is offered as a solution to the problem of Richard, his political actions are difficult to separate from Richard's political performance, for he struggles to fully extricate himself from Richard's performative tendencies to establish his own identity as a leader.

Taken on its own, *Richard II* offers many parallels to the American political landscape today, not the least of which are the expectations placed on individuals who hold the office of the president, the role of citizens in political reform, and the dangers of performative politics. The Trump White House was frequently compared to a reality television show, a genre that at once purports to be real even as the notion of reality itself gets turned into a performance. Indeed, while President Donald Trump seemed to largely elide what it means to be presidential, performativity was central to his platform. His rants on Twitter, his use of COVID-19 briefings as campaign platforms, his administration's choice to roll back trans-gender rights on the anniversary of one of the deadliest attacks on the LGBTQ community in US history, and his party's choice to hold a rally on the anniversary of the Tulsa Massacre suggested that the performance was a highly orchestrated attack on democracy. Like Richard, Donald Trump was a leader who evoked uncompromising, polarized responses precisely because he both compulsively seeks an audience and in many respects disregards his audience altogether. From the beginning, his candidacy occasioned debate about the nature of leadership and what qualities and skills an individual should possess in order to fill the office of the president. For some, his lack of experience with foreign policy and the law seemed to define his unsuitability for the job, while others looked to his background as a businessman as the model of what American politics needed. Still others saw his lack of experience in politics as precisely the thing that made him an ideal president. Those loyal to Trump's presidency heralded him as a redeemer of American values, in stark contrast to his opponents, many of whom believed that in his four years as president, democracy in the US teetered closer to authoritarianism than anyone ever thought possible. Trump's response to dissension of any kind was not unlike Richard's impulse to galvanize the authority of his office at the expense of his people. Surrounding himself with loyalists, often friends and family, Trump was more concerned with his own ratings than with the work of a president. For the four years of his presidency, the US felt the effects of what one writer called "the death of expertise."[15]

Just as Richard's performativity creates a kind of gravity that compels others to perform a role within the political play he directs, so too has Trump's performance of leadership turned the US into a theater-at-large with the American public seemingly trapped within a culture of political performance. The quick politicization of the COVID-19 health crisis in the US offers just one case study that shows the degree to which unabashed and unfettered performativity can not only be used to undermine social relations within a society, but to create the conditions in which civic responsibility collapses into performance. The nature and magnitude of the danger of Trump's disavowal of experts came to the forefront in February 2020 when the first COVID-19 cases were identified in the US. With Trump having gutted the pandemic response team, broken ties with the World Health Organization, denied the recommendations of the Centers for Disease Control and Prevention, frequently positioned himself at odds with even the members of his own task force, publicly disavowed mask wearing, indicated his preference for less testing rather than more, and advocated the use of household chemicals and unapproved drugs to combat the virus, the death of expertise was followed swiftly by death itself.

What *Richard II* provides, then, is a place to interpret and reflect upon the importance of individual judgment and resistance as an alternative form of leadership in the face of political institutions that have been supplanted by pageantry without principle and an authentic individualism that has collapsed into role playing. The question remains how a citizen can break free from the performativity of the highest-ranking government official to affect reform. In the essay that follows, I trace the creation and the perpetuation of performative culture in *Richard II*. In particular, I argue that Richard's performativity has three major consequences: it indicates the weakness of his own political leadership, it threatens to undermine the legitimacy of Bolingbroke's resistance to weak leadership, and it renders the judgment of the audience uncertain. *Richard II* reveals the dangers of weak leadership to society at many different levels, a truth that is as cogent in late sixteenth-century England as it is in twenty-first-century America.

RICHARD, BOLINGBROKE, AND THE CULTURE OF POLITICAL PERFORMANCE

Although Shakespeare's Richard is hardly a fully realized historical figure, the performative aspects in Richard's character—and the performativity he inspires in his subjects—were not far from the historical mark. Shakespeare's play ignores the historical circumstances surrounding much of Richard's reign leading up to his deposition, including the threats to his sovereignty that abounded for most of his life.[16] The clearest manifestation of these threats was the Peasants Revolt of 1381, which served as a wake-up call to the aristocracy and the monarch about the precariousness of their position. As the social structure of English medieval society was transitioning away from the feudal system to something as yet undefined, the lower classes were "aggravated by the administrative incompetence and selfishness superadded by the ruling classes to their normal display of luxury and cruelty, by the unpopularity of a government which did not work in any sense of the word, was corruptly administered, supported by heavy taxation and inclined to shift the burden of taxation, as far as it dared, from the rich on to the poor."[17] It is in the context of this popular outcry against corruption, ineptitude, and extravagance that Richard emerged as a ruler committed not to reform but to reestablishing his sovereignty by exalting ceremony and creating a language of power for his rule.[18] He not only re-envisioned the monarch's role as a political performer, but also sought to enhance his subjects' "performance of obedience."[19] Despite his youth and inexperience, he restored order to England in the wake of the Peasants Revolt.

Nevertheless, Richard's reign is characterized by a distrust and factionalism that he attempted to overcome with ritual and prerogative. Richard ascended the throne as a ten-year-old boy in 1377 after the death of his father Edward III. By the late 1380s, he declared the autonomy of his rule separate from his ambitious uncles who had carefully watched the young monarch, other political factions at the court, and Parliament, which sought to create a counsel to oversee his actions and impinge upon his prerogative. Seeking to secure his authority against Parliament, for the first time in English history a monarch pitted his judges against Parliament, asking them to make a political judgment about whether or not Parliament had overstepped its bounds.[20] Perhaps not surprisingly, the judges spoke in Richard's favor. The king's prerogative may have suggested to him that he was above the law, but the English people and aristocracy—and, in fact, English law—took a different view. By the late 1390s, Richard had gained a reputation as a king who frequently used his prerogative for his own benefit rather than the benefit of his people.[21] It was only at the end of his reign leading up to his deposition in 1399—which is when Shakespeare's play begins—that Richard started lashing out at his opponents in order to consolidate his power even further.

This historical background is useful for understanding Shakespeare's play, because it suggests a rationale for a monarch who would be highly invested in both his own political performance and that of his subjects. The historic Richard II put great stock in the performance of power as a means of maintaining his sovereignty. Richard's use of language for political performance was heightened by Shakespeare as he chose to focus on the events leading up to Richard's abdication. By focusing almost exclusively on the moment when the king loses his power, Shakespeare draws back the curtain on the cracks in Richard's political edifice.[22] In Shakespeare's play, Richard's faults are many—he is naïve, unskilled, egotistical, and given to poetics more than politics; he violates the rights of the aristocracy; he taxes people unfairly for his own interests; and, in what is perhaps the biggest of his political sins, he imprudently surrounds himself with "caterpillars" who offer him bad counsel. Despite all these flaws, he is not simply a king who "renteth right and law asunder."[23] The play cannot be called a morality play or even a tragedy, wherein a great ruler is brought low by his individual moral shortcomings. Instead, the play depicts two potentially valid forms of leadership, those of Richard and Bolingbroke.

In its staging of competing performances and performance styles, *Richard II* consistently refuses to adjudicate the Richard-Bolingbroke binary that structures this work. For example, the prophecy of the Bishop of Carlisle, a loyal member of Richard's inner circle, asks the audience to consider the actions of the play not in and of themselves, but within the context of a larger view of history. Thus, though perhaps the immediate political situation validates Bolingbroke's claim to power, the words of Carlisle to Bolingbroke and his uncle, the Duke of York, foreshadow a future for England that will be characterized by conflict as a consequence of this claim:

> **CARLISLE** If you crown him, let me prophesy
> The blood of English shall manure the ground,
> And future ages groan for this foul act.
> Peace shall go sleep with Turks and infidels,
> And in this seat of peace tumultuous wars
> Shall kin with kin and kind with kind confound.
> Disorder, horror, fear, and mutiny
> Shall here inhabit, and this land be called
> The field of Golgotha and dead men's skulls. (4.1.127–35)

Carlisle's judgment represents the play's overarching mood of dread, essentially damning England to a future of unrest and bloodshed. The crowning of Bolingbroke not only makes England vulnerable to civil war, but symbolically transforms England into a Golgotha, the place where Christ was crucified. Richard, the divinely anointed king who serves as God's deputy on earth, is likened to the martyred Christ, while Bolingbroke's actions are demonized.

Despite the testimonial of this tempting rendering of English history, however, the play also takes seriously the legitimacy of Bolingbroke's response to a failed monarch.[24] Shakespeare provides the audience with an abundance of judgments about these two men and the legitimacy of their claims to the throne, but none of these pronouncements effectively alleviates the play's atmosphere of unease.[25] The evidence of the play itself suggests that the audience should reserve judgment, or at least employ a different set of criteria than any of the overt ideological viewpoints presented in the play itself.

The first scene of *Richard II* sets the stage for the performativity of both the monarch and his court, as both Richard and Bolingbroke are rendered morally suspect characters. Because the scene that Shakespeare constructs effectively neutralizes any moral argument that could be made for or against either character, it puts the audience in the seat of judgment, as they try to untangle and assess the strengths and weaknesses of either character based on their leadership skills rather than on the strength of their individual ethics or political ideologies. Indeed, though it may seem at first that an audience is called on to weigh against each other these two leaders and their causes, in the end we see not opposition but two political choices that seem more similar than different.

The play opens with the audience seemingly sharing Richard's point of view, having to make a judgment call between two political factions. When the two aristocrats Bolingbroke and Mowbray enter, heatedly accusing each other of treason, Richard notes "yet one but flatters us" (1.1.25). Both Mowbray and Bolingbroke are hiding secrets in this scene, though on the surface they appear to be performing the obedience and loyalty due to a monarch. Mowbray is covering up the fact that Richard ordered him to murder his uncle, Thomas of Woodstock, an act that precedes the action of the play. Although Mowbray worries about Richard's partiality to Bolingbroke given that they are cousins, Richard appears to assume the part of an impartial judge in the contest, noting that both Mowbray and Bolingbroke are equal subjects under him (1.1.110–23). Setting aside the issues that both men bring to Richard's court, Richard contrives a duel to resolve the conflict, though the king ultimately discards that pretense and uses his prerogative to banish both Bolingbroke and Mowbray from England. But if the audience does not have enough information upon which to judge Bolingbroke, it also does not have the information with which to evaluate Richard. In a notoriously veiled line, Mowbray seems to allude to the possibility that Richard ordered the murder of Thomas of Woodstock, but the play does not confirm Richard's guilt until the next scene. The fact that some of Shakespeare's audience would have known the story of Richard's murder of Woodstock seems to make it all the more conspicuous that Shakespeare leaves out that information from this scene.[26]

The opening scene, then, does not establish Bolingbroke as the morally superior of the two men, but it does establish him as someone capable of producing a political performance. Indeed, as one scholar has pointed out, Bolingbroke's name may be a pun on "bulling," which meant to deceive.[27] Scholarship is decidedly split on how to interpret the character of Bolingbroke and the degree to which he represents a Machiavellian model of leadership that is ushering out an older version of leadership premised on sacred kingship.[28] His character embodies a version of leadership which is much more uncertain and difficult to interpret. Whereas Shakespeare gives Richard several moments of self-reflection throughout the play, he offers no equivalent insight into Bolingbroke's interiority.[29] One crucial detail that seems to be intentionally left in doubt throughout the play is Bolingbroke's motivation. The opening lines of the play introduce the problem of interpreting political performance when even the man who is closest to Bolingbroke, his father, John of Gaunt, can offer little insight into his son's thoughts. When Richard asks Gaunt in a private conversation whether his son's suit is motivated by "ancient malice or worthily, as a good subject should" (1.1.9–10), Gaunt says that he believes his son to be alerting the king to "some apparent danger," though he admits that this is "as near as I could sift him on that argument" (1.1.12–13). Gaunt's hardly confident response registers an uncertainty about Bolingbroke's motives that recurs throughout the play. It also makes it seem likely that the two aristocrats are involved in a courtly dumbshow, rather than an earnest challenge, to demonstrate their loyalty as subjects to the king. In other words, Act 1, Scene 1 is less about political action based on conviction than the performance of conviction.

While Bolingbroke's motivations for accusing Mowbray are obscure, Mowbray himself argues for the purity of his intent in serving Richard, and indeed by the end of the play his claim that Bolingbroke's professed loyalty to the king is just a ruse will be proven to be correct. Questions about Bolingbroke's intentions dominate the rest of the play, leading the audience to wonder whether we should view him as the protagonist we might expect him to play to Richard's antagonist or not. All Shakespeare allows us to know for certain after this scene is that Richard's court is one in which professions of loyalty are nearly impossible to differentiate from loyalty itself. Richard's handling of Mowbray and Bolingbroke within the context of his courtly theater shows him managing their entrances and their exits in an attempt to cover up his own unscrupulous leadership.

Despite the play's title, Bolingbroke is the more dynamic character within the play. Whatever Bolingbroke's failures as a leader, and however dark the shadow of usurpation, the restoration of succession in the figure of Bolingbroke's son as Henry V seems to outweigh the moral ambiguity of Bolingbroke's claim to the crown. Yet when we leave the long-term consequences of Richard's abdication aside, we are left with one of the central questions of the play. Bolingbroke is either a reformer or he is a political performer, and the play seems to suggest that he cannot legitimately be both. Richard's favoritism, financial indulgences, and murderous tendencies make reform necessary, yet the performativity that shrouds all actions within the court threatens to render Bolingbroke's actions as mere performance rather than political act. To unravel what this play has to say about leadership and performativity, we have to assess more accurately Bolingbroke's character as a leader using the information—and in some cases the lack of information—that we have.

Shakespeare provides the audience with two competing axes against which to judge Bolingbroke's leadership. On the one hand, Bolingbroke is repeatedly positioned as the foil to Richard and as his rival for the throne. In this sense, the play is inscribed with a rhetoric of opposition such as that reflected in Carlisle's highly allegorical speech. However, the evidence of the play points to the similarities rather than the differences between these two men, suggesting that this opposition is a false binary. In place of this binary, the play presents a range of responses and interpretations, including those of Bolingbroke's father, John of Gaunt; Bolingbroke's uncle, the Duke of York; and Bolingbroke himself. These responses range from the religious to the secular, and from passive conformity to active reform.

The first of these views is offered early in the play by Bolingbroke's father, John of Gaunt, in the second scene of the play. In a quaint and private encounter in which Gaunt is speaking to the Duchess of Gloucester, the widow of his murdered brother, he confirms what the first scene did not: Richard's guilt in the murder of his brother, Thomas of Woodstock. In response to her plea for revenge, Gaunt recites the most conservative version of orthodox doctrine on the subject's duty to a sovereign:

> **GAUNT** God's is the quarrel; for God's substitute,
>   His deputy anointed in his sight,
>   Hath caused his death; the which if wrongfully,
>   Let heaven revenge, for I may never lift
>   An angry arm against his minister. (1.2.37–41)

Affirming the values of sacred kingship, Gaunt defers judgment to God, because only God is the superior to an anointed king. Nevertheless, the widow makes clear that Gaunt's response is dissatisfying at best. It also may well seem dissatisfying to the audience, as "Gaunt's orthodoxy is a way of rationalizing political impotence."[30] Similar to the political views he expresses in his deathbed speech in which he nostalgically compares England to an "other Eden, demi-paradise" (2.1.42), Gaunt's ideas seem entirely utopian and out of touch with the political realities of the moment.[31] Although Gaunt is characterized as a wise and honest counsellor who speaks hard political truths, he dies early in the play, a historical fact that would seem to corroborate the sense that he no longer belongs in the political world Shakespeare constructs.[32] Hence, Gaunt's version of citizenship seems unlikely to reform the political problems that ail England.

Gaunt's last remaining brother, the Duke of York, offers a similarly conservative view of reform, but his view is rooted more in a secular ethic than

Gaunt's argument that the English should patiently suffer any and all abuse at the hand of God's anointed king. When Richard decisively and imprudently seizes Gaunt's lands just moments after the aristocrat's death is announced in order to fund his Irish wars, York immediately replaces Gaunt as the play's figure of an ideal counsellor, keen to tell Richard what he does not want to hear. He is the first to diagnose Richard's violations of Bolingbroke's right to his inheritance and their consequences for the king's hold on the throne:

> **YORK** Take Hereford's rights away, and take from Time
>   His charters and his customary rights
>   Let not tomorrow then ensue today;
>   Be not thyself, for how art thou a king
>   But by fair sequence and succession? (2.1.196–200)

Like Gaunt, York is a kind of idealist, but rather than centering his belief on England's Edenic past or sacred kingship, he grounds his arguments in English law. But while Gaunt's rhetoric reflects the certainty of his beliefs, many of York's speeches end with questions. York notes that if the king ignores the right of inheritance, he not only defies the basic tenets of English common law, but he also invalidates the foundation of his own political power. This realization leads him to the question of whether or not it is ever appropriate for a subject to rebel against a monarch who disregards law. He begins his critique of Richard's seizure of Gaunt's lands with a question that looms over the entire play: "How long shall I be patient? Ah, how long / Shall tender duty make me suffer wrong?" (2.1.164–5). While Gaunt had argued for the patient suffering of a dutiful subject, York's rhetorical questioning suggests that there must be an end to patience. At some point, then, it must be valid for a subject to judge the sovereign and to act upon that judgment. Richard's actions have gone so beyond the pale of English law that he has pushed York's "tender patience to those thoughts / Which honour and allegiance cannot think" (2.1.208–9).

York comes to the very brink of becoming a reformer, only to quickly retreat from such action. Once confronted with the reality of Bolingbroke's rebellion, he decides there must be a limit to men's actions in the face of injustice, and that patience and suffering rather than reformation may be the best stance for a dutiful subject to take. In Act 2, Scene 3, York emerges as a sharp critic of Bolingbroke's treason. Though usually a man of few words and direct language, the high rhetoric Bolingbroke employs in his response to York confirms what we have already suspected: that he too is quite capable of playing political games. When he bows before his uncle, York replies to his nephew, "Show me thy humble heart, and not thy knee, / Whose duty is deceivable and false" (2.3.83–4). When Bolingbroke appeals to his "gracious uncle," York immediately identifies and cuts off his nephew's flattery: "Tut,

tut, grace me no grace, nor uncle me no uncle. / I am no traitor's uncle, and that word 'grace' / In an ungracious mouth is but profane" (2.3.86–8). Far from viewing Bolingbroke as a reformer, York sees him as a "traitor" lacking grace, for having violated decorum and law by returning to England from exile and also because he is acting without the grace or favor of God. Offering a quick assessment of Bolingbroke's "gross rebellion and detested treason" that pulls no punches, he condemns Bolingbroke's return to England, just as he had censured the king for stealing Bolingbroke's lands. Because York has been left with insufficient powers to arrest Bolingbroke, he says that he has no choice but to remain "neuter," that is, an impartial judge (2.3.158), which may be one model of response but is not a model of reform.

With Gaunt and York as two failed models of response to Richard, we arrive at the possibility that Bolingbroke's resistance may be read as an active and justifiable model of reform. The scene ends with Bolingbroke arguing for himself as a corrective to "the caterpillars of the commonwealth, / Which I have sworn to weed and pluck away" (2.3.165–6), yet there is little to suggest that Bolingbroke is the reformer he claims to be. He does rid England of some of Richard's more expendable "caterpillars," but it is hard to see what this action has to do with his rightfully reclaiming the land Richard has taken from him. In addition to the inscrutability of Bolingbroke's political motivations and the illegality of his actions, the odd compression of Act 2, Scene 1 in which Bolingbroke's father, John of Gaunt, dies, Richard seizes his land, and Bolingbroke returns further renders Bolingbroke's motivations suspect. The compression of this timeline underscores the ambiguities surrounding Bolingbroke's motivations for his early return. And so, as Richard has broken the law of English custom, Bolingbroke responds by breaking the law as well. As the play continues, the parallels between Richard and Bolingbroke become even stronger. In Act 3, Scene 3, Bolingbroke shows himself to be more than willing to create the conditions for civil war, though he describes his position as "yielding water" that will give way to Richard's raging fire (3.3.57–9). Yet the potential for violence Bolingbroke evokes here when he threatens to "lay the summer's dust with showers of blood / Rained from the wounds of slaughtered Englishmen" (3.3.40–1) seems to echo York's earlier condemnation of Richard's flouting of English law. This at once makes Bolingbroke seem like a reformer while suggesting a parallel between his actions and those of Richard at the same time.

If Bolingbroke's lawlessness and the threat of civil war he poses were not enough evidence to confirm his similarities with Richard in a way that defies the ostensible rhetoric of opposition in the play, by the end of Act 4, when Richard abdicates, we are once again confronted with the problem of interpretation. The way in which Shakespeare blurs the line between treating Richard's downfall as a deposition caused by the threat of rebellion and an abdication caused by a monarch with limited skills as a leader is important. Richard himself is the one who first mentions deposition, though he seems to voluntarily give up the crown to Bolingbroke. The difference has a significant impact on how we interpret Bolingbroke, for not only does an abdication suggest Richard's lack of leadership, but it also suggests Bolingbroke's insofar as he becomes a kind of accidental king.

In this scene it becomes clear why this play is really Richard's play and not Bolingbroke's. Although Bolingbroke calls Richard to a public deposition scene, Richard largely choreographs his own deposition. Throughout the scene Bolingbroke is confined to single line answers, while Richard's speeches are capacious, full of pathos, and highly rhetorical. When he gives the crown and scepter to Bolingbroke, Richard commands, "Now mark me how I will undo myself":

> **RICHARD** With mine own tears I wash away my balm,
>   With mine own hands I give away my crown,
>   With mine own tongue deny my sacred state,
>   With mine own breath release all duteous oaths.
>   All pomp and majesty I do forswear. (4.1.192, 197–201)

Ironically, Richard's renunciation of his own divine kingship only reaffirms it. As a divinely anointed king, he has no superiors on earth: the only person who can dethrone him is he himself. Richard further highlights his orchestration of the scene by condemning his deposers as "Pilates" who will not be able to "wash away your sin" (4.1.230, 232). Bolingbroke's ally, the Earl of Northumberland, attempts to step in and establish order by demanding that Richard read a list of grievances that provide the rationale for his deposition. After Northumberland's fourth attempt to get Richard to take the list, Bolingbroke tells him to give up his suit. The scene concludes with Bolingbroke supplying two of Richard's final requests, a mirror in which to view his ruined self and permission to leave Bolingbroke's presence forever. Although Richard is sent to the Tower, Richard's last words in a scene that he has already dominated once again cast Bolingbroke and his allies in a negative light as he calls them "conveyors," a derogatory term indicating thievery.

The way in which Richard's deposition scene unfolds makes it seem to be a voluntary, but unjust, abdication of power. Richard's rhetorical command and performative power is unmistakable for the entire time he is on stage. The audience does witness a transfer of power, but it does not seem to be one occasioned by Bolingbroke's desire for reform; rather, it is occasioned by Richard's own weakness as a leader. This scene is easily the climax of the play, but even as Richard's performance of kingship is at its height, Bolingbroke's motivations are unclear, and they remain so in the final act. During the last moments of the play, Richard's executioner, Exton, enters with the coffin containing Richard II's murdered body.[33] The new king, Henry IV, does not thank Exton for carrying out the murder, though Exton insists, "From your own mouth, my lord, did I this deed" (5.6.37). The audience never sees Henry give this order; instead, we only hear about the coded language Henry uses when he is quoted by Exton in an early scene as saying, "Have I no friend will rid me of this living fear?" (5.4.4). The indirect way in which Shakespeare gives the audience information about Bolingbroke once again calls to our attention the skill with which Bolingbroke uses political performance. Nevertheless, the play "closes, as it had opened, on a king whose hands are stained with royal blood," and with another order for banishment, this time Exton's, that will likely cause as many problems as it solves.[34] Even Henry acknowledges his own guilt as he swears to "make a voyage to the Holy Land / To wash this blood off from my guilty hand" (5.649–50). Although his actions as a reformer cannot be read outside of Richard's display of anointed kingship, with the death of Richard, Henry is free to enjoin his own political performance or to leave political performance aside entirely.

NEGOTIATING POLITICAL PERFORMANCE

Richard II is such a painfully powerful and prescient play in the twenty-first century because, despite the historical and political differences, it speaks to important questions in our own time about leadership, the relationship between political performance and political action, and the duty of an individual confronted by inadequate leadership to work within or to rebel against a dysfunctional political system. Shakespeare's Richard is by all accounts a foolish and unskillful king: he ignores the law, abuses his people with taxation, is counselled by an echo chamber of his own creation, and rules by prerogative. When York advises Richard—for his own good—to forgo taking Gaunt's lands just moments after Gaunt has died, Richard's response is uncharacteristically short and direct: "Think what you will, we seize into our hands / His plate, his goods, his money, and his lands" (2.1.210–11). The rhyming couplet only serves to underscore Richard's flippancy: he does not even care enough about his audience to try to cover up his violation of English law. From the point of view of many Americans—the popular vote of the 2016 election would suggest that it was the majority of Americans—never before were American citizens faced with a ruler like Donald Trump: one who seemed entirely unqualified to be president, who violated, or at least loosely interpreted, constitutional law, who created a panel of advisors made up of like-minded favorites, and who used branches of government against each other for his own political gain. At the very least, *Richard II* makes us stop and wonder at what qualifies a person for political leadership beyond their ability to act a part.

Bolingbroke provides us with a model of resistance, even as he shares similarities with the system of misrule he seems to be attempting to reform. He is adept at capitalizing on his popularity with his audience, a fact that leads A. L. Rowse to remark, "Bolingbroke was a politician—he would do quite well in a democracy."[35] Bolingbroke's tendency to recognize the importance of popular support that spans various classes may be one reason why the play resonates so well with contemporary American politics. Although Richard dominates the scene of his abdication and is often taken to be the active force to Bolingbroke's more passive role, it is Bolingbroke who orchestrates the scene when he calls for Richard to come "that in common view / He may surrender. So shall we proceed / Without suspicion" (4.1.146–8). Richard may be the more obvious actor and a formidable poet, but it is Bolingbroke who is keenly aware of the audience. Richard is not a successful leader precisely because the audience for the play is made aware that they are watching Richard perform a role. By contrast, Bolingbroke is the more accomplished performer. Shakespeare uses his silence strategically and in a way that places great emphasis on the role of the audience—both within the play and within the theater itself to interpret Bolingbroke's actions. This is notable because so often when Shakespeare considers audience in political plays—most notably his Roman plays *Julius Caesar*, *Titus Andronicus*, and *Coriolanus*—the audience is seen as a dangerous and unmanageable crowd.[36] Nevertheless, Shakespeare does not give a free pass to either Richard or Bolingbroke, and the consequences of Bolingbroke's actions follow him to the last lines of the play.[37]

And so the reason why we cannot simply view Bolingbroke as an answer to the ineptitude of Richard has to do with the way in which Shakespeare forces us to pause throughout the play to consider whether we are able to feel good about our judgment of him as either a rightful king or as a rebellious usurper. Shakespeare arguably does not give the audience enough information with which to judge Bolingbroke, and the information we do have shows Bolingbroke frequently playing into the roles Richard creates for him. The challenge to Mowbray, the duel, and the abdication scene are all performative spaces controlled by Richard in which Bolingbroke plays his part. For most of the play, it is difficult to know exactly what kind of performance he is offering and whether we should see his performance as evidence of his superior skill at politics and his earnest belief in reform or as an indicator that he is not all that different from the man he is replacing on the throne. If, as I have argued, Shakespeare neutralizes moral superiority in the play by creating more similarities than differences between Bolingbroke and Richard, then the play begs the question of what grounds we might use to evaluate Bolingbroke's superiority to Richard. It would seem that the only criteria we have left is to compare Bolingbroke's performativity, which prevents us from knowing what is performance and what is real, to Richard's, in which we always know where we stand, dreadful as that may be. If such is the ground that we might apply to our modern political system, we may be left substituting one empty crown for another.

Ultimately, Bolingbroke provides a contemporary audience two different insights on leadership and politics in the twenty-first century. As a rival, counterpoint, and potential reformer, Bolingbroke offers us a critique of the death of expertise. In this light, Bolingbroke, though perhaps morally as culpable as Richard, still offers some skill as a leader that the king lacks. But the second insight is even more troubling—that is, that Bolingbroke is not really much of a reformer at all, and that with a little bit of luck and ambition he falls into the role that Richard's lack of leadership skill creates for him. If we translate these insights into our position as audience and as political subject, we are either, like Bolingbroke, judging Richard's performance and responding to it with reforms to benefit society, or we are judging both Richard and Bolingbroke and have no choice but to take away a highly skeptical view of politics and civic activism in a society in which both have collapsed into performance.

Every four years, during the presidential election, US citizens are faced with the familiar dilemma of differentiating empty campaign promises from the earnest convictions that will provide the motivation to create legislation to strengthen society. The internet age makes it increasingly difficult to see the strings and seams of performance. In many ways, our position is more fraught than that of Shakespeare's audience. Whatever the ambiguities of Shakespeare's play, ultimately history did supply the choice between Richard and Bolingbroke for their audience. However, what we are left with now is a political field full of Bolingbrokes who may or may not be what they claim to be. At the same time, the political subject in the age of Trump veers precariously toward becoming a Bolingbroke. As various social media platforms now make it possible to signal action, the armchair activism of many American citizens allows for the performance of activism rather than the work of activism itself. As Americans negotiate this performative space, failed political leadership threatens to displace proactive reform measures with reactive political performativity.

NOTES

1. For a discussion of the strength of Richard's claim to the throne compared to other monarchs in Shakespeare's history plays, see Andrew Hadfield, *Shakespeare and Renaissance Politics*, Arden Shakespeare (London: Thomson Learning, 2004), 40.
2. Charles R. Forker, introduction to *King Richard II*, by William Shakespeare, Arden Shakespeare, ed. Charles R. Forker (London: Bloomsbury, 2019), 3.
3. As Robin Headlam Wells notes, the play supports neither the "didactic assertion of an 'orthodox' doctrine of absolute obedience to kingly authority, nor, at the other

extreme, a republican justification of tyrannicide." See Robin Headlam Wells, *Shakespeare's Politics* (New York: Continuum, 2009), 139.

4. Despite its relevance to the politics of the day, Shakespeare could not have anticipated the play's role in the Essex rebellion. See Forker, introduction to *King Richard II*, 5. See also Stephen Greenblatt, *Tyrant: Shakespeare on Politics* (New York: Norton, 2018), 22.

5. Barbara Hodgdon, *The End Crowns All: Closure and Contradiction in Shakespeare's History* (Princeton, NJ: Princeton University Press, 1991), 134.

6. For a discussion of Charles's identification with Richard, see Ernst H. Kantorowicz, *The King's Two Bodies: A Study of Mediaeval Political Theology* (Princeton, NJ: Princeton University Press, 1957), 41, and Victoria Kahn, *The Future of Illusion* (Chicago: University of Chicago Press, 2017), 71.

7. Kristin M. S. Bezio, *Staging Power in Tudor and Stuart English History Plays* (Burlington, VT: Ashgate, 2015), 117.

8. This and all future quotations from *Richard II* are from *The Norton Shakespeare: Histories*, 2nd ed. Edited by Stephen Greenblatt (New York: Norton, 2008).

9. Bezio notes that Bolingbroke's success is due to his "engaging in superior performative negotiation." Bezio, *Staging Power in Tudor and Stuart English History Plays*, 116.

10. Cf. E. M. W. Tillyard's reading of *Richard II* in light of the history plays that both precede and follow it. See E. M. W. Tillyard, *Shakespeare's History Plays* (London: Chatto & Windus, 1956).

11. Warren Chernaik notes that Elizabethans had a fundamentally different orientation to the past than we do today. See Warren Chernaik, *The Cambridge Introduction to Shakespeare's History Plays* (Cambridge: Cambridge University Press, 2007).

12. Doyeeta Majumder, *Tyranny and Usurpation: The New Prince and Lawmaking Violence in Early Modern Drama* (Liverpool: Liverpool University Press, 2019), 197.

13. Wells, *Shakespeare's Politics*, 131.

14. Louise Cowan, "God Will Save the King: Shakespeare's Richard II," in *Shakespeare as Political Thinker*, ed. John Alvis and Thomas G. West (Durham, NC: Carolina Academic Press, 1981), 69.

15. Tom Nichols, *The Death of Expertise* (New York: Oxford University Press), 2017.

16. For a complete discussion of Shakespeare's sources for the play, see Geoffrey Bullough, *Narrative and Dramatic Sources of Shakespeare* (London: Routledge & Kegan Paul, 1960).

17. Anthony Steel, *Richard II* (Cambridge: Cambridge University Press, 1962), 73–4.

18. On the importance of finding a language of power, see Lynn Staley, *Languages of Power in the Age of Richard II* (University Park: Pennsylvania State University Press), 2005.

19. Nigel Saul, *The Three Richards* (New York: Palgrave Macmillan, 2005), 60.

20. Saul, *The Three Richards*, 57.

21. On the way in which his use of prerogative positioned Richard both above and subject to the law, see Donna B. Hamilton, "The State of Law in *Richard II*," *Shakespeare Quarterly* 34, no. 1 (1983): 14.

22. On Shakespeare's "unsystematic" use of history, see Jeremy Lopez, "Eating Richard II," *Shakespeare Studies* 36 (2008): 207.

23. L. B. Campbell, ed., *The Mirror for Magistrates* (New York: Barnes & Noble, Inc, 1960), 111.

24. On the play's emphasis on failure, see Robyn Bolam, *"Richard II:* Shakespeare and the Languages of the Stage," in *The Cambridge Companion to Shakespeare's History Plays,* ed. Michael Hattaway (Cambridge: Cambridge University Press, 2002), 153.
25. Comparing *Richard II* to the unflinching pessimism of Marlowe's *Edward III,* A. L. Rowse argues that Shakespeare's play offers the audience "every sort of alleviation" (236). Nevertheless, Shakespeare's play is riddled with an uncertainty that hinges upon the contest between Richard and Bolingbroke. See A. L. Rowse, *William Shakespeare: A Biography* (New York: Harper & Row, 1963).
26. Many scholars have remarked on Shakespeare's choice to leave Richard's culpability in doubt in the first scene. See Nicholas Grene, *Shakespeare's Serial History Plays* (New York: Cambridge University Press, 2002), 77.
27. Bolam, *"Richard II:* Shakespeare and the Language of the Stage," 142.
28. Some scholars see Bolingbroke as an "accomplished Machiavel"; see for example, Leon Harold Craig, *The Philosopher's English King: Shakespeare's* Henriad *as Political Philosophy* (Rochester, NY: University of Rochester Press, 2015), 29–30. Barbara Hodgdon calls him the "Machiavellian new man" (*The End Crowns All,* 130). A. D. Nuttall, on the other hand, notes that Shakespeare could have made Bolingbroke a consummate Machiavel, but chose not to. See A. D. Nuttall, *Shakespeare the Thinker* (New Haven, CT: Yale University Press, 2007), 137.
29. Craig, *The Philosopher's English King,* 68.
30. See C. G. Thayer, *Shakespearean Politics: Government and Misgovernment in the Great Histories* (Athens: Ohio University Press, 1983), 2.
31. Nicholas Grene distinguishes the "mystical form of nostalgia" (172) that characterizes *Richard II* from the Henry IV plays. See Grene, *Shakespeare's Serial History Plays.*
32. The historic Gaunt was much more ambitious than Shakespeare's version. See Peter Saccio, *Shakespeare's English Kings: History, Chronicle, and Drama* (Oxford: Oxford University Press, 1977), 20.
33. On the symbolic importance of the body of Richard II, see Imke Lichterfeld, "'Thou livest and breathest, yet art thou slain in him': The Absence of Power in *Richard II,*" *Comparative Drama* 50, no. 2–3 (Summer & Fall 2016): 2–3.
34. Saccio, *Shakespeare's English Kings,* 35.
35. Rowse, *William Shakespeare,* 239.
36. Bezio argues that Bolingbroke's popularity and military support act as a "caution to potential tyrants about the potential threat posed by the populace through rebellion." See Bezio, *Staging Power in Tudor and Stuart English History Plays,* 117.
37. Rowse, *William Shakespeare,* 237.

REFERENCES

Bezio, Kristin M. S. *Staging Power in Tudor and Stuart English History Plays.* Burlington, VT: Ashgate, 2015.
Bolam, Robyn. *"Richard II:* Shakespeare and the Languages of the Stage." In *The Cambridge Companion to Shakespeare's History Plays,* edited by Michael Hattaway, 141–57. Cambridge: Cambridge University Press, 2002.
Bullough, Geoffrey. *Narrative and Dramatic Sources of Shakespeare.* London: Routledge & Kegan Paul, 1960.

Campbell, L. B., editor. *The Mirror for Magistrates.* New York: Barnes & Noble, Inc, 1960.

Chernaik, Warren. *The Cambridge Introduction to Shakespeare's History Plays.* Cambridge: Cambridge University Press, 2007.

Cowan, Louise. "God Will Save the King: Shakespeare's Richard II." In *Shakespeare as Political Thinker*, edited by John Alvis and Thomas G. West, 63–81. Durham, NC: Carolina Academic Press, 1981.

Craig, Leon Harold. *The Philosopher's English King: Shakespeare's* Henriad *as Political Philosophy.* Rochester, NY: University of Rochester Press, 2015.

Forker, Charles R. Introduction to *King Richard II*, by William Shakespeare, Arden Shakespeare, 1–169. Edited by Charles R. Forker. London: Bloomsbury, 2019.

Greenblatt, Stephen. *Tyrant: Shakespeare on Politics.* New York: Norton, 2018.

Grene, Nicholas. *Shakespeare's Serial History Plays.* New York: Cambridge University Press, 2002.

Hadfield, Andrew. *Shakespeare and Renaissance Politics.* Arden Shakespeare. London: Thomson Learning, 2004.

Hamilton, Donna B. "The State of Law in *Richard II.*" *Shakespeare Quarterly* 34, no. 1 (1983): 5–17.

Hodgdon, Barbara. *The End Crowns All: Closure and Contradiction in Shakespeare's History.* Princeton, NJ: Princeton University Press, 1991.

Kahn, Victoria. *The Future of Illusion.* Chicago: University of Chicago Press, 2017.

Kantorowicz, Ernst H. *The King's Two Bodies: A Study of Mediaeval Political Theology.* Princeton, NJ: Princeton University Press, 1957.

Lichterfeld, Imke. "'Thou livest and breathest, yet art thou slain in him': The Absence of Power in *Richard II.*" *Comparative Drama* 50, no. 2–3 (Summer & Fall 2016): 195–207.

Lopez, Jeremy. "Eating Richard II." *Shakespeare Studies* 36 (2008): 207–8.

Majumder, Doyeeta. *Tyranny and Usurpation: The New Prince and Lawmaking Violence in Early Modern Drama.* Liverpool: Liverpool University Press, 2019.

Nichols, Tom. *The Death of Expertise*, New York: Oxford University Press, 2017.

Nuttall, A. D. *Shakespeare the Thinker.* New Haven, CT: Yale University Press, 2007.

Rowse, A. L. *William Shakespeare: A Biography.* New York: Harper & Row, 1963.

Saccio, Peter. *Shakespeare's English Kings: History, Chronicle, and Drama.* Oxford: Oxford University Press, 1977.

Saul, Nigel. *The Three Richards.* New York: Palgrave Macmillan, 2005.

Shakespeare, William. *Richard II. The Norton Shakespeare: Histories*, 2nd ed. Edited by Stephen Greenblatt. New York: Norton, 2008.

Staley, Lynn. *Languages of Power in the Age of Richard II.* University Park: Pennsylvania State University Press, 2005.

Steel, Anthony. *Richard II.* Cambridge: Cambridge University Press, 1962.

Thayer, C. G. *Shakespearean Politics: Government and Misgovernment in the Great Histories.* Athens: Ohio University Press, 1983.

Tillyard, E. M. W. *Shakespeare's History Plays.* London: Chatto & Windus, 1956.

Wells, Robin Headlam. *Shakespeare's Politics.* New York: Continuum, 2009.

2. "Liars and swearers": Shakespeare's *Macbeth* and the dissemblance of modern autocrats

Ryan Farrar

Critics faulting the policies and practices of autocratic leaders such as Recep Tayyip Erdoğan and Donald Trump speak of their brazen corruption as a threat to human rights. Governmental entities and watchdog organizations, such as the United States Justice Department, Human Rights Watch, and the United Nations, have documented numerous cases of abuse by world leaders. These include extrajudicial killings, self-enrichment through kleptocracy and extortion, scapegoating ethnic groups, and repressing political dissidents.[1] To facilitate their actions, modern administrations and regimes manipulate the flow of information people receive. Politicians are reputed for dissembling, but the degree to which they distort facts appears to be on the rise. Candidates and campaigners mislead their followers into trusting easily disproven lies, and followers consciously endorse their leaders' mendacity as a show of strength and acuity. As a result, phrases such as "alternative facts" and "fake news" trend as misinformation campaigns prioritize political ideologies over material conditions. Critics use these phrases to characterize the machinations of parties and regimes, and the latter invoke them to discredit criticism. The mobilization of disinformation has helped to foster personality cults around leaders such as Trump, Kim Jong-Un, Xi Jinping, and Bashar al-Assad. In turn, these leaders rely on doublespeak to rebut inquiries into their practices, simulating social stability and promoting dogmatic confidence in might makes right. In a climate where imperious personalities encourage cutthroat competition, looking back to William Shakespeare's play *Macbeth* (1606) can afford readers a renewed understanding of the relationship between politics, language, and dissembling, as the Macbeths' fraudulent misdirection resembles moves made in politics today.

SPECTRAL LANGUAGE AND TREACHERY IN MACBETH

One major influence on Shakespeare's portrayal of villains was the sixteenth-century Italian statesman Niccolò Machiavelli, who is primarily remembered for his practical instructions to princes for gaining and retaining power. Among them, Machiavelli advised princes to win their subjects' support through benign, though false, appearances. Their improbity, he believed, would facilitate their ability to behave ruthlessly when need arose, while still maintaining a positive image. He wrote: "One who has this capacity must understand how to keep it covered, and be a skillful pretender and dissembler. Men are so simple and so subject to present needs that he who deceives in this way will always find those who will let themselves be deceived."[2] His instructions resonate in modern times when leaders employ hyperbole and pandering to cement support. Aiding their image are partisan pundits who televise and stream propaganda to wide audiences. Through these means, confirmation bias has become a ubiquitous, malleable, and, ironically, intractable weapon. I find it worthwhile to examine how dissembling affects judgment and moves people to accept untruths as true and truths as untrue. Like the impairments that result from modern echo chambers and confirmation bias, *Macbeth* dramatizes the potential for the doubleness of language and reality to impair discernment, carrying the potential to frustrate those who try to cooperate with others with an overwhelming sense of distrust.

In *Macbeth*, Shakespeare features the corruption of a Scottish noble warrior whose deceit, regicide, and usurpation of the throne transform his homeland into a dystopia. In a society like feudal England or tanist Scotland, hierarchy and authority are structured by language and customs, and *Macbeth* centers on a gross displacement of both.[3] From the play's outset, the kingdom's decline begins with political instability held at bay. The Scottish forces of King Duncan, led by Macbeth and Banquo, successfully suppress both a rebellion and an invading force that is allied with an insurrectionary defector. Despite enduring bloody battles, the Scots' victory cheers King Duncan and his thanes, and they anticipate a peaceful postwar period. Shakespeare's tragic plot ensures that peace is short-lived. Following the prophecy of three supernatural beings, Macbeth and his wife conspire against the king and initiate a reign of terror throughout the land. In a Machiavellian manner, Macbeth sloughs his honor, conscience, and loyalty to win the kingship at all costs. Macbeth's means are of particular interest as he simulates loyalty and duty to the king and thanes to achieve his ends, tricking them into seeing him as something he is not.

A similar trickery thrives in current political climates, and studies of *Macbeth* show a kinship between the world of the play and contemporary leadership. Bryan Lowrance comments on Macbeth's ambition in a way that evokes the authoritarian trends of today:

> Ambition has its own long and complex history, from Greek concepts of hubris through widespread Elizabethan vilifications of the tendency. But Shakespeare's presentation of it in *Macbeth* gives the old concept a new twist. Macbeth's treatment doesn't just repeat the period's boilerplate ethical injunctions. It uses ambition to think through the experience of political action as being profoundly disjoined from ethico-political norms […] It is the heroic ideal spiraling off into moral anarchy, a kind of misplaced ideal of immanence along solipsistic and anti-communal lines.[4]

Shakespeare reflects on the separation between the communal values that bind a country together and the potential for leadership to utterly divorce those values from ruling while espousing those values as their bedrock. Like Macbeth, current and aspiring autocrats cultivate egoistic worldviews that only reinforce their own interests and power, regardless of worsening conditions. Once they achieve power, autocrats and Macbeth maniacally scramble to totalize their control and eliminate those who show the slightest signs of dissent, either through muzzles, repression, or murder.[5] For example, it is not improbable to imagine that the likes of Barack Obama, John McCain, and Hillary Clinton serve for Trump as Banquo's ghost did for Macbeth when the former caused the latter to act erratically fearful at a banquet.[6] The praise and legacies of others haunt leaders, intensifying their attempts to affirm their self-image in the eyes of others.

Aside from Banquo's ghost, Macbeth becomes well-acquainted with insecurity. His conscientious deliberations splinter his mind into a state of paranoia; he isolates himself, becomes desensitized to human sympathy, and thus carves a path that transforms him into an unhinged tyrant. He unflinchingly orders the slaughter of women and children, even out of petty frustration, and hurls abuses at his own troops when leading them into the play's climactic battle. Connecting Macbeth's inhumanity with twentieth-century totalitarianism, Roland Frye argues that "much of what we find under the terrorizing regimes of Hitler and Stalin is also evident in Shakespeare's presentation of the medieval Scottish tyrant Macbeth."[7] Recent productions of *Macbeth* even draw parallels between the play and the spread of nationalist populism and totalitarianism. Rupert Goold's 2010 *Macbeth*, starring Patrick Stewart, featured the characters in costumes and a setting that evoked the regimes of both Stalinist Russia and Ceauşescu's Romania. When considering the moves and policies crafted by twenty-first-century states and politicians, comparisons to Macbeth and his practices are apt, but it is also necessary to further consider how political messaging emboldens and enables tyrannical conduct. A good place to start is with the role language and customs play in both politics and *Macbeth*.

Concerns about the mutability of language and its potential for deceptive appropriation pervade the art and thought of Jacobean England. Part of the caution and far-reaching skepticism of the time incongruously stemmed from a shared desire to foster an ideal commonwealth, a harmonious kingdom. As Eric Nelson writes, "The political writers who furnished the intellectual background of Shakespeare's age were in fundamental agreement that there was a best regime for any given community, and that is was a matter of moral urgency to identify and institute it."[8] Despite this shared imperative, espionage, conspiracy, and a general sense of distrust became commonplace in the politico-religious climate that followed Henry VIII's break from the Roman Catholic Church in 1534 and the Vatican's conspiratorial attempts to reclaim England thereafter. Andrew Fitzmaurice writes that "late Elizabethans [and by extension, Jacobeans], like most Post-Reformation Europeans, believed that the world they inhabited was in decline, that it had abandoned virtue and given itself over to the treacherous politics of the court."[9] In 1587, these tensions compelled Queen Elizabeth I, a Protestant, to execute her Roman Catholic cousin, Mary Queen of Scots, for her role in the Babington Plot of 1586 to assassinate Elizabeth. Paranoia, fear, and political skepticism are not exclusive to the twenty-first century. With such duplicity, the ability to trust family or confidants becomes strained.

The intrigue of deceits and plots persisted during King James I's reign, and he invoked the metaphor of the body politic to rebuff challenges to the state and his person, arguing that there is a unity that transcends sedition.[10] Gillian Kendall hones in on King James's rhetoric following the failed Gunpowder Plot of 1605. She points to his portrayal of the conspirators as diseased appendages in need of amputation, a metaphor that in many ways lines up with the othering tactics of Donald Trump's "drain-the-swamp" rhetoric, Rodrigo Duterte's extrajudicial threats against suspects, or Hillary Clinton's "basket of deplorables" label.[11] Kendall writes: "State executions may thus be seen as a logical extension of the metaphor of the body politic, which, according to James I, dictated that 'it may very well fall out that the head will be forced to garre cut off some rotten members … to keep the rest of the body in integritie.'"[12] For James to suggest that the dissenters are diseased limbs of the body politic requiring amputation provides a salient example of how language constructs perception: the conspirators were not simply Others, but members of the unified body subverting the system from within. As the conspirators sought to unseat James I, Macbeth uses his status as a thane to unseat Duncan through clandestine means. Like them, he is an impostor who uses deception as a means to power. Macbeth's imposture extends into his rule, and his furtive methods are like those used by modern dictators and autocrats.

It is important to note that tyranny and treachery in the play do not develop from an inveterate malice on the part of Macbeth towards a political enemy.

Instead, like social media posts that catalyze mass shooters to act, there is a stochastic effect, an anomalous force that urges him toward committing the sacrilegious murder he may have otherwise never committed. The Weird Sisters embody this force as they cryptically entrance Macbeth and Banquo with portents of future prosperity. The melody and rhythm of their verses estrange them from the customs of the Scottish social order, as does their physical appearance. Looming within the wilderness, the Sisters' attire and features collapse the boundaries of distinction. When Banquo sees them, he says:

> **BANQUO** What are these,
>   So withered, and so wild in their attire,
>   That look not like th' inhabitants o'th' earth
>   And yet are on't?
>   You should be women,
>   And yet your beards forbid me to interpret
>   That you are so. (1.3.39–42, 45–7)[13]

The description shows that they bridge the earthly world with a space that is alien. Banquo observes that they both collapse inviolable boundaries, such as those between men and women, truths and lies, material and immaterial, and distort interpretation itself. When the Sisters vanish, Macbeth remarks, "What seemed corporal melted / As breath into the wind" (1.3.81–2). These transitory creatures embody the collapse of contraries that Macbeth adopts throughout the rest of the play, such as when he hysterically butchers people to retain power, a power established to protect those same people. The Sisters speak to civil matters, but they appear separate from society. Banquo's difficulty in construing them bespeaks a fuzzy effect that proceeds from them and ripples through Scotland. The words they speak symbolize the (in)security of language and its capacity for (un)stable meaning as their omens appear contradictory. As the Sisters' own shape defies identification, so do interpretative methods fail when trying to affix stability to language performance. In fact, unlike the human Scots, the Sisters speak in rhyming couplets, and at times their verse is presented in catalectic trochaic tetrameter.[14] The verse pattern is often more abrupt than the iambic pentameter of the thanes, and there is something intriguingly curious about its variations.[15] The Sisters equivocate in riddles, and some of their half-truths are reflected in their catalectic speech, such as the lines "Fair is foul, and foul is fair / Hover through the fog and filthy air" (1.1.11–12). The leaving off of syllables in the final foot of lines may suggest that a sullied order will take shape in Scotland, and, as inversions of iambs, their trochees symbolize a backward hierarchy. The Sisters' prophecies unsettle pursuits of peace, and they speak to the inherent doubleness in human affairs. This is greatly encapsulated by their chanting over the cauldron: "Double, double, toil and trouble" (4.1.35), and, despite Duncan initially prevailing over the double crosses of his kin, the fear of a recrudescence lingers and is personified through the Sisters.

It is provoking to think that three centuries prior to the popularization of Orwellian doublespeak, the Weird Sisters utter a similar paradox when they famously chant, "Fair is foul, and foul is fair" (1.1.11). Like the newspeak of *Nineteen Eighty-Four*, the verse appears denotatively contradictory, but yields a logic that compromises the notion that opposites are distinct. From the play's outset, the implosion and foundering of civil decorum besets the kingdom. "Fair" becomes "foul" in the Thane of Cawdor's rebellion, and "foul" becomes "fair" in the gruesome violence Macbeth displays combating it. The Captain reports Macbeth's victories as though penning a paean, describing how he hacked and hewed down Scotland's enemies "with his brandished steel, / Which smoked with bloody execution / Like Valour's minion" (1.2.17–19). The heroism for which Duncan and his attendants laud Macbeth reveals a doubleness inherent within social relations.

A code of virtues, such as chivalry, requires vice as a means to sustain it, such as when violence becomes a tool for peace. The Sisters may not simply reflect a wildness outside of civil society but instead may reflect an unnaturalness that inheres within it. Terry Eagleton unravels this seeming paradox, noting that the commingling of "fair" with "foul" disassembles the illusory boundary between "natural" and "unnatural":

> It is hard to see why [Lady Macbeth's] bloodthirsty talk of dashing out babies' brains is any more "unnatural" than skewering an enemy soldier's guts [...] this opposition will not hold even within *Macbeth's* own terms, since the "unnatural" – Macbeth's lust for power – is disclosed by the witches as already lurking within the "natural" – the routine state of cut-throat rivalry between noblemen [...] Nature, to be normative, must already include the possibility of its own perversion, just as a sign can be roughly defined as anything which can be used for the purpose of lying.[16]

Eagleton describes normativity and its aberrations as containing each other, and likewise, codes of honor incorporate their opposites, deceit and disloyalty. These standards subsume what they ostensibly try to leave out. For example, Macbeth speaks truthfully, but the performance of truth-telling includes lying as an equal possibility. When a lie poses as truth well enough, the difference can be indeterminate. Narratives of peace and legitimacy, then, become a kind of palliative, like laying new flooring over an old one. As Macbeth poignantly observes in his tortured ecstasy while arranging Banquo's assassination, "Better be with the dead, / Whom we, to gain our peace, have sent to peace" (3.2.21–2). He recognizes the natural contradiction that the peace of mind he seeks requires a non-peaceful act, and that while he reaps the fruits of the present moment (i.e., "we, to gain our peace"), such peace produces guilt (i.e., "better be with the dead"). As such, his peace both is and is not peace.

The equation of a word with its antonym shows itself most sharply in the language and customs that suit a dissembler's motives. Within *Macbeth*, Inverness Castle embodies expectations of hospitality and presents the opportunity for its hosts to pervert these customs. Following the victory over the Norse and the execution of Cawdor, the play offers a tentative bait-and-switch sense of rejuvenation, but the optimism is steeped in irony. King Duncan offers sage advice to his thanes, cautioning them against mistaking foes for friends. With regards to Cawdor, he remarks,

> **DUNCAN** There's no art
> To find the mind's construction in the face.
> He was a gentleman on whom I built
> An absolute trust. (1.4.11–14)

Acknowledging that he could not detect any signs of betrayal while the traitor served him, Duncan reasons that one cannot accept gestures and words as truthful expressions of others' intentions. Yet, gestures and words are all they have to gauge others' trustworthiness. Sadly, Duncan does not practice what he preaches, as he voices his wisdom at the very moment he invests a complete trust in Macbeth's loyalty. To facilitate his opportunity to murder, Macbeth encourages Duncan's trust through words, saying to him: "The service and the loyalty I owe, / In doing it, pays itself," adding "everything safe toward your love / And honour" (1.4.22–3, 27–8). Macbeth disingenuously observes the customs of fealty, and Duncan is persuaded of these displays' authenticity. Lady Macbeth goes on to urge her husband's double-cross, directing him to conjoin warm hospitality with cold malice:

> **LADY MACBETH** Your face, my thane, is as a book where men
> May read strange matters. To beguile the time,
> Look the time; bear welcome in your eye,
> Your hand, your tongue. Look like th'innocent flower,
> But be the serpent underneath it. (1.5.62–6)

In a reprisal of Duncan's theme of reading motives, Lady Macbeth observes that physical expressions are texts that others will take at face value. Her instructions recognize the playful, manipulative creativity afforded by gestures and language, where tongues and bodies can craft false stories that lull targets into complacency before being attacked, like a venomous serpent hiding underneath a bewitching flower. Lady Macbeth carries her plan off impressively, as Duncan is not suspicious at all when he approaches Inverness. He remarks, "This castle hath a pleasant seat, the air / Nimbly and sweetly recommends itself unto our gentle senses" (1.6.1–3). Following upon various threats to his kingdom, Inverness appears as an oasis to him, and Shakespeare depicts the pleasant atmosphere to emphasize that even edifices are texts to be read. Yet, their appearances may belie what waits within their walls.

When Duncan last appears on the stage, he is in the company of trusted men, but his words express wonder at Macbeth's absence, which should provoke suspicion. Poetically, Macbeth has become catalectic like the Sisters' verses, absent and socially isolated, but present nevertheless. Only Lady Macbeth consistently performs the rituals of hospitality. Despite the signs of betrayal, Duncan trusts Macbeth, and it costs him his life. Julia Reinhard Lupton astutely remarks upon the effect of the Macbeths' duplicity: "To each of these ideals [of hospitality and felicity], the Macbeths' hostile modes of dwelling and greeting will pose blistering antitypes: the act of murdering sleep replaces fertility with barrenness and atmospheric openness with claustrophobia."[17] Lupton highlights the layering of antitypes to be read into "the pleasant seat," turning it into a place that bears both welcome and death. Like an Amazonian pitcher plant, these inverse states of beauty and destruction cohabit. Noting this inversion, many scholars have suggested an intertextual relationship between the biblical myth of Lucifer's expulsion from Heaven into Hell and Macbeth's descent from most honored warrior to abhorred tyrant. As Lucifer was also a pleasing deceiver, so is Macbeth.[18]

In obtaining power, though, Macbeth becomes monomaniacal and consistently looks at those around him as potential threats to his rule. In the play, Shakespeare shows a moral degradation within Scotland that leads its subjects to feel ill at the thought of their leader's intolerance. Enraged over Macduff's desertion to Malcolm's camp, King Macbeth sends soldiers to slay the former's family in retaliation. Facing imminent death, Lady Macduff and her son exchange witty observations about what constitutes a traitor. They wonder whether Macduff qualifies as one for abandoning them to Macbeth's wrath. As they agree that traitors lie and deserve to be hanged by "honest men," the son cleverly surmises, "Then the liars and swearers are fools, for there are liars and swearers enough to beat the honest men and hang up them" (4.2.54–8). The son's comment speaks of a kingdom beset with corruption. Further, he recognizes that political power has no basis in any standard of virtue, even if power upholds the values it proclaims. Groups with the greatest numbers, coordination, and means will override those that dutifully observe mutual laws and customs, such as those based on Christianity. Thus, the son concludes that liars and swearers have practical sanction to pervert principles because their majority cannot be checked. Lady Macduff offers a similar reflection in detailing the paradox of how people who act in good faith are unilaterally targeted for being innocuous:

> **LADY MACDUFF** I have done no harm. But I remember now
> I am in this earthly world, where to do harm
> Is often laudable, to do good sometime
> Accounted dangerous folly. (4.2.76–9)

In Jacobean culture, where the audience's worldviews were shaped by beliefs in a beneficent God, Lady Macduff's words describe a world order that is upside-down; performing good deeds can lead to ruin, while practicing corruption can lead to success. When tyrants try to shape circumstances to suit their advantage, the collateral damage can be devasting and victimize parties who are deemed guilty by association. If the majority, or its leaders, permit unfettered corruption and mistreatment, moral standards of right and wrong collapse, paradoxically replaced by the rigidly imposed value of unwavering loyalty.

The tragic irony for those who still aspire to maintain ethical standards in a corrupt society rests in the viral dissemination of suspicion and distrust. When measures are taken to secure trust, it is possible for precaution to breed even more distrust. In a complex scene, Shakespeare shows Macbeth's foil, Macduff, arriving at Malcolm's camp. Responding to the betrayal of his father, Duncan, and aiming to improve upon his father's missteps, Malcolm relies on trickery to vet men seeking to ally with him so he can ensure that he can trust their intentions. As Mary Ann McGrail argues, Malcolm "serves as a correction to Duncan—there is an art to finding the mind's construction, though not through simple appearances. One must search out intentions by indirect means, such as the test of loyalty and intellect he administers to Macduff."[19] However, the trickery generates ambivalence for Macduff, as he comes to fear that he has left one tyrant only to embrace another. In truth, Malcolm's trial proves disconcerting, as Duncan's son lies to Macduff, falsely professing to him that he desires to overthrow Macbeth to satisfy a lust for wealth and power without check. The trial inversely mirrors the Macbeths' bait-and-switch snare of Duncan. As they lured Duncan into comfort, Malcolm lures Macduff into reproaching him for his intemperate desires. However, Malcolm baits Macduff too convincingly for the latter to tell if the bait is bait or genuine intention:

> **MALCOLM** All the particulars of vice so grafted
> That, when they shall be opened, black Macbeth
> Will seem as pure as snow, and the poor state
> Esteem him as a lamb, being compared
> With my confineless harms. (4.3.52–6)

Malcolm promises to make Macbeth look innocent compared to his own self-indulgences. He extends his list of vices and mentions that no one will be able to fill his "cistern of lust" (4.3.64) nor satisfy his undying hunger for material possessions. He concludes his profession with a promise to sow further disorder:

> **MALCOLM** […] had I power, I should
>   Pour the sweet milk of concord into hell,
>   Uproar the universal peace, confound
>   All unity on earth. (4.3.98–101)

Throughout the scene, Malcolm threatens to install a reign that would intensify the chaos plaguing Scotland rather than usher in the succor for which Macduff hopes. He proposes to rule as a peddler in confusion, one who will glut his personal desires and make Macbeth's rule appear a restful sleep compared to the nightmare he intends.

Resolute against flouting Christian morality, but desperate to oppose Macbeth's tyranny, Macduff initially responds with concessions to secretly cater to Malcolm's libidinous desires: "You may / Convey your pleasures in a spacious plenty, / And yet seem cold; the time you may so hoodwink" (4.3.71–3). His proposal to Malcolm echoes his wife's and son's discussion regarding injustice in government, further characterizing the time as depraved. At first, he willingly compromises his own sense of right to battle someone he views as a bigger threat and, like Machiavelli, acknowledges how easily people are deceived. However, Macduff's concessions have limits. When Malcolm ends his speech and asks if the former finds him fit to govern, Macduff exclaims:

> **MACDUFF** Fit to govern?
>   No, not to live. O nation miserable!
>   With an untitled tyrant, bloody-sceptered,
>   When shalt though see thy wholesome days again?...
>   These evils thou repeat'st upon thyself
>   Hath banished me from Scotland. O my breast,
>   Thy hope ends here. (4.3.103–6, 112–14)

Seeing his future hopes dashed, Macduff cannot abide Malcolm's wicked-ness, denounces the latter's wishes, and openly rebukes the potential king for "blasphem[ing] his breed," or royal bloodline (4.3.108). For Malcolm, his test yields the desired outcome, but the façade he erected has come at a cost. Soon after Macduff protests Malcolm's corruption, the heir interjects and admits that he merely staged his degenerate desires as a technique to gauge Macduff's own morality. Understandably, though, his dissembling leaves Macduff shaken and unsure as to whether Malcolm faithfully represents the values he endorses. Malcolm may express joy to hear Macduff abjure dissipation, dubbing Macduff a "child of integrity" (4.3.116), but Macduff perceives the latter's acting as uninterpretable, kindred to Macbeth's double-dealing. Macduff's discombobulated response to the revelation is one Shakespeare likely intends his audience to share: "Such welcome and unwelcome things at once / 'Tis hard to reconcile" (4.3.137–8). At a loss, Macduff's verses capture the dizziness caused by doubleness. The vetting process elicits a vertiginous effect, one that unbalances Macduff's grasp of what is genuine and what is show.

The tenor of Malcolm's loyalty test is an inversion of Macbeth's attempts to conceal his evil by appearing good. Reflective of the theater culture that spawned their fictional selves, both men convey that they can convincingly occupy the spheres of virtue and vice simultaneously, and, with this possibility, discerning between the two becomes difficult, as one can pose as the other. Like Macbeth, Malcolm abuses the trust of his follower, switching too casually between his professions of integrity and intemperance. As a result, Macduff fears that there can be no faith in language to represent the reality of others' intentions. Eagleton fittingly details the effects that dissembling generates with regards to communication in *Macbeth*: "Language … overwhelms and dismembers the body; desire inflates consciousness to the point where it dissevers itself from sensuous constraints and comes to consume it in a void. When language is cut loose from reality, signifiers split from signifieds, the result is a radical fissure between consciousness and material life."[20] Malcolm and Macbeth both design narratives that operate independently from their intentions and actions, which renders the stability of language as transitory and ghostly as the Weird Sisters. Like the drama between Shakespeare's political characters, the fissure between signifiers and signifieds mentioned by Eagleton persists in contemporary political discourse.

Language, with all its instabilities, shows a constancy in its flexibility and manipulability. Reading Shakespeare lends opportunities for reflection on and critique of actors within political systems for the purpose of questioning their intentions, whether in the context of specific legislation they support or (fake) news stories they share on social media. Language often grants less accessibility to reality than most people readily believe. However, awareness of its limits and uses provides a platform for inquiry that can foster a mindfulness regarding political discourse.

SPECIOUSNESS AND POISONING THE WELL

When modern political officials spin issues, they aim to discredit criticism of their governance, and their tactics are extensions of the subterfuge seen in *Macbeth*. Noticing these trends can be helpful for vetting the actions of politicians and associated entities, since so much information is expected to be taken at face value. For instance, in a 2019 interview, former White House press secretary Stephanie Grisham not only obfuscated accusations that Donald Trump had flouted laws and abused his power of office for his own self-interest but also worked to overwrite those accusations entirely. She portrayed him as a prudent leader, selflessly managing his duties and "drain[ing] the swamp" of grimy officials. When journalists raised concerns around the suspension of regular White House briefings as evidence that Trump was concealing corrupt policy making and his own abuses of office, Grisham countered with her own allegations, charging journalists with publishing criticism/fake news to serve their own ambitions. Specifically, on the program *Fox & Friends*, Grisham deflected the media's concerns about the lack of White House briefings by casting shade on the journalists:

> "I mean, ultimately, if the president decides that it's something we should do, we can do that, but right now he's doing just fine … And to be honest, the briefings have become a lot of theater. And I think that a lot of reporters were doing it to get famous. I mean, yeah, they're writing books now. I mean, they're all getting famous off of this presidency. And so, I think it's great what we're doing now … It had become, again, theater, and they weren't being good to his people. And he doesn't like that. He's very loyal to his people, and he put a stop to it."[21]

In the moment of denouncing the briefings as stage performance, both Grisham and Trump are performing; she performs by changing the subject through *ad hominem* attacks, and he performs by suspending the briefings. She took the journalists' accusations against Trump and projected them onto the media itself, diverting attention away from the issue at hand. As some have noted, there is mounting evidence that Trump family members have leveraged the presidency to benefit their private enterprises, which White House officials and other Republicans either dismiss or ignore.[22] For their base, Grisham's reversal works to discredit media outlets as projecting their own corruption onto Trump. With auditors who follow the shadow of speech more than facts, the effect goes beyond simply generating another echo chamber. Like funhouse mirrors, and like the theme of language in *Macbeth*, genuine substance and illusory images may become indistinguishable, if auditors care to differentiate between them at all.

Grisham's spin aims to safeguard the White House against critiques or questions by cloaking its dealings, as though the White House were a private entity. It reflects Macbeth's actions in deflecting attention away from his crimes. Upon the discovery of Duncan's body, there is suspicion as to who carried out his murder. To steer attention away from himself, Macbeth smears Duncan's blood onto the guards, framing them for the murder he committed. Similar to the cessation of White House briefings, which deprived media representatives of the chance to directly respond to Grisham, Macbeth summarily executes the guards to prevent their testimony. Readers know that Macbeth executes them for selfish reasons, but the thane spins a narrative to the contrary, claiming that his passion for the King moved him to act rashly. More than just deflecting, Macbeth also presents himself in a noble light. Narratives like Grisham's and Macbeth's shape reception, and audiences may take mere ornaments of recti-tude as genuine articles of intention.

In an age where nearly anyone in developed countries has access to a micro-phone, camera, and other hardware to project their beliefs with or without rigorous reflection, false stories are ripe for consumption. Contemporary communicative technology was absent during the seventeenth century, yet, the Jacobean stage, with its emphasis on orality and attendees of various social ranks mingling together, is an apt analogue for the effects that internet stories can have on users. Macbeth and Lady Macbeth are panderers of sorts. They manipulate tradition to their advantage, seemingly in accord with chiv-alric norms, to conceal their violations of it. The couple's false displays and Macbeth's eventual rage provide the contemporary era with a reference point for inspecting the practices of twenty-first-century politicians with autocratic tendencies. Like an elaborate gaslighting campaign, regimes and administra-tions in the US, Russia, China, Saudi Arabia, North Korea, and others traffic in Orwellian doublespeak while purporting to combat it. They peddle in false flags, crafting narratives and party lines that affirm preconceived values and spreading them over social media. They spur supporters to reject competing narratives, if they do not censor them completely, and any contradictory evidence that arises is dismissed as false flags in themselves. Modern leaders, including Trump, Berlusconi, Xi, Kim, Putin, and others, have exercised the same chicanery through the power of their office and associates as the Macbeths did through chivalry and secondary agents, such as Banquo's assas-sins.[23] Their misinformation amplifies both the prevailing worldviews and the radical skepticism of some of their ardent supporters, for whom nothing can be trusted except stories that confirm bias.

In the virtual domain, a vast number of people across the globe are capable of transmitting information instantly, and while the medium proves empower-ing, the spatial, political, and linguistic boundaries themselves do not disap-pear even as geographical boundaries are moderately bridged. On the contrary, these boundaries often become more obdurate. The medium for interpreting information remains shared language, which is the input and output that shapes views regarding what is real and true. Depending on the preceding sources of input, whether families, friends, schools, or churches, truth-claims can inter-nally calcify within people's minds and remain unchanged, even when faced with dissonant information. For those with access to social media, there is no longer a need to reflect on or encounter dissonance as they can completely filter it out if they please. For politicians, special interest groups, activists, marketing departments, and social media influencers, this atmosphere becomes rife for inventing and pushing bad information, as the malleable relationship between language and desire allows for direct experiences with the external world to be distorted. A steady stream of disinformation overrides rational instincts and compromises the relationship between language and reality. While professionals, journalists, scholars, and rigorous activists may exercise discretion when evaluating the quality of information, it is a pipedream to imagine everyday media users as screening the information they receive.

For ordinary citizens, perhaps more concerned with their everyday lives than with hard inquiries into morality and ethics, the immediacy of web pages, social media, and viral memes allows for propaganda and yellow journalism to give them a feeling of being informed, even if the content is spurious and contradicted by professionally verified conclusions. Communities form around these habits of communication, and often they latch on to false stories to prove that their beliefs are more correct than those of their opponents. These silos facilitate the reception of theatrics from a host of actors who distinctly aim to confirm biases. For example, actor Jussie Smollett staged his own mugging to make it appear as a hate crime driven by enmity against the LGBT community; David Daleiden recorded a video of Planned Parenthood officials and stirred up conservatives when he falsely claimed they were illegally selling fetal body parts; and, finally, Walker Daugherty alleged his gun injury on a hunting trip was perpetrated by illegal immigrants, despite the incident producing no evidence of any immigrant involvement.[24] Before facts and details are confirmed, though, partisans and officials on the left and right leap upon these stories and claim them as either incontrovertibly true or false, depending on their bias. This was the case in the recording of Planned Parenthood. Believing it was authentic, the state of Missouri called a special legislative session in response to the disinformation. Even when official accounts contradicted Daugherty's testimony, elected officials, such as Texas Agriculture Commissioner Sid Miller, continued to believe the false story. Alternately, these partisans may respond by claiming the official accounts to be deep state cover-ups.

Like Duncan trusting Macbeth, beliefs in cover-ups are not unfounded, however, even if these conclusions are mistaken. Various world governments have carried out scores of classified operations that do not respect rights or transparency.[25] These covert operations are precedents for distrusting official rhetoric and cultivate conditions in which populism can thrive in reaction to it (e.g., "drain the swamp"). And yet, these supporters do not apply the same skepticism to the politicians who claim to represent their interests. These politicians will also run on a platform that characterizes government as being mismanaged and corrupt. When elected, they sometimes sabotage bureaucratic functions to confirm those failures. This is the case with Trump's appointments of Scott Pruitt, a climate change denier, to the role of administrator of the Environmental Protection Agency, and of Betsy DeVos, a Republican billionaire and staunch supporter of school vouchers who aims to privatize education, to the role of secretary of education.

Many scholars believe that social media may be largely to blame for the proliferation of misinformation and polarization of people, but the problem's roots go beyond virtual meeting spaces. Social media is simply an amplifier of another weapon: groupthink. Language serves as a unifying system of symbols that binds people into agreement and active reciprocations of service. However, always present in these rhetorical bonds is the potential for members to skew agreed-upon meanings. In human nature, the precondition to cooperation between people is division, and in his study on rhetoric, twentieth-century scholar Kenneth Burke remarked that "identification is compensatory to division."[26] In this comment, Burke reflects on commonality as a means of overcoming the natural separation of humans, which can both forge fulfilling relationships or coax them into a kind of inflexible codependency. Because people are always physically separate, even in their most intimate situations, symbols remain the bridge through which humans negotiate meaning. This in turn requires a relative consensus on the meanings of symbols. However, as the symbols that comprise language are inherently unstable, so, too, is any consensus that forms around them.

The type of groupthink currently at work allows enterprising individuals to exploit supporters to further their own self-interests. In a neoliberal economy, politicians pander to biases, such as nativism and freedoms, while they engage kleptocracy. When campaigning, former Prime Minister Silvio Berlusconi took action to make it appear as though he had divested his assets. In reality, he restructured his business and still retained control over his media empire. With a lack of transparency and disclosure, governments across the globe leverage offices while disenfranchising minorities and lower classes without recourse. Abuses such as these are replete: Saudi Arabia's responsibility for the assassination of *Washington Post* journalist Jamal Khashoggi in 2018, tacitly supported by its business partner, President Trump; Saudi Arabia's involvement in the numerous deaths of Yemeni civilians in the Yemeni Civil War since 2015; President Trump commuting Roger Stone's prison sentence as a reward for loyalty and pardoning war criminals, such as Edward Gallagher, Clint Lorance, and Michael Behenna, as a political ploy; Turkish president Recep Tayyip Erdoğan watching as his national Counter Attack Team assaulted peaceful American protesters in Washington, DC, in 2017 with no repercussions.[27] Currently in China, there are reports of two million detained Uyghur Muslims in a campaign, indicating cultural genocide.

As has been the case for centuries, politics in the twenty-first century show leaders feeding off their supporters' fears and craven desire for dominance at the expense of others while these same leaders render their own people expend-able. For instance, Donald Trump continuously denies knowing people if their association with him would damage his reputation due to scandal. Indeed, evidence often shows he does know them, such as Ukrainian-American Lev Parnas, England's Prince Andrew, or former adviser George Papadopoulos.[28] The lack of freedom of expression in North Korea makes the country an exemplar of totalitarian abuses, echoing indirectly the remark of Macbeth's enemies that "those he commands move only in command, / Nothing in love" (5.2.19–20). While like-mindedness is unavoidable, narrow-mindedness can be evaded, and while critics debate over the genuineness of Malcom's res-toration at the end of *Macbeth*, he and his followers did resolve that tyranny would not be tolerated. Through resistance and recognition of actions that foster peaceful cooperation, people can at least recognize the choice to call out duplicity, corruption, and tyranny as it affects their own and others' lives.

While *Macbeth* features a powerful couple trying to dupe a seemingly honest court, gaming the system for their selfish ambitions at the cost of numerous lives, the twentieth and twenty-first centuries have witnessed an expansion of this dynamic. The majority of world governments are not ruled by an absolute monarch nor subscribe to older forms of government, yet neoliberalism and globalization have spread to the extent that there are scholars, critics, and bil-lionaires who remark that a new feudalism or *refeudalisation* is taking root.[29] Given the behaviors of various plutocrats and populist demagogues, deceivers position themselves as correlative to kings. In the media and in the courtroom, Donald Trump's behavior has been likened to that of a king to whom the law does not apply, and current GOP actors, such as William Barr and Senator Mitch McConnell, pay him this deference.[30] Further, as in *Macbeth*, a range of scandals shows the lengths to which people with power will go to secure it, whether through tax evasion (e.g., the Panama Papers) or voter suppression.[31] In the twenty-first century, tyranny takes the form of gagging, scarcity, yellow journalism, and laws that pardon criminality. Countries bolster narratives about their own greatness and push those narratives onto their citizenry (e.g., Chinese economic policy or Russian nationalism). Indoctrination and intoler-ance grow increasingly common, as messaging is controlled to the degree that when loyalist members deviate from party lines, their missteps are rewritten as conspiracy smears on the part of political opponents.[32] Projection of one's misdeeds onto enemies becomes a tool of deflection and camouflage. In the play, Macbeth orders men to kill Banquo and Fleance. When Fleance survives, Lennox sarcastically mentions a theory circulating about Fleance's responsi-bility for Banquo's murder: "Fleance killed, / For Fleance fled" (3.6.6–7). The explanation is likely spread by Macbeth himself. Popularizing knee-jerk the-ories resonate in populism, and rather than demagogues having to respond to allegations against them, they demonize their accusers through whataboutisms and sound bites. Yet beneath their floral narratives are forked tongues.

NOTES

1. See for instance, United States Department of Justice, *Philippines 2018 Human Rights Report*, https://www.justice.gov/eoir/page/file/1145101/download, Human Rights Watch, *World Report 2019: Events of 2018*. For cronyism and the oligarchy of the United Russia Party, see Vladislav L. Inozemtse, "Neo-Feudalism Explained," *American Interest* 6, no. 4 (2011): 73–80. For kleptocracy and the Trump administration, see Timothy K. Kuhner, "American Kleptocracy: How to Categorise Trump and His Government," *King's Law Journal* 28, no. 2 (September 2017): 201–38.
2. Niccolò Machiavelli, *The Prince*, in *The Norton Anthology of World Literature*, Vol. C, 4th ed., ed. Martin Puchner et al. (New York: W. W. Norton, 2018), 177.
3. Sandra Clark and Pamela Mason, "Introduction," in *Macbeth* (London: Bloomsbury, 2015), 35. These editors provide a concise definition of tanistry: "In medieval Scotland the monarchy had been elective and largely governed according to [a] process … whereby royal successors were named from a collateral rather than a direct branch of the family, kingship passing not from father to son, but from brother to brother, uncle to nephew or cousin to cousin."
4. Bryan Lowrance, "'Modern Ecstasy': *Macbeth* and the Meaning of the Political," *ELH* 79, no. 4 (2012): 833, 835.
5. See Alice Su, "A Doctor was Arrested for Warning China about the Coronavirus. Then he Died of it," *Los Angeles Times*, February 6, 2020, https://www.latimes.com/world-nation/story/2020-02-06/coronavirus-china-xi-li-wenliang.
6. Rebecca Ballhaus and Gordon Lubold, "White House Wanted USS John McCain 'Out of Sight' During Trump Japan Visit," *The Wall Street Journal*, May 26, 2020, https://www.wsj.com/articles/white-house-wanted-uss-john-mccain-out-of-sight-during-trump-japan-visit-11559173470.
7. Roland Frye, "Hitler, Stalin, and Shakespeare's *Macbeth*: Modern Totalitarianism and Ancient Tyranny," *American Philosophical Society* 142, no. 1 (1998): 83.
8. Eric Nelson, "Shakespeare and the Best State of a Commonwealth," in *Shakespeare and Early Modern Political Thought*, ed. David Armitage, Conal Condren, and Andrew Fitzmaurice (Cambridge: Cambridge University Press, 2009), 256.
9. Andrew Fitzmaurice, "The Corruption of *Hamlet*," in *Shakespeare and Early Modern Political Thought*, ed. David Armitage, Conal Condren, and Andrew Fitzmaurice (Cambridge: Cambridge University Press, 2009), 141.
10. The metaphor of the body politic imagined the country as a body whose parts, such as towns, villages, and fiefs, contributed to the whole of the corporeal entity. At the head of the body sat the king.
11. Elahe Izadi, "'Shoot Him and I'll Give You a Medal': New Philippine President Urges Public to Kill Drug Lords," *The Washington Post*, April 19, 2019, https://www.washingtonpost.com/news/worldviews/wp/2016/06/06/shoot-him-and-ill-give-you-a-medal-new-philippine-president-urges-public-to-kill-drug-lords/.
12. Gillian Murray Kendall, "Overkill in Shakespeare," in *Shakespearean Power and Punishment: A Volume of Essays*, ed. Gillian Murray Kendall (Cranbury, NJ: Associated University Press, 1998), 173.

13. All quotations from the play derive from William Shakespeare, *The Tragedy of Macbeth*, ed. Nicholas Brooke (Oxford: Oxford University Press, 2008).

14. The word *catalectic* in poetry indicates the leaving off a syllable in the closing foot of a verse, disrupting the regularity of the measure.

15. *Pentameter* refers to the fact that Shakespearean verse contains five (penta) sets of "feet," or rhythmic patterns (meter).

16. Terry Eagleton, *William Shakespeare* (Oxford: Basil Blackwell, 1986), 6.

17. Julia Reinhard Lupton, "Macbeth's Martlets: Shakespearean Phenomenologies of Hospitality," *Criticism: A Quarterly for Literature and the Arts* 54, no. 3 (2012): 365–76.

18. See Nick Moschovakis, "Introduction: Dualistic *Macbeth*? Problematic *Macbeth*?," in *Macbeth: New Critical Essays*, ed. Nick Moschovakis (New York: Routledge, 2008), 1–72, and Howard Felperin, "A Painted Devil: *Macbeth*," in *Macbeth*, ed. Harold Bloom (New York: Chelsea House, 2005).

19. Mary Ann McGrail, *Tyranny in Shakespeare* (Lanham, MD: Lexington Books, 2001), 22.

20. Eagleton, *William Shakespeare*, 7. In semiotic theory, the word—the *signifier*—represents the idea or object—the *signified*.

21. Quint Forgey, "White House Press Secretary Says Daily Briefings Aren't Coming Back Any Time Soon," *Politico*, September 23, 2019, https://www.politico.com/story/2019/09/23/stephanie-grisham-white-house-press-briefings-1507288.

22. See Bianca Spinosa, "Interpreting Emoluments Today: The Framers' Intent and the 'Present' Problem," *Maryland Law Review* 78, no. 4 (2019): 998–1041, and Ciara Torres-Spelliscy, "From a Mint on a Hotel Pillow to an Emolument," *Mercer Law Review* 70, no. 3 (2019): 705–47.

23. For the US, these actions have a clandestine history reaching back to twentieth-century military branches (e.g., the failed proposal of Operation Northwoods or the Gulf of Tonkin incident).

24. Eliott C. McLaughlin, Amanda Watts, and Brad Parks, "Jussie Smollett Paid $3,500 to Stage his Attack, Hoping to Promote his Career, Police Allege," *CNN*, February 22, 2019, https://www.cnn.com/2019/02/21/entertainment/jussie-smollett-thursday/index.html. Sabrina Tavernise, "Planned Parenthood Awarded $2 Million in Lawsuit Over Secret Videos," *The New York Times*, November 15, 2019, https://advance-lexis-com.library.collin.edu/api/document?collection=news&id=urn:contentItem:5XHF-6W91-JBG3-63H6-00000-00&context=1516831. Brett Barrouquere, "Fake News? That Didn't Stop Sid Miller From Spreading It," *Chron*, January 15, 2017, https://www.chron.com/news/houston-texas/texas/article/Fake-news-That-didn-t-stop-Sid-Miller-from-10859067.php.

25. Such actions are not limited to meddling in elections both domestically and internationally, pardoning war criminals (e.g., Japanese scientists in Unit 731 who undertook lethal human experimentation), and experimenting without informed consent on servicemen and citizens (e.g., Project MKULTRA, Operation Sea-Spray, Operation Fast and Furious, and the Tuskegee Experiment).

26. Kenneth Burke, *A Rhetoric of Motives* (Berkeley: University of California Press, 1969), 22.

27. See Brett Samuels, "Trump Says he Stood Up to the 'Deep State' by Intervening in War Crime Cases," *The Hill*, November 26, 2019, https://thehill.com/homenews/campaign/472201-trump-says-he-stood-up-to-the-deep-state-by-intervening-in-war-crime-cases.

28. See David Knowles, "Some of the Many People Trump Has Denied Knowing," *Yahoo! News*, December 4, 2019, https://news.yahoo.com/some-of-the-many -people-trump-has-denied-knowing-004917055.html. Natalie Colarossi, "20 People who Trump has Personally Known and Then Claimed he Didn't," *Business Insider*, January 28, 2020, https://www.businessinsider.com/people-trump-said-he -didnt-know-but-did-photos.

29. See Graham Murdock, "Refeudalisation Revisited: The Destruction of Deliberative Democracy," *Javnost: The Public* 25, nos. 1–2 (2018): 43–50, and Jürgen Habermas, *The Structural Transformation of the Public Sphere: An Inquiry into a Category of Bourgeois Society*, trans. Thomas Burger and Frederick Lawrence (Cambridge: Polity Press, 1989), 142; 158; 195. Jürgen Habermas sees the consol- idation of power in the hands of non-governmental entities, such as corporations, in the twentieth century as engulfing what he termed the "public sphere," a place where citizens can think about methods for improving the public good. The con- solidation results in the public sphere falling into the hands of the few through methods such as marketing and public relations departments. This quells dialogue and independent, critical thought through a mix of consumerism, advertisements, and debt.

30. See Jane Mayer, "How Mitch McConnell Became Trump's Enabler-in-Chief," *The New Yorker*, April 20, 2020, https://www.newyorker.com/magazine/2020/ 04/20/how-mitch-mcconnell-became-trumps-enabler-in-chief. Mayer even describes McConnell's relationship to Trump using the word "fealty." Also, see Merrit Kennedy, "Barr Accuses Democrats of Trying to 'Cripple' The Trump Administration's Power," *NPR*, November 16, 2019, https://www.npr.org/ 2019/11/16/780092237/barr-accuses-democrats-of-trying-to-cripple-the-trump -administration-s-power. Jennifer Rubin, "What to Do With an Attorney General who Disdains Justice," *The Washington Post*, December 5, 2019, NA. Gale OneFile: News (accessed May 25, 2020). https://link-gale-com.library.collin.edu/ apps/doc/A607687004/STND?u=txshracd2497&sid=STND&xid=7839e864.

31. Scott Bauer, "Trump Adviser: Expect More Aggressive Poll Watching in 2020," *Associated Press*, December 21, 2019, https://apnews.com/af2f0ede054d 8baebbe1bb6ca47b4895. Michael Wines, "Deceased G.O.P. Strategist's Hard Drives Reveal New Details on the Census Citizenship Question," *The New York Times*, May 30, 2019, https://www.nytimes.com/2019/05/30/us/census-citizenship -question-hofeller.html.

32. Kathryn Krawczyk, "Fox's Lou Dobbs Declares John Bolton, Veteran of 4 GOP Administrations, a 'Tool for the Left,'" *The Week*, January 28, 2020, https:// theweek.com/speedreads/892119/foxs-lou-dobbs-declares-john-bolton-veteran-4 -gop-administrations-tool-left.

REFERENCES

Ballhaus, Rebecca, and Gordon Lubold. "White House Wanted USS John McCain 'Out of Sight' During Trump Japan Visit." *The Wall Street Journal*, May 26, 2020. https:// www.wsj.com/articles/white-house-wanted-uss-john-mccain-out-of-sight-during -trump-japan-visit-11559173470.

Barrouquere, Brett. "Fake News? That Didn't Stop Sid Miller From Spreading It." *Chron*, January 15, 2017. https://www.chron.com/news/houston-texas/texas/article/ Fake-news-That-didn-t-stop-Sid-Miller-from-10859067.php.

Bauer, Scott. "Trump Adviser: Expect More Aggressive Poll Watching in 2020." *Associated Press*, December 21, 2019. https://apnews.com/af2f0ede054d8baebbe1bb 6ca47b4895.

Burke, Kenneth. *A Rhetoric of Motives*. Berkeley: University of California Press, 1969.

Clark, Sandra, and Pamela Mason. Introduction to *Macbeth* by William Shakespeare. London: Bloomsbury, 2015.

Colarossi, Natalie. "20 People who Trump has Personally Known and then Claimed he Didn't." *Business Insider*, January 28, 2020. https://www.businessinsider.com/ people-trump-said-he-didnt-know-but-did-photos.

Eagleton, Terry. *William Shakespeare*. Oxford: Basil Blackwell, 1986.

Felperin, Howard. "A Painted Devil: *Macbeth*." In *Macbeth*, edited by Harold Bloom, 53–72. New York: Chelsea House, 2005.

Fitzmaurice, Andrew. "The Corruption of *Hamlet*." In *Shakespeare and Early Modern Political Thought*, edited by David Armitage, Conal Condren, and Andrew Fitzmaurice, 139–56. Cambridge: Cambridge University Press, 2009.

Forgey, Quint. "White House Press Secretary Says Daily Briefings Aren't Coming Back Any Time Soon." *Politico*, September 23, 2019. https://www.politico.com/ story/2019/09/23/stephanie-grisham-white-house-press-briefings-1507288.

Frye, Roland. "Hitler, Stalin, and Shakespeare's *Macbeth*: Modern Totalitarianism and Ancient Tyranny." *American Philosophical Society* 142, no. 1 (1998): 81–109.

Habermas, Jürgen. *The Structural Transformation of the Public Sphere: An Inquiry into a Category of Bourgeois Society*. Translated by Thomas Burger and Frederick Lawrence. Cambridge: Polity Press, 1989.

Inozemtse, Vladislav L. "Neo-Feudalism Explained." *American Interest* 6, no. 4 (2011): 73–80.

Izadi, Elahe. "'Shoot Him and I'll Give You a Medal': New Philippine President Urges Public to Kill Drug Lords." *The Washington Post*, April 19, 2019. https://www .washingtonpost.com/news/worldviews/wp/2016/06/06/shoot-him-and-ill-give-you -a-medal-new-philippine-president-urges-public-to-kill-drug-lords/.

Kendall, Gillian Murray. "Overkill in Shakespeare." In *Shakespearean Power and Punishment: A Volume of Essays*, edited by Gillian Murray Kendall, 173–96. Cranbury, NJ: Associated University Press, 1998.

Kennedy, Merrit. "Barr Accuses Democrats of Trying to 'Cripple' The Trump Administration's Power." *NPR*, November 16, 2019. https://www.npr.org/ 2019/11/16/780092237/barr-accuses-democrats-of-trying-to-cripple-the-trump -administration-s-power.

Knowles, David. "Some of the Many People Trump Has Denied Knowing." *Yahoo! News*, December 4, 2019. https://news.yahoo.com/some-of-the-many-people-trump -has-denied-knowing-004917055.html.

Krawczyk, Kathryn. "Fox's Lou Dobbs Declares John Bolton, Veteran of 4 GOP Administrations, a 'Tool for the Left.'" *The Week*, January 28, 2020. https:// theweek.com/speedreads/892119/foxs-lou-dobbs-declares-john-bolton-veteran-4 -gop-administrations-tool-left.

Kuhner, Timothy K. "American Kleptocracy: How to Categorise Trump and His Government." *King's Law Journal* 28, no. 2 (September 2017): 201–38. doi:10 .1080/09615768.2017.1366156.

Lowrance, Bryan. "'Modern Ecstasy': *Macbeth* and the Meaning of the Political." *ELH* 79, no. 4 (2012): 823–49.

Lupton, Julia Reinhard. "Macbeth's Martlets: Shakespearean Phenomenologies of Hospitality." *Criticism: A Quarterly for Literature and the Arts* 54, no. 3 (2012): 365–76.

Machiavelli, Niccolò. *The Prince. The Norton Anthology of World Literature*, Vol. C. 4th ed. Edited by Martin Puchner, Suzanne Conklin Akbari, Wiebke Denecke, Barbara Fuchs, Caroline Levine, Pericles Lewis, and Emily Wilson. New York: W. W. Norton, 2018, 170–92.

Mayer, Jane. "How Mitch McConnell Became Trump's Enabler-in-Chief." *The New Yorker*, April 20, 2020. https://www.newyorker.com/magazine/2020/04/20/how-mitch-mcconnell-became-trumps-enabler-in-chief.

McGrail, Mary Ann. *Tyranny in Shakespeare*. Lanham, MD: Lexington Books, 2001.

McLaughlin, Eliott C., Amanda Watts, and Brad Parks. "Jussie Smollett Paid $3,500 to Stage his Attack, Hoping to Promote his Career, Police Allege." *CNN*, February 22, 2019. https://www.cnn.com/2019/02/21/entertainment/jussie-smollett-thursday/index.html.

Moschovakis, Nick. "Introduction: Dualistic *Macbeth*? Problematic *Macbeth*?" In *Macbeth: New Critical Essays*, edited by Nick Moschovakis, 1–72. New York: Routledge, 2008.

Murdock, Graham. "Refeudalisation Revisited: The Destruction of Deliberative Democracy." *Javnost: The Public* 25, nos. 1–2 (2018): 43–50. https://doi.org/10.1080/13183222.2017.1418993.

Nelson, Eric. "Shakespeare and the Best State of a Commonwealth." In *Shakespeare and Early Modern Political Thought*, edited by David Armitage, Conal Condren, and Andrew Fitzmaurice, 253–70. Cambridge: Cambridge University Press, 2009.

Rubin, Jennifer. "What to Do With an Attorney General who Disdains Justice." *The Washington Post*, December 5, 2019. Gale OneFile: News (accessed May 25, 2020). https://link-gale-com.library.collin.edu/apps/doc/A607687004/STND?u=txshracd2497&sid=STND&xid=7839e864.

Samuels, Brett. "Trump Says he Stood Up to the 'Deep State' by Intervening in War Crime Cases." *The Hill*, November 26, 2019. https://thehill.com/homenews/campaign/472201-trump-says-he-stood-up-to-the-deep-state-by-intervening-in-war-crime-cases.

Shakespeare, William. *The Tragedy of Macbeth*. Edited by Nicholas Brooke. Oxford: Oxford University Press, 2008.

Spinosa, Bianca. "Interpreting Emoluments Today: The Framers' Intent and the 'Present' Problem." *Maryland Law Review* 78, no. 4 (2019): 998–1041.

Su, Alice. "A Doctor was Arrested for Warning China about the Coronavirus. Then he Died of it." *Los Angeles Times*, February 6, 2020. https://www.latimes.com/world-nation/story/2020-02-06/coronavirus-china-xi-li-wenliang.

Tavernise, Sabrina. "Planned Parenthood Awarded $2 Million in Lawsuit Over Secret Videos." *The New York Times*, November 15, 2019. https://advance-lexis-com.library.collin.edu/api/document?collection=news&id=urn:contentItem:5XHF-6W91-JBG3-63H6-00000-00&context=1516831.

Torres-Spelliscy, Ciara. "From a Mint on a Hotel Pillow to an Emolument." *Mercer Law Review* 70, no. 3 (2019): 705–47.

US Department of Justice. *Philippines 2018 Human Rights Report*. https://www.justice.gov/eoir/page/file/1145101/download.

Wines, Michael. "Deceased G.O.P. Strategist's Hard Drives Reveal New Details on the Census Citizenship Question." *The New York Times*, May 30, 2019. https://www.nytimes.com/2019/05/30/us/census-citizenship-question-hofeller.html.

3. Learning about leadership from *Coriolanus* and Coriolanus

Peter Iver Kaufman

Despite critics' acclaim, Ralph Fiennes's *Coriolanus* closed in most cinemas soon after it opened in 2011. Blustery autocrats were not yet in fashion. Years before, Fiennes had played the title character on stage at the Almeida Theatre in London and did it again on screen, directing as well this new take on William Shakespeare's puzzling Roman play. Interpretive puzzles or problems have not diminished the popularity of many staged performances, but Fiennes's film had a very short run—and critic Anthony Lane thinks he knows why: audiences do not warm to a protagonist who will "not stoop to court [their] affection." Coriolanus "does not want our warmth."[1]

Lane's observation calls to mind a moment in Sergei Eisenstein's cinematic classic, *Alexander Nevsky*. As Sergei Prokofiev's score conveys the euphoria of the crowd welcoming Alexander, whom they expect to save thirteenth-century Novgorod and Russia from Teutonic crusaders, the camera catches a citizen hailing the hero. "Novgorod loves you," he calls out, according to the caption. But Alexander's caption answers that he has come to be the city's leader and not her lover.

Nevsky and Coriolanus, battle-tested soldiers, are unconcerned with warmth, and their indifference distinguishes them from those leaders who, as befits politicians, take every chance to connect with commoners. That Alexander surmounts difficulties against the Mongols, defies the odds, and succeeds in the field may have left Eisenstein's admirers with the sense that all could be well in the late 1930s, when the film debuted. Yet we now know that Germany invaded Russia to devastating effect a few years later. Shakespeare's *Coriolanus*, borrowing from Plutarch's biographical sketch, and Fiennes's film adaptation of Shakespeare's play portray the protagonist as valorous and candid—arguably, to a fault. All three—Plutarch, Shakespeare, and Fiennes— raised important questions. What value should we place on a leader's warmth? Might we demand transparency? Or should we expect leaders to pull their punches and indulge them when they are less than candid and conceal their contempt—even when citizens deserve it? And what might we learn from precocious, though flawed and failed, leaders who fail because they are frank?[2]

Plutarch's protagonist is contemptuous of commoners, but also of the Roman senate, which exploits plebeians by charging excessive interest on loans. Plutarch asserted that senators and their fellow patricians also manipulated markets, holding back supplies to pump up demand and prices. They are "wise men of Rome," but come across as crafty and cruel in Plutarch's tale, for, when citizens protest the treachery, their city's senate plans to "disburden Rome of a great number" by dispatching agitators to colonies depopulated by plagues (Plutarch, 243). Another maneuver: send plebeians to war. Preemptive attacks on Rome's neighbors serve "to cleare" the capital "of mutinous and seditious persones," while protecting (and advancing) patricians' interests (Plutarch, 243).

Caius Marcius, soon-to-be Coriolanus, excels at war. The patricians, to honor his leadership, would have made him consul, although, Plutarch tells us (Shakespeare and Fiennes do not), the senate has no qualms about leaving the government's promises to the infantry unfulfilled. Coriolanus, however, is an aristocrat, to the manor born. Notwithstanding his standing in society, he clearly is uncomfortable when, in Fiennes's film, he trades his fatigues for a dress uniform. He seems more at home in the corpse-littered streets of his enemies' cities and—generally—on campaign. At war, he appears to care for commoners; Plutarch tells us that he refuses to deplete the share of the spoils reserved for the ordinary soldier by accepting a large share for himself. But in their city, back in Rome, he frowns on the commoners' clamor for commodities at what they gauge to be fair prices. When senators make concessions to quiet complainants, Coriolanus berates them for appeasement and scolds his fellow patricians for admitting tribunes nominated by the commoners into the senate and having them participate in deliberations. He is sure "it were a great folie" to permit the plebeians a part in picking apart the government's policies. Commoners will "judge we geve and graunt them this, as abasing our selves and standing in feare of them—and glad to flatter them." They will grow bold and "never leav[e off] to practise newe sedition and uprores" (Plutarch, 246).

It is obvious to the tribunes that Coriolanus is a threat to their influence in the new republic—and to the republic itself. Such populists must pretend to watch out for their people while watching out for themselves. If Coriolanus is permitted to become consul, the citizens' powers and the tribunes' power over citizens will be curbed dramatically, if not altogether eliminated, given his contempt for the concession that produced their position in the senate and among the commoners. They are determined to undermine the senators' intent. In Plutarch's sketch and Shakespeare's play, Brutus and Sicinius, the two tribunes, step up efforts to goad Coriolanus, to prod him to display his contempt. He is easy to incite, quick to offend ordinary citizens who overreach, much as he predicts in Shakespeare's play (3.1, 109–10; 3.1, 137–8). Their "wonderfull furie" result in "newe uprores" orchestrated by the tribunes (Plutarch, 247).

The commotion nearly results in his execution. Instead of death, however, exile: Coriolanus is banished for life, a rush to judgment that violates due process as Rome then construed it.[3] Plutarch was clear that, despite the confusion that attends the "uprores" and indictments, "there needed no difference of garments ... to know plebeian[s] from patrician[s]"; the former are raucous and rancorous; the latter, "sad and honge down"; Coriolanus—estranged from both castes and sabotaged by his own stout, impetuous defiance—alone seems serene, even then contemplating revenge (Plutarch, 248). But in Shakespeare's adaptation, he is more resentful and spiteful than gloomy (3.3.119–35). Fiennes played him as snarling and ferocious (one tribune takes a tumble). He curses commoners, banishing them as they banish him (3.3.123).

Plutarch saw Coriolanus off with a few partisans, but Shakespeare and Fiennes sent him out alone. In all versions, he defects to the Volscians. His old foe Aufidius welcomes him, only to be replaced by him. As its new commander, Coriolanus leads the Volscian army to the outskirts of Rome, but his mother, Volumnia (Vanessa Redgrave in the film), becomes an insurmountable obstacle. Accompanied on stage and screen by her grandson and daughter-in-law (although she has nearly all the lines), Volumnia confronts Coriolanus before the bloodletting has a chance to begin. She preaches against vengeance. She tries to talk sense. History, she holds, would honor her son and the Volscians if they elect to end the cycle of violence and reconcile with Rome. But she also conjures frightening images: "Thou shalt no sooner march to assault thy country than to tread ... on thy mother's womb" (5.3.122–4 and Plutarch, 256–7).[4] Coriolanus knows submission will be fatal, because the Volscians will think peace a betrayal. And, on their return to base, Aufidius and his comrades do in fact kill Coriolanus. Literary historian Unhae Langis saw that actors playing Coriolanus die "decorously" to add "a new layer of conciliatory significance" to the sacrifice, the lion slaughtered as a lamb.[5] Perhaps, but neither Shakespeare nor Plutarch scripted resistance. Still, Fiennes's Coriolanus grabs a sword, for "it was not for conquerours to yeld" (Plutarch, 241–2).

His unyielding serves him well in battle, but the aggravated plebeians look to be loved by their leaders or to be led by persons who seem to want their love, or at least are good at feigning fondness for their "warmth." Arguably, all we can learn about leadership from Plutarch, Shakespeare, and Fiennes is that "features which mould the soldier ... mar the politician," as Christopher Pelling says in his study of Plutarch's sketches, which concludes that Coriolanus is "a brilliant general lost in the tricks of politics" and who—on stage and screen—is a victim of his own unyielding.[6] To be sure, that may be the most salient lesson we draw from Coriolanus and *Coriolanus*, but, just as sure, it is not the only one nor the most significant.

If we shift focus from the protagonist and his intractability to his political predicament, we get a fresh perspective on his conduct. In part, the instability that plagued Rome during the early stages of the republic was due to the administrative and military elites' efforts to accommodate, but also to contain, surges of democratic sentiment. (The situation in Coriolanus's Rome might be compared with those that confronted citizens in nation states caught up in what we now call the Arab Spring.) Coriolanus's friend Menenius Agrippa, the apologist for patricians in Plutarch's story and in Shakespeare's play, justifies the gap between ordinary citizens and the elites by likening the body politic to the human body. He tries to calm commoners upset by what they take to be the patricians' indifference to their poverty. He understands that, to "discontented members" of the body, the senate may seem as "idle and unactive" as a full, contented stomach, while arms, legs, lungs, and tongues toil so conspicuously (1.1.100). Menenius, drawing on Livy as well as Plutarch, has the belly reply by stressing its obligation to receive, sift, and distribute the goods that enable the then "mutinous parts" to do their work (1.1.112). As "storehouse and … shop," the belly in the fable—much as the patricians and senate in Menenius's city—gives "inferior[s]" their "natural competency" (1.1.139–40) (nourishment) that makes it possible for members of the body and body politic to collaborate. Critic Kenneth Burke thinks that avuncular Menenius and his analogy "function well to uphold circumspectly, reasonably, much the same position Coriolanus ... represent[s] exorbitantly"; Menenius puts the patricians' perspective "in the best light"; Coriolanus puts it bluntly and "in the worst."[7]

Fiennes cut Menenius's fable, but elsewhere Brian Cox, playing Menenius, persistently calls for calm. He seems not to think Coriolanus's contempt for commoners unjust. And he relies on their credulity. He panders to them "in precisely the way Coriolanus ... find[s] unbrookable."[8] Yet Menenius is shifty; the tribunes cannot maneuver him as easily as they ride reckless over Coriolanus or as deftly as they steer the impressionable citizens. Coriolanus is convinced that commoners are inconstant, "no surer ... than is the coal of fire upon the ice ... He that depends upon [their] favors swims with fins of lead and hews down oaks with rushes. Hang ye! Trust ye? With every minute you do change a mind and call him noble that was now your hate" (1.1.180–3). And the plot, in effect, enacts the protagonist's misgivings. Playgoers find that he has a point. The citizens initially endorse Coriolanus's candidacy for consul, but when prompted by their tribunes, they repudiate their endorsement and chase him from Rome. Historian Robert Ormsby suspects that the "erratic power" of the "onstage audience," that is, of the commoners or crowd in *Coriolanus*, corresponds with the unreliable interpretive power that early modern anti-theatricalists ascribed to their contemporaries in the audiences, to "the vulgar sort" whose "non-rational, infectious" responses to what they saw on stage often misconstrued a playwright's purposes.[9] If Ormsby is correct,

Coriolanus and Shakespeare should be registered among the Elizabethan and Stuart critics of both plays and players who mistrusted playgoers' judgments.

Yet several literary historians deny that Shakespeare shared Coriolanus's contempt for commoners. They refuse to cast the playwright as a political conservative or, worse, as an incorrigible reactionary. Denying any drift to the right, they propose that Shakespeare harbored republican sympathies.[10] Colleagues continue to make the study of the playwright's political partisanship captivating, but we are looking to use *Coriolanus* to address a different question; therefore, we ought to defer judgment on Shakespeare's political sympathies and provisionally propose that the play is politically imprecise and the protagonist's candor and contempt are dramatic achievements rather than measures of the playwright's take on either the absolutism or the participatory politics of his time.

Despite the imprecision, it is quite clear that *Coriolanus*'s Coriolanus is no joiner. That is an observation we shall have occasion to repeat and develop, but it is important now to note that Shakespeare's protagonist, though to the manor born, is also quick to criticize the patricians as "reckless" (3.1.92). The distinction that matters most to him is not the one between what will later pass as Tory and Whig, but the difference between noble and base. Aufidius, for a time, meets his standard for nobility. Rome's senators never do and definitively fall short when they judge that his contempt puts him beyond their help. He faces the citizens' surges of anger alone, as "aidless" (2.2.113) in politics as he often was in battle. Conrad Russell's elegant Trevelyan lectures on King James VI and I suggest something of a parallel, without citing Coriolanus or Shakespeare. James came to England from Scotland several years before *Coriolanus* was first performed and claimed he was unaided by his new realm's Parliament. Both houses balked at legislating a perfect union between his two kingdoms. Members, instead, let contentious commissions cope (or not) with the issue. (Francis Bacon referred to that strategy or "devise" as a "digression."[11]) The new monarch persisted, repackaging his project and pressing Parliament in successive speeches to speed up the process. He appears to have been prudent, unlike Coriolanus, who berates nearly every character who shares the stage with him. But, apparently, King James could also be indiscreet and impatient with opposition, as Russell suggests, conceding that Shakespeare's sovereign, "when he spoke without thinking," discourteously "said what he thought."[12]

James was also said to dislike display, unlike his predecessor, Queen Elizabeth I, who had processed prolifically, sat for multiple portraits, and took pleasure at being "beheld of all" subjects.[13] Coriolanus, on this count, resembles the king rather than the queen. His signature offense is his failure to oblige the citizens who want to see his scars before they confirm his appointment as consul. He only reluctantly comes to the market to solicit their support. They give it, then withdraw it when their tribunes pointedly charge that his reluctance, privacy, and ostensible humility—his awkward metamorphosis from blunt, blustery general to modest would-be consul—signals a contempt for custom and for the commoners' consent. Literary historians have been known to emphasize his social isolation, much as the tribunes did. "Standing outside the social compact," Coriolanus apparently "dismisses the transparent world of urban political ceremony."[14] And, as a result, we now know, he is dismissed—banished. On his departure, he characterizes himself as the consummate outsider, proclaiming that he leaves "like a lonely dragon" (4.1.30), a legendary monster that, despite its appearance on King Henry VII's banners at Bosworth Field more than a century earlier at the start of the Tudor dynasty, is associated with malevolence and menace. Menenius laments that Coriolanus has been changed "from man to dragon" (5.4.13), but Fiennes and his friends who formed the company financing the film seemed to find a lesson in the transformation worth underscoring, for they released their take on Shakespeare's play as "a Lonely Dragon Production."

Plutarch's Coriolanus, as noted, is somewhat less of a loner. But, more important, he "follows custom" less grudgingly, exhibiting "many woundes and cuttes upon his bodie" when required or requested to do so (Plutarch, 244). Why would Shakespeare change the story? Dramatic effect? The change makes Coriolanus's sense of honor seem more striking. To him, it is a matter of honor that candidates not recite what they have "nobly done" (2.2.68). Virtues do not need what Eve Sanders calls "visual aids" when she explains Coriolanus's unwillingness to turn his scars into a sales pitch.[15] Menenius counsels conformity: "fit you to the custom" (2.2.143), but the protagonist is certain that publicity debases nobility. Baring his wounds will misrepresent their meaning, he insinuates, convinced that public life is weighed down, not buoyed up, by rituals. And he thinks that rituals are fueled by fictions, specifically, the fiction that he received his wounds for "the hire of their breath" (2.2.150). They play to and for the prurient. Enthusiastic receptions depend on deceptions. Coriolanus imagines that broadcasting his valor and public service would come across as crude bids for popularity. What he had done will be corrupted by commemorations, celebrity, and campaigns for political rule that require what Menenius calls "bolted language" (3.1.320), rehearsed and restrained speeches delivered to flatter—occasionally to defraud. Coriolanus will not curtsey. He will not blithely have citizens gawk at his scars, and, unlike politicians today who twitter and tune in to have their egos inflated, Coriolanus refuses to attend the senate to hear his "nothings monstered" (2.2.78).

But he does not court obscurity. Within sight of the play's start, he lunges forward to meet a crowd ready to storm the city's granary. His first lines insult and intimidate:

> **CORIOLANUS** What's the matter, you dissentious rogues
>   That, rubbing the poor itch of your opinion,
>   Make yourselves scabs? (1.1.165–7)

"The matter" is hunger, yet Fiennes plays a Coriolanus whose candor and contempt preclude compassion. One could be excused for guessing from the first act and scene that we will learn little about leadership from a protagonist whose curses appear unprovoked. But "unprovoked" appears rather unfair. The crowd at the granary in Fiennes's film is a mob. Police prepare for a riot. Unlike Shakespeare's play, Fiennes's film begins with a short shot of Aufidius, sharpening his blade at the Volscian camp, peering at his television screen showing the "dissentious rogues" in his enemy's capital. The implication: unrest in Rome is an excellent occasion for an invasion. Fiennes had the camera follow one "scab" as she stalks through the backstreets to join what the viewers could understandably mistake for a terrorist cell. With as much menace as she can muster, she delivers the lines: "let us kill him" (1.1.10), referring to Caius Martius.

In other productions, Shakespeare's citizens are less threatening. Casually dressed at the National Theatre in London in 1985, the chorus of players/ citizens circulated among playgoers who, similarly attired, were invited to join the polite protest that preceded Coriolanus's (Ian McKellen's) entrance. Fiennes was having none of that. His commoners are shabby and desperate. Their cell meets in a dimly lit tenement, and discussions quickly turn to Caius Martius, who has not yet earned his surname, although his reputation precedes him onstage. He has had a distinguished military career and will retaliate in short order for Aufidius's assault. He will take the Volscians' city of Corioles for Rome. But he is, to the cell of "scabs," "the chief enemy to the [Roman] people" (1.1.8). Were they right? Were they unprovoked? Much depends on whether Coriolanus strolled or strutted onstage.

Plutarch and Shakespeare fixed it so that he could not help but attract attention. John Ripley's survey concludes that lead actors' projections of the protagonist so dominated stages that the play's "antipopulism" seldom surfaced in reviews from the seventeenth into the twentieth centuries. Reviewers commented most often on the protagonist's "stern intrepidity."[16] But dissident subjects would have troubled many contemporary playgoers. Shakespeare probably first staged his play only two or three years after England experienced home-grown terrorism. In early November 1605, officials acting on a tip discovered Guy Fawkes with nearly 40 barrels of gunpowder in an undercroft beneath the room where the House of Lords, King James, and his son Henry were scheduled to meet. Fawkes and his several accomplices hoped to remove obstacles to the re-Catholicization of their realm. Convening later than planned, in January 1606, Parliament denounced popery rather than populism. But the king, his council, the landed gentry, and urban commercial interests feared "dissentious rogues," who, to speed up religious reform (precisianists or puritans) or to reverse it, might unsettle affairs; the 1606 session of Parliament proposed precautions to avert popular "stirs."[17] They had been feared for over a generation, since the economic downturns during the 1590s had created what some historians consider a pandemic of disorder. Several strategies for religious reform argued for greater lay control over parish patronage. Some strategies for social reform called for decentralization and for greater citizen-say, although tradesmen were not widely trusted to make the most sensible magistrates. Might *Coriolanus* have been Shakespeare's brief for crowd control?[18]

Playgoers may have related "the dissentious rabble" on stage in *Coriolanus* to the scuffles and "stirs" that worried authorities in early modern England. Perhaps patrons of the theater were as curious about the playwright's sympathies as are literary historians who tirelessly sift for what they call "topical reverberations," a play's veiled references to circumstances that prevailed or to episodes that occurred prior to the play's first performances. Perhaps *Coriolanus* gestures toward agrarian difficulties (low yields, high prices, widespread unemployment) that led to unrest in the Midlands, where the playwright had invested in land, malt, and corn. Tenants' interests in cutting down hedges could morph into efforts to defy or cut down landlords. Still, no historian has yet to bundle "reverberations" in the play into a coherent, consistent assessment of socioeconomic policy we can convincingly ascribe to Shakespeare. Hence, to learn what he thought about leadership, we must tread carefully.[19]

Yet Shakespeare's concept of what colleagues in leadership studies now call *leadership challenges* does seem rather readily accessible. We could infer from *Coriolanus*, for example, that the playwright figured that the foremost challenge for a leader was to build and maintain consensus among citizens who recoil from candid pronouncements about their inconstancy. Easily led (or misled), they are incoherent as well as inconstant: "we willingly consented to [Coriolanus's] banishment, yet it was against our will" (4.6.145–6). That perplexing remark, scripted for one of the play's citizens, prompted Oliver Arnold's discerning study of the problems facing republican political cultures. Arnold maintains that "irrationality" attends political representation, because the represented are told (and come to believe) that the only way their voices can be heard is by letting others speak for them. Similarly, citizens imagine that honor accrues to them when they honor others who honor and appear to love them. Hence, republican cultures reinforce the assumption that nobility is conferred reciprocally—the ruled confer it on rulers, and rulers on the ruled—

rather than achieved by either party. Tyranny or demagoguery and broadly participatory regimes coexist as long as leaders channel commoners' participation.[20] Examples of this in the twenty-first century prove the point. Political rallies give demagogues the chance to feign their love for the crowds; the crowds embolden their candidates. Popularity is the populists' drug of choice. Unlike Coriolanus, they are prepared to go to great lengths to get their fixes. And, arguably, the suppliers—the crowds—are ennobled by their candidates' (their leaders' and would-be leaders') readiness to condescend. But different spins are defensible and have influenced the ways Shakespeare's play has been played.

Productions of *Coriolanus* sometimes come across as homilies pillorying tyranny and praising or plumping for citizen solidarity. Michael Bogdanov staged his version in a Gdansk shipyard. The tribunes were all but exonerated for manipulating sympathies. They were played as overworked union organizers. Ralph Fiennes filmed his *Coriolanus* in Serbia amidst bombed-out ruins, reminding theatergoers of the grim consequences of sprawling sectarian violence. Yet Fiennes's commoners, an ethnically and racially diverse lot, seldom squabble with each other. He ransoms them, in effect, from the passions that usually divide insurgents and dismembered the former Yugoslavia. Despite the play's two tribunes' whipping up citizens' opposition to Coriolanus, Fiennes gentles their condition. So, to declare both Bogdanov's play and Fiennes's movie transparently topical would be an understatement. Nonetheless, Shakespeare's *Coriolanus* tends to bring productions back to themes relevant to leadership in any age—and to the issues that launched our investigation—notably to the relative values of candor, affection, affectation, and independence.

Candid and independent, Coriolanus does nothing to help his cause when a citizen explains that the would-be consul is undeserving of high office because he has "not ... loved the common people" (2.3.96–7). His answer is honest, if injudicious. The affection that he feigns reveals nothing of his true feelings, he says, too candid to permit his lack of candor to go unmentioned; he comes to them hat-in-hand, "most counterfeitly" (2.3.104–5). Yet, as it happens, he can hold that pose for only so long—and so poorly that, when he hastens away, the tribunes have no trouble convincing citizens of his contempt for them. Playgoers, of course, will anticipate the outcome, for, by then, they have heard him confide to his mother his resolve not to pander, a resolve that will capsize his candidacy and turn *Coriolanus* into a tragedy: "I had rather be their servant in my way," the formidably unenthusiastic candidate says, "than sway with them in theirs" (2.1.208–9).

"Sway" was used in the late sixteenth century to signal rule as well as a wobbly, side-to-side movement. Shakespeare probably intended both. Coriolanus is responding to his mother's and Menenius's advice that he tactfully solicit high office by sabotaging his chance to become consul. And the line also refers to citizens' changeable loyalties, echoing a complaint he registers at the start. But must we connect the pronouns *them* and *theirs* exclusively to commoners? Just before Coriolanus utters his "rather-be," his mother conjures up "our Rome" (2.1.207); ordinary citizens seem remote from her interests. And we know her son has contempt for the senate. He is displeased with its concessions. He dislikes "our" Rome's ceremonies. It may be inaccurate to say that his attitude toward plebeians is "not significantly different from that of his fellow patricians."[21] For he condemns the new republic comprehensively, placing him "between the two classes," as Günter Grass suggests, or, better, beyond classes or castes, outside the system, and contemptuous of its powerbrokers.[22]

Coriolanus's mother, Volumnia, is the play's most effective broker or negotiator. She saves Rome from her son.[23] Earlier, she proves the play's most astute political (and personal) analyst. She identifies the fundamental difficulty Coriolanus has getting into government: he is "too absolute" (3.2.39). If her political fortune or that of her friends were at stake, she "would dissemble" and "should do so in honor" (3.2.62–4). Undeniably, her son is well versed in war, so he ought to know that honor and "policy" "hold companionship" (3.2.49). Volumnia has a point, which Menenius endorses. Feints, dodges, and other forms of deceit win battles. Her son is dismissive ("tush tush"; 3.2.44). It is one thing to deceive enemies disposed to mistrust their adversaries, but quite another to mislead those who trust their leaders. Dissembling for any political advantage dishonors the deceiver. Political performance is duplicitous and disgraceful; before he is banished, Coriolanus reckons Rome is both.

At the end of the third act, he leaves. "There is a world elsewhere" (3.3.135), he proclaims as he departs. But it is difficult to disagree with David Hale, who concludes that the play's "elsewhere" is anticlimactic: with the exception of Volumnia's intervention, the final two acts amount to "a progression of relatively static tableaux."[24] Coriolanus's disengagement from the commoners and senate alike constitutes the climax of this play, and it could signal a profound pessimism about politics in London or England or wherever it was staged. Critics who think so have been scolded for "disdain[ing] the drama's potential to be politically interventionist," for fancying that *Coriolanus* and the other Roman tragedies are "powerful ... because they express humanity's powerlessness."[25] Possibly, then, what we learn about leadership is not simply the dreadful political consequences of insufficient self-command, but also the futility of political involvement that takes statist structures as givens and for granted. For the structures and roles into which leaders and citizens must fit captivate and capture them, as Giorgio Agamben notices, citing the anthropometric techniques feeding citizens' and sovereigns' insatiable desires for recognition.[26] Markers abound in wallets, purses, mailing labels, and passwords; every chip or code reinforces the status quo. Political identities and expectations are set, and leaders' opportunities to try out new kit are severely restricted. What, then, of innovation and would-be leaders' ideals? Certainly, Coriolanus's "absolute allegiance to his ideals" leads to exile, but, as Norman Rabkin speculated a half-century ago, "the shortsighted selfishness" of patricians, plebeians, and tribunes—all captives to their protocols—may win him playgoers' indulgence.[27]

Fiennes's film may be pitching for such an outcome by alluding to the distance between Coriolanus's ideals and his city. The screen tells viewers as they settle in their seats that they will witness the drama unfold in "a place calling itself Rome," almost certainly a reference or homage to John Osborne, whose seldom-staged take on Shakespeare's play bears that title. Osborne gives Menenius lines complaining about "overheated" rhetoric in this play's place, yet the ostensibly amiable, avuncular senator's subtlety and tact can be construed as a milder form of the tribunes' hypocrisy. Ideal Rome, where nobility rises above necessity and where candor is valued above affectation (feigned "warmth"), may exist only in the protagonist's imagination, but it contrasts with the pomp and propaganda bracing regimes' claims to authority and allegiance, that is, the ruling fictions in our real Romes, where the polarization of political cultures perpetuates turf wars, distorts opposing positions or dismisses them as fake news, and rewards counterfeit compassion.[28]

Monitoring Coriolanus's imagination is impossible, of course, but trying to retrieve his perspective on the political predicaments in early republican Rome is a useful exercise for our imaginations, an exercise that teaches us something valuable about leadership. Coriolanus and *Coriolanus* challenge leaders' conventional attachments to politically pragmatic strategies and solutions. Historians tend to yoke their discipline to leadership studies to display antitypes and prototypes: history, literature, and drama supply stocks of models. Perhaps it is wisest to shelve Coriolanus as a specimen of what not to do to defend constituents' interests or reduce friction. Menenius tries: "on both sides more respect" (3.1.180).[29] Yet confronting Coriolanus might help us respect what we cannot fully comprehend as a realistic political position. And, as Jonathan Haidt allows, that may make a timely contribution to the study and practice of politics. For Haidt, overheated political rhetoric is symptomatic of a debilitating deficit: we seem to have lost the ability to empathize with contemporaries whose moral intuitions are very different from ours. Partisans have become as adept as Shakespeare's tribunes at turning rivals into enemies of society. We hear our statesmen decry their rivals' irrationality and improbity, and we see few, if any, efforts to learn from what Haidt calls "the moral matrices" of adversaries.[30] Opponents are cast as assailants. On that count or charge, we can hardly acquit Coriolanus, but he is more than an antitype or negative example. He and the play become a fine occasion for readers, playgoers, and filmgoers to be broadly judgmental, simultaneously appraising their own standards for candor, civility, and integrity along with those of contemporaries.

For twenty-first-century theatergoers, *Coriolanus* is a feast. It presents populism stripped of partisan arguments that either dress it up as critical for democracy or dress it down as conducive to demagoguery. Titus Livy (and Machiavelli) could see it one way; Petrarch, quite another. What is important here is that the play, as just noted, is an invitation or occasion for readers and viewers to sift and put in perspective the concessions to the crowd and the manipulation of the crowd alongside concession and manipulation in their time.

As for Coriolanus, we may agree with Menenius that he is "too noble" to lead in this world of commerce that often rewards the ignoble and under-handed. We may agree with Volumnia that he is "too absolute" to tolerate compromises leaders make. Nobility and intractability force him to seek a "world elsewhere," which—Shakespeare left no doubt—affords Coriolanus no consolation. Studying the humanities, however, occasionally introduces us to leaders who point the way out with implausible, underdeveloped, or even undeveloped elsewheres. And that, in some circumstances, may be useful and enough.

NOTES

1. Anthony Lane, "Loyalty Oaths," *The New Yorker*, January 23, 2012, 86. For the play's popularity, see John Ripley, *"Coriolanus" on Stage in England and America, 1609–1994* (London: Associated University Presses, 1998).
2. For Shakespeare's *Coriolanus*, I cite the second Signet edition (2002) of the 1623 text, the First Folio. The parenthetical references include act, scene, and lines. Shakespeare likely used Plutarch's "Life of Caius Marcius Coriolanus" in Thomas North's 1579 translation, conveniently reprinted—in the fifth volume of Geoffrey Bullough, *Narrative and Dramatic Sources of Shakespeare*, vol. 5 (New York: Columbia University Press, 1964), 132–45. This study gives page references to both North and Bullough by date parenthetically in the text.
3. James Kuzner, "Unbuilding the City: *Coriolanus* and the Birth of Republican Rome," *Shakespeare Quarterly* 58 (2007): 184.
4. Volumnia's pleas are freighted with threats in Plutarch's as well as in Shakespeare's accounts. Critics have seen her intervention as the consummate expression of her belligerence and ambition. Jill Pearce, *"Coriolanus," Cahiers Elisabéthains* 38 (1990): 95–6, commenting on Barbara Jefford's "commanding performance" in Terry Hands's late twentieth-century production, alleges that "rather than reaching tragic grandeur, [*Coriolanus*] was diminished by the sheer force of Volumnia's personality." The irony in the confrontation between Volumnia and her son is not lost on R. A. Foakes, who, prompted by Shakespeare—not Plutarch—attributes Coriolanus's unyielding character to his mother's influence, even as he "yields to [her] pleading, marking what his warrior's code utterly denies, the possibility of surrender." See R. A. Foakes, *Shakespeare and Violence* (Cambridge: Cambridge University Press, 2003), 179–80.

5. Unhae Langis, "*Coriolanus*: Inordinate Passions and Powers in Personal and Political Governance," *Comparative Drama* 44 (2010): 21.
6. Christopher Pelling, *Plutarch and History* (London: Duckworth, 2002), 240 and 401.
7. Kenneth Burke, *Language as Symbolic Action: Essays in Life, Literature, and Method* (Berkeley: University of California Press, 1966), 193–4.
8. Pelling, *Plutarch and History*, 389.
9. Robert Ormsby, "*Coriolanus*, Antitheatricalism, and Audience Response," *Shakespeare Bulletin* 26 (2008): 46–52.
10. For example, see Annabel Patterson, *Shakespeare and the Popular Voice* (Oxford: Blackwell, 1989); Andrew Hadfield, *Shakespeare and Republicanism* (Cambridge: Cambridge University Press, 2005); Chris Fitter, *Radical Shakespeare: Politics and Stagecraft in the Early Career* (London: Routledge, 2012); and Chris Fitter, ed., *Shakespeare and the Politics of Commoners: Digesting the New Social History* (Oxford: Oxford University Press, 2017). For an alternative, see Peter Kaufman, "English Calvinism and the Crowd: *Coriolanus* and the History of Religious Reform," *Church History* 75 (2006): 314–42.
11. For Bacon's remarks, see *The Parliamentary Diary of Robert Bowyer, 1606–1607*, ed., David Harris Willson (New York: Octagon, 1971), 269.
12. Conrad Russell, *King James VI and I and his English Parliaments* (Oxford: Oxford University Press, 2011), 72.
13. Kevin Sharpe, *Selling the Tudor Monarchy: Authority and Image in Sixteenth-Century England* (New Haven, CT: Yale University Press, 2011), 417–50.
14. John Archer, *Citizen Shakespeare: Freemen and Aliens in the Language of the Plays* (New York: Palgrave Macmillan: 2005), 149; Peter J. Leithard, "City of In-gratia: Roman Ingratitude in Shakespeare's *Coriolanus*," *Literature and Theology* 20 (2006): 351.
15. Eve Rachele Sanders, "The Body of the Actor in *Coriolanus*," *Shakespeare Quarterly* 57 (2006): 399.
16. Ripley, *"Coriolanus" on Stage*, 212–13.
17. Russell, *King James*, 47.
18. One perplexing document in the British Library, Additional MS. 48066, 5v-6r ostensibly favors local autonomy and commoners' empowerment but also scolds citizens for trusting offices to amateurs, suggesting it is lunacy to be so fastidiously selective stabling one's horses with good grooms while trusting one's laws to the untrained. For discontent and disorder, see Jim Sharpe, "Social Strain and Social Dislocation, 1595–1603," in *The Reign of Elizabeth I: Court and Culture in the Last Decade*, ed. John Guy (Cambridge: Cambridge University Press, 1995), 200–2.
19. For the allusion to hedges and landlords, see John Walter, "A 'Rising of the People'? The Oxfordshire Rising of 1596," *Past & Present* 107 (1985): 101.
20. Oliver Arnold, *The Third Citizen: Shakespeare's Theater and the Early Modern House of Commons* (Baltimore, MD: Johns Hopkins University Press, 2007), 218–21.
21. Warren Cherniak, *The Myth of Rome in Shakespeare and his Contemporaries* (Cambridge: Cambridge University Press, 2011), 190–1.
22. Günter Grass, *Aufsätze zur Literatur* (Darmstadt: Luchterhand Literaturverlag, 1980), 30.

23. For her wiles, consult Russell M. Hillier, "Valor Will Weep: The Ethics of Valor, Anger, and Pity in Shakespeare's *Coriolanus*," *Studies in Philology* 113 (2016): 388–93 and Nicholas Taylor-Collins, "The City's Hostile Bodies: Coriolanus's Rome and Carson's Belfast," *The Modern Language Review* 115 (2020): 39–41.
24. David Hale, "*Coriolanus*: The Death of a Political Metaphor," *Shakespeare Quarterly* 22 (1971): 202.
25. Peter J. Smith, *Social Shakespeare: Aspects of Renaissance Dramaturgy and Contemporary Society* (London: Macmillan, 1995), 220–1.
26. Giorgio Agamben, *Nudità* (Milan: Nottetempo, 2009), 77–9.
27. Norman Rabkin, "*Coriolanus*: The Tragedy of Politics," *Shakespeare Quarterly* 17 (1966): 195–206.
28. John Osborne, *A Place Calling Itself Rome* (London: Faber and Faber, 1973); for Menenius's less-than-creditable subtlety, see Hillier, "'Valor Will Weep,'" 366. For Menenius's complaint, see Osborne, *Place*, 20.
29. Ethan Shagan, "Beyond Good and Evil: Thinking with Moderates in Early Modern England," *Journal of British Studies* 49 (2010): 500–2 and 511–13, suspects play-goers might not have appreciated irenic gestures ("more respect") as do historians, that early Stuart audiences could well have identified Menenius's calls for calm in *Coriolanus* with their government's repressive measures.
30. Jonathan Haidt, *The Righteous Mind* (New York: Pantheon, 2012), 313–18.

REFERENCES

Agamben, Giorgio. *Nudità*. Milan: Nottetempo, 2009.
Archer, John. *Citizen Shakespeare: Freemen and Aliens in the Language of the Plays*. New York: Palgrave Macmillan, 2005.
Arnold, Oliver. *The Third Citizen: Shakespeare's Theater and the Early Modern House of Commons*. Baltimore, MD: Johns Hopkins University Press, 2007.
Bowyer, Robert. *The Parliamentary Diary of Robert Bowyer, 1606–1607*. Edited by David Harris Willson. New York: Octagon, 1971.
Bullough, Geoffrey. *Narrative and Dramatic Sources of Shakespeare*, vol. 5. New York: Columbia University Press, 1964, 132–45.
Burke, Kenneth. *Language as Symbolic Action: Essays in Life, Literature, and Method*. Berkeley: University of California Press, 1966.
Cherniak, Warren. *The Myth of Rome in Shakespeare and his Contemporaries*. Cambridge: Cambridge University Press, 2011.
Eisenstein, Sergei and Dmitriy Vasilev. *Alexander Nevsky*. Moscow, Russia: Mosfilm, 1938. Filmstrip, 111 min.
Fiennes, Ralph. *Coriolanus*. United Kingdom: Icon Entertainment International, 2011. Filmstrip, 123 min.
Fitter, Chris. *Radical Shakespeare: Politics and Stagecraft in the Early Career*. London: Routledge, 2012.
Fitter, Chris, ed. *Shakespeare and the Politics of Commoners: Digesting the New Social History*. Oxford: Oxford University Press, 2017.
Foakes, R. A. *Shakespeare and Violence*. Cambridge: Cambridge University Press, 2003.
Grass, Günter. *Aufsätze zur Literatur*. Darmstadt, Germany: Luchterhand Literaturverlag, 1980.

Hadfield, Andrew. *Shakespeare and Republicanism*. Cambridge: Cambridge University Press, 2005.

Haidt, Jonathan. *The Righteous Mind*. New York: Pantheon, 2012.

Hale, David. "*Coriolanus*: The Death of a Political Metaphor." *Shakespeare Quarterly* 22 (1971): 197–202.

Hillier, Russell M. "'Valor Will Weep': The Ethics of Valor, Anger, and Pity in Shakespeare's *Coriolanus*." *Studies in Philology* 113 (2016): 358–96.

Kaufman, Peter. "English Calvinism and the Crowd: *Coriolanus* and the History of Religious Reform." *Church History* 75 (2006): 314–42.

Kuzner, James. "Unbuilding the City: *Coriolanus* and the Birth of Republican Rome." *Shakespeare Quarterly* 58 (2007): 174–99.

Lane, Anthony. "Loyalty Oaths." *The New Yorker*, January 23, 2012, 86.

Langis, Unhae. "*Coriolanus*: Inordinate Passions and Powers in Personal and Political Governance." *Comparative Drama* 44 (2010): 1–27.

Leithard, Peter J. "City of In-gratia: Roman Ingratitude in Shakespeare's *Coriolanus*." *Literature and Theology* 20 (2006): 341–60.

Ormsby, Robert. "*Coriolanus*, Antitheatricalism, and Audience Response." *Shakespeare Bulletin* 26 (2008): 43–62.

Osborne, John. *A Place Calling Itself Rome*. London: Faber and Faber, 1973.

Patterson, Annabel. *Shakespeare and the Popular Voice*. Oxford: Blackwell, 1989.

Pearce, Jill. "Coriolanus." *Cahiers Elisabéthains* 38 (1990): 95–6.

Pelling, Christopher. *Plutarch and History*. London: Duckworth, 2002.

Plutarch. "Life of Caius Marcius Coriolanus." Translated by Thomas North. In *Narrative and Dramatic Sources of Shakespeare*, 5th vol., edited by Geoffrey Bullough, 132–45. New York: Columbia University Press, 1964.

Rabkin, Norman. "*Coriolanus*: The Tragedy of Politics." *Shakespeare Quarterly* 17 (1966): 195–212.

Ripley, John. *"Coriolanus" on Stage in England and America, 1609–1994*. London: Associated University Presses, 1998.

Russell, Conrad. *King James VI and I and his English Parliaments*. Oxford: Oxford University Press, 2011.

Sanders, Eve Rachele. "The Body of the Actor in *Coriolanus*." *Shakespeare Quarterly* 57 (2006): 387–412.

Shagan, Ethan. "Beyond Good and Evil: Thinking with Moderates in Early Modern England." *Journal of British Studies* 49 (2010): 488–513.

Shakespeare, William. *Coriolanus*. 1623. 2nd revised edition. New York: Signet Classic, 2002.

Sharpe, Jim. "Social Strain and Social Dislocation, 1595–1603." In *The Reign of Elizabeth I: Court and Culture in the Last Decade*, edited by John Guy, 192–211. Cambridge: Cambridge University Press, 1995.

Sharpe, Kevin. *Selling the Tudor Monarchy: Authority and Image in Sixteenth-Century England*. New Haven, CT: Yale University Press, 2011.

Smith, Peter J. *Social Shakespeare: Aspects of Renaissance Dramaturgy and Contemporary Society*. London: Macmillan, 1995.

Taylor-Collins, Nicholas. "The City's Hostile Bodies: Coriolanus's Rome and Carson's Belfast." *The Modern Language Review* 115 (2020): 17–45.

Walter, John. "A 'Rising of the People'? The Oxfordshire Rising of 1596." *Past & Present* 107 (1985): 90–143.

PART II

Truth

4. "Lies like truth": *Macbeth* and the American Dream

Anthony Presti Russell

The sense of anger and anxiety that has pervaded many communities in the United States and beyond in the first part of the twenty-first century has many sources, but much of it is reducible to the experience of threatened security. Nationalism or populism, sexism, racism, xenophobia, and religious intolerance are all fundamentally responses to the fear of loss, in particular the loss of economic or social status and privilege and the loss of cultural heritage; in other words, the loss of meaning and of predictability, the loss of all those reliable boundaries to the self which, as the complaint so often goes, "we" used to possess in the past. The permeability of cultural, economic, and political systems in a global context—exacerbated by the internet—may be bracing and stimulating to many, but it is clearly menacing to many others, and one response to this menace is to wish to control or to rectify the "time" one lives in. As Macduff shouts triumphantly at the end of *Macbeth*, holding up the tyrant Macbeth's head, "the time is free" (5.11.21).[1] Indeed, from the beginning of time the promise to properly manage, control, or redeem "lost" time has been one of the most common ways by which political leaders have sought to appeal to their followers. From Franklin Roosevelt's "happy days are here again," to Reagan's "it's morning again in America," to Trump's "make America great again," some of the most successful US presidential candidates of the last 100 years have managed to anchor their visions of the future in the "safe space" of an idealized past. The presidential candidate's role, after all, is to prophesy persuasively a secure future in which time takes on the outlines of a comedy.

Too often, however, these uttered prophecies have turned out to be hollow. In the United States, the perhaps aptly named "American Dream" has provided the fundamental plot points of our particular version of comedy. According to the Dream, in the words of James Truslow Adams, "Life should be better and richer and fuller for everyone, with opportunity for each according to ability or achievement regardless of social class or circumstances of birth."[2] The struggle to achieve that dream has been central to fictional and nonfictional American narratives of the past 200 years. In the context of the rapid growth of a capitalist economy, however, this dream has also increasingly entailed the unleashing of viciously competitive aggression between individuals and between groups.[3] In a warrior economy in which profit and survival are the primary markers of success, after all, there must be winners and losers. News stories about ambitious, successful, and sometimes corrupt "winners" such as Madoff, Zuckerberg, Bezos, and Kalanick; films such as *The Godfather* and *The Wolf of Wall Street*; and television shows such as *Survivor* and *The Apprentice* consistently have drawn huge audiences to the spectacle of ruthless competition and its aftermaths. Most recently, of course, the self-appointed embodiment of triumph in the capitalist arena has been Donald Trump, who in November of 2019 tweeted a self-apotheosis consisting of a picture of his face grafted onto the body of Rocky Balboa (Figure 4.1).[4]

Figure 4.1   Trump as Rocky Balboa

Like a latter-day Macbeth who usurped the presumptive but ultimately too "feminine" heir to the White House, Hillary Clinton, Trump's rapid and unlikely rise to power was premised on the notion of his own competitive, masculine might. As he promised during one campaign rally:

> We're going to win. We're going to win so much. We're going to win at trade, we're going to win at the border. We're going to win so much, you're going to be so sick and tired of winning, you're going to come to me and go "Please, please, we can't

win anymore" ... And I'm going to say "I'm sorry, but we're going to keep winning, winning, winning, we're going to make America great again.[5]

As our "suffering country" (3.6.48) endured the chaos generated by economic inequity, racism, gun violence, and coronavirus—a chaos that Trump reveled in and sought to intensify—it is clear that his prophecy was false. And yet for many in our electorate he "lies like truth" (5.5.43); he collapses the distinction between veracity and falsehood, creating the conditions in which reality is shaped by desire or fear. The promise of greatness, of security, is more persuasive than the evidence of fiendishness.

Equivocation, "alternative facts," lying like truth, a warrior culture defined by violence and ambition, tyranny, and the desire to control time in the interests of greatness and security are central themes in Shakespeare's *Macbeth*, and perhaps for that reason the play in recent years has seemed an apt vehicle through which to highlight and to examine some of the less savory concoctions that have emerged out of the cauldron of American culture, politics, and economics.[6] Two works in particular, William Morrissette's *Scotland, PA* and Vince Gilligan's *Breaking Bad*, have engaged with *Macbeth* in ways that address the unique tensions and contradictions defining this present moment of crisis in the United States, a crisis that embraces our leadership, our democracy, and our commitment to racial, gender, and economic equity. A crisis of faith in the American Dream. Both made before the 2016 election, their appropriations of Shakespeare's play help us to read the unfolding narrative of Trump's reign by focusing on the complex forces that generate the context in which the falsehoods and confusions enabling tyranny are activated. Indeed, though wistful comparisons between Trump and Macbeth were rife in the media, in the end, it may be much more instructive to examine the parallels between the president—a self-described victim of "witch-hunts"—and the play's "weird sisters," whose haunting refrain of "fair is foul, foul is fair, / Hover through the fog and filthy air" (1.1.9–10) defines the very collapse of moral or ethical distinctions that this false prophet engendered.

"ALTERNATIVE FACTS" AND *MACBETH*

"There's no art / To find the mind's construction in the face," says King Duncan about the traitorous Thane of Cawdor, whose defeat at the hands of Macbeth is described at the beginning of Shakespeare's tragedy (1.4.11–12). Taken at face value, *Macbeth* itself seems to be what it is not. On the surface it appears to be a morality tale, however dark and violent in its contours, in which a traitorous and violent usurper against his rightful king is finally punished for his actions by the end of the play, while Malcolm, the murdered Duncan's son and his legitimate successor, ascends to the throne. The assurances given to

Macbeth by the witches that "none of woman born" can harm him (4.1.80) and that he will not be vanquished "until / Great Birnam Wood to high Dunsinane Hill / Shall come against him" (4.1.92) turn out to be deceptive. He is foiled by "alternative facts." In the final battle of the play, the allied rebels approach Macbeth's castle camouflaged by tree branches, thereby nominally fulfilling the prophecy. And Macduff, who vanquishes Macbeth in combat, announces that he was "untimely ripped" from his mother's womb by Cesarean section and is therefore technically not of woman born. The defeated tyrant makes his final appearance in this play as a decapitated head. Macbeth may emerge as poetically sublime in his expressions of ambition, fear, guilt, cruelty, and nihilistic numbness, but ultimately he pays the price of his crimes and order is apparently restored.

And yet, many critics have not been convinced by this plot's seeming resemblance to a morality tale in which good finally prevails over evil. In a play prefaced by the witches' declarative warning that "fair is foul, and foul is fair," we may well want to be careful about embracing any facile oppositions it offers up. As David Kastan and Jonathan Goldberg have shown, the play insistently undoes such oppositions through ironic echoes, doublings, and recurrences.[7] *Macbeth* begins, for example, with the defeat of a traitorous Thane of Cawdor, who is then replaced by Macbeth, who will turn out to be another traitorous Thane of Cawdor. It begins with a gruesome account of Macbeth—a warrior who makes "strange images of death" (1.3.98)—"unseaming" the rebel Macdonwald "from nave to th' chops" (1.2.22), cutting off his head, and fixing it upon the battlements. It ends with a traitorous king and Thane of Cawdor also defeated and decapitated, his head held up to public scorn. Similarly, the play begins with Macbeth defending his king against an alliance of foreign and domestic powers (Norwegian and Scottish), and it ends with his fighting another foreign (this time English) and domestic coalition. In the latter case, Malcolm and Macduff proclaim Macbeth's illegitimacy, and yet, as has been noted, Macbeth had been formally "named" and "invested" (2.4.31–2) as king, and could therefore justifiably define the invaders as rebels.[8] These parallels suggest sameness lurking beneath difference, and indeed Shakespeare's emphasis on the brutal violence itself required of Macbeth to defend Duncan's sacred right to the throne implies that fair and foul cannot easily be differentiated in his world.[9]

Even the moral high ground claimed by Malcolm and Macduff is undermined in this play. The latter, for example, leaves behind his wife and child—to be murdered eventually—when he escapes to England. In the terrible scene of their slaughter, Lady Macduff bitterly calls her husband a traitor, defining a traitor as "one that swears and lies" (4.2.47). Her son concludes that there must then be many more traitors than honest men, to which his mother implicitly assents when she exclaims that in "this earthly world ... to do harm is often laudable" (4.3.73–4). In another disturbing scene, Malcolm tests Macduff's honesty as a potential ally by convincingly claiming that he will be a worse ruler than Macbeth. He is so lecherous, he declares, that "your wives, your daughters, / Your matrons and your maids, could not fill up / The cistern of my lust" (4.3.61–3). Macduff acknowledges this as a problem, but then surprisingly concedes that Scotland has "willing dames enough" with whom he can privately satisfy his desires. But Malcolm goes on, claiming that he is also voraciously greedy. Macduff once again compromises, promising that Scotland has plenty of wealth for him to ransack. When Malcolm doubles down, assigning to himself additional depravities, Macduff finally expresses his outrage, at which Malcolm reveals that he had really only been testing his rectitude. "Such welcome and unwelcome things at once / 'Tis hard to reconcile" (4.3.138), Macduff responds, echoing the witches' phrase that resounds throughout this play: "fair is foul, and foul is fair." How should we interpret Macduff's willingness to countenance Malcolm's unrestrained lechery and greed, and can we fully believe Malcolm's also seemingly convincing professions of unspotted virtue at the end of this exchange?

As the play multiplies these ambiguities, it becomes increasingly difficult to distinguish with certainty hero from villain, justified from unjustified violence, legitimate power from tyranny, truth from lies. The play perhaps presents us with just one episode in a wider, vicious, and recurring cycle of violence and betrayal, rather than with an aberrant event in a redemptive political eschatology. Taken together, all these equivocations suggest an alternative vision of the world in which Macbeth "struts and frets his hour" (5.5.24). If the official version celebrated at the play's conclusion requires a clear dichotomy between good and evil, between moral and immoral, between truth and falsehood, the "alternative facts" of this world may align more closely with the witches' proclamation that there is no real distinction between fair and foul, and in this world Macbeth is simply a consequence of his environment. Terry Eagleton goes so far as to assert that "the witches are the heroines of the piece ... It is they who, by releasing ambitious thoughts in Macbeth, expose a reverence for hierarchical social order for what it is, as the pious self-deception of a society based on routine oppression and incessant warfare."[10] Almost as if the play itself were a version of its protagonist, who "mock(s) the time with fairest show" (1.7.82) when plotting murder, *Macbeth* offers us at its conclusion a vision of time redeemed that may in fact be a mockery disguising the reality of chaos, of the "hurly-burly" (1.1.3), which was there from the beginning.

"THE FUTURE IN THE INSTANT": *SCOTLAND, PA*

Billy Morrissette's film adaptation of *Macbeth*, *Scotland, PA* (2001) begins by promising the same kind of easy contrast between good and evil that

Shakespeare's play seems to end with. Indeed, in the opening credits we are presented with the concluding shots of a 1970s cop show, *McCloud*, in which a cowboy-hat-wearing good guy gets the bad guy.[11] As it turns out, however, Morrissette's film delivers a satirical critique of the capitalist economy embedded in the American Dream that does not leave us with any morally sanitized conclusions. Just as Shakespeare's tragedy suggests that Macbeth is simply the product of a world in which violence and betrayal undergird all power, however apparently legitimate, so Morrissette's adaptation draws our attention to a comparable contradiction between the sacralized ideals of the American Dream and the Darwinian reality of competition and consumption that undermines this mythology.

Set in a small town in central Pennsylvania in 1975, Morrissette turns *Macbeth* into a dark comedy centered around the "invention" of the drive-through fast-food restaurant. Joe "Mac" McBeth, a hamburger prep cook, and his wife, Pat, a waitress, both work at a diner owned by "Norm" Duncan. In Morrissette's drab vision of rural America, Mac and Pat might well be among those whom Hillary Clinton would later define as "deplorables."[12] They live in a trailer, have little education, and work dead-end jobs. They pass the time drinking cheap beer, going hunting, and playing pool and Yahtzee at the local bar. Having heard Norm's idea, partly inspired by Mac, for turning his modest burger joint into a drive-through restaurant, Pat persuades her husband they must kill Norm and take over the establishment. "We're not bad people," she tells her husband the night before the murder, "just underachievers that have to make up for lost time."

In evoking the McBeths' yearning for success (and meaning) in terms of the recovery of time, Morrissette develops a theme that is central to Shakespeare's original. As has been noted, Macbeth's ambitions are rarely expressed in terms of a yearning for wealth and power. Rather, what seems most to excite his and his wife's imagination is the idea of shaping or controlling time through the murder of King Duncan.[13] When Lady Macbeth greets Macbeth after reading about his encounter with the witches, she exclaims, "Thy letters have transported me beyond / This ignorant present, and I feel now / The future in the instant" (1.5.56–8). The murder, she assures her husband, "shall to all our nights and days to come / Give solely sovereign sway and masterdom" (1.5.69–70). They will become masters of their time, free from the limitations of contingency. When at the beginning of the play the witches greet Macbeth as Thane of Glamis and Thane of Cawdor, he interprets these words as "two truths" told "as happy prologues to the swelling act / of the imperial theme" (1.3.129–31). He imagines himself, in other words, as the triumphant protagonist of a drama in which time is ordered according to his desires. By the end of the play, however, Macbeth discovers that the freedom to dominate "his" time, which he thought the witches had promised, was just the opposite.

Reality is a random sequence of tomorrows ("Tomorrow, and tomorrow, and tomorrow") that creep "from day to day / until the last syllable of recorded time" (5.5.18–20). Imagined as an unintelligible sequence of syllables, the passage of time is like incoherent speech. With this insight, Macbeth returns to the metaphor of the theater, but now as only meaningless performance:

MACBETH Life's but a walking shadow, a poor player
    That struts and frets his hour upon the stage
    And then is heard no more. It is a tale
    Told by an idiot, full of sound and fury
    Signifying nothing. (5.5.23–7)

The "swelling act / of the imperial theme" was just meaningless drama.

By reimagining Macbeth and Lady Macbeth as "underachievers" who need to make up for "lost time," Morrissette's film situates them within the fraught context of the American Dream, in which time is measured by gain, and in which failure betrays the incapacity or unwillingness to manage time productively. In an American democracy, supposedly, "opportunity" is available to all, and ultimately all are judged by their capacity or failure to realize it. Interestingly, like their predecessors, neither Mac nor Pat spend much time imagining what exactly they will gain by taking over Duncan's business. What seems to drive them is simply the imperative to achieve, and in Morrissette's film, achievement is tied to "winning" in the capitalist marketplace.

In this respect, the McBeths' drive-through fast-food restaurant—clearly evocative of McDonald's—is a fitting metaphor of the film's central concerns. As would-be entrepreneurs, Mac and Pat develop a business model that embodies the frenetic pace of production and consumption at the heart of a capitalist economy. This industry, with its cheap, high-fat, and addictive fare, became responsible for startling levels of obesity and diabetes among the poor, and its celebration of convenience and speed in fact contradicted the ideals of hearth and home—"small town" American family values—that have been so often touted by American politicians supportive of capitalist ideals. In this particular business venture, the marketplace claims to bestow on us free time, while in fact depriving us of quality time. It promises efficiency, while creating health crises.

McDuff, in the film, is the lone alternative to the future-driven McBeths. Played by Christopher Walken as the detective sent to solve Norm's murder, he is a vegetarian who listens to pseudo-Buddhist self-help tapes about living in the present ("tomorrow is tomorrow, tomorrow is not today, today is who I am ...") and who views the greasy food served by the McBeths as a drug. The film thus shapes up as a confrontation between the vegetarian and the capitalist carnivore, concluding with a fight in which Mac tries to suffocate McDuff with a burger and is eventually impaled on the steer's horns that decorate the hood of his Camaro. In the last shot of the film, we see that McDuff has taken over the McBeths' restaurant and turned it into a vegetarian establishment. He waits patiently outside, spatula in hand, but there are no customers to be seen. Mac may have been caught and punished, but we know what the reality is: fast food will grow to become a parasitic, carnivorous empire, feeding on the fleshly desires of an often ignorant and vulnerable public.

The witches in Morrissette's film are a relatively pallid presence, but this is largely due to the fact that, from the beginning, Mac and Pat are in the grasp of the determinism that underlies a capitalist economy premised on constant expansive movement.[14] Pat's very affirmation that she and her husband are "underachievers" denotes that a sense of meaning or fulfillment is not available to them outside the American value system. It is that value system, ultimately, that renders the political idealization of small-town America a seeming "fair" that is actually "foul." Outside of the "real" time in which "real" wealth is produced and distributed— mostly in the large urban centers on the East and West coasts—towns like Scotland, Pennsylvania, are in fact destined for the decay associated with lack of education, low wages, unemployment, insufficient healthcare, and more recently, the scourge of opioid addiction. Even as they struggle to be winners by the standards of success they have inherited, the McBeths are also destined to be losers by the very fact that the time they seek to redeem has in fact passed them by. Whatever entrepreneurial spirit they enact in this narrative, their inability to use their profits for anything better than an above-ground pool, a tawdry car, and a basement bar, condemns them to being "losers." Macbeth's moral failings in Shakespeare's original become failures of taste in Morrissette's version. The very products that Mac and Pat consume are cheap, garish expressions of the same marketplace to which their fast-food drive-through belongs. Rather than becoming "masters" of time through their success, they reveal themselves unwitting or unconscious pawns of a system that controls them.

"FAIR IS FOUL, AND FOUL IS FAIR": *BREAKING BAD*

Between 2008–13, during Barack Obama's administration and not long before Trump's rise to power, Walter White took center stage in the American cultural imagination as a mild, middle- to lower-middle-class Everyman whose gradual embrace of the dark side is, as in *Scotland, PA*, provoked by the broken promises of the American Dream. Critics have often pointed out parallels between the television show and Shakespeare's *Macbeth*.[15] Vince Gilligan, the show's creator, has explicitly acknowledged that this play haunts the series, noting in an interview that "we steal from the best, we writers do, and the best has to be Shakespeare."[16] *Breaking Bad* is not an explicit adaptation of *Macbeth*, and yet the parallels between the television show and the play are intriguing: both Walter White and Macbeth are men with extraordinary abilities—the former intellectual and the latter military. Both are married to women whom they love and who challenge their sense of masculinity. Both make choices leading them down a path of moral depravity which they are initially horrified by but become gradually inured to. Both make their choices in pursuit of self-transcendence and mastery over time.

As in Morrissette's film, *Breaking Bad* is concerned centrally with a faltering American Dream, but it figures the failure to realize this dream in terms of emasculation. Macbeth is famously spurred to act by Lady Macbeth, who expresses concern that her husband is "too full o' th' milk of human kindness" (1.5.17) to bring himself to murder Duncan. When Macbeth begins to back away from their plan, Lady Macbeth calls in question his manhood: "Art thou afeard / To be the same in thine own act and valor / As thou art in desire?"; to which Macbeth answers that he dares "do all that may become a man, / Who dares do more is none." Lady Macbeth, in turn, exclaims, "When you durst do it, then you were a man" (5.7.39–49). The exchange yields two different definitions of manhood that are important to our understanding of *Breaking Bad*. From Macbeth's perspective, manhood is tied up with respect for those moral and ethical rules that define the social contract: in this case hospitality, honor, and fealty to the king. For Lady Macbeth, manhood is defined by the unleashing of a will to power that dismisses all social restraints and conventions. This is manhood understood in terms of that unrepressed "act and valor" that Macbeth displays as a warrior in battle and that potentially yields "sovereign sway and masterdom" over time itself.

Walter White's compromised masculinity is thematized throughout the first season of the series. His meager salary as a high school teacher to indifferent students requires him to work a humiliating second job at a car wash run by a Russian whose bushy eyebrows betoken his virility. He drives a drab car and owns a shabbily furnished house with a malfunctioning water heater. His only son, Walter Junior, is disabled, and will later drop his father's name for the cinematically masculine Flynn. His well-intentioned wife, Skyler, is domineering, coaxing him to eat veggie bacon on his fiftieth birthday because he is now aging.[17] In one particularly pathetic moment from the same episode, Skyler is clearly more excited by tracking her online sale of a "faux-Lalique vase" purchased from Super Swap than she is in the hand job she's giving her perplexed and ultimately un-stimulable husband. When Walt's DEA agent brother-in-law, Hank, later shows off his gun and Walt remarks on its heaviness, Hank exclaims, "That's why they hire men." Walt's emasculation, the series makes clear, is closely linked to the fact that he lacks the resources to realize anything more than a threadbare, fragile version of the American Dream. To make things worse, he lives with the knowledge that he could have been a privileged member of the 1 percent. Having sold for a pittance his share in a biotech company he co-founded and that is now worth billions, he lives as an exile from the Eden of the Corporate Kingdom of Heaven, where his genius and talents should have earned him his rightful place. Walt, it is clear, has been "too full o' th' mik of human kindness" to succeed in the capitalist arena.

Breaking Bad presents to us an America in which, despite the promises of its Dream, merit and worth are not necessarily rewarded; in which those without the means may be fated to die for lack of affordable healthcare; in which capitalist market forces yield the sterility of suburban blandness and urban blight; in which drugs, twelve-step programs, and therapy fail to keep the unhappiness of the 99 percent at bay. From this perspective, the title "Breaking Bad" may describe something quite different than simply Walter White's fall into crime. It may also designate the disruption itself of moral categories in today's America, such that "bad" has been rendered meaningless. In this series, too, the distinction between "fair" and "foul" is often unclear. Gilligan brilliantly captures this overlap by locating Walt's first base of operations in the house his young partner Jesse inherited from his aunt. It is in this beautiful two-story Spanish Colonial Revival home in the middle of an upscale and well-tended suburban neighborhood that Walt and Jesse will gruesomely dissolve their first "kill" in acid. This ironic blurring of distinctions is centrally highlighted throughout the series by the exacting scientific process through which Walt produces his meth, sought after and consumed precisely for its purity: pure is impure, impure is pure. In this America, the "underworld" of drug trafficking is perhaps no better than one in which a brilliant chemist is forced to teach apathetic students and then wash their cars.

When Walt is diagnosed with cancer, the precariousness of his world is exposed. Lacking the necessary healthcare benefits that could guarantee him the best chances of survival, Walt will turn to cooking and selling meth to pay for his treatment and to guarantee his family's future financial stability. Walt's diagnosis functions as an analogue to the witches' prophecies in *Macbeth*. It is only after he learns what his likely future will be that he gradually embraces the freedom of self-determination that cooking meth promises. Walt's cancer is also a metaphor for his existential condition. His vision of undergoing chemotherapy that will only delay his death also seems to describe his life prior to his diagnosis: "Me, some dead man—artificially alive—just marking time" (1/5). Now confronted with limited time, Walt decides to shape it on his own terms, and indeed time, and timing, are at the heart of this series. From the moment of his diagnosis, the energies of this narrative are largely produced by the temporal predicaments in which Walt finds himself. Again and again, he manages to devise ways of controlling the various contingencies he confronts through his plots and improvisations. In one memorable occasion, he manages at the very last moment to prevent his own execution by having Jesse kill the chemist who would have replaced him as meth cook (4/13).

The criminal persona that Walt takes on is the pork-pie-hat-wearing Heisenberg, the name of the scientist who formulated the "uncertainty principle." A core principle of quantum mechanics, the uncertainty principle essentially states that the position and the speed of a particle cannot be simultaneously known with certainty. Unpredictability thus underlies all being-in-the-world. As Heisenberg, Walt on the one hand manages to master events in their chaotic and unexpected unfolding, and on the other hand understands that his reality is ultimately unknowable—a tale, perhaps, told by an idiot. From this vantage one might see Walt's Heisenberg as revealing (and reveling in) the contingent nature of the world we take for granted. The show's frequent depictions of the "strange images of death" that Walt, like Macbeth, brings about, underscores this point. As we witness bodies liquefying in acid, choking on their own vomit, falling in pieces from the sky, and shredded by bullets, one may well be tempted to echo Jesse's words as he tries to gather the courage to dispose of a corpse: "It's just meat" (1/2). In Walt's new life, this reality—consistent with the ongoing corrosion in his lungs, with the despair of meth addicts, with his wife's infidelity—may be more "true" than the papier-mâché optimism of the American Dream. This reality, in which "fair" only seems so, is captured with delicious irony by the office décor of Walt's corrupt lawyer. Located in a depressing strip mall, the interior presents with empty grandeur a semi-circle of plastic ionic columns behind which is displayed a wallpaper version of the Declaration of Independence. It is in one of the plywood panels of this shabby theatrical backdrop that Saul keeps some of the drug money that needs laundering. In this America perhaps all money is dirty, and "laundering" takes place on a much larger scale than we realize.

This dark vision receives confirmation in a number of ways throughout the series, but perhaps most clearly when we discover that a German corporation is the parent company of the fast-food franchise through which the drug lord Gustavo Fring distributes his meth. Gus Fring himself, an upstanding citizen of the community with philanthropic ties to the police department, embodies the blurring of boundaries between the legal and the illegal. His spectacular death in the last episode of season 4 also reinforces the overlap of fair and foul that this series insists on. Aware that Gus wants to kill him, Walt manages to have him blown up in the room of a nursing home. In the shot immediately following the blast, Gus slowly exits the room, seemingly unharmed. Dapper as always in a blue plaid suit, he straightens his tie, and as he does so, the camera pans in front of him to reveal the other half of his head, reduced to a bloody skull with an empty eye socket. In that brief image, in which we see Gus as both elegant and successful businessman and ruined carcass, Gilligan captures the dualities of the world in which Walt operates.

"DOUBLE, DOUBLE, TOIL AND TROUBLE": *BREAKING BAD*'S REQUIEM FOR A DEAD WHITE MALE

In the end, however, Walt never achieves the tragic stature of a Macbeth, whose closing sublime nihilism somehow elevates him beyond his world. The reasons for this have to do with a "doubleness" at the heart of this series that its makers may not have intended. If as Heisenberg this character is the consequence of a failed American Dream, as Walter White he struggles to remain throughout the series a family man who somewhat archaically uses "son" to address his boy, who tries to hold his marriage together, and who justifies his criminal actions by claiming that everything he does is for his family. Indeed, part of the show's appeal is in seeing the acrobatics performed by Walt as he moves from his role as the "foul" Heisenberg to that of a "fair" family man barbecuing with his brother- and sister-in-law, making breakfast, teaching his son to drive, or tenderly observing his wife with their newborn. However brutishly "masculine" Heisenberg becomes in his career as a maker and trafficker of drugs, as Walter White he continues to nurture an ideal of manhood as husband and father that has a whiff of 1950s nostalgia about it. He is still attached to a vision of the "perfect" nuclear family, as popularized in those ideals of postwar American suburban bliss that he has failed to realize.[18] Manhood, in this context, is about taking charge, being responsible, guaranteeing the security of "his" family.

The same two versions of manhood we identified in *Macbeth* are thus delineated in this series: man as amoral warrior and man as subject to social and ethical obligations. As warrior, Heisenberg has seen through the illusions of the American Dream and understands that the difference between a drug empire and a pharmaceutical company may be that the former sells its drugs on the black market (something that has become even clearer to us during the opioid crisis).[19] Both are willing to kill their customers, either through withholding or by selling the drugs they need. As self-styled patriarch and provider for his family, on the other hand, Walt is still nostalgically attached to the American Dream of lawn-tending security. Where does the series leave us with respect to these two competing perspectives?

Here, we must turn to a centrally defining characteristic of Walt's that is not relevant to our understanding of Macbeth. Unlike Shakespeare's tragic hero, Walter White ... is white. The last name Gilligan assigns his protagonist, one might argue, simply underscores his status as an "average Joe," but why should it be necessary to highlight his whiteness? Perhaps because in our history the American Dream has largely been an ideological construct inhabited by white Americans, and in particular by white males. As James Baldwin made so devastatingly clear in a talk delivered in 1961, the "fat" and "sleek" and "safe" and "happy" suburban home, with its Plymouth, its wife, and its children going to college, a home in which father "knows best," was a white home.[20] Walt is not just an American Everyman confronting the puncturing of his dreams and ambitions in an America that has failed him. He is, more specifically, a literally and metaphorically dying white man facing the breakdown of *his* promised privileges, a breakdown that marginalized others in our American experiment have been familiar with for centuries.

Seen from this perspective, Walt comes across as a doomed but heroic specimen of his race, making a stand against the "dark" forces that undermine his right to primacy. If we consider his career throughout the season, Walt is presented to us as a brilliant mind whose superior intellectual abilities and scientific skills allow him to prevail over adversaries who, more often than not, are associated with the "brown" cartels from south of the border and are hyperbolically alpha-male Latinxs or African American gangbangers, none of whom stand a chance against Walt's powers of reason. Demonstrating truly "White" supremacy, Walt not only teaches the Mexican cartel "natives" how to make meth of far greater purity than they're capable of, but he also manages to create a drug empire which will not rely on help from Mexico. He builds a wall. Walt's obsession with the cleanliness of his equipment, so as to make the purest meth, might be read as a displaced trope of the white man whose colonization of the natives is justified by his superior hygiene—both spiritual and physical.

The series' finale (5/16) confirms that *Breaking Bad*, perhaps unconsciously, voices the resentments of the white American male, breaking with *Macbeth*'s more universalizing preoccupations. Interestingly, the final scene of the penultimate episode of the series provides the most explicit allusion to Shakespeare's play (5/15). Walter is dying of cancer and is hiding out in the New Hampshire wilderness. After his handler departs, Walter stuffs his coat with money, walks out to the gate of his compound, and considers leaving. After hesitating, he mutters to himself "tomorrow, tomorrow ..." and returns to his shack. His muttered "tomorrow" does not yield a philosophical meditation on the vanity of human striving. Rather, Walt's "tomorrow" is ultimately purposive. "Tomorrow" he will indeed achieve his most remarkable mastery over time—despite his terminal cancer—whereby mere "chronos" will become "kairos"—time redeemed, made meaningful.[21]

The finale delivers on this teasing promise. First, Walt cleverly manipulates his former friends and business partners into giving his remaining millions to his son when he turns 18. He has provided for his family. Next, showing his usual technological mastery, he assembles a machine gun, rigs it to a rotating device in his car trunk, and kills all the members of the Aryan brotherhood who had robbed him of his empire. In the mêlée, Walt throws Jesse down to save him from the hail of bullets, though he is mortally wounded in the process. In the final shots of the episode, Walt limps over to the lab he had created, smiling as he caresses the polished tanks where he made the purest meth. He sinks to the ground, spread-eagled, a faint smile lingering on his face. As the camera slowly pans back to give us a bird's-eye view of Walt's body, we see it framed by a grid of squares and rectangles formed by the iron beams crisscrossing the ceiling (Figure 4.2). In our last sight of him, he is both Da Vinci's *Vitruvian Man* and Christ (Figure 4.3).

Figure 4.2   Breaking Bad

As Christ, he has sacrificed himself to guarantee some kind of future to his son and to save Jesse. As Vitruvian Man, he embodies and celebrates the nobility of white, Western "man," a nobility founded morally on his self-sacrifice and intellectually on the infinite resources of his genius. Walt has redeemed time, proven his masculinity, demonstrated White's supremacy.[22]

Breaking Bad thus leaves us with a troubling and problematic doubleness. On the one hand, it provides an often incisive and poignant critique of the failures of the American Dream; on the other hand, it activates an ideologically and racially tinted nostalgia for the values and hierarchies that Dream was founded on. From this latter perspective, the series perhaps prophesied

Figure 4.3   Vitruvian Man

the successful rise of another unlikely contender to greatness who has been frequently compared to Macbeth.

"THE EQUIVOCATION OF THE FIEND THAT LIES LIKE TRUTH": DONALD TRUMP

Not long after *Breaking Bad*'s run, Donald Trump ran for and achieved the presidency of the United States on a platform that explicitly spoke to the anger and frustrations of the "average" white male. In an echo of the doubleness we find in *Breaking Bad*, Trump both described and decried the collapse of the American Dream for white, mostly lower-middle-class Americans and promised to restore it as their birthright. Corporate America, he argued, had undercut the American worker's financial security by shifting jobs offshore while unfairly benefitting from lucrative government contracts, and all the while, corruption was rampant among the political elites who did the bidding of those wealthy billionaires—including Trump himself—who could afford to pay them off through campaign donations. A failing infrastructure, danger- ously porous national borders, Christian values threatened by Islam and trans rights, all these contributed to the unraveling of America's promise. "Sadly," Trump wrote in a Facebook post from July 2016, "the American Dream is dead."[23] At his inaugural address, he offered up a bleak vision of this American reality: as "politicians prospered," Trump declared, "the jobs left, and the factories closed ... The wealth of our middle class has been ripped from their homes and then redistributed across the entire world." Speaking to his base, Trump-as-warrior promised that "this American carnage stops here and stops right now ... The forgotten men and women of our country will be forgotten no longer ... America will start winning again, winning like never before."[24]

Trump's bleak vision, as usual, contradicted a number of facts, including that the country had experienced six years of job growth, that unemployment was at historic lows, that the economy was growing, and that crime rates were falling.[25] But those facts were not directly relevant to his base, whose members often did live among "rusted-out factories scattered like tombstones across the landscape of our nation," whose wages for part-time or low-paid jobs had not increased in decades, who were in the midst of a ravaging opioid crisis, and who had been defined as deplorable.[26] To these forgotten people, Donald Trump promised to "Make America Great Again," to return to them "their" American Dream.

This clearly meant restoring "lost" white male supremacy. Making America great again required building a wall to keep out "rapist" Mexicans, Muslims, and other immigrants from "shit-hole" countries that contaminate our purity. It meant celebrating gun-toting, virile defenders of "law and order," a metaphor, really, for the suppression of political, racial, sexual, and religious difference. It meant describing peaceful protesters horrified by violence against African Americans as domestic terrorists, while inciting armed protesters carrying nooses, Confederate flags, and swastikas to resist the coronavirus stay-at-home orders in Michigan. It is therefore understandable if—as the blustering, self-styled victor over "this American carnage," champion of the forgotten, bleach-wielding conqueror of coronavirus, Bible-brandishing Moses parting angry seas of protesters, swaggering soul mate of Vladimir Putin and Kim Jong-Un, defier of the deep state, and capitoline insurrectionist impervious to impeachment—Trump was wistfully viewed by some as a version of the tyrant Macbeth.

Googling "Macbeth and Trump" yields dozens of links to essays, articles, posts, and blogs that tease out similarities between the two.[27] While acknowledging that Macbeth is a vastly more interesting personality than Trump, for example, Eliot Cohen prophetically claimed that, "In the moment of losing power, the two will be alike. A tyrant is unloved, and although the laws and institutions of the United States have proven a brake on Trump, his spirit remains tyrannical—that is, utterly self-absorbed and self-concerned, indifferent to the suffering of others, knowing no moral restraint. He expects fealty and gives none."[28] For most of these commentators, Macbeth is, after all, one of the most memorable examples of "breaking bad," a powerful and successful warrior who allows his dark ambitions to transform him into a regicide and then a tyrant. Drawing this parallel, of course, also implied a certain hopeful anticipation regarding the conclusion to Trump's narrative arc. Surely the impostor, narcissist president, whose actions and Twitters "each new morn" (4.3.4) further destabilized our democracy, was destined, like all tyrants or would-be tyrants, to meet his retribution? Surely *Macbeth* teaches us that "fair," in the end, wins out over "foul"?

As I have suggested, however, the play provides no such easy or hopeful answers, and the parallels between Macbeth and Donald Trump are perhaps less instructive to consider than those between the MAGA president and the witches that so profoundly influence our sense of the play's atmosphere. One of Trump's most common slogans in response to accusations of unethical and/ or illegal behavior leveled against him is "witch hunt!" It is more accurate, in fact, to think of Trump as a version of the witches in *Macbeth*, and by an ironic twist of fate, "maga" in Italian means female witch or sorceress. As we have seen, the most famous verses the weird sisters utter in the course of the play speak to a reality that is unfixed, unstable, unmoored:

> Fair is foul, and foul is fair.
> Hover through the fog and filthy air. (1.1.9–10)

> Double, double, toil and trouble;
> Fire burn and cauldron bubble. (4.1.10–11)

This is the befogged and obfuscating "reality" that Trump has embodied through his duplicity, mendacity, and "alternative facts."[29] From this vantage, it is Trump's base that has been playing the role of Macbeth, mesmerized by a prophecy—the restoration of the American Dream—that "lies like truth." Like Mac in Morrissette's film and Walter White in *Breaking Bad*, this "Macbeth" is the white American Every*man* to whom future greatness is promised through the realization of a dream that was fraudulent from the beginning. He is the white Everyman who seeks an illusory security in a country where economic inequality is growing, in which a few billionaires possess more wealth than the bottom half of the entire nation. As weird sister, Trump promises his followers control over and renewal of the future—mastery over time—by appealing to the white male's destined superiority. And as his Macbeth-ian base embraced this promise of greatness, he also ensured its betrayal by working to deny health insurance to those who can't afford it, by slashing the welfare programs that constitute our social safety net, by cutting taxes for the wealthiest, by deregulating those very industries he had previously critiqued, by privileging Wall Street returns over the threat of coronavirus, by denying the reality of climate change, by enacting the political corruption he had decried.

Beclouded by the spreading "fog and filthy air" released through Twitter, Facebook, and Instagram by Trump and his other weird sisters—including Fox Television, Steve Bannon, Rudy Giuliani, Mitch McConnell, William Barr, and even, ironically, a doctor from Houston who peddled hydroxychloroquine as a cure for COVID-19 and believes that gynecological problems can stem from sex with demons—fair and foul, truth and falsehood, are increasingly difficult to distinguish.[30] "Truth is not truth," Giuliani infamously stated in an interview in 2018, and indeed when "truth" is available only through the filter bubbles brewed in the social media cauldron, we are left with only the doubleness of perspectivism and, to use a word Shakespeare uniquely employs in *Macbeth*, of equivocation.[31] What *Macbeth* reveals, as we have seen, is its tragic protagonist as the product of a world inherently compromised by violence and the will to power. It is, *Scotland, PA* and *Breaking Bad* suggest, a world not so different from the one we find ourselves in today, in which the ideals of democracy and the American Dream are undercut by the realities of economic and racial inequities, of religious intolerance, of violence wrought under false pretexts, of environmental devastation. As "maga," or "weird sister," Trump is indeed an "imperfect speaker" (1.3.70) who greets many of us "with present grace and great prediction / Of noble having and of royal hope" (1.3.55–6). Our culture—our media and social media, our politicians, our commercials, our sitcoms, our "reality" shows, our celebrities, our self-help books, our narratives of happiness and of success—all these have conjured this being who tempts many American Macbeths with narcissistic images of self-fulfillment. "We are cruelly trapped," wrote James Baldwin some years ago, "between what we would like to be and what we actually are. And we cannot possibly become what we would like to be until we are willing to ask ourselves just why the lives we lead on this continent are mainly so empty, so tame, so ugly."[32] The trajectory from "what we would like to be" to "what we actually are" succinctly describes the arc of Macbeth's career in Shakespeare's play. In his final words, Macbeth bravely lifts the veil from his life and his world and reveals it as hollow. Though we are not necessarily asked to embrace Macbeth's radical disillusionment ourselves, I would suggest that the experience of disillusionment is a necessary step in the search for truth. In this respect, one may nurture the hope that unlike Walter White, who leaves us with the nostalgic dream of white greatness, the white Everyman caught in the fog of Trump's American Dream will, eventually, painfully awaken from it.

NOTES

1.　William Shakespeare, *Macbeth*, ed. Sandra Clark and Pamela Mason, Bloomsbury Arden Shakespeare (London: Bloomsbury, 2015). All parenthetical play citations in this chapter will be from *Macbeth*. References are to act, scene, and line.

2. James Truslow Adams, *The Epic of America* (New York: Little, Brown, 1931), 404.

3. On capitalism and the American Dream, see Lee Artz and Bren Ortega Murphy, *Cultural Hegemony in the United States* (Thousand Oaks, CA: Sage, 2000), 275. See also Lawrence R. Samuel, *The American Dream: A Cultural History* (Syracuse, NY: Syracuse University Press, 2012).

4. Abby Ohlheiser, "A Short Journey into the MAGA Internet's Obsession with Swole Trump," *washingtonpost.com*, November 27, 2019, sec. Internet Culture.

5. Tom Lutey, "Trump: 'We're going to win so much, you're going to be so sick and tired of winning,'" *billingsgazette.com*, May 26, 2016, https://billingsgazette.com/news/state-and-regional/govt-and-politics/trump-we-re-going-to-win-so-much-you-re/article_2f346f38-37e7-5711-ae07-d1fd000f4c38.html.

6. The phrase "alternative facts" was made infamous by Kellyanne Conway, President Trump's senior White House adviser, when defending Trump press secretary Sean Spicer's false claims about the size of Trump's inauguration crowds. See Jim Rutenberg, "'Alternative Facts' and the Costs of Trump-Branded Reality," *nytimes.com*, January 22, 2017.

7. David Scott Kastan, "*Macbeth* and the 'Name of the King,'" in *Shakespeare after Theory* (New York: Routledge, 1999), 151–67; Jonathan Goldberg, "Speculations: *Macbeth* and Source," in *Shakespeare Reproduced: The Text in History and Ideology*, ed. Jean E. Howard and Marion F. O'Connor (New York: Methuen, 1987), 242–64.

8. Kastan notes that King James VI and I had admitted in the *The True Law of Free Monarchies* that monarchical authority often was first derived from the right of conquest ("Macbeth and the 'Name of the King,'" 156). This of course risked undercutting the notion of kingship as divinely sanctioned.

9. Regarding Macbeth's violence, Kastan notes that it also calls into question Duncan's very legitimacy ("Macbeth and the 'Name of the King,'" 152). For a similar reading, see Alan Sinfeld, "*Macbeth*: History, Ideology, and Intellectuals," *Critical Quarterly* 28, no. 1–2 (1986): 63–77.

10. Terry Eagleton, *William Shakespeare* (Oxford: Blackwell, 1986), 2. Karin S. Coddon makes a similar point, arguing that "Macbeth, then, is not the victim so much as the *effect* of a disorder that manifestly precedes and, I would suggest, produces him." Karin S. Coddon, "'Unreal Mockery': Unreason and the Problem of Spectacle in *Macbeth*," *ELH* 56, no. 3 (Autumn 1989): 491.

11. Billy Morrissette, *Scotland, PA* (Lot 47 Films, 2001), 104 min.

12. Katie Reilly, "Read Hillary Clinton's 'Basket of Deplorables' Remarks About Donald Trump Supporters," *time.com*, September 10, 2016.

13. On time in *Macbeth*, see Donald W. Foster, "Macbeth's War on Time," *English Literary Renaissance* 16, no. 2 (Spring 1986): 319–42 and Howard Marchitello, "Speed and the Problem of Real Time in *Macbeth*," *Shakespeare Quarterly* 64, no. 4 (Winter 2013): 425–48.

14. On the subject of capitalism and determinism in this film, see George Moore, "*Macbeth* Goes to Carnival: *Otium* and Economic Determinism in *Scotland, PA*," *Literature/Film Quarterly* 45, no. 3 (2017), https://lfq.salisbury.edu/_issues/45_3/macbeth_goes_to_carnival.html. See also Eric C. Brown, "Shakespeare, Class, and *Scotland, PA*," *Literature/Film Quarterly* 34, no. 2 (2006): 147–53.

15. One of the best discussions of these parallels is in Paul A. Cantor's chapter, "The Macbeth of Meth: *Breaking Bad* and the Tragedy of Walter White," in *Pop Culture and the Dark Side of the American Dream: Con Men, Gangsters, Drug*

Lords, and Zombies (Lexington: University Press of Kentucky, 2019), 88–131. I disagree, however, with his conclusion that the show reveals the dangers of denying "the value of masculinity" (131). See also Ray Bossert, "Macbeth on Ice," in *Breaking Bad and Philosophy: Badder Living through Chemistry*, ed. David R. Koepsell and David Arp (Chicago and LaSalle, IL: Open Court, 2012), 65–74.

16. Vince Gilligan, interview by Mark Lawson, *Front Row*, BBC Radio 4, August 21, 2013, https://www.bbc.co.uk/sounds/play/b038hghh.

17. Vince Gilligan, *Breaking Bad* (AMC, 2008–13), season 1, episode 1. All sub-sequent references to the series will provide the season and episode number in parentheses.

18. Heath A. Diehl offers a compelling analysis of the ways in which Walt is haunted by postwar models of fatherhood. See "Breaking Dad: Reimagining Postwar Models of American Fatherhood in *Breaking Bad*," in *Pops in Pop Culture: Fatherhood, Masculinity, and the New Man*, ed. Elizabeth Podnieks (New York: Palgrave, 2016), 179–94.

19. Malcolm Harris, "The White Market," *thenewinquiry.com*, September 12, 2012, https://thenewinquiry.com/the-white-market/.

20. James Baldwin, "From Nationalism, Colonialism, and the United States: One Minute to Twelve—A Forum," in *The Cross of Redemption*: *Uncollected Writings*, ed. Randall Kenan (New York: Pantheon Books, 2010), 12.

21. On "chronos" and "kairos," see Frank Kermode, *The Sense of an Ending: Studies in the Theory of Fiction* (New York: Oxford University Press, 2000).

22. It matters little that the enemies Walt vanquishes here are actual white suprema-cists. They serve, I would argue, as a red herring that distracts an audience from the more subterranean race politics of the show.

23. Donald Trump, "Sadly, the American dream is dead. But if I ever get elected president, I will bring it back, bigger and better than ever. DJT," Twitter, July 9, 2016, https://www.facebook.com/DonaldTrump/posts/sadly-the-american-dream -is-dead-but-if-i-ever-get-elected-president-i-will-brin/10157280885660725/.

24. Donald Trump, "The Inaugural Address: Remarks of President Donald J. Trump— As Prepared for Delivery" (address given in Washington, DC, January 20, 2017). https://www.whitehouse.gov/briefings-statements/the-inaugural-address/.

25. Michael A. Cohen, "Trump's Dark Vision of America," *bostonglobe.com*, January 20, 2017.

26. Donald Trump, "Remarks of President Donald J. Trump."

27. Among these, see Maureen Dowd, "Double, Double, Trump's Toil, Our Trouble: Demon sperm meets alien D.N.A., as President Trump Teeters," *nytimes.com*, August 1, 2020; Eliot Cohen, "How This Will End. Sooner or Later, Tyrants are Always Abandoned by their Followers," *theatlantic.com*, August 24, 2018; Brent Budowski, "Mueller and Trump Star in a Shakespearean Drama that Grips US," *thehill.com*, February 27, 2018; George Wead, "Trump is a Real-Life Macbeth," *dnronline.com*, June 3, 2017; and Stephen Greenblatt, "The Instigator," in *Tyrant: Shakespeare on Politics* (New York: W. W. Norton, 2018), 96–112.

28. Eliot Cohen, "How This Will End."

29. On Trump's systematic mendacity, see Glen Kessler, Salvador Rizzo, and Meg Kelly (*Washington Post* Fact Checker Staff), *Donald Trump and his Assault on Truth: The President's Falsehoods, Misleading Claims and Flat-Out Lies* (New York: Scribner, 2020).

30. Will Sommer, "Trump's New Favorite COVID Doctor Believes in Alien DNA, Demon Sperm, and Hydroxychloroquine," *thedailybeast.com*, July 27, 2020,

https://www.thedailybeast.com/stella-immanuel-trumps-new-covid-doctor-believes-in-alien-dna-demon-sperm-and-hydroxychloroquine. Hydroxychloroquine was shown to be ineffective as a treatment for COVID-19, despite Trump's stubborn promotion of it.
31. Rebecca Morin and David Cohen, "Giuliani: 'Truth isn't Truth,'" *politico.com*, August 19, 2018, https://www.politico.com/story/2018/08/19/giuliani-truth-todd-trump-788161.
32. James Baldwin, "Mass Culture and the Creative Artist: Some Personal Notes," in *The Cross of Redemption: Uncollected Writings*, ed. Randall Kenan (New York: Pantheon Books, 2010), 5–6.

REFERENCES

Adams, James Truslow. *The Epic of America*. New York: Little, Brown, 1931.

Artz, Lee, and Bren Ortega Murphy. *Cultural Hegemony in the United States*. Thousand Oaks, CA: Sage, 2000.

Baldwin, James. "From Nationalism, Colonialism, and the United States: One Minute to Twelve—A Forum." In *The Cross of Redemption: Uncollected Writings*, edited by Randall Kenan, 9–15. New York: Pantheon Books, 2010.

Baldwin, James. "Mass Culture and the Creative Artist: Some Personal Notes." In *The Cross of Redemption: Uncollected Writings*, edited by Randall Kenan, 3–6. New York: Pantheon Books, 2010.

Bossert, Ray. "Macbeth on Ice." In *Breaking Bad and Philosophy: Badder Living through Chemistry*, edited by David R. Koepsell and David Arp, 65–74. Chicago and LaSalle, IL: Open Court, 2012.

Brown, Eric C. "Shakespeare, Class, and *Scotland, PA*." *Literature/Film Quarterly* 34, no. 2 (2006): 147–53.

Budowski, Brent. "Mueller and Trump Star in a Shakespearean Drama that Grips US." *thehill.com*, February 27, 2018.

Cantor, Paul A. "The Macbeth of Meth: *Breaking Bad* and the Tragedy of Walter White." In *Pop Culture and the Dark Side of the American Dream: Con Men, Gangsters, Drug Lords, and Zombies*, 88–131. Lexington: University Press of Kentucky, 2019.

Coddon, Karin S. "'Unreal Mockery': Unreason and the Problem of Spectacle in *Macbeth*." *ELH* 56, no. 3 (Autumn 1989): 485–501.

Cohen, Eliot. "How This Will End. Sooner or Later, Tyrants are Always Abandoned by their Followers." *theatlantic.com*, August 24, 2018.

Cohen, Michael A. "Trump's Dark Vision of America." *bostonglobe.com*, January 20, 2017.

Diehl, Heath A. "Breaking Dad: Reimagining Postwar Models of American Fatherhood in *Breaking Bad*." In *Pops in Pop Culture: Fatherhood, Masculinity, and the New Man*, edited by Elizabeth Podnieks, 179–94. New York: Palgrave, 2016.

Dowd, Maureen. "Double, Double, Trump's Toil, Our Trouble: Demon Sperm Meets Alien D.N.A., as President Trump Teeters." *nytimes.com*, August 1, 2020.

Eagleton, Terry. *William Shakespeare*. Oxford: Blackwell, 1986.

Foster, Donald W. "Macbeth's War on Time." *English Literary Renaissance* 16, no. 2 (Spring 1986): 319–42.

Gilligan, Vince. *Breaking Bad*. AMC, 2008–13.

Gilligan, Vince. Interview by Mark Lawson. *Front Row*, BBC Radio 4, August 21, 2013. https://www.bbc.co.uk/sounds/play/b038hghh.

Goldberg, Jonathan. "Speculations: *Macbeth* and Source." In *Shakespeare Reproduced: The Text in History and Ideology*, edited by Jean E. Howard and Marion F. O'Connor, 242–64. New York: Methuen, 1987.

Greenblatt, Stephen. "The Instigator." In *Tyrant: Shakespeare on Politics*, 96–112. New York: W. W. Norton, 2018.

Harris, Malcolm. "The White Market." *thenewinquiry.com*, September 12, 2012. https://thenewinquiry.com/the-white-market/.

Kastan, David Scott. "*Macbeth* and the 'Name of the King.'" In *Shakespeare after Theory*, 151–67. New York: Routledge, 1999.

Kermode, Frank. *The Sense of an Ending: Studies in the Theory of Fiction.* New York: Oxford University Press, 2000.

Kessler, Glen, Salvador Rizzo, and Meg Kelly (*Washington Post* Fact Checker Staff). *Donald Trump and his Assault on Truth: The President's Falsehoods, Misleading Claims and Flat-Out Lies.* New York: Scribner, 2020.

Lutey, Tom. "Trump: 'We're going to win so much, you're going to be so sick and tired of winning.'" *billingsgazette.com*, May 26, 2016. https://billingsgazette.com/news/state-and-regional/govt-and-politics/trump-we-re-going-to-win-so-much-you-re/article_2f346f38-37e7-5711-ae07-d1fd000f4c38.html.

Marchitello, Howard. "Speed and the Problem of Real Time in *Macbeth*." *Shakespeare Quarterly* 64, no. 4 (Winter 2013): 425–48.

Moore, George. "*Macbeth* goes to Carnival: *Otium* and Economic Determinism in *Scotland, PA*." *Literature/Film Quarterly* 45, no. 3 (2017). https://lfq.salisbury.edu/_issues/45_3/macbeth_goes_to_carnival.html.

Morin, Rebecca, and David Cohen. "Giuliani: 'Truth isn't Truth.'" *politico.com*, August 19, 2018. https://www.politico.com/story/2018/08/19/giuliani-truth-todd-trump-788161.

Morrissette, Billy. *Scotland, PA*. Lot 47 Films, 2001. 104 min.

Ohlheiser, Abby. "A Short Journey into the MAGA Internet's Obsession with Swole Trump." *washingtonpost.com*, November 27, 2019, sec. Internet Culture.

Reilly, Katie. "Read Hillary Clinton's 'Basket of Deplorables' Remarks About Donald Trump Supporters." *time.com*, September 10, 2016.

Rutenberg, Jim. "'Alternative Facts' and the Costs of Trump-Branded Reality." *nytimes.com*, January 22, 2017.

Samuel, Lawrence R. *The American Dream: A Cultural History.* Syracuse, NY: Syracuse University Press, 2012.

Shakespeare, William. *Macbeth*. Edited by Sandra Clark and Pamela Mason. Bloomsbury Arden Shakespeare. London: Bloomsbury, 2015.

Sinfeld, Alan. "*Macbeth*: History, Ideology, and Intellectuals." *Critical Quarterly* 28, no. 1–2 (1986): 63–77.

Sommer, Will. "Trump's New Favorite COVID Doctor Believes in Alien DNA, Demon Sperm, and Hydroxychloroquine." *thedailybeast.com*, July 27, 2020. https://www.thedailybeast.com/stella-immanuel-trumps-new-covid-doctor-believes-in-alien-dna-demon-sperm-and-hydroxychloroquine.

Trump, Donald. "Sadly, the American dream is dead. But if I ever get elected president, I will bring it back, bigger and better than ever. DJT." Twitter, July 9, 2016. https://www.facebook.com/DonaldTrump/posts/sadly-the-american-dream-is-dead-but-if-i-ever-get-elected-president-i-will-brin/10157280885660725/.

Trump, Donald. "The Inaugural Address: Remarks of President Donald J. Trump—As Prepared for Delivery." Address given in Washington, DC, January 20, 2017. https://www.whitehouse.gov/briefings-statements/the-inaugural-address/.

Wead, George. "Trump is a Real-Life Macbeth." *dnronline.com*, June 3, 2017.

5. When it is wise to play the fool: a lesson in servant leadership, courtesy of *King Lear*

Katey Roden

> I will have such revenges on you both
> That all the world shall – I will do such things –
> What they are yet I know not, but they shall be
> The terrors of the earth! (2.2.468–71)
> (King Lear, *King Lear*)[1]

> They [North Korea] will be met with fire and fury like the world has never seen ...
> They will be met with fire, fury and frankly power the likes of which this world has
> never seen before.
> (President Donald Trump, press conference, August 8, 2017)[2]

Donald Trump's White House has often been called "Shakespearean," as an ever-rotating cast of characters invites modern audiences to meditate on a storyline rife with tyrants, madmen, and fools.[3] Ever since Trump declared his candidacy for president, a host of media outlets has been quick to label him a fool.[4] When candidate Trump became President Trump, the accusation of Shakespearean foolishness became even more ubiquitous, as former advisors, pundits, and politicians debate whether the American president is an absolute fool or a Machiavel clever enough to play one. The polarizing 45th president's all-too-public rages and televised cabinet meetings replete with sycophantic speeches have certainly drawn direct comparison to the titular character of Shakespeare's *King Lear*.[5]

With these parallels in mind, Shakespeare offers potent criticism of the folly of self-serving politicians, particularly so in *King Lear*. Since its first performance in December of 1606, *King Lear* challenged audiences to reconcile with the play's brutal portrayal of political gamesmanship, its moral desolation, and its absolute refusal to offer consolation to a country riven by vying political factions. Shakespeare's theater company brought *Lear* to the stage on the heels of the November 5, 1605, Gunpowder Plot, an act of home-grown terrorism intended to decimate the whole of Parliament along with England's Protestant monarch, James I, and both his sons. The terrible image of the Catholic recusant Guy Fawkes arrested with a lit match and long fuse leading to barrels of gunpowder stacked below the House of Lords would have been fresh in the nation's mind at the time of the play's production; if not, surely, Fawkes's drawn-and-quartered body served as a grisly reminder of the nation's political and religious divides. The national mood must have been one of anxious uncertainty, much as it is today.

The parallels between 1606 London and the 2020 United States are conspicuous. 1606 London was beset with plague and politico-religious discord; America also finds itself a nation divided. The acrimony between America's progressive left and religious right appears as entrenched as the Catholic-Protestant divide. This is perhaps most evident in the presidential response to the global pandemic, which has become a partisan issue exemplified by Trump's Tulsa, Oklahoma, political rally wherein Trump's desire for public adulation outweighed the considerable risk of contagion.[6] Extant national tensions have only heightened as the outburst of Black Lives Matter protests and calls to defund the police prompted local right-wing militias to mobilize throughout the United States.[7] While 1606 London was awash with political uneasiness, 2020 America appears just as turbulent. Shakespeare's great tragedy captures the madness of the times, both then and now. Discomfiting as these parallels may be, *King Lear* presents more than just the story of a ruler whose narcissism and self-serving political decisions create dire consequences for his country.

This chapter focuses on the ways *King Lear* offers contemporary and early modern audiences a lesson in the value of self-sacrifice and service by examining the myriad ways Lear's loyal servants, the Fool and Kent, as well as Gloucester's politically disenfranchised son Edgar, masquerading as the mad beggar Poor Tom, bring their king into greater consciousness of his leadership failures. By tracing the ways Shakespeare diffuses the archetypal figure of the wise fool across these faithful servants, I argue that *King Lear* features a dynamic commentary on the wisdom of empathetic and service-oriented leadership that is particularly relevant in Donald Trump's America. To do so, I first consider the biblical and literary legacy of the wise fool, a didactic figure intended to teach the value of spiritual wisdom over worldly ambition.

Next, I explore the play's various fools in relation to their social stations as servants in the deeply hierarchical world of Renaissance England. I consider how their foolishly faithful service to Lear facilitates his momentary, but powerfully wrought, awakening to his leadership failures that resulted in the "houseless heads," "unfed sides," and "looped and windowed raggedness" (3.4.30–1) of his populace. Utilizing the philosophy of servant leadership, I examine the service done for Lear and his own recognition that true leadership is selfless. Reading *King Lear* through the framework of servant leadership, I argue, offers a valuable new way of interpreting not only the play's portrayal of the faithful and self-sacrificing servants who follow King

Lear, but also its adaptation of the tradition of the Christian fool. Ultimately, by stitching together the seemingly paradoxical figures of the wise fool and the servant leader in *King Lear*, Shakespeare's bleakest play offers a timeless lesson in the spirit of true leadership and the folly of valuing personal power over social well-being.

FOOLS FOR GOD AND THE WORLDLY WISE

> If any man among you seem to be wise in this world, let him be a fool, that he may be wise. For the wisdom of this world is foolishness with God; for it is written, He catcheth the wise in their own craftiness. (1 Corinthians 3:18–19, Geneva Bible (1599))[8]

The Christian church did not hold a monopoly on the figure of the holy fool, a common enough image in many cultures, but the Christian tradition of the holy fool provides two noteworthy examples: Christ and the apostle Paul. The ultimate holy fool is, of course, Christ. The paradigm of Christ's sinless body voluntarily sacrificed offers a profoundly affective illustration of holy folly, since privileging the afterlife of the soul appears potentially foolish in this world. This seeming foolishness opposes the materialistic or fleshly "wisdom" of the world that often leads humanity to sin in the first place. In the following section, I will introduce the biblical and literary traditions of holy and wise fools at Shakespeare's disposal when composing *King Lear*.

Aside from Christ, the most important biblical figure to illustrate holy folly is Paul, who followed Christ's example and sacrificed physical well-being for the spirit. The hardships Paul encountered on his apostolic mission enact the paradox of the wise fool, which he clarifies:

> Let no man deceive himself: If any man among you seem to be wise in this world, let him be a fool, that he may be wise. (1 Cor. 3:18)

Paul admonishes individuals whom the world regards as successful by reframing their so-called "wisdom" as actually illustrating foolish attachments to earthly accomplishment. Paul inverts the value system associated with wisdom and foolishness such that interest in earthly gains reveals true foolishness. In Paul's view, having the wisdom to value spiritual gains over worldly success is the only form of wisdom worth pursuing. All other pursuits are simply foolish.

The Christian commitment to holy folly was manifested in medieval monasticism's vocational emphasis on turning away from worldly concerns.

This spiritual principle was modeled after Paul's apostolic leadership, which endorsed personal sacrifice for greater good:

> For though I be free from all men, yet have I made myself servant unto all men, that I may win the more. (1 Cor. 9:19, 22–3)

The tradition of holy folly is also reflected in popular early modern satires like Sebastian Brant's *Ship of Fools* (1494), which portrayed a pilotless ship manned by an irrational crew who catalogue the varieties of human folly, and Erasmus of Rotterdam's influential *Moriae Encomium* or *The Praise of Folly* (1509–11), which juxtaposes the moral failings of humanity against the moral integrity of the spiritually wise in a devastating satire with wide appeal. Following in Paul's stead, both Brant's and Erasmus's narrators claimed foolishness as they spoke otherwise unspeakable social truths with a deeply didactic agenda.

The wise fool could also be found in the courts of monarchs where "the court fool or jester … was allowed to satirize the morals of the powerful and comment on the affairs of the state with impunity."[9] The wise fools who occupied service-level positions in the great houses of Renaissance England were expected to use their wit to speak truth to power. Shakespeare's frequent portrayal of these figures invites consideration over how his wise fools might present models of servant leadership that hold a mirror to ineffective leaders within the highly regimented, class-based, authoritarian structures of early modern governance.

SERVANT LEADERSHIP

The term *servant leadership* was first used in 1977 by Robert Greenleaf (1904–90), a professional in the field of management research and development in the AT&T corporation.[10] In that venue, and as a consultant for non-profit entities, Greenleaf worked to counteract what he identified as a growing "crisis of leadership" during the social upheaval of 1960s–1970s-era America. As Greenleaf describes it, servant leadership "begins with the natural feeling that one wants to serve, to serve first. Then conscious choice brings one to aspire to lead."[11] This desire to become a servant leader, to become "a person of character who puts people first," aligns with the selfless valuation of immaterial virtue over material profit inherent in the holy folly and wise fool traditions.[12] Greenleaf asserts that servant leaders should assess their impact on the world by asking:

> do those served grow as persons; do they, *while being served*, become healthier, wiser, freer, more autonomous, more likely themselves to become servants? And,

what is the effect on the least privileged person in society; will she or he benefit, or at least, not be further deprived? No one will knowingly be hurt, directly or indirectly?[13]

In this simple servant leader test, concern for the least privileged and most vulnerable in society is paramount. This selfless vision of how one ought to deploy worldly power would doubtlessly appear a foolish mode of leadership to those whom the holy folly tradition would call the worldly wise or to individuals who care more for personal power and advantage over ethical concerns. The apostle Paul affirms this by characterizing Christ's early followers as fools:

> For brethren, you see your calling, how that not many wise men after the flesh, not many mighty, not many noble are called. But God hath chosen the foolish things of the world to confound the wise, and God hath chosen the weak things of the world, to confound the mighty things. (1 Cor 1. 26–7)

When Paul directs early Christians to examine their calling to become leaders, he also admonishes them to abandon the value-standards of the world represented by desires for material gain. If, as Greenleaf argues, "humility is one of the distinguishing traits of the true servant," then servant leadership also directs leaders to turn away from the material trappings of power.[14] Proponents of servant leadership claim that theirs is a leadership philosophy grounded in *love*, which "sounds strange in the context of *business* … But here the emphasis is not on sentimentality but on acting intentionally in ways that support the health, wisdom, freedom, autonomy of persons, with the motive of meeting *their* most critical needs rather than our narrow ego needs."[15] While not explicitly Christian, servant leadership parallels the emphasis on loving service as the path toward empathetic leadership capable of improving society.

Given the socio-politico-religious crisis in *King Lear*, a crisis brought about by the selfish concerns of the play's leaders and resolved through foolish servants willing to sacrifice their own well-being for the greater good, I will now turn to *King Lear*, a play that serves as a powerful vehicle to reflect on the tenets of good leadership and ultimately proffers a vision of servant leadership responsive to the ethical and social dilemmas of Shakespeare's England.

THE WISDOM OF FOOLS AND SERVANTS: SERVANT LEADERSHIP IN *KING LEAR*

Service, in its many forms, touched every element of early modern social organization. Be it staff and officials in noble households or apprentices living with their masters, servants could be found in roughly 29 percent of all early modern households.[16] Buttressed by encouragement from social historians to reread sources with an eye toward marginalized or invisible populations, early modern scholars are applying service studies to Shakespeare to reassess social and economic relations among previously overlooked side characters occupying service positions. This critical trend began with *King Lear*, a play that draws attention to the mutual obligations of the serving and ruling classes and the catastrophic consequences of either side abandoning their service obligations. *King Lear* has been a crucial touchstone in examining the significance of service in early modern England, but little attention has been given to the ways in which the play stages successful service around the paradoxical figure of the wise fool, a character that exposes the familial and political tensions of *King Lear* and facilitates the play's ultimate advocacy for servant leadership.[17]

From *King Lear*'s outset, Shakespeare's audience is presented with an array of foolish behaviors. Lear's inaugural declaration that he will divide his kingdom between his children and "shake all cares and business from our age / Conferring them on younger strengths, while we / Unburdened crawl toward death" (1.1.38–40) is a study in foolishness. At first glance, Lear's desire to renounce the duties of governance might be misconstrued as a desire to relinquish the material luxuries that accompany political power by making the "wise" choice to reject the world and better attune himself toward an impending afterlife. However, Lear's decision to "divest us both of rule, / Interest of territory, cares of state" and also "retain / The name, and all th'addition to a king" (1.1.49–50, 135–6) leaves his country in the precarious position of multiple parties jockeying for power. What is more, Lear demands to keep a retainer of 100 knights, whose only apparent purpose is to illustrate Lear's royal power, despite having just given this up.

Lear's foolhardy narcissism forces those closest to him into taking up a range of foolish positions. Lear desires public adulation, and so devises a contest to see which daughter can best profess her love for him; she who loves him most will receive the most prized parcel of land. Driven by worldly "wisdom," Goneril and Regan offer obsequious speeches. Goneril declares that Lear is "dearer than eyesight, space and liberty, / Beyond what can be valued, rich or rare, / No less than life" (1.1.56–8). Regan escalates the saccharine-sweet compliments, countering that Goneril expresses "my very deed of love," only falling short in that Regan is "an enemy to all other joys ... And find I am alone felicitate / In your dear highness' love" (1.1.71–5). Awash in the glow of such toadying speeches, Lear becomes enraged when Cordelia, his youngest and dearest daughter, offers him nothing. Publicly refusing to pay homage, she confesses, "I love your majesty / According to my bond, no more nor less" (1.1.92–3). Embarrassed by a truthful response, Lear disowns, disinherits, and banishes Cordelia.

While reflecting on the foolishness of this pivotal scene, it is worth noting that the English "fool" comes from the Latin *follis*, meaning "a bellows or windbag."[18] The hot air Goneril and Regan emit to secure political capital reveal them to be, like Lear, windbags void of care for the common good. Lear's foolish desire for empty compliments presents an unsettling parallel to twenty-first-century America, wherein President Trump so desires public adulation that, like Lear, he is willing to manufacture it. Whether that praise comes via awkward speeches from political appointees in a televised cabinet meeting, his own braggadocious tweeting, or the use of coronavirus press briefings to demand praise, Trump certainly appears as demanding of and responsive to complimentary bombast as Lear.[19] The intemperate insults with which he has treated individuals who defect from his administration reveal a similarly Lear-like instinct for hot-headed political calculus.[20]

Cordelia's forthright explanation that she loves Lear exactly as she should exhibits the type of godly service that contemporary conduct manuals advised between a daughter and her *paterfamilias*, the male head of a family, and in Lear's case, the father of a kingdom and earthly representative of God the Father.[21] Lear's rash rejoinder against Cordelia reflects a terrible rejection of the service obligations that bound contemporary social systems together. The noble Earl of Kent underscores the importance of service relations in his explicit attempt to remind Lear of his own dutiful service to the crown: "Royal Lear, / Whom I have ever honoured as my king, / Loved as my father, as my master followed, / As my great patron thought on in my prayers" (1.1.140–3). Kent's formal address emphasizes his own participation in the reflexive service obligations between the nobility and monarchs, insofar as his successive naming of Lear as "king," "father," and "master" calls attention to his role as royal *paterfamilias*, a position that carries its own service obligations to subjects. Kent defines this relationsnip when he reminds Lear of the honor he has paid him, the love he has shown him, and the faith with which he serves Lear before advising the king to reconsider Cordelia's banishment. Kent reminds Lear that if he desires love, honor, and faith from those below him in the social hierarchy, if he expects the respect and service due to a king, father, and master, then he must lead them with love, honor, and good faith. Kent's forthright attitude appeals to the ideals of good service when he identifies his own public rebuke of Lear's decision-making as "unmannerly" and subsequently inquires, "What wouldst thou do, old man? / Think'st thou that duty shall have dread to speak, / When power to flatter bows? To plainness honour's bound / When majesty falls to folly" (1.1.146–50).

Kent's shift away from formal appellations acknowledging Lear's position of power to "old man" emphasizes the vulnerable identity awaiting Lear once he divests himself of crown and kingdom. Kent demands that Lear recognize the reciprocal nature of a servant-master relationship by juxtaposing the artificiality of Goneril's and Regan's claims to love and honor Lear with his plain, dutiful speech intended to lead his master away from folly.

Kent thus models good service through what can only be described as an act of foolish disobedience intended to lead Lear into better leadership practices. Kent's foolishness displays true wisdom insofar as he chooses service over servility, a distinction best illustrated by the servile, self-serving behaviors of Lear's eldest daughters and Kent's service-oriented motivations. Kent is forced to "give up the conventionally conceived role of servant for that of master— and teacher."[22] To guide Lear, Kent must take up the position of servant leader. In this way, Kent models behavior that one might attribute to an individual like General James Mattis, whose public rebuke of President Trump appears to stem from a conscientious desire to do the country good service by holding his former "master" accountable.[23] This service-oriented perspective demands leaders willing to risk their own good fortune for the sake of the greater good. Just as Mattis received backlash for his public criticism of Trump, Kent is banished for his desire to serve rather than be servile. The parallels between the opening scenes of *King Lear* and the present-day White House are unsettling precisely because a true servant leader still embedded within the administration has yet to emerge. *King Lear*'s opening scenes emphasize master-servant relations and the importance of having individuals willing to remind leaders that power comes with an obligation to serve.

Kent's refusal to abandon the role of servant duty-bound to provide his master with good counsel demonstrates precisely how foolish selfless service might look in regard to worldly expectations to safeguard the self. Kent's stringent devotion to the master-servant relationship wherein "the authority of masters was both authorized and constrained by their relation to God" reveals the pressure placed upon servants to serve their master's pleasure and also hold their betters to the standards of a divinely established social order.[24] Ultimately, *King Lear* stages a clash between worldly and spiritual wisdom via Goneril's and Regan's seemingly wise service to the self, Lear's self-oriented worldly "wisdom" that disintegrates the social bonds of his family, court, country, and Kent's seemingly foolish choice to resist his banishment and continue to serve Lear in disguise. As the play progresses, the value of service-oriented leadership becomes even more apparent as Lear tips into madness and must rely on the faithful service of Kent and his Fool to lead him into realizing his leadership failures.

Some of the play's most potent commentary on the value of sacrificial leadership comes, unsurprisingly, from Lear's Fool, who, dressed in motley and employed in Lear's household, most clearly embodies the paradoxical positions of wise fool and servant leader. The emphasis servant leadership places on leaders considering the needs of the most marginal populations when making decisions is reflected quite clearly in Lear's Fool, a character who draws the audience's attention to the broader social impact of Lear's intractable behavior. When he encounters Kent suffering in the stocks outside of Regan's home, a punishment Kent receives for insulting one of Regan's servants in defense of Lear's honor, the Fool remarks, "Fortune, that arrant whore, / Ne'er turns the key to the poor" (2.4.242–3). The Fool's blithe estimation of Kent's circumstances, having been reduced so swiftly from a nobleman to a common servant so easily punishable, so easily made to suffer, offers a startling condemnation of a social system that provided little safety net for servants caught up in the quarrels of their masters. The Fool's observation that good fortune is as faithful to the poor as a common prostitute would have resonated with an early modern audience acutely aware of the distinctions between the haves and have-nots. His assessment of Kent's degraded position aims at more than simple laughs; it is a form of truth-telling, a reminder to the elites in Shakespeare's audience that their excessive fortune, in both monetary terms and the ease with which they navigate life, is a privilege denied to the poor. Given the stark divisions between those who have and those who have not in America, divisions made all the more apparent in times of pandemic, protests demanding racial equity, and Trump-era tax policies that favor the rich, it seems the Trump administration is in need of a Fool to draw the president's attention to these steep divisions.

Shortly thereafter, the Fool instructs Kent on the nature of true service: "That sir which serves and seeks for gain, / And follows but for form, / Will pack when it begins to rain, / And leave thee in the storm; / But I will tarry, the fool will stay, / And let the wise man fly" (2.2.267–72). Noting the distinction between Goneril's steward Oswald, a man who serves only with an eye toward personal gain and whom Kent is being punished for insulting, and Kent's fool-hardy loyalty to Lear, the Fool's prophetic vision of the stormy heath draws a sharp distinction between Oswald's selfish concerns and the personal danger Kent and the Fool encounter by serving Lear. The sacrificial tenor of the Fool's remark to Kent acknowledges how readily they both take up the mantle of holy folly in support of a leader still fixating on worldly concerns.

Lear's self-absorption is on full display when seeing Kent in the stocks; his outrage stems more from a sense of personal affront than indignation at his servant's significant suffering. In an exclamation exhibiting Lear's foolish pride, he rages: "They could not, would not do't – 'tis worse than murder / To do upon respect such violent outrage" (2.2.212–13). Lear's hyperbolic reaction reveals that he still foolishly attaches his sense of self to socio-political and economic power, which is underscored when he pointedly emphasizes that he is Kent's master. Confronting Regan, Lear queries, "Who put my man i'the stocks?" then, "Who stocked my servant?" and again, "How came my man i'the stocks?" (2.2.371, 377, 387). Repeating the possessive adjective "my" reminds both Regan and the audience that "a well-trained and loyal servant became part of his master … the liveried man was not merely clothed in his master's identity but absorbed into his social body, to be fed as his own body was fed."[25] An injury to Kent certainly amounts to an insult to Lear, but this formulation of service effectively obscures Kent's actual suffering. Shakespeare, however, ensures that we see Kent suffer. Kent spends a night stocked, talks to the Fool stocked, talks to Lear stocked, and is released from that painful position after almost 170 lines of dialogue.[26] Giving such stage time to a servant suffering for the sake of their leader highlights how narcissism shapes Lear's response. Lear reveals himself an unempathetic master who doesn't authentically care for the well-being of others. As Lear's twenty-first-century counterpart, President Trump has also been accused of lacking the capacity for empathetic leadership in times of personal and national suffering.[27] Trump's desire to brand his response to the pandemic a "great success story" just as the nation edged towards 60,000 dead from COVID-19 echoes not only Lear's desire for public praise, but also Lear's utter inability to respond emotionally to human suffering.[28] This self-absorbed leadership style is on full display when Lear describes the disrespect directed at him as being "worse than murder," a statement that further reveals self-centeredness rather than a sense of obligation to those who serve him. Only the violence of the storm and an unexpected encounter with true poverty can shake Lear from his egotism and teach him to condemn self-serving leadership.

Accompanied by Kent and his Fool, and exposed to a brutal storm on a barren heath, Lear struggles to reconcile a sense of self defined by mastery over those around him with an emerging vision of himself as a man who is still yet a master, but a master who is called to serve rather than be served. Lear's first moment of authentic and empathetic leadership comes when he has nothing except the capacity to recognize the suffering of those less fortunate. As they discover a hovel that might provide some relief from the elements, Lear asks the Fool, "How dost my boy? Art cold? I am Cold myself"; turning to Kent, he inquires, "Where is this straw, my fellow?" and back to the Fool, "Poor fool and knave, I have one part in my heart that's sorry yet for thee" (3.2.69, 70, 73). While Lear continues to apply the possessive adjective "my" to his servants, the emotional register differs significantly from his egocentric response to Kent's stocking. These personal appellations, while still indicating mastership, evince concern for his servants' condition, for their suffering. Lear's concern indicates an emerging sense of responsibility for lower social orders; it is the seedbed of a desire to serve, not the self, but others.

Lear's emerging servant leader consciousness crystallizes when he self-lessly invites the Fool to enter the hovel before him:

> **LEAR** In boy, go first. You houseless
> Poverty—
> Nay, get thee in. I'll pray, and then I'll sleep.
> [*Kneels*] Poor naked wretches, wheresoe'er you are,
> That bide the pelting of this pitiless storm,
> How shall your houseless heads and unfed sides,
> Your looped and windowed raggedness, defend you
> From seasons such as these? O, I have ta'en
> Too little care of this. Take physic, pomp,
> Expose thyself to feel what wretches feel,
> That thou mayst shake the superflux to them
> And show the heavens more just. (3.4.26–36)

Indigent and exposed to the elements, Lear transcends his narcissism by confessing his poor leadership and acknowledging its effects on the poor. Not only does he voice empathy for his Fool's suffering by inviting the Fool to take shelter before him, but Lear also proffers an expansive concern for all the people suffering in his kingdom by wondering how those who have gone longer than he without food, clothing, and shelter are weathering the storm. He recognizes his responsibility, his failure to serve these communities. Desiring to "feel what wretches feel," he displays empathy that prompts acknowledge-ment of his leadership failures. By confessing that heretofore he has paid little attention to poverty, Lear voices a crucial principle of servant leadership: accountability for one's actions while exhibiting care for others. This emergent social consciousness is a by-product of Lear's exposure to those lower on the socio-economic scale. Bearing witness to the suffering of his foolishly faithful servants brings him into greater consciousness of his obligations to them. Without such exposure, Lear would likely remain oblivious to such suffering because he, like Trump surrounded by wealthy cabinet appointees and servile family and staff, would simply be unable to understand true need.

This nascent sense of social responsibility deepens when Poor Tom emerges from the hovel and both Lear and the audience are forced to reckon with true poverty. Gloucester's forsaken son Edgar, disguised as the mad beggar Poor Tom, triggers Lear's most authentic recognition of his foolishness. Seeing

Tom's near-naked body besmeared with mud and shivering with cold, Lear directs the audience to take stock of the suffering before them:

> **LEAR** Is man no more than this? Consider him well. Thou
>   Ow'st the worm no silk, the beast no hide, the sheep
>   No wool, the cat no perfume. Ha? Here's three on's
>   Are sophisticated; thou art the thing itself,
>   Unaccommodated man is no more but such a poor,
>   Bare, forked animal as thou art. Off, off, you lendings:
>   Come, unbutton here. (3.4.101–7)

As Lear tears at his clothes, Shakespeare invites the audience to consider the foolishness of social arrangements distinguishing the rich from the poor through "sophisticated" material markers of worldly success like fine clothes and perfume. Suddenly self-reflective, Lear views himself, Kent, and the Fool as pretending to be more than what they are. The trappings of wealth and status blind them to seeing their shared humanity with Poor Tom, whom Lear describes as "the thing itself." Struggling to undress, Lear not only recognizes human suffering, but desires to share in it as he comes to see his party of fools as vulnerable and disenfranchised as the naked wretch before them. But it is too late for Lear to become a true service-oriented leader; at this moment of revelation, Lear slips into madness.[29]

While Lear's tragic epiphany arrives too late to correct his leadership failures, his painful descent into madness engenders a desire to serve in those around him. When Lear becomes an actual fool, the progressive social consciousness of holy folly and servant leadership already at work in characters like Lear's Fool and Kent manifests itself in Edgar, who disguised as the mad beggar Poor Tom propelled Lear into his servant leader revelation. In an aside directed at the audience, Edgar responds to Lear's suffering, "My tears begin to take his part so much / They mar my counterfeiting" (3.6.58–9). Edgar's empathetic wisdom stems not only from the old king's obvious torment, but from a sense of obligation to serve evident in the following soliloquy, wherein Edgar reevaluates his own substantial suffering:

> **EDGAR** When we our betters see bearing our woes,
>   We scarcely think our miseries our foes.
>   Who alone suffers, suffers most i'the mind,
>   Leaving free things and happy shows behind.
>   But then the mind much sufferance doth o'erskip,
>   When grief hath mates and bearing fellowship.
>   How light and portable my pain seems now,
>   When that which makes me bend makes the King bow,
>   He childed as I fathered. Tom, away;
>   Mark the high noises, and thyself bewray
>   When false opinion, whose wrong thoughts defile thee,
>   In thy just proof repeals and reconciles thee. (3.6.99–110)

Recognizing the social contract between the powerful and the poor, Edgar expounds upon how it is easier to bear misfortune when he observes his "betters" sharing in the burdens of the less fortunate. Watching Lear's solitary descent into madness, seeing him isolated from the fellowship of even his most faithful servants, Edgar reinterprets his own suffering as "light and portable," precisely because Lear has been "childed" as Edgar has been "fathered," diction that emphasizes how Lear's children and Edgar's father have mutually abandoned their familial obligations. Edgar's phrasing also suggests a sense of social responsibility to care for an infirm old man "childed" by mental instability and no longer able to perform his role as *paterfamilias*. In the speech's final lines, Edgar acknowledges that as a man of virtue, he must "repeal" selfish concerns for his own safety that drove him to create the Poor Tom disguise and "reconcile" himself to his estranged father, serve his ailing king, and take a more active role in righting the many wrongs of his fractured fatherland. Edgar takes up the mantle of servant leadership.

Contemporary audiences of *King Lear* might note the crucial role empathy plays in developing a conscious desire to serve the social good. Without his recognition of Edgar's true suffering in the storm, Lear might not have acknowledged his leadership failures and neglected social obligations. He might not have come to understand true need. This revelation may have expedited Lear's transformation into a pitiful creature untethered from reality, but Lear's swift descent into madness also inspires Edgar's empathetic response and decision to reclaim his true identity. The sense of responsibility and social care Edgar voices in response to Lear's suffering presents a vision of sacrificial leadership, as Edgar chooses to take the hard but true path reclaiming his rightful identity and punishing wrongdoing rather than continuing safely on in his disguise as Poor Tom. Selfless leadership and care for the common good, *King Lear* evinces, are tightly wound up with proximity to suffering, recognition of the social contract that the haves ought to care for the have-nots, and most crucially, the simple willingness of leaders to open themselves up to "feel what wretches feel."

The remainder of the play is marked by intense violence and moral turpitude as Goneril and Regan battle for power. Edgar's father, Gloucester, who has been tricked into believing Edgar is plotting to kill him, takes pity on Lear and tries to help; in return for this disloyalty to Goneril and Regan, both of Gloucester's eyes are gouged out. Blinded and wandering the heath, Gloucester encounters Edgar disguised as Poor Tom, who agrees to lead his father to a cliff so he may throw himself over. Edgar then tricks his father into believing that he has survived his suicide attempt and should no longer despair, declaring his life a miracle. Cordelia, now Queen of France, returns with an army intent on saving her father. She finds the now entirely mad Lear just as her army is defeated and they are imprisoned. Regan and Goneril compete for the love of Edmund, Gloucester's bastard son who tried to cheat Edgar out of his rightful inheritance by turning Gloucester against him. Goneril poisons Regan, then commits suicide when she learns that Edmund has been mortally wounded battling Edgar. Prior to the brothers' battle, Edmund orders Cordelia to be hanged. When the audience next sees Lear, in the final scene of the play, he is inconsolable with grief, howling as he carries Cordelia's body, and futilely asking for his collar to be unbuttoned as he gasps his last breath (5.3.308). The desolation at the end of *King Lear* overwhelms characters and audience alike. Lear's kingdom is so broken by self-serving leaders that none of the remaining characters desires the absolute power of the crown for themselves. *King Lear* stages personal and national suffering to such effect that audiences, both then and now, might wonder how to interpret the fact that the play begins and ends with a divided kingdom. The portrait of political power and self-serving ambition modeled by Lear, Goneril, and Regan has soiled the throne such that even the nobles who are invited to rule recoil from the ultimate seat of power. It is a damning renunciation of self-serving leadership that invites audiences to rally their support around leaders who have the capacity for empathy, care for those less fortunate, and the selflessness to serve.

Shakespeare gives the play's final words to Edgar, who instructs the audience in the value of empathetic leadership. He advises: "The weight of this sad time we must obey, / Speak what we feel, not what we ought to say" (5.3.522–3). In his directive to feel rather than speak, to acknowledge shared trauma, Edgar confirms the horrors of the political world engendered by self-serving leaders who might offer empty platitudes at such a moment. Indeed, the leadership vacuum at the end of the play reveals that none of the remaining characters care to be the fool in pursuit of worldly power. Goneril and Regan, like Lear before them, have demonstrated that absolutist, strongman models of leadership are destructive precisely because they are disconnected from the moral authority of leaders commited to empathetic leadership. Edgar's final instruction to speak and feel truly reminds us that social relations and political structures must be built on foundations of trust generated through the emotional exchanges that bind human beings together. The urgency of these final lines, spoken by a character whom we have seen utterly debased by this system, a character who has deliberately acted a fool, brings the ethic of servant leadership fully to bear. Edgar's call for authentic emotional connection brings the play full circle and encourages audiences to demand that their political leaders expose themselves to human suffering, feel that suffering deeply, and be guided by concern for others. The consequences of having leaders who simply seek out compliments and empty praise are too dire.

King Lear refuses to offer solace, but the rawness of the play's familial, social, and political wounds presents a compelling endorsement of sacrificial, selfless, and service-oriented leadership. The play revolves around departures from the expected emotional responses between children and parents, siblings, monarchs and subjects, as well as servants and masters. The prodigious suffering in *King Lear* would not occur if not for unempathetic political leaders insulated from the true cost of their poor leadership, because they are surrounded by servile individuals offering empty praise, rather than servants who speak hard truths. Both in early modern England and now, particularly in times of national strife and great suffering, *King Lear* teaches audiences that the individuals our leaders surround themselves with are vitally important; these are the servants who will either help lead their masters to grow in empathy or enable them to rage publically over perceived slights. Just as the play stages profound tragedy, it also models the paradoxical tensions of servant leadership, wise fools, and holy folly through a range of characters who answer the call to lead through selfless service, even if they are not themselves politically powerful. In a world gone mad, *King Lear* continues to remind audiences that it can be a challenge to distinguish between folly and true wisdom, but leaders who attune themselves to the role of servant are wise enough to play the fool.

NOTES

1.   All quotations from the play derive from William Shakespeare, *King Lear*, ed. R. A. Foakes, Arden Shakespeare, 3rd series (London: Bloomsbury, 1997). References are to act, scene, and line.
2.   Peter Baker and Choe Sang-Hun, "Trump Threatens 'Fire and Fury' Against North Korea if it Endangers U.S," *The New York Times*, August 8, 2017.
3.   Stephen Greenblatt, "Shakespeare Explains the 2016 Election," *The New York Times*, October 8, 2016; Peter Conrad, "Shakespeare in the Age of Brexit and Trump: The Play's Still the Thing," *The Guardian*, September 29, 2018; Gregg Opelka, "Would Shakespeare Impeach Trump? The President Is No More Corrupt than King Lear," *The Wall Street Journal*, September 27, 2019; Steven Greenblatt,

Tyrant: Shakespeare on Politics (New York: Norton, 2018); Jeffrey Wilson, *Shakespeare and Trump* (Philadelphia: Temple University Press, 2020).

4. Michael Hayden, "Former CIA Chief: Trump Is Russia's Useful Fool," *The Washington Post*, November 3, 2016; Christina Silva, "Chinese State Media Suggests President Trump Is a 'Fool,'" *Newsweek*, June 16, 2018; William McRaven, "This Is What Happens When a Stable Genius Leads a Stupid Country," *The Washington Post*, November 19, 2018; Sydney Ember, "Biden, Urging Face Masks, Calls Trump a 'Fool' for Not Wearing Mask in Coronavirus Crisis," *The New York Times*, May 26, 2020.

5. Jennifer Finney Boylan, "The Madness of King Donald," *The New York Times*, February 20, 2019; Henry Olsen, "Trump Is Looking a Lot Like King Lear—but This Tragedy Is Far from Over," *The Washington Post*, October 2, 2019; Laurence Dodds, "'A Dog's Obeyed in Office!' Seven Ways Donald Trump Is Just Like King Lear," *The Telegraph*, June 13, 2017.

6. Rex Huppke, "Trump's Tulsa Coronavirus Rally: Deep-fried Hydroxychloroquine, a 'Joyous Festival of Narcissism, Anger and Disease,'" *Chicago Tribune*, June 19, 2020.

7. Isaac Stanley-Becker, "As Protests Spread to Small-Town America, Militia Groups Respond with Armed Intimidation and Online Threats," *The Washington Post*, June 18, 2020.

8. All biblical references come from the Geneva Bible, an edition that was first printed in 1560. Shakespeare had access to various biblical editions, but his biblical references most often mirror the Geneva Bible.

9. Peter Phan, "The Wisdom of Holy Fools in Postmodernity," *Theological Studies* 62 (2001): 732.

10. Robert Greenleaf, *The Power of Servant Leadership*, ed. Larry C. Spears (San Francisco: Berrett-Koehler, 1998), 3.

11. Robert Greenleaf, *Servant Leadership: A Journey into the Nature of Legitimate Power and Greatness* (New York: Paulist Press), 13.

12. J. W. Sipe and D. M. Frick, *Seven Pillars of Servant Leadership: Practicing the Wisdom of Leading by Serving* (1989; repr., New York: Paulist Press, 2009), 4.

13. Greenleaf, *The Power of Servant Leadership*, 123, italics in the original.

14. Greenleaf, *The Power of Servant Leadership*, 41.

15. Sipe and Frick, *Seven Pillars of Servant Leadership*, 44, italics in the original.

16. Mark Thornton Burnett, *Masters and Servants in English Renaissance Drama and Culture: Authority and Obedience* (London and New York: Macmillan and St. Martins, 1997), 1.

17. The first critical treatment of "service" in Shakespeare is Jonas A. Barish and Marshall Waingrow, "'Service' in *King Lear*," *Shakespeare Quarterly* 9, no. 3 (Summer 1958): 347–55. Other influential works include: Mark Thornton Burnett, *Masters and Servants in English Renaissance Drama and Culture*; Michael Neill, *Putting History to the Question: Power, Politics, and Society in English Renaissance Drama* (New York: Columbia University Press, 2000); Linda Anderson, *A Place in the Story: Servants and Service in Shakespeare's Plays* (Newark: University of Delaware Press, 2005); and David Evett, *Discourses of Service in Shakespeare's England* (New York: Palgrave Macmillan, 2005).

18. Kinch Hoekstra, "Hobbes and the Foole," *Political Theory* 25, no. 5 (1997): 642 n. 10.

19. John Wagner, "Praise for the Chief: Trump's Cabinet Tells Him It's an 'Honor' and 'Blessing' to Serve," *The Washington Post*, June 12, 2017; Jeremy Peters,

Elaina Plott, and Maggie Haberman, "260,000 Words, Full of Self-Praise, from Trump on the Virus," *The New York Times*, April 27, 2020; Ashley Parker and Anne Gearan, "Coronavirus Crisis Highlights Trump's Resistance to Criticism — and His Desire for Fervent Praise," *The Washington Post*, April 8, 2020.
20. Morgan Chalfant, "Trump Calls Mattis 'Overrated,'" *The Hill*, June 3, 2020.
21. Mark Thornton Burnett, "*King Lear*, Service, and the Deconstruction of Protestant Idealism," *The Shakespeare International Yearbook, Volume 5: Special Section: Shakespeare and the Bonds of Service*, edited by Michael Neill (Aldershot, UK and Burlington, VT: Ashgate Press, 2005), 66–85.
22. Barish and Waingrow, "'Service' in *King Lear*," 349.
23. Jeffrey Goldberg, "James Mattis Denounces President Trump, Describes Him as a Threat to the Constitution," *The Atlantic*, June 2, 2020.
24. Neill, *Putting History to the Question*, 23.
25. Neill, *Putting History to the Question*, 23.
26. Stage directions indicate that Kent is stocked at 2.2.148 and released at 2.2.316.
27. Unempathetic responses to human suffering have plagued Trump's presidency. For instance, Trump has failed to offer unifying or even emotionally sensitive responses to the staggering American death toll amidst the 2020 global COVID-19 pandemic, but he has publically mourned its toll on America's economy.
28. Jared Kushner, interview by Steve Doocy, Ainsley Earhardt, and Brian Kilmeade, *Fox & Friends*, April 29, 2020.
29. Concern over Trump's mental health is exemplified in Charles Blow's "Mental Health Professionals Warn about Trump," *The New York Times*, February 13, 2017, wherein 35 psychologists question the president's mental fitness.

REFERENCES

Anderson, Linda. *A Place in the Story: Servants and Service in Shakespeare's Plays*. Newark: University of Delaware Press, 2005.

Baker, Peter, and Choe Sang-Hun. "Trump Threatens 'Fire and Fury' Against North Korea if it Endangers U.S." *The New York Times*. August 8, 2017.

Barish, Jonas A., and Marshall Waingrow. "'Service' in *King Lear*." *Shakespeare Quarterly* 9, no. 3 (Summer 1958): 347–55.

Blow, Charles. "Mental Health Professionals Warn about Trump." *The New York Times*. February 13, 2017.

Boylan, Jennifer Finney. "The Madness of King Donald." *The New York Times*. February 20, 2019.

Brant, Sebastian. *The Ship of Fools, Volume 1*. Translated by Alexander Barclay. Urbana, IL: Project Gutenberg. https://www.gutenberg.org/files/20179/20179-h/20179-h.htm.

Burnett, Mark Thornton. "*King Lear*, Service and the Deconstruction of Protestant Idealism." In *The Shakespearean International Yearbook, Volume 5: Special Section: Shakespeare and the Bonds of Service*, edited by Michael Neill, 66–85. Aldershot, UK and Burlington, VT: Ashgate Press, 2005.

Burnett, Mark Thornton. *Masters and Servants in English Renaissance Drama and Culture: Authority and Obedience*, Early Modern Literature in History Series. London and New York: Macmillan and St. Martin's, 1997.

Chalfant, Morgan. "Trump Calls Mattis 'Overrated.'" *The Hill*. June 3, 2020.

Conrad, Peter. "Shakespeare in the Age of Brexit and Trump: The Play's Still the Thing." *The Guardian*. September 29, 2018.

Dodds, Laurence. "'A Dog's Obeyed in Office!' Seven Ways Donald Trump Is Just Like King Lear." *The Telegraph*. June 13, 2017.

Ember, Sydney. "Biden, Urging Face Masks, Calls Trump a 'Fool' for Not Wearing Mask in Coronavirus Crisis." *The New York Times*. May 26, 2020.

Erasmus, Desiderius. *The Praise of Folly*. London: Penguin Classics, 1994. (Penguin Classics; Reprint edition, March 1, 1994)

Evett, David. *Discourses of Service in Shakespeare's England*. New York: Palgrave Macmillan, 2005.

Evett, David. "The Year's Work in Service Studies: Shakespeare, 2005." *Modern Philology* 104 (February 2007): 412–29.

Geneva Bible. Edited by Gerald Sheppard. New York: Pilgrim Press, 1989.

Goldberg, Jeffrey. "James Mattis Denounces President Trump, Describes Him as a Threat to the Constitution." *The Atlantic*. June 2, 2020.

Greenblatt, Stephen. "Shakespeare Explains the 2016 Election." *The New York Times*. October 8, 2016.

Greenblatt, Stephen. *Tyrant: Shakespeare on Politics*. New York: Norton, 2018.

Greenleaf, Robert. *Servant Leadership: A Journey into the Nature of Legitimate Power and Greatness*. New York: Paulist Press, 1977.

Greenleaf, Robert. *The Power of Servant Leadership*. Edited by Larry C. Spears. San Francisco: Berrett-Koehler Publishers, 1998.

Hayden, Michael. "Former CIA Chief: Trump Is Russia's Useful Fool." *The Washington Post*. November 3, 2016.

Hoekstra, Kinch. "Hobbes and the Foole." *Political Theory* 25, no. 5 (1997): 620–54.

Huppke, Rex. "Trump's Tulsa Coronavirus Rally: Deep-fried Hydroxychloroquine, a 'Joyous Festival of Narcissism, Anger and Disease.'" *Chicago Tribune*. June 19, 2020.

Kushner, Jared. Interviewed by Steve Doocy, Ainsley Earhardt, and Brian Kilmeade. *Fox & Friends*. April 29, 2020.

McRaven, William. "This Is What Happens When a Stable Genius Leads a Stupid Country." *The Washington Post*. November 19, 2018.

Neill, Michael. *Putting History to the Question: Power, Politics, and Society in English Renaissance Drama*. New York: Columbia University Press, 2000.

Olsen, Henry. "Trump Is Looking a Lot Like King Lear—but This Tragedy Is Far from Over." *The Washington Post*. October 2, 2019.

Opelka, Gregg. "Would Shakespeare Impeach Trump? The President Is No More Corrupt than King Lear." *The Wall Street Journal*. September 27, 2019.

Parker, Ashley, and Anne Gearman. "Coronavirus Crisis Highlights Trump's Resistance to Criticism—and His Desire for Fervent Praise." *The Washington Post*. April 8, 2020.

Peters, Jeremy, Elaina Plott, and Maggie Haberman. "260,000 Words, Full of Self-Praise, from Trump on the Virus." *The New York Times*. April 27, 2020.

Phan, Peter C. "The Wisdom of Holy Fools in Postmodernity." *Theological Studies* 62 (2001): 730–52.

Shakespeare, William. *King Lear*. In *The Arden Shakespeare*, 3rd series, edited by R. A. Foakes. London: Bloomsbury, 1997.

Silva, Christina. "Chinese State Media Suggests President Trump Is a 'Fool.'" *Newsweek*. June 16, 2018.

Sipe, J. W., and D. M. Frick. *Seven Pillars of Servant Leadership: Practicing the Wisdom of Leading by Serving.* New York: Paulist Press, 2009.

Stanley-Becker, Isaac. "As Protests Spread to Small-Town America, Militia Groups Respond with Armed Intimidation and Online Threats." *The Washington Post.* June 18, 2020.

Wagner John. "Praise for the Chief: Trump's Cabinet Tells Him It's an 'Honor' and 'Blessing' to Serve." *The Washington Post.* June 12, 2017.

Wilson, Jeffrey R. *Shakespeare and Trump.* Philadelphia: Temple University Press, 2020.

6. Post-truth and pre-truth: how rhetoric shapes reality in Boyle's *Certain Physiological Essays*, Shakespeare's *Othello*, and the language of Donald Trump

Samantha Dressel

We are supposedly living in a post-truth world. *Post-truth* was the Oxford Word of the Year in 2016, and numerous related coinages, including *fake news* and *alternative facts*, have come to dominate political discourse in the United States.[1] Similar to President Donald Trump's tagline of "Make America Great Again," the term *post-truth* seems to hearken back to a mythical moment in time when America was great and truth was reliable. Did these times ever actually exist, however? I argue that they did not; truth is always filtered through rhetoric and must be so filtered when everyone does not have equal access to the facts. To engage this issue, I look back to Renaissance England, a time before Twitter and PizzaGate and COVID-19.[2] Rather than considering this era as a golden age in which truth was present, I dub it, somewhat facetiously, a "pre-truth" era. This was a time before the Scientific Revolution, when accurate measurements were all but impossible, and scientific results were frequently unreproducible. Given the lack of empirical certainties, probable outcomes and actions became a way of assessing the world, though this approach has the dark potential to lead to essentializing stereotypes. This sort of probabilistic thinking infiltrates both fiction and nonfiction writing of the Renaissance and it continues to underpin much of modern discourse.

To look at the rhetorical treatment of truth in this period, I examine two very different texts. I will explore the rhetoric of Iago, the archetypal prince of alternative facts, from William Shakespeare's *Othello* (1604). I will also consider a scientific source, Robert Boyle's *Certain Physiological Essays* (1661). These two texts are in stark contrast if we juxtapose the fictional context of *Othello* with Boyle's factual approach and Iago's evil motivations with Boyle's knowledge-driven ones. And yet, bringing these two texts into conversation with Donald Trump's speeches, I will trace clear similarities in the ways these rhetors address their audiences.[3] Despite three very different rhetorical situations—a play in which a fictional character tries to pollute his enemy's mind, a scientific tract, and political rhetoric—the texts share striking similarities of goals and style. All are faced with the task of convincing audiences of situations for which they cannot offer evidence; in Iago's and Trump's cases, this is because the described "facts" do not actually exist, while Boyle simply lacks reliable reproducibility. All three rhetors approach the problem through similar tactics: building ethos[4] with their audience, highlighting the deceptive or fickle nature of the world by emphasizing the need for probabilistic assumption, and presenting a highly detailed account of their story which, in Renaissance terms, resembles judicial testimony. These similarities, spanning upwards of 400 years, suggest that there is not and has never been a "true" narration of ideas accessible to an audience; instead, the question is whether these rhetorical strategies are being used to communicate the world as it truly seems or to obfuscate that truth. This chapter will argue that these strategies are highly effective at molding perceptions, and that they ultimately may be used by science communicators for persuasion as much as they are used by rhetors with more suspect motivations.

Before I explore these texts and the rhetorical strategies and assumptions that characterize them, I will briefly summarize the works themselves. Shakespeare's *Othello* traces the downfall of the titular character, a black Venetian general. His love for his white wife Desdemona is undermined by the machinations of Iago, who plants suspicions of Desdemona's infidelity for unknown reasons. Robert Boyle is an early scientist, probably most famous for developing Boyle's law, which relates the pressure of a gas to its volume. He is a significant figure among early modern scientists because of his emphasis on testable hypotheses.[5] His *Physiological Essays* consider a range of chemical experiments, biological dissections, and more. The details of these experiments are not relevant to this chapter; I am interested in the way he frames and describes the experiments themselves rather than their actual goals and outcomes.

It has been well established that President Donald Trump speaks in ways that hide, obscure, or alter the facts, and this sort of discourse has grown ubiquitous in contemporary media. Trump notably "relies on hearsay, anecdote, and suspect information in partisan media but also shifts the burden of proof to those who oppose his conclusions and shuns responsibility for distributing faulty information."[6] According to Stephen Heidt and Damien Pfister, Trump's language results in "people passing around a rumor with the feel of truthiness until a story just becomes part of the enthymematic backdrop of a particular social network."[7] In other words, a discourse composed entirely of heavily flawed assumptions is created. Trump's refusal to substantiate his own claims has resulted in others feeling justified in doing the same. Trump's supporters, in particular, will latch onto his claims, propagate them, and sometimes even expand on them.[8] Notably, though, the post-truth spread of information is not necessarily about contradicting accepted truths so much as suggesting that these truths do not matter.[9] Instead, hyperbole is normalized in the service of arguments steeped in pathos and ethos.[10] If the *feeling* evoked is true, the details are incidental.

Today's fake media, according to Robert Gutsche, attempts to propagate false facts in order to undermine truth itself. He claims a vast departure from a past in which hoaxes were designed to simply test the limits of technology or create entertainment.[11] To me, this framing contributes to a falsely glorified past. As Robert Mejia et al. argue, for people outside of the hegemonic group, the truths presented to them have always been suspect.[12] Mejia et al. articulate the ways in which the hegemony foists narratives upon those outside of the ruling elite, such as drug policies that tacitly target people of color.[13] Their argument focuses particularly on the racial component of the issue; but their argument can also be generalized to any hegemonic discourse—the narratives of men, of the rich, etc., hold more public truth value than those of subjugated classes. This argument is vital because it emphasizes the degree to which there has not been a sea change in the way facts are presented or distorted in the world.

This idea that the world and the way it is presented may be deceptive or inconsistent was strongly held during the English Renaissance and dates back to the classical period. Renaissance thinkers saw the world in probabilistic terms rather than certain ones.[14] Joel Altman defines probability as "the contingent, strictly unknowable quality of human behavior," a definition which can be expanded to encompass the unknowable aspects of the natural world.[15] Much of the world appeared "unknowable" at this point in time, given that many of the major ways we understand the natural world, such as germ theory, gravity, and calculus, were not yet conceived.[16] With an imperfect understanding of the world, observers were left relying on probabilities rather than data-driven (near) certainties that give our modern world an assumption of objective truth when it comes to knowledge generation. This fallibility was recognized; as Barbara Shapiro notes, humans and their senses were considered imperfect, and, therefore, so too were their observations and conclusions.[17] One option to compensate for this fallibility was to construct probabilities based on multiple testimonies; Altman argues that collected wisdom leads to "an interpretation that renders a past act intelligible and a future event relatively predictable and morally acceptable."[18] In other words, the more people observed the same circumstances and outcomes, the more likely that those circumstances and outcomes were causally linked, and the more predictable the same event could be in the future. When this probability is extended to human action, the observer risks stereotyping and essentializing. Framing the world in terms of probabilities informs the rhetoric used to engage with it, particularly as the rhetor positions himself within that uncertain world. While our modern world no longer explicitly frames truth probabilistically (outside of certain scientific disciplines), similar approaches continue to be used and to prove persuasive.

In an uncertain world, the audience needs a reason to believe the rhetor as having a more certain grasp of a situation than they do. Therefore, the rhetor must find a way to establish his ethos. One common strategy used to appeal to ethos in the Renaissance was the humility *topos*, through which the speaker paradoxically establishes himself as an authority by downplaying his abilities. This strategy emphasizes the speaker's awareness of the need not to express too much pride in his eloquence.[19] Boyle situates himself among the other orators and scientists of his day: "I am sufficiently sensible both to how unlearned I am, and in how learned an Age I presume to write."[20] This sort of modest positioning is similar to Othello's rhetoric in Shakespeare's play; he begins his defense of his marriage to Desdemona by assuring his unwilling father-in-law: "Rude am I in my speech / And little blest with the soft phrase of peace /... / And therefore little shall I grace my cause / In speaking for myself" (1.3.82–3, 89–90).[21] In both cases, these modest introductions ring false, if expectedly so. Boyle's introductory arguments for the essay form are erudite and well-constructed, and his essays themselves reveal extensive familiarity with the scientific properties and materials he explores. Likewise, despite his claim of lacking rhetorical mastery, Othello's subsequent monologue describes his own storytelling as able to evoke "a world of sighs" (1.3.160) from Desdemona, along with her love, proving to the white Venetian society that he wooed her honestly, without magical aid.

Similarly, Shakespeare writes Iago as reluctant and apparently unsure of himself when he is introducing a new idea to Othello. While he is not introducing himself as a trustworthy rhetor for the first time, his goal of drawing attention away from the power of his suggestion is similar. Iago tries to persuade Othello of Desdemona's infidelity by casting doubt on the virtue of Cassio, Othello's second-in-command. When he does so, he does not directly accuse Cassio of adultery, but instead, speaks in fragments, making Othello think that his suspicions are his own rather than Iago's suggestion:

> **OTHELLO** Is [Cassio] not honest?
> **IAGO** Honest, my lord?
> **OTHELLO** Honest? Ay, honest.
> **IAGO** My lord, for aught I know.
> **OTHELLO** What dost thou think?
> **IAGO** Think, my lord? (3.3.103–8)

In this passage, Iago positions himself as reluctant, needing to be drawn out to betray his supposed comrade. Iago wants Othello to think that his speech against Cassio is unwilling so that Othello will not interpret it as jealousy, but instead see it as truth. When he is finally drawn into speaking, Iago frames himself as suspicious and untrustworthy:

> **IAGO** Though I perchance am vicious in my guess
> – As I confess it is my nature's plague
> To spy into abuses, and oft my jealousy
> Shapes faults that are not. (3.3.148–51)

He suggests that his words cannot be trusted based on his personality flaws, and he calls his own supposed observations "scattering and unsure" (3.3.154). Iago sets himself up as a highly *unreliable* narrator (which he actually is), but that is exactly the opposite message that he wants to transmit to Othello.

So, why begin an argument with a claim that undermines it? One explanation is that plain speaking gained prominence as a move against empty rhetoric and sophistic argument in both literary and scientific endeavors during the long Renaissance.[22] Boyle himself speaks to his intention to avoid rhetoric, "desiring that my expressions should be rather clear and significant, than curiously adorned."[23] He claims that he is not trying to be persuasive—he does not want his readers to take his word for granted, but instead to perform their own experiments.[24] However, as he presents these claims to a general audience in the vernacular, it seems that he does intend persuasion: surely his audience will take at least some of his claims at face value, and surely that cannot be surprising to the author.

Iago uses the same strategy more insidiously, bringing plain speaking to the point of the absurd through repetition. Shakespeare creates a strong irony here: Othello has a flamboyant speech style, but is easy to understand, whereas Iago speaks plainly in theory, but his simplicity is so exaggerated as to become opaque. In the exchange quoted above (3.3.103–8), Iago and Othello repeat "honest" four times and "think" twice. While Othello is the major offender in this case, his repetitions are provoked by Iago's brief and repetitive utterances, a tendency Othello himself notes and interprets as Iago being intentionally coy: "Alas, thou echo'st me / As if there were some monster in thy thought / Too hideous to be shown" (3.3.109–11). Iago employs repetition throughout the play, both in his own repetitions of words and by encouraging others to repeat themselves. This sort of repetition *ad absurdum* creates an instability in language in which the repeated words begin to lose meaning because of their very frequency.[25] However, on the surface, Iago speaks plainly—he uses brief, uncomplicated phrases in these exchanges, saying no more (or, indeed, far less) than is required to answer his interlocutors.

While Trump certainly does not present himself humbly, he does use similar tactics of plain speaking and rhetorical fallibility to create a bond between himself and his audience. Trump does not denigrate the knowledge he provides; in fact, he often positions himself as an authority. However, he links himself to his audiences by creating an impression of authenticity through a rejection of political correctness, communicating primarily through informal channels such as Twitter and through his use of choppy sentences and repeated words. These strategies create an impression of authenticity much as Boyle's erudite denials of his erudition and Iago's coy omissions do for their respective audiences. One way of communicating this genuineness is a rejection of political correctness, as many scholars of the president's rhetoric have noted.[26] Neville-Shepherd argues that this rejection is a highly intentional strategy in which Trump violates the generic norms of presidential language to convey authenticity, a strategy that Rachel Dubrofsky links to the president's history in reality television, where curated but apparently off-the-cuff moments are prized.[27]

Heidt suggests that the viability of this strategy can be traced in part to the changing media landscape, which enables the president far more informal communication opportunities, most notably Twitter, which can circulate widely.[28] Because of the many casual media opportunities that he is afforded, the president can communicate informally to his followers, evoking a perception of authenticity. For example, when protests broke out following the murder of George Floyd, the president tweeted on May 28, 2020, "These THUGS are dishonoring the memory of George Floyd, and I won't let that happen ... Any difficulty and we will assume control but, when the looting starts, the shooting starts. Thank you!"[29] This tweet was so inflammatory that Twitter flagged it as glorifying violence, though it continued to allow access to the tweet. President Trump builds his credibility among his base by blatantly calling for the execution of protestors. To some, this tweet would clearly continue to escalate racial tensions and race-based violence, but to Trump's supporters, this sort of language highlights Trump's willingness to 'call it like he sees it' regardless of social norms.

In addition to creating an impression of authenticity through bluntness, Trump also achieves this effect by using speech markers similar to Iago's. In particular, Kirsten Theye and Steven Melling note that Trump's speeches tend to be characterized by parataxis (the removal of words suggesting causal links between clauses), extremely short sentences, frequent repetition, and single-syllable words.[30] This style contributes to the evocation of an authentic, unscripted persona—what presidential speech-writer would use broken sentences and monosyllabic vocabulary? For example, on October 12, 2019, President Trump told the Family Research Council's Values Voter Summit:

> They're coming after me because I'm fighting for you. It's a big part of it. And I'm fighting for all Americans and our way of life, but I'm fighting for you. And they

don't like you. They don't like you. And you explain why. You explain why. Your values are so incredible. They don't like you.[31]

In this single paragraph of a much longer speech, Trump repeats "you" seven times (plus one "yours"). He repeats the phrase "they don't like you" three times. And yet, with all of this repetition, his meaning is obscure. Much as Iago hints at deep knowledge with brief sentences that lack context, so too Trump defines his audience and their values. He notes that he is "fighting for all Americans … but fighting for you," suggesting that there is a difference between those categories. What that difference is, however, is left to audience members' imaginations.[32] Trump's audience can fill in the blank for what they most want him to be referring to—perhaps an anti-abortion perspective, or a hatred of gay marriage, or something as benign as weekly church attendance. Just as Iago plants the idea of Desdemona's infidelity in Othello's head by repeatedly using brief phrases and allowing Othello to insert his greatest fears, so too does the president create affiliation with his audiences by encouraging them to read their own goals and values into his vagaries.

All of these cases of plain speaking work to place the rhetor in a probabilistic world, a world without objective knowledge and the certainty that would arise from it. In such a world, the rhetor shows their own authority by recognizing that no one can be better informed than they, since ultimately the world is unknowable anyway. Robert Boyle highlights the probabilistic nature of the world around him most benignly, his goal being largely to explain why his readers' experiments may fail to produce the expected results. Boyle emphasizes the numerous "Contingencies" and "Circumstances" that, while seeming minor, may influence the execution of the experiment.[33] These range from the quality of the substances and containers used, to the correct proportions of the solutions (which he rarely presents in quantitative terms), to unknown astrological influences. Boyle insists, however, that, "though some of the Experiments I have deliver'd may prove Contingent, yet I have not deliver'd them unfaithfully in reference to what I thought I observed in them and remembered of them."[34] Boyle says that he has recorded his observations as faithfully as he could, even though they may deliver discrepant results based on the above types of "Contingencies." Boyle emphasizes that his audience should trust him to relate truthfully what he perceived; however, he allows doubt that his perceptions accurately capture the occurrences. Boyle can promise to faithfully report only what he "thought" he observed and what he "remembered"—in both cases, there is a potential for information to be mis-transmitted. The probability of results does not mean future certainty, and, anyway, the fallible human eye may have reported "alternative facts" to begin with.

The darker side of an approach to the world as probabilistic is the tendency to essentialize, creating generalizations because of a desire to predict individual actions.[35] Iago does this in spades, casting Othello and Desdemona in racist and misogynistic roles, encouraging Othello to cave in to the stereotype threat and to believe in those roles despite himself. At the start of the play, Othello casts himself as an individual to be judged on his individual merits. He trusts that "My parts, my title and my perfect soul / Shall manifest me rightly" (1.2.31–2) when he is charged with bewitching Desdemona. Othello highlights his exceptionality, framing himself as an exemplary military leader and rhetorician. Iago, by contrast, looks upon the world in terms of probabilistic categories and creates essentialized assumptions based on those perceived probabilities. Iago uses the drive for certainty as an excuse for racism and sexism, which inform his presuppositions. He tells Roderigo that Othello's marriage will not last because "these Moors are changeable in their wills" (1.3.347). Similarly, as a young woman, Desdemona's own affections are most likely to waver: "She must / change for youth; when she is sated with his body, / she will find the error of her choice: she must / have change, she must" (1.3. 350–2). In each case, Iago uses oddly imperative language: Othello, as a Moor, will grow tired of Desdemona, and she, as a (white) woman, in turn "must change," with "must" being repeated three times in a single sentence. Whether he is speaking to his own biases or Roderigo's, Iago essentializes Desdemona as a woman and Othello as a black man, couching both categories in negative assumptions and then predicting that both individuals will be true to type.[36] Ultimately, Othello succumbs to the stereotype threat, murdering Desdemona and acting exactly like the overly emotional, violent Moor that Iago constructs over the course of the play.

Iago performs this essentializing directly before Othello, leading to his changing self-perception. Like Boyle, Iago encourages Othello to experiment: "I speak not yet of proof: / Look to your wife, observe her well with Cassio" (3.3.199–200). He reminds Othello that he and his wife are different types, that Desdemona did not "affect many proposed matches / Of her own clime, complexion and degree" (3.3.233–4). In doing so, Iago draws attention to the supposedly unnatural difference between Othello's and Desdemona's "clime, complexion and degree," and implies that these may signify larger differences. Indeed, by the end of the scene, Othello participates in Iago's essentializing, classing himself in the category of cuckolded husband: "O curse of marriage / That we can call these delicate creatures ours / And not their appetites!" (3.3. 272–4). No longer is Othello an individual of exemplary characteristics who married a similarly unique individual. Instead, he is one of many cuckolds who could not satisfy their numberless voracious wives.

Donald Trump rhetorically constructs a United States that is defined by essentializing stereotypes of the type Iago uses; in order to do so, Trump must invalidate other narratives of the state of the country. Boyle points to a fallibility in human perception; Trump points to a fallibility in expertise. In referring to the Obama administration's trade policies, for example, Trump talks about "the usual so-called experts who've been wrong about every trade deal for decades," with his phrasing of "so-called" experts casting doubt on the validity of what expertise even means.[37] Trump has additionally taken care to delegitimize the news media, meaning that his followers can no longer believe in authoritative sources. As Neville-Shepherd argues, "In such a world, there is no right or wrong form of argument, but just a series of on-the-spot judgments made by 'amateur experts.'"[38] In such an expert-less world, no one's word can be trusted above another's, meaning that while Trump himself is also such an "amateur expert," he is no more fallible than any other, but perhaps more trustworthy because he is willing to reveal the fallibility of scientists. By highlighting the potential failings of the world and those reporting it, Trump, like Boyle, allies himself with an audience that has the same ability to judge the world as he himself.

While the president creates a perception of a world that is essentially unknowable, and therefore universally accessible, he also frames that world in terms of probabilistic stereotype. In his remarks announcing his candidacy in 2015, Trump notoriously claimed that Mexico was "sending" its worst citizens to the United States: "They're bringing drugs. They're bringing crime. They're rapists. And some, I assume, are good people."[39] This phrasing is both essentializing and probabilistic. First, Trump creates an equivalence between Mexicans and criminals.[40] This false equivalence is reinforced and broadened when Trump claims later in the speech that immigrant criminality is "coming from more than Mexico. It's coming from all over South and Latin America, and it's coming probably—probably—from the Middle East."[41] Here, Trump goes beyond suggesting that Mexicans are criminals and begins to essentialize all immigrants (of color). Trump creates an essentialized, racialized view of the world as Iago does. Also following Iago, Trump highlights the possibility that he could be wrong, drawing attention to just how small a chance that could be. Rather than claiming outright that *all* Mexicans are criminals and rapists, he mediates the point by noting his "assumption" that some are good people—probabilistically, some must be. Trump's syllogistic logic is flawed for rhetorical effect: some Mexicans are criminals, some immigrants are Mexicans, therefore, most immigrants are criminals.[42] Obviously, this syllogism is seriously flawed, but Trump's intention is to create an emotional response, not to display sound logical acumen.

In all three cases in question, then, the rhetor is faced with a problem of evidence presentation. All have allied themselves with their audience as reputable speakers, and all have covered their bases by framing the world around them as probabilistic. As they present their cases, however, they all are trying to argue for things that cannot be accessed by the audience. In *Othello*, Othello demands that Iago provide him with "the ocular proof" (3.3.363) of Desdemona's affair, which is clearly impossible in a world where no such affair exists. Even the nature of the proof is elusive—how can a woman tangibly demonstrate her chastity? A similar, if less deadly, problem is presented in Boyle's writing—despite Boyle's level of reproducible detail, most people would not have access to his exact equipment or have witnessed the original event of his experiment.[43] He is faced with a multi-layered problem of transmission: he must describe events to an audience that has no direct access to them; he does not use extensive mathematical proofs that could be double-checked with sufficient knowledge because such an approach was only just developing; and even if similar scientific instruments were available to others, there was no fidelity in production to ensure identical construction, quality, etc. Trump also cannot present proof to back up many of his claims, frequently because they are exaggerations or just not true. For example, Trump frequently repeats his claim about the criminality of undocumented immigrants, but, as Michael Light and Ty Miller have demonstrated in a 24-year longitudinal study, undocumented immigration does not correlate with a change in crime rate.[44] Just as Iago cannot give direct proof of Desdemona's affair because it does not exist, so too Trump cannot give proof of the criminality of immigrants.

One way these rhetors attempt to counteract the problem of tangible proof is by giving lush descriptions of the (supposed) event. Boyle's stated intention is to provide detail so that his audience can replicate his experiments with fidelity, saying that he "would incourage You to make tryal also of more nice and difficult experiments."[45] His rich descriptions mean, however, that while the reader could choose to recreate the experiment, he could also experience it imaginatively, a process described by Stephen Shapin as "virtual witnessing."[46] Boyle himself implicitly draws attention to this disconnect between literal and imaginative witnessing through an essay on non-reproducible experiments—he claims to include detail to allow others to perform their own tests, but in this essay no degree of detail will allow for recreation. He discusses the irregularities that can be found in different bodies, and states:

> I remember that a while since being present at the dissection of a lusty young Thief, we had opportunity to observe among other things, that the interval betwixt two of his ribs was near the back-bone fill'd up with a thick bony substance, which seem'd to be but an expansion of the ribs, and appeared not to have grown there upon occasion of any fracture, or other mischance.[47]

In this passage, Boyle discusses an odd, bony protrusion found in a thief's cadaver. He highlights the believability of his story by presenting himself as the original witness to this strange dissection. And yet, the story he tells is inherently unbelievable because it is a medical abnormality and therefore also inherently unreproducible. While I do not think there is a reason to distrust that Boyle experienced this medical abnormality, we cannot prove or disprove such a claim without access to the body itself.

Iago similarly presents a first-hand account that seems trustworthy but is inherently suspect. Othello demands that Iago "Give me a living reason she's disloyal" (3.3.412). In such a case, the expected answer would be something Othello can verify, something Desdemona might unwillingly corroborate. Instead, Iago responds by relating a dream that Cassio supposedly had. Like Boyle, he begins by establishing his first-hand knowledge, gained during a sleepless night: "I lay with Cassio lately / And being troubled with a raging tooth / I could not sleep" (3.3.416–18). He then elaborates upon this circumstance, describing how the dreaming Cassio addresses him as Desdemona, "lay his leg o'er my thigh, / And sigh, and kiss, and then cry 'Cursed fate / That gave thee to the Moor!'" (3.3.426–8). This tale is suspicious in many ways: the only evidence for this dream having occurred is Iago's word, and, even if it took place, there is nothing to suggest that Cassio was reenacting reality as opposed to living out a completely fantastical encounter. However, Iago brings so many details to bear—the placement of Cassio's body in relation to his own, the tone of Cassio's speech, and so on—it is as though Othello himself were witness to it. Through Iago's rich description, Othello imaginatively lives the event. Imaginative witnessing takes the place of physical witnessing; because Othello can envision the interaction so clearly, it is as though he actually saw it.

Boyle creates a similar effect in his description of the body: it is not any cadaver being dissected, but specifically that of a "lusty young Thief."[48] The next abnormal body he discusses was dissected "about the same time"—this temporal detail, and the biographical detail above about the thief, have no bearing on the body or the scientific findings it produced, but instead create a sense of fidelity through extraneous detail, much as Iago's presumably fictional toothache does.[49] According to Lorna Hutson, detailed reports of off-stage events are vital because they "[encourage] audiences and readers to conjure or imagine what cannot be staged."[50] The importance of this technique can be broadened beyond the stage: audiences are beguiled into believing that Othello has a rich inner life by the same means that Iago beguiles Othello into believing in a dream, by the same means Boyle persuades his audience that he was in fact privy to medical prodigies.

When creating his arguments for various policies, President Trump similarly includes extraneous details to add a sense of fidelity. At his "Keep America Great" rally in Cincinnati in August 2019, the president claimed,

> So, we've got thousands of people standing outside, and I asked the officials can we sneak some up along the aisles? Can they sit on the stairs? But I'll tell you what, this is some crowd, some turnout. We've sold tens of thousands of tickets.[51]

According to the *Cincinnati Enquirer*, however, the venue of the rally held a crowd of 17,000—not "tens of thousands."[52] However, to people in the venue, this was surely a believable statement. They were in a packed stadium, and the president recounted a conversation he had with people outside.[53] We do not know who these people are, but if he talked to them, the conversation must have happened. If he says "tens of thousands of tickets" have been sold, why question that?

Each speaker's attention to minor, even seemingly irrelevant detail can be described as an attention to circumstance. Hutson defines circumstances as "the topics that made any human action intelligible and able to be narrated and enquired into."[54] In other words, these are the types of details that make stories narratable, creating both narrative texture and greater understanding through the logical links they seem to fill in. In Shakespeare's day, circumstantial narrative was particularly important to court cases; a persuasive circumstantial narrative functioned as solid forensic evidence given the lack of actual forensics available.[55] The more detailed a description, the more factual it seems. Given that a circumstantial forensic narrative was an accepted form of evidence, Othello's acceptance of Iago's story is not naive, but reflects judicial prudence. In recounting the story of Cassio's dream, Iago adds to his coherent narrative of betrayal.

While "circumstantial narrative" was a term generally used to refer to human action, a similar technique could be used to narrativize natural events.[56] Boyle details one experiment on the movement of smoke in glass: "The mouth being fill'd with the smoak of Rosemary (that happening to be at hand when I made the experiment) if this smoak be plentifully blown into a glass Pipe of an indifferent size," and so on.[57] This passage presents a strange mix of precision and casualness with which Boyle reinforces his assertion that the reader attempt the experiment at home; yet, likewise, that assertion is again questioned. By implying the irrelevance of the pipe's size and stating that the use of rosemary was incidental, Boyle creates circumstances that are simple for a layperson to reproduce. At the same time, he who attempts the experiment with a different type of smoke might do so at his own risk; Boyle can attest only to the efficacy of his own smoke in this experiment. By including these small details, Boyle creates a narrative in which the experiment should succeed—if it does not, failure can easily be explained by the chance in circumstance. Circumstance makes the narrative believable, but also removes liability from the speaker. If the event cannot be reproduced, circumstances can easily be held at fault.

Donald Trump uses circumstantial description in a similar way, in that he mixes vague platitudes with a surprising amount of detail. It is widely noted that Trump expresses himself in broad terms, particularly when discussing intended policies.[58] However, scholars have not focused on the evocative pictures he paints when discussing those general policies. As Hutson argues, as well as enhancing credibility, circumstantial narratives "enable the bringing of a scene before the mind's eye."[59] For example, when tilting against windmills, Trump claims:

> If it's anywhere near your house, your house is way down in value … They make noise. They kill all the birds. The energy is intermittent. If you happen to be watching the Democrat debate and the wind isn't blowing, you're not going to the see the debate. "Charlie, what the hell happened to this debate?" He says: "Darling, the wind isn't blowing. The goddamn windmill stopped. That windmill stopped."[60]

This excerpt demonstrates two main strategies Trump uses to paint clear, affective pictures for his audience. First, as with Boyle and Iago, he includes a lot of unconfirmable detail, and these very details add a sense of authenticity. Presumably, few if any people at the Republican Conference Member Retreat Dinner in Baltimore will find a windmill to hear how loud it is or to see if birds are dying.[61] Second, Trump frequently creates brief, imaginary dialogues to support his points. Unlike the example of his rally where he was referring to a conversation he had (in theory), this is a purely fictional conversation between two hypothetical wind power users. These lines got laughs in his talk—regardless of the fact that they do not remotely reflect how windmills work, Trump paints a funny and evocative picture of a hapless tree-hugging Democratic couple whose green intentions backfire. At another point in the same speech, the president imagines what would happen in a Biden presidency sit-down with Chinese president Xi Jinping: "Here's Xi: 'Hwah!' And here's Sleepy Joe, 'What? Where am I? Where am I?' 'Just sign here, Sleepy Joe. Just sign here.'"[62] Trump again creates a fictional conversation to comic effect. As in the more Quixotic moments of this speech, this imagined dialogue is funny specifically because it builds on the audiences' fears, in this case, a presidency in which the elderly president is confused enough to sign any deal put in front of him. By adding extraneous detail and creating easily imagined conversations, Donald Trump adds circumstantial believability to the most unbelievable narratives.

The strategies by which rhetors persuade their audience of a claim to whose truth the audience has no direct access are shockingly similar across time periods and disciplines. Across the span of 60 years in Renaissance England, a fictional character and a scientist use the same rhetorical tactics to make their point. These tactics are also adopted by a modern president. From this similarity, I hope to draw two main lessons for the modern world. First, it is incorrect, and even detrimental, to think that the "post-truth" world is anything new. Such nostalgia downplays the role rhetoric has always held in mediating the truth. This role leads to my second conclusion: the importance of remembering that these strategies are rhetorically effective, but morally neutral. Rhetoric mediates the truth that is passed from person to person; this is inevitable. However, as the contrast between Boyle and the other rhetors demonstrates, the sort of rhetoric that allows for argumentation without tangible evidence need not be used in pursuit of evil. Perhaps modern scientists can take a page out of their predecessor's book. Politicians use rhetoric to create racist metonymies and speeches full of fictive details. Why should other modern speakers not use the same strategies to communicate scientific fact to an audience who responds so well to these strategies? Most Americans cannot and will not read and understand scientific calculations of climate change. They can convince themselves that the recent obvious climate fluctuations are instead localized temperature fluctuations. It is illogical for experts to approach these people with claims that the sea level will rise by X meters in Y years; these claims may be data driven and accurate, but they lack an acknowledgment of most people's perception of the world as probabilistic rather than certain, and they lack circumstantial details that can give the layperson a visceral image of what lies ahead. Perhaps climate change scientists (and doctors developing vaccines, and experts in any number of other regimes) will achieve more success fighting fire with fire, using circumstantial and probabilistic language to engage audience emotion and imagination and, therefore, persuade people of facts they cannot fully access, however true. Rhetoric shapes perceived truth, and effective rhetoric should not be sidelined because it has the potential for creating "alternative facts." Instead, it must be leveraged to emphasize actual facts and real news, to the greatest extent possible.

NOTES

1.   "Word of the Year 2016," Oxford Languages, accessed January 14, 2020, https://languages.oup.com/word-of-the-year/2016/.
2.   I refer to Twitter here because of Trump's ubiquitous use of it as well as its general capacity for spreading information and misinformation. PizzaGate refers to a conspiracy theory developed during the 2016 presidential election cycle, leading to an armed man breaking into a pizza parlor under the belief that it was a front for a sex-trafficking ring linked to Hillary Clinton. It was not. The COVID-19 pandemic began to reach the United States in early 2020, while this chapter was under revision. Given its recency, this chapter will not extensively deal with the

tension between medical fact and political rhetorical goals, but that is certainly in the background of this discussion.

3. I refer to all three as rhetors in that they are the purveyors of speech or text; given that Boyle's communication is solely written, I cannot accurately refer to them as speakers.
4. Here, I refer to the rhetorical appeal to authority, as contrasted with pathos (the appeal to emotion) and logos (the appeal to logic).
5. Barbara Shapiro, *Probability and Certainty in Seventeenth-Century England: A Study of the Relationships Between Natural Science, Religion, History, Law, and Literature* (Princeton, NJ: Princeton University Press, 1983), 53.
6. Kathleen Hall Jamieson and Doron Taussig, "Disruption, Demonization, Deliverance, and Norm Destruction: The Rhetorical Signature of Donald J. Trump," *Political Science Quarterly* 132, no. 4 (Winter 2017): 620, https://doi .org/10.1002/polq.12699.
7. Stephen J. Heidt and Damien Smith Pfister, "Trump, Twitter, and the Microdiatribe: The Short Circuits of Networked Presidential Public Address," in *Reading the Presidency: Advances in Presidential Rhetoric*, ed. Stephen J. Heidt and Mary E. Stuckey, vol. 43, Frontiers in Political Communication (New York: Peter Lang, n.d.), 174.
8. For further discussion of how Trump's rhetoric leads to his followers' shifting belief systems, see Douglas Kellner, "Donald Trump and the War on the Media: From Election '16 into the Trump Presidency," in *The Trump Presidency, Journalism, and Democracy*, ed. Robert E. Gutsche Jr., Routledge Research in Journalism 20 (New York: Routledge, 2018), 19–38; Robert E. Gutsche Jr., "Introduction: Translating Trump: How to Discuss the Complications of Covering New Presidential Politics," in *The Trump Presidency, Journalism, and Democracy*, ed. Robert E. Gutsche Jr., Routledge Research in Journalism 20 (New York: Routledge, 2018), 1–15; Frank Durham, "The Origins of Trump's 'Alternative Reality': A Brief History of the Breitbart Effect," in *The Trump Presidency, Journalism, and Democracy*, ed. Robert E. Gutsche Jr., Routledge Research in Journalism 20 (New York: Routledge, 2018), 181–91.
9. Sorin Suciu, "The Rhetoric of Post-Truth," *PCTS Proceedings (Professional Communication & Translation Studies)* 10 (June 2017): 40–1.
10. The following critics establish Trump's use of hyperbole in an attempt to excite emotional response: Mary E. Stuckey, "American Elections and the Rhetoric of Political Change: Hyperbole, Anger, and Hope in US Politics," *Rhetoric & Public Affairs* 20, no. 4 (Winter 2017): 667–94, https://doi.org/10.14321/rhetpublaffa.20 .4.0667; Orly Kayam, "Donald Trump's Rhetoric," *Language & Dialogue* 8, no. 2 (May 2018): 183–208, https://doi.org/10.1075/ld.00012.kay; Douglas Kellner, *American Nightmare: Donald Trump, Media Spectacle, and Authoritarian Populism* (Rotterdam, The Netherlands: Sense Publishers, 2016).
11. Robert E. Gutsche Jr., "News Boundaries of 'Fakiness' and the Challenged Authority of the Press," in *The Trump Presidency, Journalism, and Democracy*, ed. Robert E. Gutsche Jr., Routledge Research in Journalism 20 (New York: Routledge, 2018), 41.
12. Robert Mejia, Kay Beckermann, and Curtis Sullivan, "White Lies: A Racial History of the (Post)Truth," *Communication and Critical/Cultural Studies* 15, no. 2 (2018): 109–26, https://doi.org/10.1080/14791420.2018.1456668.
13. Mejia, Beckermann, and Sullivan, "White Lies," 116–17.

14. For a discussion on probabilistic thinking in the Renaissance, see Stephen Shapin, "Pump and Circumstance: Robert Boyle's Literary Technology," in *The Scientific Revolution*, ed. Marcus Hellyer (Malden, MA: Blackwell Publishing, 2003), 72–100; Joel Altman, *The Improbability of Othello: Rhetorical Anthropology and Shakespearean Selfhood* (Chicago: University of Chicago Press, 2010); Lorna Hutson, *Circumstantial Shakespeare* (Oxford: Oxford University Press, 2015); Shapiro, *Probability and Certainty*.
15. Altman, *The Improbability of Othello*, 22.
16. In this chapter, I refer broadly to the world, as the rhetorical upshots of a probabilistic approach to nature and human nature are very similar in their effects.
17. Shapiro, *Probability and Certainty*, 62.
18. Altman, *The Improbability of Othello*, 3.
19. Neill Rhodes, *The Power of Eloquence and English Renaissance Literature* (New York: Harvester Wheatsheaf, 1992), 32, 41 passim.
20. Robert Boyle, "Certain Physiological Essays and Other Tracts Written at Distant Times, and on Several Occasions by the Honourable Robert Boyle; Wherein Some of the Tracts Are Enlarged by Experiments and the Work Is Increased by the Addition of a Discourse about the Absolute Rest in Bodies" (London: Printed for Henry Herringman, 1669), Wing/B3930, Cambridge University Library, https://search.proquest.com/docview/2248558009?accountid=163371, 1.
21. William Shakespeare, *Othello*, ed. E. A. J. Honigmann, 3rd ed., The Arden Shakespeare (London: Cengage Learning, 1997). All quotations are drawn from this edition.
22. Shapiro, *Probability and Certainty*, 232.
23. Boyle, "Certain Physiological Essays," 12.
24. Boyle, "Certain Physiological Essays,"16.
25. Both of the following authors discuss Iago's rhetorical repetitions in further depth: Thomas Moisan, "Repetition and Interrogation in Othello: 'What Needs This Iterance?' Or, 'Can Anything Be Made of This?,'" in *Othello: New Perspectives*, ed. Virginia Mason Vaughn and Kent Cartwright (Rutherford, NJ: Fairleigh Dickinson University Press, 1991), 48–73; Ken Gross, *Shakespeare's Noise* (Chicago: University of Chicago Press, 2001).
26. Among others, Kirsten Theye and Steven Melling, "Total Losers and Bad Hombres: The Political Incorrectness and Perceived Authenticity of Donald J. Trump," *Southern Communication Journal* 83, no. 5 (October 20, 2018): 322–37, https://doi.org/10.1080/1041794X.2018.1511747; Jamieson and Taussig, "Disruption, Demonization, Deliverance, and Norm Destruction"; Ryan Neville-Shepard, "Genre Busting: Campaign Speech Genres and the Rhetoric of Political Outsiders," in *Reading the Presidency: Advances in Presidential Rhetoric*, ed. Stephen J. Heidt and Mary E. Stuckey, vol. 43, Frontiers in Political Communication (New York: Peter Lang, n.d.), 86–105; Rachel E. Dubrofsky, "Authentic Trump: Yearning for Civility," *Television & New Media* 17, no. 7 (November 1, 2016): 663–6, https://doi.org/10.1177/1527476416652698; Kayam, "Donald Trump's Rhetoric."
27. Neville-Shepard, "Genre Busting," 93; Dubrofsky, "Authentic Trump," 664.
28. Stephen J. Heidt, "Introduction: The Study of Presidential Rhetoric in Uncertain Times: Thoughts on Theory and Praxis," in *Reading the Presidency: Advances in Presidential Rhetoric*, ed. Stephen J. Heidt and Mary E. Stuckey, vol. 43, Frontiers in Political Communication (New York: Peter Lang, n.d.), 1–19.

29. Donald Trump, tweet, May 28, 2020, https://twitter.com/realDonaldTrump/status/ 1266231100780744704.

30. Theye and Melling, "Total Losers and Bad Hombres," 326.

31. Donald Trump, "Remarks at the Family Research Council's Values Voter Summit," October 12, 2019, The American Presidency Project, https://www .presidency.ucsb.edu/documents/remarks-the-family-research-councils-values -voter-summit-0.

32. Stuckey, "American Elections and the Rhetoric of Political Change," notes this tendency as well, suggesting voters can "[find] in him a reflection of their own preferences" (682).

33. Boyle, "Certain Physiological Essays," 75.

34. Boyle, "Certain Physiological Essays," 110.

35. Matthew C. MacWilliams, *The Rise of Trump: America's Authoritarian Spring*, Public Works (Amherst, MA: The Amherst College Press, 2016), 5, describes this sort of argumentative move as an ascriptive argument, discusses Iago's essential-izing as well, describing his habit of mind as "the tendency to assimilate the apt to the true" (90). He notes the tension throughout the play between the individual and the categorical.

36. Altman, *The Improbability of Othello*, discusses Iago's essentializing as well, describing his habit of mind as "the tendency to assimilate the apt to the true" (90). He notes the tension throughout the play between the individual and the categorical.

37. Donald Trump, "Remarks to the Detroit Economic Club," August 8, 2016, The American Presidency Project, https://www.presidency.ucsb.edu/documents/ remarks-the-detroit-economic-club-1.

38. Ryan Neville-Shepard, "Post-Presumption Argumentation and the Post-Truth World: On the Conspiracy Rhetoric of Donald Trump," *Argumentation and Advocacy* 55, no. 3 (2019): 182.

39. Donald Trump, "Remarks Announcing Candidacy for President in New York City," June 16, 2015, The American Presidency Project, https://www.presidency .ucsb.edu/documents/remarks-announcing-candidacy-for-president-new-york -city.

40. Theye and Melling, "Total Losers and Bad Hombres," also note Trump's frequent use of metonymy (the figure of speech in which an attribute is substituted for the actual name of the item or person talked about), closely tying enemies to evil traits (326). Scott Astrada and Marvin Astrada, "Truth in Crisis: Critically Re-Examining Immigration Rhetoric & Policy under the Trump Administration," *Harvard Latinx Law Review* 22 (August 2019): 17, similarly note Trump's propensity to synonymize South American immigrants with "drugs, crime, and violence."

41. Trump, "Remarks Announcing Candidacy for President in New York City," https://www.presidency.ucsb.edu/documents/remarks-announcing-candidacy-for -president-new-york-city.

42. Stephen J. Heidt, "Scapegoater-in-Chief: Racist Undertones of Donald Trump's Rhetorical Repertoire," in *The Trump Presidency, Journalism, and Democracy*, ed. Robert E. Gutsche Jr., Routledge Research in Journalism 20 (New York: Routledge, 2018), 215, notes this sort of flawed syllogistic logic in other speeches.

43. Marcus Hellyer, *The Scientific Revolution* (Malden, MA: Blackwell Publishing, 2003), 72.

44. Michael T. Light and Ty Miller, "Does Undocumented Immigration Increase Violent Crime?," *Criminology: An Interdisciplinary Journal* 56, no. 2 (May 2017): 370–401, https://doi.org/10.1111/1745-9125.12175.

45. Boyle, "Certain Physiological Essays," 16.

46. Shapin, "Pump and Circumstance," 82–3.

47. Boyle, "Certain Physiological Essays," 94.

48. Boyle, "Certain Physiological Essays," 94.

49. Boyle, "Certain Physiological Essays," 94.

50. Hutson, *Circumstantial Shakespeare*, 10.

51. Donald Trump, "Remarks at a 'Keep America Great' Rally in Cincinnati, Ohio," August 1, 2019, The American Presidency Project, https://www.presidency.ucsb.edu/documents/remarks-keep-america-great-rally-cincinnati-ohio.

52. Cameron Knight et al., "'I'm Here to Support the President.' Heat, Long Lines Don't Keep Supporters from Trump Rally," *Cincinnati Enquirer*, August 1, 2019, sec. News, https://www.cincinnati.com/story/news/2019/08/01/president-trump-supporters-protesters-turn-out-cincinnati-rally/1889804001/.

53. Jamieson and Taussig, "Disruption, Demonization, Deliverance, and Norm Destruction," 628, note Trump's propensity for "reflexively" citing unnamed, potentially fictive individuals. Neville-Shepard, "Post-Presumption Argumentation," 183–4, also observes Trump's reliance on vague sourcing.

54. Hutson, *Circumstantial Shakespeare*, 2.

55. Shapiro, *Probability and Certainty*, 187.

56. Shapiro, *Probability and Certainty*, 168. Shapiro notes the similarity between law and science in their increasing emphasis on evaluating the reliability and probability of evidence presented.

57. Boyle, "Certain Physiological Essays," 166.

58. Emma Frances Bloomfield and Gabriela Tscholl, "Analyzing Warrants and Worldviews in the Rhetoric of Donald Trump and Hillary Clinton: Burke and Argumentation in the 2016 Presidential Election," *The Journal of the Kenneth Burke Society* 13, no. 2 (2018): 5, https://doi.org/10.1111/psq.12490; Robert C. Rowland, "The Populist and Nationalist Roots of Trump's Rhetoric," *Rhetoric and Public Affairs* 22, no. 3 (2019): 350, https://doi.org/10.14321/rhetpublaffa.22.3.0343; and Stuckey, "American Elections and the Rhetoric of Political Change," 682, for example, all note the vague nature of Trump's policy discussions.

59. Hutson, *Circumstantial Shakespeare*, 5.

60. Donald Trump, "Remarks at the House Republican Conference Member Retreat Dinner in Baltimore, Maryland," September 12, 2019, The American Presidency Project, https://www.presidency.ucsb.edu/documents/remarks-the-house-republican-conference-member-retreat-dinner-baltimore-maryland.

61. They are not. As of 2015, cats are the top killer of birds, with numbers in the *billions*, whereas windmills are responsible for hundreds of *thousands* of bird casualties. Scott R. Loss, Tom Will, and Peter P. Marra, "Direct Mortality of Birds from Anthropogenic Causes," *Annual Review of Ecology, Evolution, and Systematics* 46, no. 1 (December 4, 2015): 99–120, https://doi.org/10.1146/annurev-ecolsys-112414-054133.

62. Donald Trump, "Remarks at the House Republican Conference Member Retreat Dinner in Baltimore, Maryland."

REFERENCES

Altman, Joel. *The Improbability of Othello: Rhetorical Anthropology and Shakespearean Selfhood*. Chicago: University of Chicago Press, 2010.

Astrada, Scott, and Marvin Astrada. "Truth in Crisis: Critically Re-Examining Immigration Rhetoric & Policy under the Trump Administration." *Harvard Latinx Law Review* 22 (August 2019): 7–36.

Bloomfield, Emma Frances, and Gabriela Tscholl. "Analyzing Warrants and Worldviews in the Rhetoric of Donald Trump and Hillary Clinton: Burke and Argumentation in the 2016 Presidential Election." *The Journal of the Kenneth Burke Society* 13, no. 2 (2018): 1–12. https://doi.org/10.1111/psq.12490.

Boyle, Robert. "Certain Physiological Essays and Other Tracts Written at Distant Times, and on Several Occasions by the Honourable Robert Boyle; Wherein Some of the Tracts Are Enlarged by Experiments and the Work Is Increased by the Addition of a Discourse about the Absolute Rest in Bodies." London: Printed for Henry Herringman, 1669. Wing/B3930. Cambridge University Library. https://search.proquest.com/docview/2248558009?accountid=163371.

Dubrofsky, Rachel E. "Authentic Trump: Yearning for Civility." *Television & New Media* 17, no. 7 (November 1, 2016): 663–6. https://doi.org/10.1177/1527476416652698.

Durham, Frank. "The Origins of Trump's 'Alternative Reality': A Brief History of the Breitbart Effect." In *The Trump Presidency, Journalism, and Democracy*, edited by Robert E. Gutsche Jr., 181–91. Routledge Research in Journalism 20. New York: Routledge, 2018.

Gross, Ken. *Shakespeare's Noise*. Chicago: University of Chicago Press, 2001.

Gutsche Jr., Robert E. "Introduction: Translating Trump: How to Discuss the Complications of Covering New Presidential Politics." In *The Trump Presidency, Journalism, and Democracy*, edited by Robert E. Gutsche Jr., 1–15. Routledge Research in Journalism 20. New York: Routledge, 2018.

Gutsche Jr., Robert E. "News Boundaries of 'Fakiness' and the Challenged Authority of the Press." In *The Trump Presidency, Journalism, and Democracy*, edited by Robert E. Gutsche Jr., 39–58. Routledge Research in Journalism 20. New York: Routledge, 2018.

Heidt, Stephen J. "Introduction: The Study of Presidential Rhetoric in Uncertain Times: Thoughts on Theory and Praxis." In *Reading the Presidency: Advances in Presidential Rhetoric*, edited by Stephen J. Heidt and Mary E. Stuckey, 43: 1–19. Frontiers in Political Communication. New York: Peter Lang, n.d.

Heidt, Stephen J. "Scapegoater-in-Chief: Racist Undertones of Donald Trump's Rhetorical Repertoire." In *The Trump Presidency, Journalism, and Democracy*, edited by Robert E. Gutsche Jr., 206–28. Routledge Research in Journalism 20. New York: Routledge, 2018.

Heidt, Stephen J., and Damien Smith Pfister. "Trump, Twitter, and the Microdiatribe: The Short Circuits of Networked Presidential Public Address." In *Reading the Presidency: Advances in Presidential Rhetoric*, edited by Stephen J. Heidt and Mary E. Stuckey, 43: 171–94. Frontiers in Political Communication. New York: Peter Lang, n.d.

Hellyer, Marcus. *The Scientific Revolution*. Malden, MA: Blackwell Publishing, 2003.

Hutson, Lorna. *Circumstantial Shakespeare*. Oxford: Oxford University Press, 2015.

Jamieson, Kathleen Hall, and Doron Taussig. "Disruption, Demonization, Deliverance, and Norm Destruction: The Rhetorical Signature of Donald J. Trump." *Political Science Quarterly* 132, no. 4 (Winter 2017): 619–50. https://doi.org/10.1002/polq .12699.

Kayam, Orly. "Donald Trump's Rhetoric." *Language & Dialogue* 8, no. 2 (May 2018): 183–208. https://doi.org/10.1075/ld.00012.kay.

Kellner, Douglas. *American Nightmare: Donald Trump, Media Spectacle, and Authoritarian Populism*. Rotterdam, The Netherlands: Sense Publishers, 2016.

Kellner, Douglas. "Donald Trump and the War on the Media: From Election '16 into the Trump Presidency." In *The Trump Presidency, Journalism, and Democracy*, edited by Robert E. Gutsche Jr., 19–38. Routledge Research in Journalism 20. New York: Routledge, 2018.

Knight, Cameron, Hannah Sparling, Briana Rice, and Rachel Berry. "'I'm Here to Support the President.' Heat, Long Lines Don't Keep Supporters from Trump Rally." *Cincinnati Enquirer*, August 1, 2019, sec. News. https://www.cincinnati.com/story/ news/2019/08/01/president-trump-supporters-protesters-turn-out-cincinnati-rally/ 1889804001/.

Light, Michael T., and Ty Miller. "Does Undocumented Immigration Increase Violent Crime?" *Criminology: An Interdisciplinary Journal* 56, no. 2 (May 2017): 370–401. https://doi.org/10.1111/1745-9125.12175.

Loss, Scott R., Tom Will, and Peter P. Marra. "Direct Mortality of Birds from Anthropogenic Causes." *Annual Review of Ecology, Evolution, and Systematics* 46, no. 1 (December 4, 2015): 99–120. https://doi.org/10.1146/annurev-ecolsys-112414 -054133.

MacWilliams, Matthew C. *The Rise of Trump: America's Authoritarian Spring*. Public Works. Amherst, MA: The Amherst College Press, 2016.

Mejia, Robert, Kay Beckermann, and Curtis Sullivan. "White Lies: A Racial History of the (Post)Truth." *Communication and Critical/Cultural Studies* 15, no. 2 (2018): 109–26. https://doi.org/10.1080/14791420.2018.1456668.

Moisan, Thomas. "Repetition and Interrogation in Othello: 'What Needs This Iterance?' Or, 'Can Anything Be Made of This?'" In *Othello: New Perspectives*, edited by Virginia Mason Vaughn and Kent Cartwright, 48–73. Rutherford, NJ: Fairleigh Dickinson University Press, 1991.

Neville-Shepard, Ryan. "Genre Busting: Campaign Speech Genres and the Rhetoric of Political Outsiders." In *Reading the Presidency: Advances in Presidential Rhetoric*, edited by Stephen J. Heidt and Mary E. Stuckey, 43, 86–105. Frontiers in Political Communication. New York: Peter Lang, n.d.

Neville-Shepard, Ryan. "Post-Presumption Argumentation and the Post-Truth World: On the Conspiracy Rhetoric of Donald Trump." *Argumentation and Advocacy* 55, no. 3 (2019): 175–93.

Oxford Languages. "Word of the Year 2016." Accessed January 14, 2020. https:// languages.oup.com/word-of-the-year/2016/.

Rhodes, Neill. *The Power of Eloquence and English Renaissance Literature*. New York: Harvester Wheatsheaf, 1992.

Rowland, Robert C. "The Populist and Nationalist Roots of Trump's Rhetoric." *Rhetoric and Public Affairs* 22, no. 3 (2019): 343–88. https://doi.org/10.14321/ rhetpublaffa.22.3.0343.

Shakespeare, William. *Othello*. Edited by E. A. J. Honigmann. 3rd ed. The Arden Shakespeare. London: Cengage Learning, 1997.

Shapin, Stephen. "Pump and Circumstance: Robert Boyle's Literary Technology." In *The Scientific Revolution*, edited by Marcus Hellyer, 72–100. Malden, MA: Blackwell Publishing, 2003.

Shapiro, Barbara. *Probability and Certainty in Seventeenth-Century England: A Study of the Relationships Between Natural Science, Religion, History, Law, and Literature.* Princeton, NJ: Princeton University Press, 1983.

Stuckey, Mary E. "American Elections and the Rhetoric of Political Change: Hyperbole, Anger, and Hope in US Politics." *Rhetoric & Public Affairs* 20, no. 4 (Winter 2017): 667–94. https://doi.org/10.14321/rhetpublaffa.20.4.0667.

Suciu, Sorin. "The Rhetoric of Post-Truth." *PCTS Proceedings (Professional Communication & Translation Studies)* 10 (June 2017): 40–4.

Theye, Kirsten, and Steven Melling. "Total Losers and Bad Hombres: The Political Incorrectness and Perceived Authenticity of Donald J. Trump." *Southern Communication Journal* 83, no. 5 (October 20, 2018): 322–37. https://doi.org/10.1080/1041794X.2018.1511747.

Trump, Donald. "Remarks Announcing Candidacy for President in New York City," June 16, 2015. The American Presidency Project. https://www.presidency.ucsb.edu/documents/remarks-announcing-candidacy-for-president-new-york-city.

Trump, Donald. "Remarks to the Detroit Economic Club," August 8, 2016. The American Presidency Project. https://www.presidency.ucsb.edu/documents/remarks-the-detroit-economic-club-1.

Trump, Donald. "Remarks at the Family Research Council's Values Voter Summit," October 12, 2019. The American Presidency Project, https://www.presidency.ucsb.edu/documents/remarks-the-family-research-councils-values-voter-summit-0.

Trump, Donald. "Remarks at the House Republican Conference Member Retreat Dinner in Baltimore, Maryland," September 12, 2019. The American Presidency Project. https://www.presidency.ucsb.edu/documents/remarks-the-house-republican-conference-member-retreat-dinner-baltimore-maryland.

Trump, Donald. "Remarks at a 'Keep America Great' Rally in Cincinnati, Ohio," August 1, 2019. The American Presidency Project. https://www.presidency.ucsb.edu/documents/remarks-keep-america-great-rally-cincinnati-ohio.

Trump, Donald. Tweet, May 28, 2020. https://twitter.com/realDonaldTrump/status/1266231100780744704.

PART III

Resistance

7. Much ado about me too: the personal and political activism of Shakespeare's women

Jess Landis

In October of 2017, two bombshell reports from the *New Times* and the *New Yorker* exposed over a dozen accusations of sexual misconduct against film producer Harvey Weinstein. Following the publication of these articles, many more women came forward to describe similar experiences with the powerful entertainment executive. These allegations netted results: in late February of 2020, Weinstein was convicted of criminal sexual assault and rape in New York, and he was sentenced to serve 23 years in prison. One of the issues that has emerged in this high-profile case is the courage it takes for victims of sexual assault and harassment to publicly accuse their abusers. After all, Weinstein wielded great power over budding actors' careers, which he might have easily thwarted were they to speak out. Weinstein and the accusations against him have been at the center of the rise of the #MeToo movement, which seeks to raise awareness about and end sexual assault and sexual harassment against women. #MeToo has called attention to the silence that often surrounds sexual assault, as well as the power dynamics that influence that silence. Even after his conviction, Weinstein has continued to deny his culpability, claiming that the accounts of the women who accuse him simply cannot be believed. His dismissal of the accusations highlights a long-standing tenet of the patriarchy: the believability of women's accounts of sexual misconduct against their persons is always already suspect. The emergence of the #MeToo movement, however, highlights another phenomenon that spans across history: women will resist this "truth."

The cultural perception of women's collective untrustworthiness and their pushback against it were certainly both present in early modern England. In his play *Measure for Measure* (ca. 1603–4), Shakespeare explores this very issue of the credibility of women's voices. Isabella, the heroine of this problem play, or "comedy" (although in many ways it violates the early modern conventions of this genre), finds herself pleading for her brother's life after he has been convicted for getting his beloved Julietta pregnant out of wedlock. Isabella must appeal to the strict Angelo, a judge who has recently been left in charge of Vienna and tasked with cleansing it of sin. In exchange for allowing Claudio to live, Angelo demands that the exceptionally chaste Isabella sleep with him. She refuses and threatens to expose his ungodly request. Angelo, however, reminds her that her word is worth little in comparison to his. He says,

> **ANGELO** Who will believe thee, Isabel?
>   My unsoil'd name, the austereness of my life,
>   My vouch against you, and my place I' th' state,
>   Will so your accusation overweigh,
>   That you shall stifle in your own report,
>   And smell of calumny. (2.4.154–9)[1]

One can imagine present-day victims hearing these words from similarly powerful men, such as Weinstein or Bill Cosby, whose conviction for sexual assault in some ways helped to kick off the #MeToo movement. Clearly, threats of this kind are not new. These words remind us that there is a lot of history to overcome in order to get women's voices heard.

The #MeToo movement and other similar initiatives have much work to do in order to undo the patriarchal, misogynistic thinking that shapes rape culture, or a culture that normalizes violence against women. Yet the initiative has also revealed its power to make headway in the fight against this entrenched history. In her 1997 book, Irene Dash reads the relationship between Angelo and Isabella in *Measure for Measure* with an eye toward this kind of history, saying, "It exemplifies what we now recognize as 'sexual harassment.'"[2] In a note, she adds, "I believe it is significant that following [the Anita Hill hearings] students, for the first time, understood Isabella's plight, and, without exception, could hear the modern resonances in her exchange with Angelo."[3] Dash here recognizes the shift in the collective American understanding of sexual harassment caused by the Anita Hill hearings and their impact on the reception of Shakespeare's play.[4] I argue that the #MeToo movement is causing a similar shift. While *Measure for Measure* certainly demonstrates that the problem of sexual harassment has been ever present in our culture, this chapter seeks to extend this example to show that the #MeToo movement can help us to think through how Shakespeare represents sexual misconduct in other works in his canon and perhaps simultaneously push us toward understanding these problems from a historical *and* contemporary perspective, thereby increasing the culture's capacity to create much-needed change.

Measure for Measure has enjoyed something of a performance revival because of its relevance to the conversations happening within and because of the #MeToo movement. The Public Theater in New York staged a production in November 2017, just weeks after stories about the sexual assault accusations against Harvey Weinstein gained major international traction. In a piece for

Vox that was inspired by the production, Tara Isabella Burton writes, "It still may be one of the most relevant plays ever written about sexual harassment and abuse against women, and the stakes for women who speak up about it."[5] About a year later, the Donmar Warehouse Theatre in London staged the play in the immediate aftermath of the Brett Kavanaugh hearings.[6] *New Yorker* writer Rebecca Mead spoke with director Josie Rourke, the theater's first female artistic director, and concludes, "The aftermath of [Hillary] Clinton's loss to Donald Trump also informed Rourke's *Measure for Measure*—a play that, though four hundred years old, might have been written for the era of #MeToo."[7] The play seems relevant in an era marked by political polarity and influenced by conservative policy (put forth, of course, by a president who himself has faced allegations of sexual harassment and misconduct) that many believe is eroding the progress made toward equal rights and protections for women. Professional and amateur productions of *Measure*, some modernized, some traditional, followed in several cities, including Santa Barbara, Milwaukee, and London (again) in 2019.

People are turning to Shakespeare for help in understanding this specific issue in our specific moment, but why? What can plays by a long-dead white man add to the exploding and important conversations that are part of #MeToo? I argue that Shakespeare's work offers insightful perspectives about the conditions that create and perpetuate harmful ideas about women that lead to their subjugation. He presents strong heroines who do not necessarily conform to gender norms, but instead resist the cultural conditions that lead to the violence against them. In a 2018 TED Talk, #MeToo movement founder Tarana Burke describes feeling "numb" and "tired" because disheartening events related to sexual assault and misogyny keep happening, despite the great momentum behind the movement. She attributes these feelings to the huge task we face in moving forward, saying, "We have to dramatically shift a culture that propagates the idea that vulnerability is synonymous with permission and that bodily autonomy is not a basic human right. In other words, we have to dismantle the building blocks of sexual violence: power and privilege."[8] Shakespeare's plays also implicitly recognize the great amount of work that must happen to dismantle widespread and institutionalized attitudes that continually force women into harm's way.

While Shakespeare writes a lot about sexual assault and early modern attitudes toward it, the word "rape" appears just 21 times in his canon, and 15 of those instances occur in *Titus Andronicus*, which features Lavinia's exceptionally brutal and politicized rape against a backdrop of extreme violence. Rape is certainly implied in Angelo's appeal to Isabella, but the word does not actually appear in *Measure for Measure*. In fact, the word *rape* rarely appears in Shakespeare's comedies, though his canon includes several works that are as similarly relevant as *Measure* to current discussions influenced by #MeToo.[9] The plot of *Much Ado About Nothing* hinges on men's refusals to hear or believe a woman's (Hero's) denial of involvement in sexual betrayal that deeply affects her prospects in life. Claudio refuses to give Hero the opportunity to speak on her own behalf, instead choosing to believe dubious men's accounts of her sexual interaction with another man. However, this play also stages the attempts of women's collective voices to battle and destabilize patriarchal dominance. Shakespeare's canon certainly contains more overtly violent representations that express the pervasiveness of sexual assault and rape, much like the high-profile exposure of celebrities has done in the current #MeToo movement. However, *Much Ado* speaks to the subtler but equally dangerous consequences of sexual slander on women, showing just how entrenched misogyny is in early modern English culture, but also the extent to which women resisted it. This chapter establishes that resistance as a pervasive force that extends across history by putting the play in conversation with some of the goals of the #MeToo movement. It seeks to increase awareness of women's voices in their fight against a culture of sexual violence and misconduct.

EARLY MODERN RAPE CULTURE ON AND OFF STAGE

The legal and cultural approaches to sexual assault in early modern England differed, of course, from our contemporary treatment of the issue, but those approaches still constitute an essential basis on which contemporary ideas about and attitudes toward rape are formed. As Barbara J. Baines says, "For an inquiry into the history and thus the idea of rape, the Renaissance is an ideal period because it both re-presents medieval and classical assumptions and lays the foundation for what we recognize as our own modern concerns. Then as now, the heart of the matter is the concept of consent."[10] In Shakespeare's day, rape was illegal, but its definition was somewhat tenuous and circumstantial. Understanding how sexual assault was perceived in the period provides insight into misogynistic attitudes that shaped the cultural relationship women had with sex and sexual reputation. Citing historian Susan Brownmiller's important 1977 study, *Against Our Will: Men Women, and Rape*, Garthine Walker—another important voice in the historical study of crimes against women—points out that "sexual violence was neither attributable only to the uncivilized inhabitants of past societies nor to be explained in the present in terms of deviant pathological behaviour. Rather, it resided at the core of modern Western patriarchy."[11]

In *Law's Resolutions for Women's Rights, or the Law's Provision for Women* (1632), a publication often cited in discussions of what constituted sexual assault in the period, confusion surrounds attempts to articulate the slippery nature of ravishment. Baines points out the text's "amazing combination of indifference and misunderstanding concerning the woman's experience of rape, but also the fact that the very meaning of rape eludes its author."[12] *Law's Resolutions* lays out detailed explanations of the laws that related to rape and other crimes against women, but it is unclear when it comes to pinning down exactly what constituted the illegal act. The anonymous author distinguishes two kinds of rape with little explanation of what makes them different in legal or cultural terms. The first kind involves coercing a woman against her will and abandoning her, driven by "a hideous, hateful kind of whoredom in him which comitteth it."[13] Here, the author identifies rape as an act driven by the depravity of the rapist, but does not seem to consider the consequences of the act for the woman involved. The second kind described acknowledges, at least faintly, the implications of rape for the female victim by insinuating that her reputation might be damaged. It includes forcibly abducting "a woman of honest reputation whether a virgin, widow, or nun against the will of those under whose power she is."[14] Given the different emphases of these descriptions, *Law's Resolutions* might be pointing to divergences in the perception of rape when it was acted upon women of different social statuses, the latter insinuating that the rape of a woman of status affected not only her reputation, but also the reputations of those to whom she "belonged," like her father or her husband.

According to *Law's Resolutions*, both acts potentially carried death sentences, the first "unless the woman ravished were unbetrothed so that the ravisher might marry her," which indicates that a man might avoid punishment if his female victim were single and he could therefore marry her to perhaps in some way legitimize the rape as marital consummation.[15] The second type of rape described was punishable by death if "the ravished woman were of free-birth," meaning that a death sentence could be applied only if the woman were not a slave or a servant.[16] Notably, the author makes sure to emphasize the consequences of the latter act for the ravished woman's guardians: "Once she has been ravished, willingly or unwillingly, the violence done to the parents or guardians seems to be of the highest degree."[17] The reference to the level of willingness here is interesting because it suggests that violating virginity rather than sexual violence is the biggest concern in punishing the act. Additionally, *Law's Resolutions* almost makes rape seem inevitable. In the section that precedes these distinctions, the author notes, "So drunken are men with their own lusts … that if the rampier of Laws were not betwixt women and their harms, I verily think none of them, being above twelve years of age and under a hundred, being either fair or rich, should be able to escape ravishing."[18] In other words, the author states that only laws can deter men from raping women at will, because their inherently lustful natures will push them to satisfy their sexual needs any way they can. One thing is clear from this discussion: there was a perception of sexual assault that normalized it in terms of men's regular sexual urges.

There is a lot to unpack in *Law's Resolutions* as it relates to the #MeToo movement and what the movement is fighting against. First, it demonstrates that, like today, definitions and distinctions surrounding sexual assault are problematic in their ambiguity; it is difficult to understand the difference between two distinct acts of rape. It fails in its attempts to draw a line between a "hideous" act committed by a clearly devilish man and the common compulsions that continuously threaten to lead otherwise good men astray. Despite the author's clear belief in the necessity of laws against rape, he seems to explain away rape as a momentary lapse in judgment that is almost inescapable for even the most promising of young men, much like the defenses used by rapist Brock Turner in his 2016 trial.[19] After all, as the author claims, "fair or rich" women "above twelve years of age and under a hundred" are not only susceptible to men's lust, but cannot "escape" it. In fact, according to *Law's Resolutions*, women are more likely to be made prisoners by "lust's thieves," or men using "rough handling, violence, or plain strength of arms," than by "honest lovers."[20] Based on the somewhat restrictive criteria outlined for offenders who could incur the death penalty, the author might even imply that men's lives should not be ruined by the inconvenience of accusations. In this way, *Law's Resolutions* also somewhat aligns with the modern sense of fear that surrounds women's sexuality, implying that women's bodies and reputations are in constant danger because of their inability to defend themselves against the "natural" impulses of men.[21] Not only that, but they put their families' reputations and economics in jeopardy as well, simply by being a woman who is capable of being ravished.[22]

Shakespeare and his contemporary playwrights clearly participated in the cultural work of forming and being informed by some of these early modern perceptions of rape. David Mann estimates that "something of the order of seven out of every ten plays presented on the Elizabethan adult stage include at least one, and often several, [scenes of violence toward women]," including rape.[23] This theatrical trend reflects an increasingly normalized acceptance of sexual assault, which was clear in other literary representations as well. In her study of sexual consent in the English lyric, Cynthia E. Garrett argues that in English culture "the idea that women want to be forced into sex gained popular currency in 1590–1610."[24] Garrett's compelling study includes sussing out connections between the attitudes expressed in late-sixteenth-century poetry and Ovid's *Ars Amatoria*, a popular translation of which was published by writer Thomas Heywood at the beginning of the seventeenth century. She posits that this translation helped to introduce the idea of "licensed comic rape" into English culture.[25] While Mann is not specific in his estimations and does not identify how many staged instances of violence against women occur in comedies, several Shakespearean comedies, including the aforementioned *Measure for Measure*, are often haunted by the specter of sexual assault. In *Much Ado About Nothing*, for example, Shakespeare expresses an understanding of the always real, though sometimes imperceptible, damage that sexual misconduct can do, a kind of damage similar to that which the #MeToo movement is striving to expose and undo.

SEXUAL ASSAULT AND SLANDER IN *MUCH ADO ABOUT NOTHING*

#MeToo resonates in several ways in relation to Shakespeare's *Much Ado About Nothing.* Like the movement, the play, at least in some ways, values the power of women's voices. The play features one of Shakespeare's most beloved outspoken heroines in Beatrice, who seems to eschew marriage and men's advances in favor of her independence. Because of these qualities, she can easily be read as a sort of proto-feminist icon. The play seems most often remembered for the romance between her and the equally clever and funny Benedick, which in most ways seems exceptionally egalitarian by early modern standards. Yet even Beatrice's clever wit, sharp tongue, and unconventional ideas about marriage cannot quell the misogyny and real threat to women's bodies, reputations, and voices contained within the play. *Much Ado*'s plot pivots on the fate of Beatrice's quieter, more obedient cousin, Hero, who is falsely accused of sexual promiscuity. After a whirlwind romance with the handsome, seemingly honorable young soldier Claudio, Hero agrees to marry him. However, a vicious plan to stop the marriage is plotted, and Claudio is tricked into thinking he sees Hero with another man. Enraged, Claudio then refuses to marry Hero at the altar and publicly shames her by revealing that she has been spoiled by another man, essentially accusing her of promiscuity. Overtaken with grief, Hero faints. After being told Hero is dead, Claudio expresses regret, and so promises he will marry another of Leonato's (Hero's father) relations. At this ceremony, the mystery bride is revealed to be Hero, alive and well, and the couple marries.

The play emphasizes just how difficult it is for women to be heard when their sexualities are involved. Accused of being with a man the night before she is to marry the heralded soldier Claudio, Hero is left speechless at the wedding altar. She is of course shocked by the false claims, but her silence results more directly from being denied a chance to speak for or defend herself. Like so many victims in contemporary rape and sexual assault cases, Hero's perspective is simply not valued, even if someone other than herself, in this case the Friar, calls attention to it. This silence has dire consequences, for Claudio does not merely deny Hero, he pointedly humiliates her and her family. At the wedding ceremony, when asked if there is a reason the couple should not marry, Claudio pushes his bride-to-be back onto her father Leonato, exclaiming, "Give not this rotten orange to your friend; / She's but the sign and semblance of her honor" (4.1.30–1).[26] This line amplifies the accusation partly because it escalates the consequences for Hero; oranges were associated with prostitutes, so the line acts to foreshadow Hero's disgraced future. But as the scene goes on, there is little indication that any man—save perhaps the Friar—has any concern for Hero's future. After this humiliation, she has few options because her honor, her most attractive quality on the marriage market (save perhaps her dowry), has been destroyed. And yet Hero faints rather than fighting. Garthine Walker offers a potential explanation for this inaction: "Because women's honour has effectively been imagined in terms of dishonour, constructions of shame—especially those associated with sexuality and sexual behaviour—have been privileged over, or compounded with, those of affront."[27] The power of humiliation effectively inhibits a woman's ability to defend herself. Indeed, her shame actually sanctions the actions of men embarrassed by their wives' (or betrotheds') supposed indiscretions, even if those indiscretions never occurred.

Because of the shame *she* has brought to *him*—the shame, essentially, of a cuckold—Hero, as a person, becomes irrelevant to Claudio, and he can see only the consequences her supposed action brings to his reputation. Believing that she had a rendezvous with Borachio, Claudio rails against her and claims that her intemperate behavior has forever turned "all beauty into thoughts of harm" (4.1.107) for him, a sentiment that minimizes the impact that the accusation has on a young woman, and instead privileges his own victimhood. The latent misogyny in the play becomes explicit in this scene. Claudio implicates all women in the sexual sins he assigns to Hero, for he can no longer appreciate their beauty or goodness. Don Pedro, who plays matchmaker for the couple earlier in the play, also sees Hero's alleged sin as a personal affront, though he is neither the jilted nor the jiltee. His words are perhaps even more revealing of the real concern behind the perceived infidelity: "I stand dishounoured that have gone about / To link my dear friend to a common stale" (4.1.63–4). Rather than focusing on how the allegations of wrongdoing hurt Hero's or even Claudio's reputation, Don Pedro is instead worried about damage to his own honor merely by having encouraged the match. In fact, he adds salt to the wound by calling her a "stale," another term for a prostitute that recalls Claudio's "orange." Even Leonato, Hero's father, cannot see beyond his own situation. When Hero fails to deny the accusation in a way that will satisfy the angry mob of men who surround her, Leonato exclaims, "Hath no man's dagger here a point for me?" (4.1.109). He seeks to end *his* anguish as the father of a disgraced daughter through suicide rather than tending to his daughter's heartbreak, which causes her to faint directly after his plea for relief. As Irene Dash succinctly explains, "The man's life is primary. The implications of rape or the threat of rape to a woman are irrelevant."[28] Although the accusation in *Much Ado* is not one of rape, but infidelity, women are being victimized because they are silenced; men's words are primary because women's words are disallowed or ignored. Dash's statement is applicable in that Claudio and the other male characters fixate on the humiliation brought upon *him* by potential cuckoldry rather than on the real consequences of shame brought upon Hero by this accusation. The ease with which the men in the play believe that Hero has been unfaithful reflects their anxieties about unregulated femininity, much like the modern tendency of men to be skeptical of women's accusations of sexual assault.

The irrelevance of the consequences of sexual shaming for women resonates with the #MeToo movement, especially given its goal to increase awareness of, and attention to, female victims' stories. I am reminded of one particular contemporary voice: Monica Lewinski's. She, of course, was the intern involved in an extramarital affair with then-President Bill Clinton from 1995–7. Twenty years after the scandal that decimated Lewinsky's reputation and would lead to Clinton's impeachment, Lewinski penned a piece for *Vanity Fair* in which she links the events from the late 1990s with the modern #MeToo movement. She says, "I've also come to understand how my trauma has been, in a way, a microcosm of a larger, national one. Both clinically and observationally, something fundamental changed in our society in 1998, and it is changing again as we enter the second year of the Trump presidency in a post-Cosby-Ailes-O'Reilly-Weinstein-Spacey-Whoever-Is-Next world."[29] She characterizes that change as an "upheaval," a real turn in how we approach public accusations of sexual misconduct. Lewinsky goes on to address the personal loneliness that resulted from her oh-so-public involvement in the Clinton ordeal. Highlighting the importance of a supportive community and the hope for change, she says,

> Isolation is such a powerful tool to the subjugator. And yet I don't believe I would have felt so isolated had it all happened today. One of the most inspiring aspects of this newly energized movement is the sheer number of women who have spoken up in support of one another. And the volume in numbers has translated into volume of public voice … Virtually anyone can share her or his #MeToo story and be instantly welcomed into a tribe.[30]

Like so many women who have come forward with their stories of sexual assault or mistreatment since the #MeToo movement began, Lewinski finds solace in numbers because others' support and understanding make her feel less alone. While Shakespeare's heroines did not have hashtags or Facebook groups to look to for support, they did have networks of women who helped them navigate the dangerous field of sexual interactions.

In *Much Ado*, Hero's agency is rendered moot by Claudio's slanderous accusation, so Beatrice rises up to act on her behalf, becoming her (small) network of supportive women. Hero's relative silence suggests more than merely her compliance with period gender expectations. Her silence ensures she will not object or present evidence to clear her name; she will not put Claudio (or any man) in a position in which it is her word against his, because she does not have a word at all. Beatrice, on the other hand, is potentially dangerous because not only does she have a well-established voice, but also a receptive audience in Benedick, a man respected for his command of language and his masculinity. He empowers her because his love for her compels him to act on her behalf. Despite her lack of agency to act, her words do indeed prove powerful, especially her instruction to Benedick to "kill Claudio" (4.1.288). The delivery of this line can shape the tenor of any production of this play; if it is played for comedy, the production decreases the impact of Claudio's accusation, but if it is played for shock, Beatrice emphasizes the weight and dire consequences of his claim.[31] I quote the passage at length here to underscore Beatrice's increasing anger with Claudio—and men in general—as well as her increasing empathy for her cousin's situation:

> **BENEDICK** Come, bid me do any thing for thee.
> **BEATRICE** Kill Claudio.
> **BENEDICK** Ha! not for the wide world.
> **BEATRICE** You kill me to deny it. Farewell.
> **BENEDICK** Tarry, sweet Beatrice.
> **BEATRICE** I am gone, though I am here: there is no love in you: nay, I pray you, let me go …
> **BENEDICK** Beatrice,--
> **BEATRICE** In faith, I will go.
> **BENEDICK** We'll be friends first.
> **BEATRICE** You dare easier be friends with me than fight with mine enemy.
> **BENEDICK** Is Claudio thine enemy?
> **BEATRICE** Is he not approved in the height a villain, that hath slandered, scorned, dishonoured my kinswoman? O that I were a man! What, bear her in hand until they come to take hands; and then, with public accusation, uncovered slander, unmitigated rancour, --O God, that I were a man! I would eat his heart in the marketplace.
> **BENEDICK** Hear me, Beatrice,--
> **BEATRICE** Talk with a man out at a window! A proper saying!
> **BENEDICK** Nay, but, Beatrice,--
> **BEATRICE** Sweet Hero! She is wronged, she is slandered, she is undone.
> (4.1.287–310)

Scrutinizing the word *kill* in this passage reveals the power that genuine words can have over unsubstantiated perception. Beatrice's command to "kill Claudio" contrasts with Hero's meek reaction to Claudio's accusations at the altar, but it also may recall her cousin's supposed death at his hands; he, in effect, killed her. In the few seconds that the characters believe Hero to be dead, killed by the heartbreak of the accusation, Leonato professes, "Death is the fairest cover for her shame / That may be wished for" (4.1.116–17). Better she were dead than dishonored in his eyes. Yet her dishonor *is* a sort of death; being labeled promiscuous renders Hero unmarriageable and useless to her father, so she essentially has no place in society. Death here is associated with reputation, so it stands to reason that Beatrice's direction to "kill Claudio" could also refer to the ruin of his reputation. After all, she wants to "kill" him publicly, or "eat his heart in the *marketplace*." Beatrice understands her world enough to know that her own word alone probably could not damage Claudio's reputation, but she recognizes that Benedick could.

Her feat in this scene is getting a man to agree to speak and act on Hero's behalf, since within an early modern context, only a man can revive Hero's reputation and give her life. Beatrice's words and actions illustrate one of the central precepts of the #MeToo movement: women's insistence on being believed. From its inception, the movement has worked to break the silence around sexual assault and violence against women, as several feminist initiatives had done before it.[32] Likewise, Beatrice demands that Benedick believe her. Her—and other women's—historical circumstances necessitate a man's help, a sentiment echoed in her repeated line, "O that I were a man!" Benedick proves himself worthy of this strong woman and decides to work on her and Hero's behalf because he believes her:

> **BENEDICK** Think you in your soul that Count Claudio hath wronged Hero?
> **BEATRICE** Yea, as sure as I have a thought or a soul.
> **BENEDICK** Enough, I am engaged. (4.1.325–7)

Ultimately, her word is "enough." Benedick's devotion to Beatrice yields a commitment to believing women, making him an essential ally in the fight against sexual slander.

In the desperate situation at hand, words are the only tools that may help Hero and women in general. Although their words most often fall on deaf ears, acts and visuals that are supposed to serve as evidence are shown to be contrived and deceptive. The false scene staged by the bitter Don John and his crony Borachio to incriminate Hero proves that acts can be easily feigned. Claudio's conclusion about Hero's chastity is based on the orchestrated scene he witnessed in which Margaret, Hero's waiting woman, posed as Hero to "talk with a man out a window" (4.1.307–8). Beatrice simply scoffs at the suggestion that Hero would be involved in such an encounter, whereas the patriarchal paradigm, or the systems working to ensure and protect men's supremacy, privileges questionable visual evidence over women's vehement and true professions of innocence. Nova Myhill writes that perception "becomes a problem in the play because the male characters accept that women should be, as Hero is, silent and defined by the ways in which they are seen."[33] Hero's exoneration can happen only when Claudio really *sees* her innocence, hence the success of the second wedding ceremony when the mystery bride is revealed to be Hero by her lifting the veil that obscures her image. Through its treatment of Margaret, co-conspirator in Don John's plot, the play is careful to remind us, however, that the standard for absolution is set by men. Once Leonato is convinced of his daughter's virtue, he calls Margaret to task, despite Borachio's proclamation that "by my soul she was not [packed in all this wrong], / Nor knew not what she did when she spoke to me, / But always has been just and virtuous / In anything that I do know by her" (5.1.290–3). Though Leonato ostensibly accepts that Margaret was not in full cahoots with Don John and friends in this scene, he later continues to express skepticism about her culpability, declaring, "But Margaret was in some fault for this, / Although against her will, *as it appears* / In the true course of all the question" (5.4.4–6). Her part in the plot is never settled because it continues to *appear* suspect. There is no way to prove the veracity of the claims of her innocence; that instead depends on Leonato's personal construal.

Much Ado is very much concerned with the importance and impact of interpretation in situations of potential sexual slander and misconduct. The play asks whether interpretation through one set of eyes is enough to condemn another person, and it comes dangerously close to concluding that one (false) interpretation can effectively ruin a woman's life. The central dilemma comes down to "her word against his," a classic complaint about sexual assault cases that lack physical evidence or reliable outside witness accounts, and one that continues to be pervasive despite strides made in the earlier feminist and the #MeToo movements. According to the recent article "Why So Few Rapists Are Convicted" in *The Economist*, polls show "that in the aftermath of #MeToo people are more worried than before about false allegations of harassment and rape."[34] This fear may be due to several factors, including an erroneous sense that women are creating stories because there are more allegations being made. Negative cultural perceptions of the "feminist agenda" and the pervasive stereotype of feminists as man-haters certainly contribute, as well. The power of women's words to convict or even slander a man who is accused of sexual misconduct indeed may be increasing in the wake of #MeToo, but, as this sta-tistic shows, that power is more often perceived as the power to lie rather than the power to reveal the truth. *Much Ado* calls into question the fear of vocal women and the general unwillingness to believe them by severely restricting Hero and Beatrice from speaking at all, at least in a public forum. Instead, they can legitimate their voices only by giving them over to men via marriage.

In *Much Ado*, as in other Shakespearean comedies, marriage essentially erases women's subversive agency. The bride trick at the second wedding ceremony concedes some of the power to Hero and Beatrice, who have a part in planning and enacting it, though it must be noted that the Friar is actually the mastermind behind the plot. In spite of her broken heart, Hero must actively participate in the wedding trick for it to work, and Beatrice must actively decide to acquiesce to the idea of marriage even when she rages against the damage men can enact upon women. Both need the weddings in order to be legitimate themselves, for the women are no one if they are not wives. Hero's willingness to marry a man who treated her so poorly may seem particularly disturbing to modern audiences, but it does help to illustrate the desperate life circumstances faced by women whose sexual reputations were ruined.

The men in this play also believe that marriage is a legitimizing force; both Claudio and Don Pedro seem to see it as an inevitable and welcome step that launches men into maturity. Even the once marriage-averse Benedick acknowledges, "When I said I would die a bachelor, I did not think I would live till I were married" (2.3.233–5). However, what Shakespeare includes of the wedding itself does not actually validate anything of the sort because he substitutes cultural rituals for the actual ceremony. As Nathaniel Leonard points out, "Shakespeare does not simply avoid the staging of marriage performatives in his comedies: his plays go to great lengths to construct elaborate stand-ins for the marriages that serve as capstones to their comic arcs."[35] When Benedick calls out, "Strike up, pipers!" (5.4.126) in the final line of the play, the wedding is replaced by a celebratory dance, leaving Hero and Beatrice with a liminal status, if only for a moment. Lisa Hopkins's idea that Shakespearean marriage is both "redemptive and painful" is relevant here.[36] Marriage can indeed redeem Hero's reputation and provide Beatrice with a socially sanctioned place. But a threat remains. Right before Benedick instructs the pipers, it is announced that Don John, the architect behind the scheme that brought Hero down, has fled unpunished. In a way, his unknown whereabouts keep open the possibility of further pain.

For modern audiences, the play's ending is not just unsatisfying, but, rather, *dis*satisfying. It literally stops women's voices and opts instead for ritualized silence and willful blindness. The trick brides are veiled, and though both Hero and Beatrice speak after this happens, they are also essentially silenced by the patriarchal marriage ritual. This time, it is not Benedick's kiss that stops Beatrice's mouth, which has been the case not once, but twice before in the play, but Leonato's passing of her to Benedick. Leonato exclaims, "Peace! [*to Beatrice*] I will stop your mouth [*hands her to Benedick*]" (5.4.97). While this line is often given to Benedick in performance, Claire McEachern, the editor of the third Arden Shakespeare edition of the play, chooses to insert these stage directions in part to untangle the unclear and somewhat chaotic action of this final scene. More importantly, however, her choice to have Leonato hand Beatrice to Benedick at this line symbolically transfers any power Beatrice's voice may have carried as she orchestrated her cousin's redemption over to Benedick. In essence, Leonato here reifies the idea that women must be ruled by the men in their lives, an ethos that drives the male characters' behavior throughout the play. Paul Innes hints at this move when he assesses the veiling of the play's trick brides in the final scene as "visually condensing the moment of their recuperation"; Innes identifies the handing over moment as "a gestus to epitomize the patriarchal moment," and Leonato as "functioning to contain the threats to patriarchy that have emerged during the play."[37] Innes insists that Leonato and the other older men in the play "serve to ensure that there will be no more … alternative possibilities, and that the play's nothings will be noted and safely and securely policed … order is restored, but the price is the unveiling of its hidden mechanisms."[38] In some ways, for an audience who has at least been exposed to the tenets of modern feminism, the ending is frustrating for its containment. Yet, if examined closely, it is also oddly optimistic in its implicit acknowledgment that the patriarchal system at work in the world of the play is a construct that requires protection and maintenance, rather than an inescapable reality, and that the construct can be threatened and perhaps even dismantled.

In the absence of an actual rape or sexual misconduct in this play, *words* assault women instead. In *Much Ado*, slanderous words "kill" Hero and threaten Margaret, demonstrating how dangerous rumor can be to women. Beatrice attempts to capture that power of words in instructing Benedick to "kill Claudio." Benedick's response to this command is initially resistant because adhering to it would mean relinquishing his membership in a group of men whose bond is ostensibly as soldiers, but who over the course of the play have proven to be more connected by their fear of female sexuality. However, these specific words, and their deployment as a command, underscore that only men's actions can truly redeem a woman. The #MeToo movement also depends on words and their reception. Its aim is to provide a safe platform for victims to give words to their experiences. Yet words are also at the center of opposition to the movement. When the hashtag itself took off, #MeToo seemed to offer respite in a politically divided women's movement. Conservative and liberal women alike praised the efforts to make it easier for victims of sexual assault and harassment to speak out in a space made safe by the staggering number of women who saw themselves in the stories of others. But soon some women wanted to make a space for men's voices and opposition. #NotAllMen emerged, a movement that seemed to indicate women's words were in fact still not enough to implicate a patriarchal culture in the crimes it performs against the bodies of women. Not *all* men rape, they claimed, therefore *some* men can discredit an entire movement's ethos that depends on valuing women's voices. In his initial resistance to Beatrice's request, Benedick comes dangerously close to employing an ethos similar to this counter-movement.

Ultimately, however, his willingness to believe Beatrice—and by extension, Hero—trumps his desire to belong. As *Much Ado* and its dissatisfying ending demonstrate, #NotAllMen essentially just makes an old problem new again. This defense of the patriarchy has existed for many, many years.

Yet in the face of the pushback, the #MeToo movement continues to grow and influence the culture. Its reach is apparent in the convictions of Harvey Weinstein and others like him who commit sexual assault crimes, offenses that likely would have been swept under the rug even just a decade ago. The culture is beginning to take men to task and believe women. In fact, several powerful, well-known men—not the women who accuse them—have come to understand what Angelo in *Measure for Measure* calls "the smell of calumny." Their power and careers have been cut short as a consequence of their actions. In a real way, the movement has awakened a consciousness that is more aware of the issues women face on a daily basis as they move through the world. Such a new orientation to women's experiences influences not just the way we see the present and the future, but how we see the past in artifacts like Shakespeare's plays. It opens up new interpretive possibilities. Just as Beatrice and Hero find a way to survive, and perhaps even thrive, in the early modern culture of misogyny, the movement trudges on to create opportunities and new understandings.

NOTES

1. Quotations from *Measure for Measure* are taken from William Shakespeare, *Measure for Measure*, ed. J. W. Lever (London: Thompson Learning, 2006).
2. Irene Dash, *Women's Worlds in Shakespeare* (Newark: University of Delaware Press, 1997), 23.
3. Dash, *Women's Worlds in Shakespeare*, 23.
4. During the congressional confirmation hearing for soon-to-be Supreme Court Justice Clarence Thomas, Anita Hill testified that Thomas, her former supervisor at the Department of Education, sexually harassed her on multiple occasions. Though she provided credible testimony, Thomas was appointed. The hearings, and especially Hill's role in them, were widely televised and are credited for bringing the term and concept *sexual harassment* to the mainstream public consciousness.
5. Tara Isabella Burton, "What a Lesser-Known Shakespeare Play Can Tell Us about Harvey Weinstein: Before #MeToo There Was *Measure for Measure*," *Vox*, November 15, 2017, https://www.vox.com/culture/2017/11/15/16644938/ shakespeare-measure-for-measure-weinstein-sexual-harassment-play-theater.
6. Before Brett Kavanaugh was confirmed as a Supreme Court Justice in 2018, Christine Blasey Ford, Kavanaugh's childhood friend, came forward to accuse him of sexual assault. Like Anita Hill, Blasey Ford testified during Kavanaugh's confirmation hearings, but despite her compelling testimony, Kavanaugh, like Clarence Thomas before him, was appointed to the position. The hearings were

widely reported in the media, and the decision to confirm Kavanaugh has been held up as an example of how much work is left to do in the feminist movement.

7. Rebecca Mead, "Josie Rourke's Shakespeare for the #MeToo Era," *The New Yorker*, December 20, 2018, https://www.newyorker.com/magazine/2018/12/10/josie-rourkes-shakespeare-for-the-metoo-era.

8. Tarana Burke, "Me Too Is a Movement, Not a Moment," TED video, 16:07, filmed November 2018, https://www.ted.com/talks/tarana_burke_me_too_is_a_movement_not_a_moment#t-2272.

9. *All's Well That Ends Well* is the only comedy that contains the word; it appears as an abstract concept during the prank played on Parolles, when the vulgar soldier describes Captain Dumaine as a cad who has done many "rapes and ravishments" (4.3.246). This quotation is taken from William Shakespeare, *All's Well That Ends Well*, ed. Suzanne Gossett and Helen Wilcox (London: Bloomsbury Publishing, 2019).

10. Barbara J. Baines, "Effacing Rape in Early Modern Representation," *English Literary History* 65, no. 1 (1998): 69.

11. Garthine Walker, "Everyman or a Monster? The Rapist in Early Modern England, c.1600–1750," *History Workshop Journal* 76, no. 1 (2013): 5.

12. Baines, "Effacing Rape," 77.

13. T. E., ed., *The Law's Resolutions for Women's Rights, or the Law's Provision for Women* (1632), in Sexuality and Gender in the English Renaissance: An Annotated Edition of Contemporary Documents, ed. Lloyd Davis (New York: Garland, 1998), 398.

14. T. E., *Law's Resolutions*, 398.

15. T. E., *Law's Resolutions*, 398.

16. T. E., *Law's Resolutions*, 398.

17. T. E., *Law's Resolutions*, 398.

18. T. E., *Law's Resolutions*, 398.

19. Turner's father famously penned an appeal to the judge in the trial, arguing that his son should receive probation and not serve time when he was convicted. In it, he says of potential jail time, "That is a steep price to pay for 20 minutes of action out of his 20 plus years of life," implying that Brock's actions were a momentary lapse in a life otherwise well lived. See Michael E. Miller, "'A Steep Price to Pay for 20 Minutes of Action': Dad Defends Stanford Sex Offender," *The Washington Post*, June 6, 2016, https://www.washingtonpost.com/news/morning-mix/wp/2016/06/06/a-steep-price-to-pay-for-20-minutes-of-action-dad-defends-stanford-sex-offender/.

20. T. E., *Law's Resolutions*, 398.

21. I am thinking here of the ways in which fear of sexual assault alters women's lives. One example is the idea that women adhere to a "rape schedule," or that they plan their days around avoiding situations that could make them vulnerable to sexual assault. See Jessica Valenti, *Full Frontal Feminism: A Young Woman's Guide to Why Feminism Matters* (Berkeley, CA: Seal Press, 2014), 63, for an explanation of this phenomenon.

22. Of course, the fear associated with women's sexuality is also experienced by men, but for a different reason: cuckoldry. For a thorough discussion of this kind of sexual fear, see Carol Cook, "'The Sign and Semblance of Her Honor': Reading Gender Difference in *Much Ado About Nothing*," *PMLA* 101, no. 2 (1986): 186–202.

23. David Mann, *Shakespeare's Women: Performance and Conception* (Cambridge: Cambridge University Press, 2008), 186.
24. Cynthia E. Garrett, "Sexual Consent and the Art of Love in the Early Modern English Lyric," *Studies in English Literature, 1500–1900* 44, no. 1 (2004): 38.
25. Garrett, "Sexual Consent," 28.
26. All quotations of *Much Ado about Nothing* are taken from William Shakespeare, *Much Ado About Nothing*, 2nd ed., Arden Shakespeare, 3rd Series, ed. Claire McEachern (London: Bloomsbury Arden Shakespeare, 2016).
27. Garthine Walker, "Expanding the Boundaries of Female Honour in Early Modern England," *Transactions of the Royal Historical Society* 6 (1996): 235–6.
28. Irene Dash, *Women's Worlds in Shakespeare*, 21.
29. Monica Lewinsky, "Emerging from 'The House of Gaslight' in the Age of #MeToo," *Vanity Fair*, February 25, 2018, https://www.vanityfair.com/news/2018/02/monica-lewinsky-in-the-age-of-metoo.
30. Lewinsky, "Emerging."
31. For an interesting and comprehensive discussion of the delivery and staging of this line, see J. F. Cox, "The Stage Representation of the 'Kill Claudio' Sequence in *Much Ado About Nothing*," *Shakespeare Survey* 32 (1980): 27–36.
32. Specifically, I am thinking here of initiatives like Take Back the Night and the establishment of rape crisis centers and hotlines in the 1970s.
33. Nova Myhill, "Spectatorship in/of *Much Ado About Nothing*," *Studies in English Literature, 1500–1900* 39, no. 2 (1999): 294.
34. "Why So Few Rapists Are Convicted," *The Economist*, January 4, 2020, https://www.economist.com/international/2020/01/04/why-so-few-rapists-are-convicted.
35. Nathaniel C. Leonard, "Circling the Nuptial in *As You Like It* and *Much Ado About Nothing*," *SEL* 57, no. 2 (2017): 320.
36. Lisa Hopkins, *The Shakespearean Marriage: Merry Wives and Heavy Husbands* (Basingstoke: Macmillan, 1998), 9.
37. Paul Innes, "Sensory Confusion and the Generation Gap in *Much Ado About Nothing*," *Critical Survey* 25, no. 2 (2014): 16–17.
38. Innes, "Sensory Confusion," 18.

REFERENCES

Baines, Barbara J. "Effacing Rape in Early Modern Representation." *English Literary History* 65, no. 1 (1998): 69–98.
Burke, Tarana. "Me Too Is a Movement, Not a Moment." Filmed November 2018. TED video, 16:07. Accessed January 3, 2020. https://www.ted.com/talks/tarana_burke_me_too_is_a_movement_not_a_moment#t-2272.
Burton, Tara Isabella. "What a Lesser-Known Shakespeare Play Can Tell Us about Harvey Weinstein: Before #MeToo There Was *Measure for Measure*." *Vox*, November 15, 2017. Accessed January 12, 2020. https://www.vox.com/culture/2017/11/15/16644938/shakespeare-measure-for-measure-weinstein-sexual-harassment-play-theater.
Cook, Carol. "'The Sign and Semblance of Her Honor': Reading Gender Difference in *Much Ado About Nothing*." *PMLA* 101, no. 2 (1986): 186–202.
Cox, J. F. "The Stage Representation of the 'Kill Claudio' Sequence in *Much Ado About Nothing*." *Shakespeare Survey* 32 (1980): 27–36.

Dash, Irene. *Women's Worlds in Shakespeare*. Newark: University of Delaware Press, 1997.

The Economist. "Why So Few Rapists Are Convicted." January 4, 2020. Accessed January 14, 2020. https://www.economist.com/international/2020/01/04/why-so -few-rapists-are-convicted.

Garrett, Cynthia E. "Sexual Consent and the Art of Love in the Early Modern English Lyric." *Studies in English Literature, 1500–1900* 44, no. 1 (2004): 37–58.

Hopkins, Lisa. *The Shakespearean Marriage: Merry Wives and Heavy Husbands*. Basingstoke: Macmillan, 1998.

Innes, Paul. "Sensory Confusion and the Generation Gap in *Much Ado About Nothing*." *Critical Survey* 25, no. 2 (2014): 1–20.

Leonard, Nathaniel C. "Circling the Nuptial in *As You Like It* and *Much Ado About Nothing*." *SEL* 57, no. 2 (2017): 303–23.

Lewinsky, Monica, "Emerging from 'The House of Gaslight' in the Age of #MeToo." *Vanity Fair*, February 25, 2018. Accessed January 12, 2020. https://www.vanityfair .com/news/2018/02/monica-lewinsky-in-the-age-of-metoo.

Mann, David. *Shakespeare's Women: Performance and Conception*. Cambridge: Cambridge University Press, 2008.

Mead, Rebecca. "Josie Rourke's Shakespeare for the #MeToo Era." *The New Yorker*, December 20, 2018. Accessed January 12, 2020. https://www.newyorker.com/ magazine/2018/12/10/josie-rourkes-shakespeare-for-the-metoo-era.

Miller, Michael E. "'A Steep Price to Pay for 20 Minutes of Action': Dad Defends Stanford Sex Offender." *The Washington Post*, June 6, 2016. Accessed January 14, 2020. https://www.washingtonpost.com/news/morning-mix/wp/2016/06/06/a-steep -price-to-pay-for-20-minutes-of-action-dad-defends-stanford-sex-offender/.

Myhill, Nova. "Spectatorship in/of *Much Ado About Nothing*." *Studies in English Literature, 1500–1900* 39, no. 2 (1999): 291–311.

Shakespeare, William. *All's Well That Ends Well*. Edited by Suzanne Gossett and Helen Wilcox. London: Bloomsbury Publishing, 2019.

Shakespeare, William. *Measure for Measure*. Edited by J. W. Lever. London: Thompson Learning, 2006.

Shakespeare, William. *Much Ado About Nothing*. Edited by Claire McEachern. London: Bloomsbury Arden Shakespeare, 2016.

T. E., ed. *The Law's Resolutions for Women's Rights, or the Law's Provision for Women* (1632). In *Sexuality and Gender in the English Renaissance: An Annotated Edition of Contemporary Documents*, edited by Lloyd Davis, 371–406. New York: Garland, 1998.

Valenti, Jessica. *Full Frontal Feminism: A Young Woman's Guide to Why Feminism Matters*. Berkeley, CA: Seal Press, 2014.

Walker, Garthine. "Everyman or a Monster? The Rapist in Early Modern England, c.1600–1750." *History Workshop Journal* 76, no. 1 (2013): 5–31.

Walker, Garthine. "Expanding the Boundaries of Female Honour in Early Modern England." *Transactions of the Royal Historical Society* 6 (1996): 235–45.

8. The importance of highlighting the rotten state: a study of Vishal Bharadwaj's *Haider* (2014) and its subversive strategies

Debaditya Mukhopadhyay

Immediately after its release in 2014, Vishal Bharadwaj's Indian adaptation of *Hamlet*, entitled *Haider*, became the focus of a number of remarkable critical studies that explored the film from a variety of perspectives. Despite the substantiality of these discussions, an analysis of this film focusing on its use of Shakespeare to offer a nuanced portrayal of the three issues recurrently discussed throughout this volume—politics, leadership, and culture—has yet to be sufficiently developed. Despite having a troubled state as its setting, *Hamlet* rarely draws attention to the impact of this on its residents; only the line "Something is rotten in the state of Denmark" (1.4.85), uttered by Marcellus, hints at the presence of corruption beneath the apparent stability of Denmark.[1] Taking its cue from this mention of disorder beneath order, Bharadwaj's film achieves its distinction by focusing on how the corrupted condition of Kashmir is sustained as well as concealed by its politics, leadership, and culture, just as the corruption of Denmark was covered up by Claudius's apparently sound ruling policies.

Though *Hamlet* and its numerous Anglo-American film adaptations do address the close links between the play's tragic events and the corruption of Denmark (or equivalent settings), *Haider* foregrounds, with explicit insistence, this tragedy's potential to reveal Shakespeare's views about the problems of a rotten state by adapting its key plot elements and characters for the sake of a nuanced exposé of problems in present-day Kashmir. It should be noted, however, that *Haider* does not condemn Kashmir as a state rotten to the core, beyond recovery. Rather, it shows this corruption to be resistible and the result of a vicious circle created by the coming together of problematic models of politics and leadership. These models aggravate each other, and are also influenced by a hegemonic culture that aids this circle by normalizing corruption. This confluence lends itself to being understood through the lens of Shakespeare's work in order to find possible solutions to the challenges of the moment. By analyzing the film's portrayal of the role played by these factors in creating Kashmir's current problematic conditions, this chapter will explain how *Haider* gives a new direction to the politicizing of Shakespeare's plays.

A NOTE ON SUBVERSION

Before reading the film's engagement with the three issues mentioned above, a note on its subversion of Shakespeare's play seems necessary. Among the many interesting differences between *Haider* and *Hamlet*, one particular change appears to be most relevant to the present discussion. In *Hamlet*, the inner conflict as well as the past actions of the royal family appear to be largely responsible for the troubled state of Denmark, but in this film it is the troubled state of Kashmir that destroys these two families and many others. The plot of *Haider* makes adequate room for portraying inner familial conflicts by featuring all of the major characters of the play *Hamlet* except Horatio; but instead of being shaped solely by the decisions they make due to their respective family situations, their lives are shown to be controlled by the socio-political problems of the place in which they reside. Hamlet's family members are represented in this film by the Meer family, namely Dr. Hilal Meer (Hamlet's father); his wife, Ghazala Meer (Gertrude); and his younger brother, Khurram Meer (Claudius). Ophelia's family appears as the Lone family governed by Pervez Lone (Polonius); his son, Liaqat Lone (Laertes); and daughter, Arshia Lone. Just as in *Hamlet*, in this film the Meer family is torn apart because the younger brother betrays his elder brother; but since this betrayal is shown to be a result of the corrupted condition of the state instead of being its cause, the film begins by reversing the dynamic of the Shakespearean tragedy. To put it differently, in *Hamlet* it is the royal family that affects the futures of the characters as well as the overall state of Denmark, but in *Haider* individuals as well as their families are bound by the circumstances of Kashmir.

Hamlet's theme of families affecting individuals' lives may be understood by referring to Joseph Barnett's interpretation of this play as primarily "set in motion" by what he calls "the family ideology" and as tracing "the tragic consequences that may arise in those situations which involve catastrophic disillusionment with the family ideology."[2] According to Barnett's assessment, *Hamlet* reveals the inescapability of the ramifications of faulty family values, mainly through Hamlet and Ophelia. Though they differ significantly in their responses to problematic family values, they meet the same fate. While Hamlet keeps debating whether he must "reinsta[te] the family ideology by simply following his father's instructions," or whether he should "overthro[w] the family ideology" after discovering what is wrong with his family, Ophelia remains unable to "free herself of the suspicions that marked her family's view of the world" and which taught her to doubt everyone.[3] Still, by the end of the play, both of them are devastated. Representatives of the new generation are shown to be devastated in *Haider*, too, but unlike the inescapability of family values in *Hamlet*, these devastations reveal how ineluctable the effects of a rotten state can be.

Along with affecting the lives of individuals, Shakespeare's play shows that the royal family affects the nation as a whole, too. In *Hamlet*, the state of Denmark faces an external threat in the form of Fortinbras, because Hamlet senior had agreed to gamble with Fortinbras's father. In the words of William Witherle Lawrence, "The elder Hamlet [...] appears as a reckless champion, risking life and lands on personal valor, rather than as a careful guardian of his domain."[4] The situation is further complicated when Hamlet tries to kill Claudius, the person who tried to resolve the dispute started by his elder brother. Fortinbras's unchallenged victory at the end of *Hamlet*, therefore, is intimately related to the inner turmoil of Hamlet's family. In *Haider*, this whole dynamic is replaced by a situation in which instead of a state being ruined by a family, families are devoured by the turmoil of the state. The characters of *Hamlet* act as villains, victims, or avengers mostly due to their individual natures, thereby turning Denmark into a rotten state. By contrast, each of their Indian counterparts in *Haider* plays similar roles because the rotten condition of Kashmir obliges them to do so. In short, in *Haider* the rotten state and its politics become the only major theme, and thus it seems crucial to study this politicized version of *Hamlet* by focusing on its portrayal of Kashmir's problematic situation and the consequences that result from it.

THE KASHMIR PROBLEM: A BRIEF OVERVIEW IN RELATION TO *HAIDER*

The history of the ongoing problem in Kashmir spans nearly a century, and an extensive account of this history is outside the purview of this chapter; besides, the film *Haider* is not a documentary concerned with historical accuracy. Rather, as pointed out by Preti Taneja, the film has multiple moments when the "manipulation of time and events" takes place.[5] Taneja opines that the film mixes real events with imaginary ones in order to map "events that resonate across time" and adds that these events enable this film to reach its viewers in 2014, despite the declaration at the film's onset that the events shown are set in 1995.[6] Instead of providing a chronological account of Kashmir's historical as well as political condition, *Haider* actually draws attention to a number of perennial problems in Kashmir that have haunted this state ever since it became a contested territory.[7] Taking this selective principle into account while discussing *Haider*'s use of Shakespeare in portraying the politics of Kashmir, this chapter will focus mostly on those recurrent issues that have played key roles in shaping Kashmir's problematic condition since the beginning of the tussle between India and Pakistan over its control. Prior to that, this section will offer a brief overview of Kashmir's problems resulting from its status as a contested territory.

Sumantra Bose's monograph on Kashmir and four other regions disturbed by conflicts over legal territorial control refers to these places as "contested lands," defining them as places that do not have "political stability […] anchored in ties of regional integration and cross-border cooperation that spill across national sovereignties and frontiers."[8] Bose describes Kashmir as a place "caught […] in the crosshairs of the India-Pakistan conflict," and his account of the genesis of this conflict shows how a politics of suppressing the voice of the general public has shaped Kashmir since the decolonization of India.[9] During decolonization, all princely states under British rule were given the option to align either with India or Pakistan "on the basis of two considerations: the location of their fief in relation to the territories of the two emergent sovereign polities, and the preferences of their population of subjects."[10] In the case of Kashmir, the first criterion did not suffice, because "it was geographically contiguous to both India and Pakistan," and, according to Bose's account and the chronology featured in *Kashmir: The Case for Freedom*, despite the decision in favor of a plebiscite in 1949, both India and Pakistan have continuously attempted to ignore the opinion of Kashmiris.[11] Describing this situation, Patrick Colm Hogan comments: "Almost no one who has any authority seems to take seriously the idea of Kashmiri independence."[12]

Pakistan's approach has been to attempt to secure Kashmir or win support of Kashmiris chiefly by kindling militancy in Kashmir through infiltration. Even articles like Samina Yasmeen's "Pakistan's Kashmir Policy: Voices of Moderation?" which sheds light on the emergence of moderate policy proponents in Pakistan, mention in significant detail how problematic Pakistan's approach to Kashmir has been in the past. According to Yasmeen, these policy proponents started arguing in favor of resolving the Kashmir issue through "accommodation and negotiation with India" in the late 1990s, but prior to their emergence, Pakistan had been "engaged in promoting/turning a blind eye to the *Jihadi* infiltration across the Line of Control into the Indian part of Kashmir."[13] India, on the other hand, dealt with the situation by encouraging movements like the Prasad protest movement of 1952 and by attempting legal inclusion of Kashmir into India.[14]

The special autonomy granted Kashmir since 1950 through Article 370 of the Constitution of India was fully revoked on August 5, 2019; but, as Jill Cottrell suggests, "In reality Kashmir never effectively enjoyed anything like the autonomy that article 370 seemed to promise, and hardly anyone involved intended, at least in the late 1940s […] that it should do so."[15] A sense of the ineffectiveness of Article 370 may be gathered from the passage in 1965 of the "Integration Bill," which "formally [made] Kashmir a province of India."[16]

Cottrell opines that by passing Article 370, Jawaharlal Nehru basically wanted to make Kashmir a part of India, "essentially like any other state," and hoped to get it done through "a willing acceptance by Kashmir."[17] India's promises of plebiscite and autonomy to the people of Kashmir, therefore, appear to have been façades behind which lurked the motive of winning Kashmir through diplomacy.

Bose's monograph outlines India's subsequent strategy toward Kashmir, stating that "from 1953 onward Indian governments embarked on a strategy of incrementally revoking Indian-controlled Kashmir's self-ruling powers and of governing the territory through client politicians [...] subservient to New Delhi."[18] Overall, the Indian government dealt with Kashmir by using what Bose terms "the strategy of hegemonic control"; from his description of its ramifications, it becomes clear that this hegemonic control over Kashmir was achieved chiefly through using "compliant politicians [...] at the mercy of their patrons in Delhi" and by "turning Indian-controlled Kashmir into a draconian police state."[19] As a result, Kashmiris literally started disappearing because the two rival nations created a scenario in which one could survive only by taking the side of one or the other of these nations. Kashmiris had to act either as Indians or as Pakistanis, and if they tried to act neutrally, or more importantly, as Kashmiris who treat their fellow residents simply as Kashmiris irrespective of their political ideology, they would literally disappear, just as happens to Haider's father, Dr. Hilal Meer, in the film. In short, the major problem of Kashmir has been a relentless silencing of its residents, because neither India nor Pakistan has been interested in allowing Kashmiri people to speak for themselves.

From the prefatory note to the script of this film by director Vishal Bharadwaj, it becomes clear that the earnest intention to tell the story of Kashmir's problems through an authentic Kashmiri perspective significantly drove the making of this film. In the words of Bharadwaj, during all stages of the film he collaborated with the Kashmiri writer-cum-journalist Basharat Peer, who is credited as his co-writer because, he "did not want to write or direct through imagination."[20] The film itself is therefore an attempt to speak out against this silencing strategy of the two rival nations, and, as mentioned before, it portrays the troubles of Kashmir as an outcome of problematic aspects of politics, leadership, and culture that pervade this region. The subsequent sections of this chapter will trace the ways in which *Haider* portrays these three factors as impacting the state of affairs in Kashmir.

THE PROBLEMATIC ROLE OF POLITICS, LEADERSHIP, AND CULTURE IN KASHMIR

The enduring problems of politics and leadership in Kashmir are portrayed in *Haider* by presenting three different kinds of leaders and the toxic political strategies behind each of their standpoints. The allied pair of Khurram and Pervez represents leadership marked by opportunism and exploitation of helpless Kashmiris. Abhishek Sarkar comments on the relation between these two, suggesting that Pervez "is not an obtuse and loquacious dotard, but the cold-blooded lynchpin of a network involving the police, the army, and the anti-separatist militia, who manipulates the Claudius figure like a puppeteer."[21] Though a degree of manipulation is certainly shown to govern a portion of Pervez's and Khurram's interactions in the film, there are moments that make them look more like partners in the overall process of exploiting the Kashmiris. They are both professionally involved with the Kashmiri institutions of law and order, and they are shown to establish a vicious circle together, through which they entrap Kashmiris for their nefarious purposes. While announcing the approval of "Operation Bulbul," Brigadier Murthy, the army officer who represents the Indian government's involvement in Kashmir, openly declares that Pervez will be playing the chief role in this operation, which involves the creation of a counterinsurgency force against militants backed by various extremist organizations and Pakistan. The brigadier informs the audience that the force will have complete support from Delhi, and he asks the officials, particularly Pervez, to head as well as enlarge the force by recruiting prisoners and militants who have given themselves up, thereby giving Pervez the opportunity to harness a lot of power. Exploiting his position as an entrusted lawyer, Khurram is shown to aid Pervez in this process. He creates a steady supply for the force Pervez is permitted to lead by advising his clients that if anyone is detained by the military, the only way that a person can be saved from disappearing is to be registered as a prisoner. Subsequently, Pervez also helps Khurram to gain power by ensuring that he wins the election. They create the counterinsurgency force together, and, after Pervez's death at the hands of Haider, Khurram uses it to hunt individuals branded as enemies of the state like Haider.

Exploitation and manipulation of a comparable type is portrayed through the group of militants that the Indian government tries to wipe out through Operation Bulbul. This second group is led by Zahoor Hussain, who, according to Sarkar, plays a role similar to Fortinbras in the film (played by Ashwath Bhatt).[22] While the Indian government uses Khurram as the face of democracy in the election campaign, Zahoor unites people against the Indian government, openly critiquing its policies. In each of his appearances, he is shown to spread hatred against the Indian government. Though people like Haider's grandfather, Hussain Meer, remain unaffected by his hate-speeches, the vastness of Zahoor's network and his persistence throughout the film make it clear that people like him have a lasting, widespread influence over Kashmiris. If Khurram tries to win people's sympathy by reminding them how his own brother, Dr. Hilal, and their family have been victims of Kashmir's turmoil, Zahoor gathers them by posing as a rebel with a proper cause. Just like the Khurram-Pervez duo, Zahoor tries to build a force by manipulating the exploited people of Kashmir. While Khurram and Pervez keep destroying lives and shattering families in order to rise to power, Zahoor approaches those victims in order to channel their hatred against their exploiters for the purpose of his own terrorist activities.

Interestingly, the Indian army officer Brigadier Murthy's Operation Bulbul, which is supposed to establish a resistance against people like Zahoor, does not seem to differ much from Zahoor's strategies. In fact, Zahoor and Murthy both use the politics of whataboutism.[23] Zahoor justifies his actions in the scene where he meets Dr. Hilal and Hussain Meer by claiming that violence continues because of India; and when, at a press conference, a journalist asks Brigadier Murthy to comment on the disappearance of Kashmiris, Murthy replies sharply by asking him whether he counts the Kashmiri Pundits, who were forced to leave their home after being attacked by the Pakistan-backed militants and their supporters, as disappeared people. Though Murthy does not lie, his question is problematic because it implies that the present disappearances of Kashmiri Muslims are nothing compared to the troubles faced by Kashmiri Hindus in the past. Murthy's response shows that just like Zahoor, he justifies the violence of the present by recalling the past.

Apart from presenting these exploitative and manipulative leaders, the film also provides ideas about the kind of leadership that can resist such exploitations and make the Kashmiris aware of their fundamental rights through Haider Meer. Unlike the three scheming leaders, he is shown as the true face of the suffering public because he experiences their plight himself. He undergoes everything a young Kashmiri goes through after being identified as a civilian with militant connections. Yet his inherent ability to think against the grain makes him realize that the freedom that people like Pervez or Zahoor, and, by extension, the two rival nations India and Pakistan, promise to offer the Kashmiris is a scam. He emerges as a potential leader for Kashmir because he shares these insights with common people who are unable to see through the web of lies spread all over Kashmir.

In Shakespeare's *Julius Caesar* and *Hamlet*, E. A. J. Honigmann categorizes Brutus and Hamlet as "intellectual hero [es]" and describes the plays in which they feature as "tragedies of thought" where the intellectual hero is "summoned to the world of action; duty."[24] In Honigmann's opinion, while writing the character of Hamlet, Shakespeare tried to ensure that his second "intellectual hero" did not turn into a recluse like the first, that is, Brutus. Hence, Hamlet was endowed with an "outgoing, all-embracing temperament," whereas Brutus was shown to "shrin[k] from human contact."[25] *Haider* pushes this transformation further by making its Hamlet figure constantly roam around Kashmir, interacting with a wide range of people from the very beginning. Hamlet's inactivity and procrastination made him an unapproachable figure, thereby making him unfit for leadership despite his intelligence, but Haider's ability to make decisions quickly and mix with the crowd makes him a worthy representative of the common people.

It is very significant that this film begins with the disappearance, not death, of Haider's father and the demolition of their residence at the hands of the Indian army. Shakespeare's Hamlet rarely steps out of Elsinore, but Haider is never at home, firstly, because there is nothing left of his home and, secondly, because he is always driven by the hope that his father might be alive. His relentless wanderings and interactions enable him to feel the pangs of every oppressed resident of Kashmir. Drawing upon this insider's view of Kashmir, he regularly tells people what is wrong with Kashmir and, since it is clear that the words he speaks about Kashmir come out of his own experiences, he becomes a more reliable commentator on the rotten state than Hamlet is on Denmark. For instance, when Hamlet tells Rosencrantz and Guildenstern that Denmark is like a prison, he gives only a metaphoric opinion because he was not actually being treated like a prisoner. Therefore, after sharing such a poignant observation, he immediately has to add that "nothing is either good or bad but thinking makes it so. To me it [Denmark] is a prison" (2.2.249–50). Haider, however, tells his friends Salman and Salman (playing Rosencrantz and Guildenstern in the film) about Kashmir being a prison only after being frisked by the army twice without any definite reason.

Through Haider's character, Bharadwaj attempts to show how Hamlet could have influenced people around him if he had uttered his numerous words of wisdom in the form of public speeches instead of soliloquies. Therefore, unlike Hamlet, Haider is never shown to utter any soliloquies. Instead, he repeatedly tells people what is wrong with Kashmir, using a language that is less philosophical and more intelligible than Hamlet's. The film's version of the famous "to be or not to be" soliloquy is an interesting example of this. Hamlet's soliloquy might appeal to a philosophical mind for its engagement with the value of life itself, but it makes little reference to the specific problems of Denmark. Haider, however, is shown to be more concerned about the world he lives in than with thinking about "what dreams may come" during the "sleep of death" (3.1.66).

After a large public gathering at Lal Chowk, Haider does not encourage his audience to wonder whether life is worth living or not, as the Prince of

Denmark does; instead, while addressing the crowd, he offers a speech that is an interesting mix of the famous soliloquy of Act 3, Scene 1 and authentic legal information. In one breath he mentions UN Council resolution no. 47 of 1948, Article 2 of the Geneva Convention, and Article 370 of the Indian Constitution, and then he states that all of these simply ask whether Kashmiris exist or not. Preti Taneja calls this scene a critique of "the written international and national instruments of officialdom that trap Kashmiris" and explains how all the legal resolutions Haider refers to imply that the Indian government should allow Kashmiris to be themselves.[26] Since India keeps imposing restrictive policies on the Kashmiris despite all these regulations, it indeed becomes important to ask whether the Kashmiris actually exist or not. By posing this question, Haider emerges as a true leader of the Kashmiris, because instead of telling them how important it is to support India or Pakistan, like Khurram or Zahoor, he reminds them that their Kashmiri identity is facing an existential crisis due to the conflict between India and Pakistan. Haider does not seek to win public support by selling victimhood, like Khurram, or spreading hatred against India, like Zahoor. Rather, he tries to unite the oppressed Kashmiris by reminding them that neither India nor Pakistan is allowing them to express their own opinions and demands. Unfortunately, even Haider falls prey to the webs spread by militants who brainwash him by revealing how Khurram betrayed Haider's father. Haider embodies a politics of resistance that has the potential to resolve the Kashmir problem, but throughout the film he remains unaware of this potential because the vicious politics that pervade Kashmir profoundly affect his ideals, too.

Instead of making room in Kashmir for the emergence of genuinely democratic minds like Haider's, India and Pakistan directly or indirectly collaborate in the eroding of the Kashmiris' right to autonomy, which Patrick Colm Hogan explains as usurpation of "self-determination in Kashmir" by "the competing 'external' colonialisms" of Indian and Pakistani origin.[27] Addressing this issue, *Haider* shows both the nations using a common method for metaphorically and literally erasing the voice of the Kashmiris as explained before. Both the propagandist language of Pakistani militants that Zahoor speaks and the false promises made by the emerging politician Khurram, who acts as a stooge for the Indian government, have the same function in this film. Zahoor and Khurram keep repeating their words until their listeners lose their ability to think for themselves and start thinking what the Pakistani militants or the Indian government wants them to think. The politics and leadership embodied by Zahoor, Khurram, and Pervez therefore are shown as enacting the erasure of Kashmiri voices in both literal and metaphorical senses. Moreover, their efforts are shown to be aided by Bollywood, which ensures that both the Kashmiris and the people of larger India remain oblivious to the actual situation of Kashmir.

The next section of this chapter will explore the way *Haider* draws attention to this cultural politics of Bollywood films.

BOLLYWOOD AND *HAIDER*

Typical Bollywood films are rarely found to offer portrayals of the actual history of India. Rather, as suggested by Priya Joshi, "The India that Hindi film addresses is no more real than the vagabond Raj or the dacoit Gabbar Singh."[28] Such fictitious portrayals appear deeply problematic, particularly when Bollywood sticks to producing artificial narratives dominated by song, dance, and romance instead of engaging with ongoing crises. For instance, none of the Bollywood films of 1993 or 1994 engaged with the religious tension between the Hindu and Muslim communities that ensued from the demolition of Babri Masjid on December 6, 1992.[29] Bollywood took a similar stance regarding the issue of Kashmir as well, and *Haider* addresses this issue by breaking away from Bollywood's attempts to stereotype Kashmiris as well as by highlighting how Bollywood films of late 1980s and early 1990s diverted the attention of Indian people in general and Kashmiri people in particular from the problematic situation in Kashmir.

Commenting on the typical ways Bollywood has represented Kashmir so far, Nishat Haider observes: "If we trace Bollywood's shifting gaze on Kashmir, we find that its imaginings of the Valley transform from an Elysian territory of desire, romance and innocence ... to a terrain which stages a dialectic encounter between Islam, the Kashmir insurgency, and the Indian nation."[30] Nishat Haider categorizes Bollywood's Kashmir films into four main categories, namely the romantic films that appeared in the 1960s, films of the early 1990s that "focused on the Kashmiri as Muslim," the Kashmir films of mid-1990s "set against the backdrop of Kargil war," and, lastly, the films of late twentieth and early twenty-first centuries where "terrorists" appear as "objects of desire."[31] Grouping *Haider* with Vidhu Vinod Chopra's *Mission Kashmir*, Nishat Haider classifies these two as "vigilante-terrorist films" in which the survival of the terrorist figure, as in the case of Haider, gives the figure of the otherized militant Kashmiri the status of "a legitimate adversary."[32] Despite the aptness of Nishat Haider's observation on *Haider*, it seems important to explore this film's significance further, since, along with making a departure from stereotyping terrorists, Bharadwaj's film appears to offer a subtle critique of the way typical Bollywood films keep diverting the public with larger-than-life romances even in times of crisis.

Abhishek Sarkar's and Preti Taneja's analyses of *Haider* take note of the film's critical take on Bollywood from two different perspectives. After describing *Haider*'s relationship with "the heritage of Bollywood" to be "ambiguous" and taking note of the presence of commercial elements like "choreographed song and dance sequences" and what in Sarkar's opinion is an "unnecessary song between Haider and Arshia in the snow when he is recuperating from the trauma of discovering his father's killing," Sarkar opines that *"Haider* ultimately adheres to the Bollywood idiom of film-making."[33] Taneja's analysis offers an alternative reading by suggesting that the film *Haider* "questions what gets known, heard, and seen, and how and by whom" through the "deconstruction" of both "the intricate territory of international humanitarian law and action" and "its own cinematic peers."[34] *Haider*, according to Sarkar, never loses sight of its own "commercial prospects"; instead of being overt, it opts for showing "the incipient equation between Bollywood and the totalizing tendencies of the Indian state" by making veiled suggestions about the problematic role played by Bollywood films through portrayals of the Rosencrantz-Guildenstern figures.[35] In Sarkar's opinion, the film's references to the famous actor Salman Khan by the duo named "Salman and Salman" are at best a "moot point," because their addiction to unrealistic Bollywood films is only indirectly suggested.[36] Besides, the romantic song in the snowy lands of Kashmir is viewed by Sarkar as uncalled for and a sign of the film's adherence to Bollywood's norms. Taneja, however, views all these allusions to be the film's way of conveying the irresponsibility and unrealistic nature of conventional Bollywood films. Since Salman and Salman keep indulging in watching Salman Khan's *Maine Pyar Kiya* (1989) and keep referring to it and other similar films in their conversations, they are, according to Taneja, obsessed with "a compelling spectacular, light entertainment" that "promotes ... nation in its true patriotic vein." They become reminiscent of the Indian audience in general, who preferred to watch films like these during 1989, while the people of Kashmir lived under the threats of the violence ensuing from the ongoing insurgency in Kashmir.[37] The romantic song "Khul Kabhi" is shown to function in a similar manner by Taneja, as she finds the song to engage with and subvert a particular time-honored tradition of Bollywood. It begins by "echoing the many Bollywood films that use the Kashmiri landscape as a mere backdrop for love stories," but ends "with Haider and Arshia naked," which according to Taneja, "marks a critique of Bollywood prurience."[38] Taneja sums up her perspective by stating, "A critique of cinema's role in culture is here."[39] Drawing upon this particular observation and revisiting the moments referred to in her study, the present discussion will attempt to trace what other cultural role of cinema might have been critiqued by *Haider*.

Brigadier Murthy keeps mentioning the Indian government's mission of bringing normalcy to Kashmir and explains that elections are a step toward this goal. In a larger sense, Bollywood's typical Kashmiri films, which Nishat Haider discusses, in addition to the Salman Khan films referred to in Bharadwaj's film, contribute to establishing this normalcy in an indirect yet notable manner. Taneja discusses at length the way films like *Maine Pyar*

Kiya distracted the audience of larger India outside Kashmir during Kashmir's crisis, but there also are moments in *Haider* that show the people of Kashmir being affected by these films in the same manner. Salman and Salman are Kashmiris, and it is clear that the films of their idol, Salman Khan, help them escape from their reality. Even military officers watch similar films like *Sangdil Sanam* (1994) when they relax. It is also to be noted that *Haider* shows these people always watching the song-and-dance sequences in these films. According to Ajay Gehlawat, "The song in the Bollywood narrative functions as a type of 'resolution' or interruption to what has come before."[40] In *Haider*, these Salman Khan songs start functioning similarly, but, in both cases, subvert the Bollywood tradition as explained by Gehlawat. It is the tense situation of Kashmir that cuts these songs short. Salman and Salman are forced to mute their video player because Pervez calls and rebukes them for being distracted by song and dance. Likewise, the second song from *Sangdil Sanam* also gets interrupted by the army officers because a group of arrested Kashmiris are brought in. Taken together, these two songs and the manner in which they are cut short seem to represent metaphorically the inefficacy of Bollywood film escapism in regions like Kashmir.

Typical Bollywood films may be made with the aim of promoting normalcy or happiness during troubled times, but Bharadwaj shows that these attempts ultimately fail to conceal such troubles in these moments. This is also true of the romantic song sequence, which ends with Haider bursting into tears despite Arshia's attempts to distract him by dancing like typical Bollywood heroines. To sum up, just as Indian government or Pakistani militant groups attempt to replace Kashmir's actual voices with their own, so typical romantic Bollywood films in general and traditional Bollywood films about Kashmir serve to conceal the rotting state of Kashmir, which, until *Haider*'s release, only Kashmiri films like *Jashn-E-Azadi* (2008) and *Harud* (2011) at times managed to portray, because they presented "the reality in Kashmir" from the Kashmiris' perspective. *Haider* brought a notable change to this trend by making a sincere attempt to combine typical Bollywood film conventions with an authentic portrayal of Kashmir, thereby becoming the first film to bridge the difference between Bollywood's Kashmiri films and Kashmiris' films about Kashmir.[41]

Zahr Said Stauffer, in his essay "The Politicisation of Shakespeare in Arabic in Youssef Chahine's Film Trilogy," concludes his discussion on Chahine's films in which "Shakespearean allusions and characters shape personal motivations and drive the overall plot" by saying that "the character of Hamlet acts as a vehicle for a subtle resistance to a variety of norms," adding that "Chahine finds a language in Shakespeare" that enables him to speak about things which "he would not have been able to discuss if he remained in non-Shakespearean Arabic."[42] As shown in the discussion above, *Haider* may be viewed as a similar kind of adaptation, because it uses both the Prince of Denmark himself and the play in which he is featured to expose those problems of Kashmir to which false leaders and unrealistic Bollywood films never gave expression.

NOTES

1. William Shakespeare, *Hamlet*, ed. Harold Jenkins (Bangalore, India: Thomson Asia Pvt. Ltd., 2000). References in the text to act, scene, and line numbers are to this edition.
2. Joseph Barnett, "Hamlet and the Family Ideology," *Journal of the American Academy of Psychoanalysis* 3, no. 4 (October 1975): 416.
3. Barnett, "Hamlet and the Family Ideology," 413, 415.
4. William Witherle Lawrence, "Hamlet and Fortinbras," *PMLA* 61, no. 3 (1946): 673.
5. Preti Taneja, "Breaking Curfew, Presenting Utopia: Vishal Bharadwaj's *Haider* Inside the National and International Legal Framework," in *Indian Cinema Beyond Bollywood: The New Independent Cinema Revolution*, ed. Ashvin Immanuel Devasundaram, (New York: Routledge, 2018), 53.
6. Taneja, "Breaking Curfew," 54.
7. The conflict arguably started with the first Indo-Pakistani War in October 1947, when Maharaja Hari Singh formally allowed India to enter Kashmir and fight the Pakistanis who had joined the revolting Kashmiris' revolt against the Maharaja.
8. Sumantra Bose, *Contested Lands: Israel-Palestine, Kashmir, Bosnia, Cyprus, and Sri Lanka* (Cambridge, MA: Harvard University Press, 2007), I.
9. Bose, *Contested Lands*, 163.
10. Bose, *Contested Lands*, 166.
11. Tariq Ali et al., *Kashmir: The Case for Freedom* (London: Verso, 2011), vii–xiv.
12. Patrick Colm Hogan, *Imagining Kashmir: Emplotment and Colonialism* (Lincoln: University Press of Nebraska, 2016), 2.
13. Samina Yasmeen, "Pakistan's Kashmir Policy: Voices of Moderation?" *Contemporary South Asia* 12, no. 2 (2003): 187, 188.
14. The politician Dr. Syama Prasad Mukherjee had been vocal against Nehru's policies regarding Kashmir even before he formally began this movement for the inclusion of Kashmir to India. Reportedly, after meeting Prem Nath Dogra, who served as the leader of a Kashmiri group that supported Kashmir's inclusion to India, Syama Prasad decided to launch a full-fledged movement around this issue.
15. Article 370 of the Indian Constitution gave special status to Jammu and Kashmir prior to the passing of the Jammu and Kashmir Reorganisation Act, 2019 on August 5, 2019, which formally revoked this special status. Jill Cottrell, "Kashmir: The Vanishing Autonomy," in *Practising Self-Government: A Comparative Study of Autonomous Regions*, ed. Yash Ghai and Sophia Woodman (Cambridge: Cambridge University Press, 2013), 166.
16. K. Sarwar Hassan, "The Real Issue in the Present Indo-Pakistan War (1965)," in *50 Years of Indo-Pak Relations*, vol. 1, ed. Verinder Grover and Ranjana Arora (New Delhi: Deep & Deep Publications, 1999), 374.
17. Cottrell, "Kashmir," 167.
18. Bose, *Contested Lands*, 169.
19. Bose, *Contested Lands*, 171.

20. Basharat Peer, presently a New York-based writer, was born and brought up in Anantnag, the Kashmir region where the majority of *Haider*'s action takes place. His memoir about his birthplace, *Curfewed Night: A Frontline Memoir of Life, Love and War in Kashmir* (2010), was a major source of inspiration for Vishal Bharadwaj. Vishal Bharadwaj, *Haider: The Original Screenplay* (Noida, India: HarperCollins, 2014), vi.
21. Abhishek Sarkar, "*Haider* and the Nation State: Shakespeare, Bollywood, and Kashmir," *South Asian Review* 37, no. 2, (2016): 35.
22. Sarkar, "*Haider* and the Nation State," 36.
23. Whataboutism is a method of tackling accusations by making counter-accusations.
24. E. A. J. Honigmann, *Shakespeare: Seven Tragedies Revisited: The Dramatist's Manipulation of Response* (New York: Palgrave, 2002), 54.
25. Honigmann, *Shakespeare*, 55.
26. Taneja, "Breaking Curfew," 50.
27. Hogan, *Imagining Kashmir*, 5.
28. Priya Joshi, *Bollywood's India: A Public Fantasy* (New York: Columbia University Press, 2015), 2.
29. A crowd of Hindu fundamentalists, claiming the Babri Masjid built during the sixteenth century to be an encroachment of the original birthplace of Ram, the hero of the epic Ramayana, destroyed the entire mosque on December 6, 1992. As a result, severe tensions between the Hindu and the Muslim communities spread throughout India.
30. Nishat Haider, "Explorations in History, Films, and the Nation: A Study of the Representations of Kashmir Insurgency in the Hindi Mainstream Cinema," *South Asian Review* 37, no. 2 (2014): 101.
31. Haider, "Explorations," 106.
32. Haider, "Explorations," 109.
33. Sarkar, "*Haider* and the Nation State," 38.
34. Taneja, "Breaking Curfew," 55.
35. Sarkar, "*Haider* and the Nation State," 38.
36. Sarkar, "*Haider* and the Nation State," 38.
37. The insurgency signifies the revolt against the Indian government to achieve autonomy in Kashmir. The movement created a turbulent situation in 1989. Reportedly, a large number of government officials as well as common people suspected of being Indian spies were killed by the rebels for overthrowing the ruling government of Kashmir.
38. Taneja, "Breaking Curfew," 56.
39. Taneja, "Breaking Curfew," 56.
40. Ajay Gehlawat, *Reframing Bollywood: Theories of Popular Hindi Cinema* (New Delhi: Sage, 2010), 2.
41. Somjyoti Mridha, "Interrogating the Idea of India: A Study of Cinematic Representations of Kashmir Conflict from Bollywood and Beyond," *DUJES* 27 (2019). https://www.academia.edu/40035003/Interrogating_the_Idea_of_India_A_Study_of_Cinematic_Representation_of_Kashmir_Conflict_from_Bollywood_and_Beyond.
42. Zahr Said Stauffer, "The Politicisation of Shakespeare in Arabic in Youssef Chahine's Film Trilogy," *English Studies in Africa* 47, no. 2 (2004): 52.

REFERENCES

Ali, Tariq, Hilal Bhatt, Angana P. Chatterji, Habbah Khatun, Pankaj Mishra, and Arundhati Roy. *Kashmir: The Case for Freedom*. London: Verso, 2011.

Barnett, Joseph. "Hamlet and the Family Ideology." *Journal of the American Academy of Psychoanalysis* 3, no. 4 (October 1975): 405–17.

Bharadwaj, Vishal. *Haider: The Original Screenplay*. Noida, India: HarperCollins, 2014.

Bharadwaj, Vishal, dir. *Haider*. Mumbai: VB Pictures, 2014. DVD, 160 min.

Bose, Sumantra. *Contested Lands: Israel-Palestine, Kashmir, Bosnia, Cyprus, and Sri Lanka*. Cambridge, MA: Harvard University Press, 2007.

Cottrell, Jill. "Kashmir: The Vanishing Autonomy." In *Practising Self-Government: A Comparative Study of Autonomous Regions*, edited by Yash Ghai and Sophia Woodman, 163–99. Cambridge: Cambridge University Press, 2013. doi:10.1017/CBO9781139088206.006.

Gehlawat, Ajay. *Reframing Bollywood: Theories of Popular Hindi Cinema*. New Delhi: Sage, 2010.

Haider, Nishat. "Explorations in History, Films, and the Nation: A Study of the Representations of Kashmir Insurgency in the Hindi Mainstream Cinema." *South Asian Review* 37, no. 2 (2014): 95–115.

Hassan, K. Sarwar. "The Real Issue in the Present Indo-Pakistan War (1965)." In *50 Years of Indo-Pak Relations*, vol. 1, edited by Verinder Grover and Ranjana Arora, 369–76. New Delhi: Deep & Deep Publications, 1999.

Hogan, Patrick Colm. *Imagining Kashmir: Emplotment and Colonialism*. Lincoln: University Press of Nebraska, 2016.

Honigmann, E. A. J. *Shakespeare: Seven Tragedies Revisited: The Dramatist's Manipulation of Response*. New York: Palgrave, 2002.

Joshi, Priya. *Bollywood's India: A Public Fantasy*. New York: Columbia University Press, 2015.

Lawrence, William Witherle. "Hamlet and Fortinbras." *PMLA* 61, no. 3 (1946): 673–98.

Mridha, Somjyoti. "Interrogating the Idea of India: A Study of Cinematic Representations of Kashmir Conflict from Bollywood and Beyond." *DUJES* 27 (2019). https://www.academia.edu/40035003/Interrogating_the_Idea_of_India_A_Study_of_Cinematic_Representation_of_Kashmir_Conflict_from_Bollywood_and_Beyond.

Peer, Basharat. *Curfewed Night: A Frontline Memoir of Life, Love and War in Kashmir*. Random House, 2010.

Sarkar, Abhishek. "*Haider* and the Nation State: Shakespeare, Bollywood, and Kashmir." *South Asian Review* 37, no. 2 (2016): 29–46.

Shakespeare, William. *Hamlet*. Edited by Harold Jenkins. Bangalore, India: Thomson Asia Pvt. Ltd., 2000.

Stauffer, Zahr Said. "The Politicisation of Shakespeare in Arabic in Youssef Chahine's Film Trilogy." *English Studies in Africa* 47, no. 2 (2004): 41–55.

Taneja, Preti. "Breaking Curfew, Presenting Utopia: Vishal Bharadwaj's *Haider* Inside the National and International Legal Framework." In *Indian Cinema Beyond Bollywood: The New Independent Cinema Revolution*, 46–65, edited by Ashvin Immanuel Devasundaram. New York: Routledge, 2018.

Yasmeen, Samina. "Pakistan's Kashmir Policy: Voices of Moderation?" *Contemporary South Asia* 12, no. 2 (2003): 187–202.

9. The Shakespeare Company Japan and regional self-fashioning

Tetsuhito Motoyama and Fumiaki Konno

Japan continues to struggle with a rapidly declining rurality with no effective solution in sight. In 2014, the Japan Policy Council released the "Masuda Report," which warned that half of all Japanese municipalities will disappear by 2040.[1] Some blame this dire prospect on former prime minister Koizumi Jun'ichirō's (1942–; in office 2001–2006) structural reforms that made it the responsibility of the already enervated municipalities to save themselves; in other words, reforms that "amount to nothing more than a 'cutting off and throwing away' of rural areas."[2] Others criticize the "clearly top-down structure in the plans" to revitalize these areas teetering on the brink of collapse.[3] The actual situation is a little more complex. According to sociologist Yamashita Yūsuke, the central government, through such pronouncements as the "Masuda Report," paralyzes provincial areas with the fear of no longer being able to operate as a municipality; it then offers substantial economic investments for projects that will not necessarily benefit that particular region but will further the interests of the central government.[4] At the root of the problem is the undoing of the ties among local people. Without these ties, municipalities will become nothing more than targets for the central government and corporations looking to exploit them for local resources and geographical advantages.[5]

One region that has been experiencing this especially intensely is Tohoku, which consists of the six prefectures on the northern end of mainland Japan. Years of rapid population decline had already taken its toll on the region when the Great East Japan Earthquake (also known as 3.11) on May 11, 2011, left it in a state of devastation. The government and officials responded to this tragedy by proposing policies and measures oblivious to the actual needs of the locals.[6] What such official policies have failed to accomplish, a theater company has continued to do since its inception in 1992. This was when Shimodate Kazumi (1955–) formed the Shakespeare Company Japan (SCJ) in Sendai, the capital of Miyagi Prefecture. What sets the SCJ apart from other troupes is the fact that Shimodate translates Shakespeare into the local dialect and transposes the plays to the historical past of the Tohoku region. They have toured most of their productions across Tohoku, reaching out to people who otherwise would never have seen Shakespeare on stage. What is also of interest is that none of the 30 founding members or the 300 supporters of the company were actors; they were simply people interested in seeing Shakespeare performed.[7] With its focus thus on the general public, the SCJ staged 12 plays before 3.11; a trilogy set in a fictitious hot spring resort immediately following the earthquake; and most recently, an adaptation of *Othello*.[8] A look at the SCJ's work from these three periods will demonstrate the role art can play in tackling the kinds of problems provincial regions face by bringing people together as a community, bringing to light their shared experiences, and breathing new life into the local culture.

SCJ productions before the Great East Japan Earthquake challenged the cultural and political dominance that the capital has enjoyed over the Tohoku region. By translating Shakespeare into the Tohoku dialect, Shimodate hoped not only to celebrate a dialect that has long been deemed inferior to "standardized Japanese," but also to elevate it into a literary language. These adaptations, by being set in Tohoku's historical past, impressed upon the audience the resilience of local identity by bringing attention to how the recalcitrant people of Tohoku had historically resisted the control of the central government.

Shimodate has identified playwright Kinoshita Junji (1914–2006), who adapted the Sado Island dialect to write *Twilight Crane* (1949), as an inspiration for his decision to translate Shakespeare into the Tohoku dialect.[9] According to Shimodate, Kinoshita did so with the conviction that it was the playwright's duty to "discover the strength, character, and fecundity of a dialect and to incorporate its appeal into the Japanese language."[10] Kinoshita is also known for translating 15 Shakespeare plays. When doing so, he focused upon Shakespeare's ability to integrate the everyday vernacular of the groundlings into sophisticated language, which, he believed, awakened them to the breathtaking vibrancy of their own language.[11] Shimodate, likewise, attempts to dazzle his audience with the richness of the Tohoku dialect through his translations of Shakespeare. As Sauzier-Uchida Emi writes, "Language is so deeply linked to our thoughts, lives, and culture that it is the source of our self-identity."[12] An individual who uses a dialect is attempting "to 'construct' and 'deconstruct' their identities … as well as 'stage' their identity … by drawing on salient linguistic resources associated with a known local identity."[13] Moreover, a performance of a text written in a dialect brings to the fore "the shared cultural associations the performer aims to convey by using salient features" of the dialect.[14] This can very much be seen in Shimodate's translations, which are an affirmation of both the language and the identity of the Tohoku people.

Use of the local dialect in the translations also carries political implications that impact the identity of people from the provinces. In the eighteenth century, scholars and poets such as Motoori Norinaga (1730–1801) and Koshigaya Gozan (1717–88) celebrated provincial dialects as being a more authentic form of Japanese, unadulterated by the influence of Chinese that was seen in the central areas.[15] The pressure to modernize the nation in the mid-nineteenth century, however, led the government to unify the language into a single, standardized mother tongue. What resulted was "the educated citizens of Tokyo enjoying the privileges of the linguistic ruling class while the aberrant forms of the language and those who spoke them being associated with the backward, the uncultured, and the parochial and becoming subjected to calls for eradication and outright discrimination."[16] In other words, the dialect carries with it memories of the suppression that the central government inflicted upon the provincial regions; Shimodate, through his translations, not only reclaims the linguistic heritage of the Tohoku region, but also rejoices in its diversity.

A quick look at *Macbeth of Mt. Osore* (1999), as an example from an early SCJ production, illustrates Shimodate's craft in bringing together the disparate variations of the local vernacular. He combines expressions from three different dialects of the Tohoku region to translate the multiple meanings of "Fair is foul, and foul is fair" (1.1.9):[17] "*Ē wa warī, warī wa ē/ megoi wa meguse, meguse wa megoi/ mandoro wa kurasumi, kurasumi wa mandoro.*" *Ē* and *warī* respectively mean *good* and *bad* in the Sendai dialect, while, throughout the Tohoku region, *megoi* describes that which is visually pleasing and *meguse* that which is unsightly; and *mandoro* and *kaurasumi* are the equivalent of *bright* and *dark* in the Tsugaru dialect.[18] As will be discussed later, the woman who delivers these lines serves as a medium for the dead; the mixing of the dialects, therefore, suggests she is channeling the voice of dead souls from across the region. A multitude of distinct dialects co-exist in Tohoku, and Shimodate creates a language for the theater that, while being an artificial construct in that it mixes expressions that are not found together in everyday speech, reflects this linguistic diversity. What may appear to be, on one level, appropriation, is actually a reminder of the regional diversity which official policies have attempted to obliterate by promoting the idea of a unified nation.

The use of dialects is not the only way *Macbeth of Mt. Osore* underscores this marginalization of the provincial; it does so by transposing Shakespeare's play to a region in Tohoku where tensions persisted between the court in Kyoto and the Ezo people in the eleventh century.[19] A number of critics have discussed Shakespeare's play in terms of the unification of Scotland and England under James I (1566–1625), though there is no consensus as to where the play stands on this issue.[20] In a 1604 parliamentary speech, a few years prior to the staging of *Macbeth*, James voiced his desire to bring together the two nations by referring to them as the two halves of his life, with nothing "so injurious to me ... as to cut asunder the one half of me from the other."[21] Tiffany Grace argues that the play "supported James's own rhetorical strategies, confronting British divisiveness by locating regenerative power in the figure of the royal Anglo-Scottish male."[22] Others argue that the play questions or even discounts James's "imperialist and absolutist thought" by focusing on Macbeth's description of the witches' predictions of his becoming king, "happy prologues to the swelling act / Of the imperial theme" (1.3.130–1), and on Shakespeare's excision of the support Macbeth receives for the regicide in Holinshed, the source of the play; and there are those who perceive the play as forcing upon James, who claimed to possess a "quasi-divine perspective" that could thwart treasonous acts, the role of a passive audience member witnessing Macbeth's treason, so as to impress upon him "the limits of proper rule and authority."[23] In more recent discussions, the play has been read as presenting "colliding and contradictory positions on the Union"; or as reworking the source material so it could "bear double implications that allowed the playwright to equivocate with his pro-union monarch and largely anti-union audience."[24]

In any case, the unification of the provincial outskirts with the central government is a pivotal issue in *Macbeth of Mt. Osore*, as well. At the opening of the play, Fujiwara Danka (Duncan), who is of mixed ancestry, belonging both to the Fujiwara clan that controls the court and to the Ezo, rules over the Oshu region in Tohoku. Kiyohara Kōdō (Cawdor) conspires with the Ezo to overthrow Danka. As in Shakespeare's version, mayhem follows until Makubesu (Macbeth) is defeated and order is restored: Maroka (Malcolm), Danka's first-born and, thus, a symbol of the union between the court and the Ezo, becomes lord of the region.

The play's political stance toward unification, however, is much less ambiguous than in Shakespeare's version, mainly because of the *itakos* (witches). An itako is a shamanistic figure closely linked with Mt. Osore, one of the three most important spiritual spots of Japan; she is a blind woman who performs prayers, delivers oracles, and, most famously, channels the dead in acts known as *kuchiyose*.[25] This act of kuchiyose differentiates her from a witch. Clark Stuart notes, "All writers, including James ... admitted that in witchcraft the real agent of *maleficium*, true or illusory, was the Devil," while Garry Wills describes them as serving the "order of Hell," and Anthony Harris explains that they were seen as plotting "the ultimate triumph of Satan."[26] Itakos, however, do not serve a demon, but give voice to those who are no longer living. It is particularly significant that when they first appear in the play, the Buddhist chant used to pray for the salvation of dead souls is heard (Shimodate, 2016, vol. 3, 6). Then Banko (Banquo), encountering them with Makubesu, remarks, "They are itakos. It's said that the souls of the dead all gather on Mt. Osore. Rumor has it, though, that the voices of the dead can't be heard until forty-nine days after they've died. It won't work if you've just kicked the bucket" (Shimodate, 13).[27] The implication is that these itakos are doing the bidding of the local people who have, in the past, lost their lives in struggles against the forces from the court. That the play began its run in the Osore-zan Bodai-ji Temple of Mt. Osore in August 1999 adds to the reality effect of these voices from the past. It is telling that the play ends not with Maroka (Malcolm), heir to the Fujiwara clan, assuming control over the realm, but with the itakos predicting that Makudafu (Macduff) of the Ezo people will rise to power. After Maroka announces that his coronation will take place in Taga Castle, the scene changes, and the itakos chant amidst fog and wind. A spinning windmill on the stage suggests there will be another change in political tides. The itakos' words describe the act of being dragged through four different kinds of hell and of rowing toward the gokuraku-jōdo paradise. They narrate the fate of not only Makudafu, who then appears, but also the local people who have been killed in battle and thus been silenced. The play ends with Makudafu grinning as he hears the words, "It shall come to be, that you the great lord will be" (Shimodate, 111). Assimilation of the region under the reign of a lord who is himself an embodiment of the unification of the court and the Ezo is not to be. The souls of the locals have been stirring unrest in the region from beyond the grave to ensure that it is not subjugated to the court. *Macbeth of Mt. Osore*, thus, is a work that aims to restore the voice of the region and remind the people of their history of resistance against the meddling forces of the central government.

Though still focused on the identity of the local people, the Hot Spring Trilogy that the SCJ produced immediately after the Great East Japan Earthquake of 2011 was not so much about Tohoku regaining its voice as it was about bringing the people torn asunder back together as a community.[28] Tohoku has faced countless calamities and challenges since the Great East Japan Earthquake, ranging from the nuclear power plant meltdown in Fukushima to the eviction of evacuees from temporary housing. The reconstruction of areas devastated by the disaster has proven to be a disaster in itself because it has been driven by central government officials instead of local residents. Yamaori Tetsuo suggests that the name chosen for the earthquake epitomizes the root of the problem. The Japan Meteorological Agency first referred to it as the Off the Pacific Coast of Tohoku Earthquake, yet the name that has stuck makes no mention of the specific region where it occurred. This omission is a sign of the mindset at work: one that is concerned with the good of the nation, which is a synecdoche for Tokyo, the center of the nation's political and economic power.[29] While some bureaucrats and experts dismissively asserted that it was not worth investing in regions that had already been on the verge of collapse because of their dwindling population, others have insisted on "creative reconstruction" that aims not to restore but improve through a new stage of industrialization.[30] Journalist Furukawa Miho has documented the various plans proposed by governor Murai Yoshio (1960–; in office 2005–) of Miyagi Prefecture and the central ministries, which determine what kind of projects are worthy of financial aid; these plans, ranging from the Tohoku Medical Megabank Project, whose mission is to collect the genetic data of the local people, to the creation of a fishery revival zone that would allow outside capital access to waters hitherto protected by regional fishing rights, are designed to stimulate the local economy in the short run at the expense of the needs of the local people and a more fundamentally sustainable development of the region.[31] Of particular interest is the privatization of Sendai Airport, which may maximize efficiency and generate profit, but, at the same time, undermines the lives of the local people by forcing local businesses to close and increasing the numbers of underpaid precarious workers.[32] All this is in line with former prime minister Abe Shinzo's (1954–; in office 2006–2007 and 2012–2020) plan to create national strategic special zones and boost industrial and economic competitiveness. During the 2014 World Economic Forum, Abe announced his determination to see this plan through by remarking, "Over the next two years, no vested interests will remain immune from my drill." Furukawa notes that included among such "vested interests" are "the communities that the local people have established over long periods of time and the very foundations for their livelihoods."[33]

One of the main reasons the locals have not been able to take the initiative in rebuilding their towns is because they can no longer function as a community. Yamashita is of the opinion that despite Tohoku's long history of refusing to succumb to central authorities, as seen with the Ezo, the Tohoku people now rely on the government to solve their problems; this has allowed the government to take the reins in proposing these projects.[34] A look at another case helps explain why locals have become so compliant after 3.11. The city of Shiogama, located at the southern end of Miyagi's Matsushima Bay, became a special zone for reconstruction in August 2012. This allowed the AEON Group, a corporate group of retail and financial businesses, to receive substantial tax incentives and open a mall there in March 2014.[35] Although AEON set up talks with the local shop associations prior to building the mall, local business owners had been hit so hard by the earthquake and tsunami that they were unable to put up a united front against disaster capitalism.[36] Furukawa explains that local markets are where people gather spontaneously and "the land itself and the people are brought together and become a 'space' for the *locals* instead of for *producers* and *consumers*"; in other words, these projects are severing the bonds among the locals.[37] Authorities and corporations exploit disaster-stricken areas because the locals are unable to come together as a community and protest. Without an effective community, locals are at the mercy of large corporations and governmental policies, which then further disband the community. Yamashita warns, "When other bodies take over because the disaster-stricken community is unable to function, what results is a puppet government or a colony."[38]

It is this "space" where local people can feel connected as a community that the SCJ provided with its productions of the Hot Spring Trilogy. The SCJ toured the trilogy throughout community centers, welfare centers, schools, museums, and temporary housing sites across Tohoku, in areas hard-hit by the earthquake, and offered the performances free of charge.[39] Shimodate, who had been ready to leave behind the theater after the disaster, recounts the moment he realized he could not do so: in Sendai, immediately after the earthquake, an elderly woman accosted him on the street and bid him, "Are you quitting Shakespeare? Don't quit. It's something I always look forward to. But stage something that's not sad and not long."[40] What followed were repeated requests from residents of areas where the SCJ toured for the company to return with more performances.[41] Unlike the policies that the government introduced after 3.11, the trilogy was produced in response to a clear demand from the locals. The works aimed to lift the spirits of the people, but they achieved much more than this. Shimodate took *The New Romeo and Juliet*, an abridged version of Shakespeare's play with a happy ending, to Onagawa-cho, a fishing port on the south end of Matsushima Bay. After the performance, an elderly woman came up to him. This woman, who had lost her shop and everyone she had known in the tsunami, told him she felt the play was about her and her late husband when they had been young.[42] Someone who had been completely at a loss found a world with which she could connect. Even more significantly, though, Shimodate's work in the theater had given these people opportunities to interact with him, the young actors, and the staff of his company.[43] A class on theater that Shimodate teaches at Tohoku University attracted over 250 students in 2011; when he asked them, "Why the theater now?" many of them told him that the disaster made them realize the significance of human interaction.[44] Yamashita argues that the key to reviving these communities is understanding the importance of "human interaction, festivals, culture, school, and work," and what the productions of SCJ's Hot Spring Trilogy inspired was just such contact among people.[45] It was not simply the performances, though, that brought people out of their isolation; the plays themselves, by remembering the earthquake and triggering a sense of nostalgia for a shared local history as well as the "happier times" of the Showa period (1926–89), made audience members aware of their connection with each other, as will be made clear by examining *The New Romeo and Juliet* (2012–13).

In the play, the *matagi* hunter (Friar Lawrence) remembers an earthquake and tsunami from the past: "With that catastrophic earthquake, the mountain before me collapsed like it had turned to water, like the mountain became the sea. My dad was in Sendai and survived, but my mum hung her three-year-old child from that big beech tree and was washed away."[46] He then consoles his friend with a failing memory: "It's not a bad thing, to have your ears shut off and your mind go foggy. We can't go on living without forgetting." To this his friend replies, "Forgetting's not good. We could be washed away by the tsunami again" (Shimodate, 2016, vol. 1, 48). This reference to an earthquake and tsunami would be a reminder for the audience of the tragedy they themselves had just experienced. What adds even more significance to this scene is the fact that it is the matagi who speaks about the past. Matagi hunters, with their worship of the mountain gods, incantations, and ritualistic skinning of the animals they hunt, are mystical figures closely tied to the land.[47] With the building of dams, which destroyed their settlements, most have disappeared and been replaced by faux hunters who cater to tourists.[48] Matagis have thus become figures associated with the sacred past of the region, which has for the most part become a memory. Ory Bartal explains that through traumatic memories represented in art, private memory finds "its context in the narrative of collective memory," for the representation "formulates a living connection with the past as it gives presence to the memory, which is vital to the foundation and shaping of a sense of identity of individuals and groups."[49] Bracha Lichtenberg Ettinger discusses this in much more abstract terms when proposing that works that deal with trauma trigger "a certain jointness … co-emergence with-one-another that is not assimilation and fusion … a web of connections inside and outside the individual's limits."[50] In other words, art is a means to connect the individual to the common memory and transform the traumatic memory into something shared; to forget would wash the individual away both literally, when the next tsunami hits, and figuratively, back into his or her isolation.

It is not only with this nod to 3.11 that the play impresses upon audience members their interconnectedness. The names of pop stars, songs, films, and television programs from the mid-1950s to the mid-1970s abound in *The New Romeo and Juliet*. These two decades from the Showa period have come to hold a special place in the popular imagination, in what is called Showa nostalgia. Fred Davies notices that in the face of "some untoward historic event or intrusive social change, it can be seen how at the most elemental level collective nostalgia acts to restore ... a sense of socio-historic continuity."[51] In his seminal study, Hidaka Katsuyuki describes Showa nostalgia as "a search for any fundamental meaning or lesson that would be helpful for contemporary people who live in an uncertain modernity."[52] In the case of Tohoku post-3.11, this uncertainty originates in the isolation of individuals. One of the features of Showa nostalgia in the new millennium, according to Kōno Kōhei's extensive survey of the phenomenon, is a sense of familiarity experienced, not on an individual level, but shared across society.[53] It is this experience of individuals brought together through a sense of continuity with others that the play taps into with the countless nods to Showa period popular culture. What the official policies and projects have disregarded and destroyed, the Hot Spring Trilogy aimed to restore.

The SCJ's most recent work, *Ainu Othello*, has delved deeper into the question of what comprises the local community and where it stands in relation to the world in order to strengthen and reinvigorate it. It focuses on the presence of the indigenous Ainu in the history of the region. Although the Ainu are most commonly associated with Hokkaido, the northern island of Japan, remains of Ainu culture have been found in the Tohoku region from the fourth century, when it is believed cold weather forced the people to migrate from Hokkaido. The persecution of the Ainu, which began in the fifth century, also occurred in the Tohoku region. Most notably, in 1756 and 1809, the Hirosaki Domain in the northernmost area of Tohoku implemented an assimilation policy that attempted to erase the culture from the region. Only recently have the Ainu begun to reclaim their identity and rights. The Ainu were finally officially recognized as an indigenous people, first by the Sapporo District Court in a 1997 lawsuit regarding land for a dam, then by the Japanese Diet in 2008.[54]

Shimodate sets his play in the nineteenth century when Russia frequently attacked the northern part of Japan called Ezogashima; Osero (Othello) is an Ainu admiral who, with the help of 2,000 samurais and their families, protects the region (2016, vol. 5, 4–5). The play, initially called *Atuy Othello*, went through several incarnations.[55] The first production, which began in late 2010, was cut short by 3.11. A chance meeting with Ainu artist Akibe Debo in 2016 drastically altered the work. At the suggestion of Akibe, Yago (Iago), the villain who plants the seed of doubt in Osero's mind and destroys his life, came to be partly Ainu; Akibe co-directed the new version, now called *Ainu Othello* and brought in Pirikap, an Ainu dance troupe, to introduce traditional dance and music into the play.[56] In 2019, the SCJ took the play to the Tara Arts Theatre in London. Jatinder Verma, artistic director of Tara Arts, reshaped the production, integrating the Ainu performances into the narrative; he dispersed the Ainu performances, which had been grafted onto the beginning of the play as a non-diegetic opening act, to crucial moments in the action, turning the Pirikap dancers into a kind of chorus.

While Akibe's initial aim in giving Yago an Ainu background was to avoid a romanticized portrayal of the Ainu, Verma gave new significance to the racial issue by highlighting the tension between the Ainu and those who are mixed-race.[57] For example, in the opening scene, Yago's wife, Emiria (Emilia), observed from afar the Ainu nuptial ceremony that the Ainu chorus celebrated for Osero and Dezuma (Desdemona). Although the ceremony was part of her cultural heritage, she would not step out of the shadows and into the festivities.

Similarly, although Bianka (Bianca), the mistress of one of Osero's men, was partly Ainu, she entered the stage mockingly humming the music of the Ainu chorus and cast a disdainful glance toward them. Such scenes transform the nature of Yago's denunciation of Osero, repeated twice in the play: "I can't endure Osero. I am *rataskep*, or rather half so, but look at me. And look at him, he is wise, *pawetok*—eloquent, *rametok*—brave, *siretok*—dashing, and with dignity."[58] With the mixed-race characters constantly rejecting the indigenous in the play, Yago's lines seem not so much to be about his resentment toward the discrepancy in their social standing despite a shared heritage. Instead, his desire to obliterate the Ainu within himself drives him to loathe even the most admirable of the indigenous people, as if even the greatest virtues will not make up for this ethnic heritage. *Ainu Othello* thus serves as a reminder of how Tohoku has failed to embrace the Ainu culture that had, for centuries, been part of the region. The SCJ's most recent work has drawn attention to the Ainu presence in the Tohoku region as it recognizes the diversity that has existed in, yet long been erased from, the community.

The SCJ's production of *Ainu Othello*, while bringing to light what has been suppressed within the regional history in this way, also looked outwards; by engaging with the wider world, it has become a successful example of how the arts of an endangered culture can be revitalized. Shimodate's initial aim in creating this play was to respond to a challenge that came to him in a dream during a trip to Hokkaido: "Are the Ainu simply serving an ornamental purpose for you? Come on, make it about the Ainu."[59] Through his collaboration with Akibe and Verma, however, the work became more than just an effort to grasp the reality of a marginalized culture; it heralded the potential of that culture to evolve. Akibe incorporated into the performance Ainu dance and music, which Verma, through discussions with and input from the dance troupe, then made part of the narrative. With their contributions, not only was the diversity of the regional identity brought to the forefront, but the Ainu cultural traditions also took on new meanings. For example, when Yago declared his resolve to destroy Osero, "The die is cast and the plan has come thus far … To bring this monstrous birth to light, I'll need help from hell and night," the Ainu chorus surrounded him and danced the *futtare cuy*, which involves the dancers repeatedly flipping their long hair up and down. The choreography represents a gust blowing through pine trees; in this scene, however, it came to convey both the tragedy approaching with tempestuous momentum and the dark forces descending upon Yago to propel him forward with his scheme. Similarly, the chorus danced the *haraki*, a reenactment of cranes flapping their wings, when Osero sealed the fate of Dezuma with the words, "Blood, blood, blood!" The cranes became a harbinger of evil, and the cries that accompanied the dance were later repeated as Osero strangled his wife. By becoming part of the narrative, these dances took on new life and the dancers explored new possibilities and meanings for their art without uprooting it from its traditions. When Shimodate welcomed Akibe into his creative process, the generally unacknowledged presence of the marginalized came to the forefront of the play; Shimodate then placed the work in the hands of Verma, who, approaching the Ainu culture from an outsider's viewpoint, succeeded in breathing new life into their traditions by suggesting ways in which the traditions could engage with other forms of art and evolve.

This creative process is a lesson for governmental projects that declare that Tohoku's future depends upon its globalization. To give a much debated example, in May 2014 the Japan Policy Council released a proposal promoting global research centers in provincial areas as a means to generate employment. As a result, governor Tasso Takuya of Iwate Prefecture in Tohoku has offered land for the International Linear Collider, an international project to build a tunnel where the Big Bang can be artificially recreated. Not only does this disregard the lessons that should have been learned from the Fukushima nuclear meltdown, but it also fails to consider what the local community needs in the long run. Yamashita criticizes the governmental chicanery that inveigles provincial areas into conceding vested rights in exchange for the promise of foreign investment.[60] The Masuda Report clearly states that the only provincial areas worth saving are those with "the capacity to procure foreign currency."[61]

SCJ's *Ainu Othello*, on the other hand, has shown that globalization must start with an eye on local people, their environment, and their history. Internationalization driven by national agendas can be, as Anthony Kwame Appiah writes, "charged with effacing local partialities and solidarities, with promulgating norms that undermine local traditions and customs—with being a force of homogeneity."[62] The creative process of *Ainu Othello* demonstrates how "a citizen of the world can make the world better by making some local place better, even though that place need not be the place of her literal or original citizenship."[63] One of the driving forces behind the SCJ has been its plan to build a "Globe Theatre" in the Tohoku region; Shimodate envisions this as a space that will give birth to the kind of synergy created during the London production of *Ainu Othello*. In a personal interview during the rehearsals in London, Shimodate spoke of hopes that it would attract productions from across Asia and beyond. Works that tackle local issues from around the world may evolve in unexpected ways as they, in turn, revitalize the arts in Tohoku.[64]

By engaging with the local communities, along with their cultural and historical heritage, in ways that authorities and the central government have failed to do, the SCJ demonstrates what the arts have to offer toward making a difference for struggling communities. They have been encouraging the Tohoku people to regain their voice, especially in relation to the central government; to come together as a community; and to reevaluate their identity in terms of both their own history and the global community. SCJ's works have shown that Shakespeare can be a catalyst through which the local language, history, and culture produce "cultural hybridities"; and it is through this productive liminality that "a subversive strategy of subaltern agency … negotiates its own authority."[65] By adhering to their belief that "Shakespeare belongs not to Tokyo, scholars, or thespians, but to everyone," the SCJ transforms the works into something that represents the voice of the marginalized and points to the potential that lies therein.[66]

Whether because of the long history of the reception of his works in Japan or the appreciation of the works as cultural capital, Shakespeare, perhaps more than any Japanese playwright, has continued to appeal to and inspire the people. To experience their voice and their history reshaping Shakespeare's works is, for those who have been marginalized, to recognize the power their voice holds and to be given a chance to come together again as a community. It is also to witness one's own cultural heritage converging with an outward-looking perspective and to be presented with a means to evolve and be heard. In other words, with the SCJ's productions of Shakespeare, the Tohoku people can reconfirm their ties to one another and to the world and see, as has not been possible with governmental policies, a way forward into the future.

NOTES

1. Yūsuke Yamashita, *Chihō shōmetsu no wana: "Masuda Report" to jinkō genshō shakai no shōtai* [The Extinction of Provincial Communities as a Trap: The "Masuda Report" and the Truth about a Society Undergoing Depopulation], Chikuma Shinsho 1100 (Tokyo: Chikuma Shobō, 2014), 12. The name of this report derives from former minister of general affairs Masuda Hiroya. All Japanese names in the text (except for those of the two authors), following the Japanese practice, will be in the order of the family then the given name.
2. Luke Dilley, Sae Shinzato, and Mitsuyoshi Ando, "Revitalising the Rural in Japan: Working through the Power of Place," *Electronic Journal of Contemporary Japanese Studies* 17, no. 3 (2017), http://japanesestudies.org.uk/ejcjs/vol17/iss3/dilley.html.
3. Makoto Sakamoto, "'Chihō sōsei' to nōson: Nōson chiiki no kadai to tembō" ['Regional Revitalization' and Agricultural Villages: The Problems and Prospects of Agricultural Areas], in *Chihō sōsei to jichitai* [Regional Revitalization and Municipalities], ed. the Japan Association for the Study of Local Government, Chihō Jichi Sōsho [Local Government Series] 29 (Tokyo: Keibundō, 2018), 6.
4. Yamashita, *Chihō shōmetsu no wana*, 83–4.
5. Yamashita, *Chihō shōmetsu no wana*, 281. Yūsuke Yamashita and Toshiyuki Kanai, *Chihō sōsei no shōtai: Naze chiiki seisaku wa shippai suru no ka* [*The Truth about Regional Revitalization: Why Regional Policies Fail*], Chikuma shinsho 1150 (Tokyo: Chikuma Shobō, 2015), 138.
6. There are some areas within Tohoku, such as Iwate Prefecture, where the locals have successfully taken it upon themselves to rebuild their community. Miho Furukawa, *Tohoku Shock Doctrine* (Tokyo: Iwanami Shoten, 2015), 49.

7.   Kazumi Shimodate, *Hamuretto, Tohoku ni tatsu: Tohoku-ben Shakespeare gekidan no bōken* [Hamlet, on the Tohoku Stage: The Adventures of the Tohoku Dialect Shakespeare Theater Company] (Tokyo: Kokusho Kankōkai, 2017), 17.
8.   The Hot Spring Trilogy consists of *The New Romeo and Juliet* (2012–13), *The New King Lear* (2013–14), and *The New Merchant of Venice* (2014–15). For further details see footnote 28 below. For details about the SCJ and its work, see Fumiaki Konno, "General Introduction," "*The New Romeo and Juliet*," and "Appendix 1," in *Re-imagining Shakespeare in Contemporary Japan: A Selection of Japanese Theatrical Adaptations of Shakespeare*, ed. Tetsuhito Motoyama, Rosalind Fielding, and Fumiaki Konno (London and New York: Bloomsbury, 2021).
9.   Kazumi Shimodate, *Tohoku Shakespeare Kyakuhonshū* [Selected Scripts from Shakespeare in Tohoku], vol. 3 (Tokyo: Koko Shuppan, 2016), iv.
10. Kazumi Shimodate, "Kinoshita Junji no 'geijutsugo': *Othello* shoyaku (1947 nen) kara *Hamlet* (1970 nen) made" [The 'Artistic Language' of Kinoshita Junji: From the First Translation of *Othello* (1947) to the Translation of *Hamlet* (1970)]," *Tohoku Gakuin Daigaku eigo eibungaku kenkyūjo kiyō* [*Tohoku Gakuin University Journal for English and English Literature*], 26 (1997): 96.
11. Shimodate, "Kinoshita Junji no 'geijutsugo,'" 93–4. In addition to translating and publishing 15 Shakespeare plays with Kōdansha, Kinoshita also released a translation of *Richard III* with Iwanami Bunko in 2002 and a translation of John Barton's and Peter Hall's *The War of the Roses*, which contains *Henry VI*, in 1997. Kenji Ōba, *Shakespeare no hon'yaku* [Translating Shakespeare] (Tokyo: Kenkyūsha, 2009), 204.
12. Emi Sauzier-Uchida, "Nihon no gengo seisaku ni okeru tōitsusei to tayōsei" [Unity and Diversity of Language Policy in Japan], *Kyōyō shogaku kenkyū* [*Journal of Liberal Arts*] 125 (2008): 51.
13. Reem Bassiouney, "Introduction," in *Identity and Dialect Performance: A Study of Communities and Dialects*, ed. Reem Bassiouney (London and New York: Routledge, 2018), 3.
14. Bassiouney, "Introduction," 3.
15. Hiraku Shimoda, "Tongue-Tied: The Making of a 'National Language' and the Discovery of Dialects in Meiji Japan," *The American Historical Review* 115, no. 3 (2010): 720.
16. Sauzier-Uchida, "Nihon no gengo seisaku ni okeru tōitsusei to tayōsei," 59. Shimoda in "Tongue-Tied" explains that there was a turning of the tide once more in the Showa era (1926–89), "when the politics of rural revitalization redefined 'regions' and their practices once more." For example, in 1935, "the editors of The Fukushima Dialect Dictionary could proudly declare, 'The greatness of this region's dialect is the greatness of our ancestors'" (730–1). The works of the SCJ can be considered as an extension of this movement to revalorize the provincial areas of Japan.
17. All references to this play are from *Macbeth*, ed. Sandra Clark, and Pamela Mason, The Arden Shakespeare Third Series (London and New York: Bloomsbury, 2015).
18. Shimodate, *Hamuretto, Tohoku ni tatsu*, 71.
19. *Ezo* or *Emishi* referred to northern people who were not part of the centralized, hierarchical state known as *ritsuryō kokka* between the seventh and the eleventh centuries. Initially, the term did not point to a single ethnic group, but it later became synonymous with the indigenous people known today as the Ainu. Isao Tsutsui, *Ainugo chimei to Nippon rettō-jin ga kita michi* [Ainu Place Names and

the Path Travelled by the People of the Japanese Isles] (Tokyo: Kawade Shobō ShinshaTsutsui, 2017), 209.

20. James IV (1473–1513) of Scotland had married Margaret Tudor (1489–1541), daughter of Henry VII (1457–1509). When Henry's granddaughter Elizabeth I (1533–1603) died without leaving an heir, James VI of Scotland (1566–1625) became her successor based on his connection to the Tudors through his great-grandmother. James attempted to unify England and Scotland but met with opposition on both sides.

21. Quoted in Arthur F. Kinney, *Lies Like Truth: Shakespeare,* Macbeth*, and the Cultural Moment* (Detroit, MI: Wayne State University Press, 2001), 89.

22. Tiffany Grace, "*Macbeth*, Paternity, and the Anglicization of James I," *Studies in the Humanities* 23, no. 2 (December 1996): 157.

23. Arthur F. Kinney, "Scottish History, the Union of the Crown and the Issue of Right Rule: The Case of Shakespeare's *Macbeth*," in *Renaissance Culture in Context: Theory and Practice*, ed. Jean R. Brink and William F. Gentrup (Aldershot: Scolar Press, 1993), 39. Kinney, *Lies Like Truth*, 99; Steven Mullaney, *The Place of the Stage: License, Play, and Power in Renaissance England* (Chicago and London: The University of Chicago Press, 1988), 133.

24. Sharon Alker and Holly Faith Nelson, "*Macbeth*, the Jacobean Scot, and the Politics of Union," *SEL* 47, no. 2 (Spring 2007): 382; Jonathan Baldo, "'A Rooted Sorrow': Scotland's Unusable Past," in *Macbeth: New Critical Essays*, Shakespeare Criticism Volume 32, ed. Nick Moschovakis (New York and London: Routledge, 2008), 97. According to Baldo, Shakespeare does this by, on the one hand, appealing to James by emphasizing the large number of Scotsmen who fought alongside the English against Macbeth, while on the other, being careful not to alienate those opposed to a union by portraying Scotland "as a brutally violent land …" (Baldo, 97–8).

25. Haruka Ōmichi, *'Itako' no tanjō: Mass media to shūkyō bunka* [The Birth of the 'Itako': Mass Media and Religious Culture] (Tokyo: Kōbundō, 2017), 37 and 52.

26. Clark Stuart, "King James's *Daemonlogie*: Witchcraft and Kingship," in *The Damned Art: Essays in the Literature of Witchcraft*, ed. Sydney Anglo, Routledge Library Editions: Witchcraft Vol. 1 (London and New York: Routledge, 2011), 170; Garry Wills, *Witches and Jesuits: Shakespeare's* Macbeth (New York and Oxford: Oxford University Press, 1995), 43; Anthony Harris, *Night's Black Agents: Witchcraft and Magic in Seventeenth-Century English Drama* (Manchester: Manchester University Press, 1980), 37. Mary Floyd-Wilson offers an alternative view by proposing that "the witches and evil spirits in *Macbeth* are predominantly elemental" and connected to the land and climate of Scotland. Mary Floyd-Wilson, "English Epicures and Scottish Witches," *Shakespeare Quarterly* 57 (2006): 136.

27. This is when the *gokuraku jōdo* paradise decides whether to open its gates to or reject the soul of the deceased.

28. *The New Romeo and Juliet* toured 11 locations; *The New King Lear* toured five locations; and *The New Merchant of Venice* toured seven locations.

29. Tetsuo Yamaori and Norio Akasaka, *Hanyokubō no jidai e: Daishinsai no sanka o koete* [Towards an Age of Anti-Excess: Having Overcome the Calamity of a Great Earthquake] (Tokyo: Tokyo Kyōiku Kenkyūjo, 2011), 36.

30. Furukawa, *Tohoku Shock Doctrine*, vii–viii.

31. Furukawa, *Tohoku Shock Doctrine*, 7, 47, and 65.

32. Furukawa, *Tohoku Shock Doctrine*, 102.

33. Furukawa *Tohoku Shock Doctrine*, 111.
34. Yūsuke Yamashita, *"Fukkō" ga ubau chīki no mirai: Higashi nihon daishinsai / genpatsu jiko no kenshō to teigen* [The Future Erased by "Reconstruction Measures": Examination of and Suggestions for the Great East Japan Earthquake and Nuclear Meltdown] (Tokyo: Iwanami Shoten, 2017), 46–7.
35. Furukawa, *Tohoku Shock Doctrine*, 139.
36. Furukawa, *Tohoku Shock Doctrine*, 148. The Tohoku Medical Megabank Project and the fishery revival zone were decided under similar circumstances.
37. Furukawa, *Tohoku Shock Doctrine*, 176; our italics.
38. Yamashita, *"Fukkō" ga ubau*, 56.
39. See footnote 28.
40. Shimodate, *Hamuretto, Tohoku ni tatsu*, 7.
41. Shimodate, *Hamuretto, Tohoku ni tatsu*, 151.
42. Shimodate, *Hamuretto, Tohoku ni tatsu*, 9–10.
43. Shimodate, *Hamuretto, Tohoku ni tatsu*, 150–1.
44. Shimodate, *Hamuretto, Tohoku ni tatsu*, 152–3.
45. Yamashita, *"Fukkō" ga ubau*, 54.
46. *Matagi* hunters have resided in the northern regions of Japan for centuries and have their own language, religion, and methods of hunting. There were two major earthquakes followed by tsunamis in modern times before 3.11: the Meiji Sanriku Earthquake (June 15, 1896) and the Showa Sanriku Earthquake (March 3, 1933). It is not clear if these lines refer to one or the other. In a scene corresponding to the one in Shakespeare's play when Juliet's nurse mentions an earthquake (1.3.24), Onasu (nurse) reminisces about an earthquake without a tsunami (Shimodate, 2016, vol. 1, 16).
47. Katsusuke Chiba, *Kieta Yamabito: Shōwa no dentō matagi* [Extinct Mountaineer: The Traditional Matagi Hunter in the Showa Period] (Tokyo: Nōsangyoson Bunka Kyōkai, 2019), 24–7, 122–30.
48. Chiba, *Kieta Yamabito*, 2. Makoto Nebuka, *Shirakamisanchi matagi den: Suzuki Tadakatsu no shōgai* [Stories from a Matagi Hunter in Shirakami Sanchi: The Life of Suzuki Tadakatsu] (Tokyo: Yama to Keikokusha, 2018), 25–58, 328–33.
49. Ory Bartal, "From Hiroshima to Fukushima: Comics and Animation as Subversive Agents of Memory in Japan," in *Interdisciplinary Handbook of Trauma and Culture*, ed. Yochai Ataria et al. (Cham, Switzerland: Springer International, 2016), 114, 103–4, https://link-springer-com.ez.wul.waseda.ac.jp/chapter/10.1007/978-3-319-29404-9_7.
50. Bracha Lichtenberg Ettinger, "Art as the Transport-Station of Trauma," in *Interdisciplinary Handbook of Trauma and Culture*, ed. Yochai Ataria et al. (Cham, Switzerland: Springer International, 2016), 152, https://link-springer-com.ez.wul.waseda.ac.jp/book/10.1007%2F978-3-319-29404-9.
51. Quoted in Katsuyuki Hidaka, *Japanese Media at the Beginning of the 21st Century: Consuming the Past*, Routledge Contemporary Japan Series (London and New York: Routledge, 2017), 73.
52. Hidaka, *Japanese Media*, 21.
53. Kōhei Kōno, *Shōwa nostarujī kaitai—natsukashisa wa dō tsukurareta no ka* [Deconstructing Showa Nostalgia: How the Sense of Familiarity Was Constructed] (Tokyo: Sōbunsha, 2018), 271.
54. Yōsuke Kosaka, *Ainu, Nihonjin, sono sekai* [The Ainu and the Japanese: Different Ground Gives Life to Different Spirits] (Tokyo: Fujita Insatsu Excellent Books, 2019), 196–7.

55. *Atuy* is an Ainu word that means *sea*.
56. After Akibe proposed an Ainu Yago, Shimodate discussed the idea with Verma, who saw dramatic potential in a mixed-race Yago. Kazumi Shimodate, "Watashitachi no *Othello* o sagashite: Shakespeare Company no bōken" [Searching for Our *Othello*: The Adventures of the Shakespeare Company], in *Katari tsumugu beki mono: "Bungaku no chikara" to wa nani ka: Satō Yasumasa sensei tsuitōronshū* [That Which Should Be Spun into a Narrative: What "the Power of Literature" Is: Essays in Memory of Professor Satō Yasumasa], ed. Shinji Nakano (Tokyo: Kasama Shoin, 2018), 163–5; The Shakespeare Company Japan and Pirikap, *Ainu Othello* (theater program, August 7–10, 2019).
57. Shimodate, "Watashitachi no *Othello*," 163.
58. All quotations from this play are from the unpublished supertitles translation for the London production, by Motoyama and Konno.
59. Shimodate, "Watashitachi no *Othello*," 155.
60. Yamashita and Kanai, *Chihō sōsei no shōtai*, 70–2.
61. Yamashita, *Chihō shōmetsu no wana*, 117.
62. Anthony Kwame Appiah, *The Ethics of Identity* (Princeton, NJ and Oxford: Princeton University Press, 2005), 239.
63. Appiah, *The Ethics of Identity*, 241.
64. Shimodate is now in talks with Tagajo, which was the political center of Tohoku until the early ninth century, for permission to build his Globe Theatre there.
65. Homi Bhabha, *The Locations of Culture* (London and New York: Routledge, 2004), 265.
66. Shimodate, *Hamuretto, Tohoku ni tatsu*, 7.

REFERENCES

Alker, Sharon, and Holly Faith Nelson. "*Macbeth*, the Jacobean Scot, and the Politics of Union." *SEL* 47, no. 2 (Spring 2007): 379–401.
Appiah, Anthony Kwame. *The Ethics of Identity*. Princeton, NJ and Oxford: Princeton University Press, 2005.
Baldo, Jonathan. "'A Rooted Sorrow': Scotland's Unusable Past." Chapter 3 in *Macbeth: New Critical Essays*, Shakespeare Criticism Volume 32, edited by Nick Moschovakis, 88–105. New York and London: Routledge, 2008.
Bartal, Ory. "From Hiroshima to Fukushima: Comics and Animation as Subversive Agents of Memory in Japan." In *Interdisciplinary Handbook of Trauma and Culture*, edited by Yochai Ataria, David Gurevitz, Haviva Pedaya, and Yuval Neria, 101–15. Cham, Switzerland: Springer International, 2016.
Bassiouney, Reem. "Introduction." In *Identity and Dialect Performance: A Study of Communities and Dialects*, edited by Reem Bassiouney, 1–14. London and New York: Routledge, 2018.
Bhabha, Homi. *The Locations of Culture*. London and New York: Routledge, 2004.
Chiba, Katsusuke. *Kieta Yamabito: Shōwa no dentō matagi* [Extinct Mountaineer: The Traditional Matagi Hunter in the Showa Period]. Tokyo: Nōsangyoson Bunka Kyōkai, 2019.
Dilley, Luke, Sae Shinzato, and Mitsuyoshi Ando. "Revitalizing the Rural in Japan: Working through the Power of Place." *Electronic Journal of Contemporary Japanese Studies* 17, no. 3 (2017). Accessed April 8, 2020. http://japanesestudies.org.uk/ejcjs/vol17/iss3/dilley.html.

Ettinger, Bracha Lichtenberg. "Art as the Transport-Station of Trauma." In *Interdisciplinary Handbook of Trauma and Culture*, edited by Yochai Ataria, David Gurevitz, Haviva Pedaya, and Yuval Neria, 151–60. Cham, Switzerland: Springer International, 2016. Accessed January 20, 2020. https://link-springer-com.ez.wul .waseda.ac.jp/book/10.1007%2F978-3-319-29404-9.

Floyd-Wilson, Mary. "English Epicures and Scottish Witches." *Shakespeare Quarterly* 57 (2006): 131–61.

Furukawa, Miho. *Tohoku Shock Doctrine*. Tokyo: Iwanami Shoten, 2015.

Grace, Tiffany. "*Macbeth*, Paternity, and the Anglicization of James I." *Studies in the Humanities* 23, no. 2 (December 1996): 148–62.

Harris, Anthony. *Night's Black Agents: Witchcraft and Magic in Seventeenth-Century English Drama*. Manchester: Manchester University Press, 1980.

Hidaka, Katsuyuki. *Japanese Media at the Beginning of the 21st Century: Consuming the Past*. Routledge Contemporary Japan Series. London and New York: Routledge, 2017.

Kinney, Arthur F. *Lies Like Truth: Shakespeare,* Macbeth*, and the Cultural Moment*. Detroit, MI: Wayne State University Press, 2001.

Kinney, Arthur F. "Scottish History, the Union of the Crown and the Issue of Right Rule: The Case of Shakespeare's *Macbeth*." In *Renaissance Culture in Context: Theory and Practice*, edited by Jean R. Brink and William F. Gentrup, 18–53. Aldershot: Scolar Press. 1993.

Konno, Fumiaki. "General Introduction," "*The New Romeo and Juliet*," and "Appendix 1." In *Re-imagining Shakespeare in Contemporary Japan: A Selection of Japanese Theatrical Adaptations of Shakespeare*, edited by Tetsuhito Motoyama, Rosalind Fielding, and Fumiaki Konno. London and New York: Bloomsbury, 2021.

Kōno, Kōhei. *Shōwa nostarujī kaitai—natsukashisa wa dō tsukurareta no ka* [Deconstructing Showa Nostalgia: How the Sense of Familiarity Was Constructed]. Tokyo: Sōbunsha, 2018.

Kosaka, Yōsuke. *Ainu, Nihonjin, sono sekai* [The Ainu and the Japanese: Different Ground Gives Life to Different Spirits]. Tokyo: Fujita Insatsu Excellent Books, 2019.

Mullaney, Steven. *The Place of the Stage: License, Play, and Power in Renaissance England*. Chicago and London: The University of Chicago Press, 1988.

Nebuka, Makoto. *Shirakamisanchi matagi den: Suzuki Tadakatsu no shōgai* [Stories from a Matagi Hunter in Shirakami Sanchi: The Life of Suzuki Tadakatsu]. Tokyo: Yama to Keikokusha, 2018.

Ōba, Kenji. *Shakespeare no hon'yaku* [Translating Shakespeare]. Tokyo: Kenkyūsha, 2009.

Ōmichi, Haruka. *'Itako' no tanjō: Mass media to shūkyō bunka* [The Birth of the 'Itako': Mass Media and Religious Culture]. Tokyo: Kōbundō, 2017.

Sakamoto, Makoto. 2018. "'Chihō sōsei' to nōson: Nōson chiiki no kadai to tembō" ['Regional Revitalization' and Agricultural Villages: The Problems and Prospects of Agricultural Areas]. In *Chihō sōsei to jichitai* [Regional Revitalization and Municipalities], edited by the Japan Association for the Study of Local Government, Chihō Jichi Sōsho [Local Government Series] 29, 1–40. Tokyo Keibundō, 2018.

Sauzier-Uchida, Emi. 2008. "Nihon no gengo seisaku ni okeru tōitsusei to tayōsei" [Unity and Diversity of Language Policy in Japan]. *Kyōyō shogaku kenkyū* [*Journal of Liberal Arts*] 125 (2008): 47–73.

The Shakespeare Company Japan, and Pirikap. *Ainu Othello*. Theater program. (August 7–10, 2019).

Shakespeare, William. *Macbeth*. Edited by Sandra Clark and Pamela Mason. The Arden Shakespeare Third Series. London and New York: Bloomsbury, 2015.

Shakespeare, William. *Romeo and Juliet*. Edited by René Weis. The Arden Shakespeare Third Series. London and New York: Bloomsbury, 2012.

Shimoda, Hiraku. "Tongue-Tied: The Making of a 'National Language' and the Discovery of Dialects in Meiji Japan." *The American Historical Review* 115, no. 3 (2010): 714–31.

Shimodate, Kazumi. *Ainu Othello*. Translated by Tetsuhito Motoyama and Fumiaki Konno. Unpublished translation for the Tara Arts Theatre production, London, August 2019.

Shimodate, Kazumi. *Hamuretto, Tohoku ni tatsu: Tohoku-ben Shakespeare gekidan no bōken* [Hamlet, on the Tohoku Stage: The Adventures of the Tohoku Dialect Shakespeare Theater Company]. Tokyo: Kokusho Kankōkai, 2017.

Shimodate, Kazumi. "Kinoshita Junji no 'geijutsugo': *Othello* shoyaku (1947 nen) kara *Hamlet* (1970 nen) made" [The 'Artistic Language' of Kinoshita Junji: From the First Translation of *Othello* (1947) to the Translation of *Hamlet* (1970)]. *Tohoku Gakuin Daigaku eigo eibungaku kenkyūjo kiyō* [*Tohoku Gakuin University Journal for English and English Literature*] 26 (1997): 81–102.

Shimodate, Kazumi. *Tohoku Shakespeare Kyakuhonshū* [Selected Scripts from Shakespeare in Tohoku]. Volumes 1, 3, and 4. Tokyo: Koko Shuppan, 2016.

Shimodate, Kazumi. "Watashitachi no *Othello* o sagashite: Shakespeare Company no bōken" [Searching for Our *Othello*: The Adventures of the Shakespeare Company]. In *Katari tsumugu beki mono: "Bungaku no chikara" to wa nani ka: Satō Yasumasa sensei tsuitōronshū* [That Which Should Be Spun into a Narrative: What "the Power of Literature" Is: Essays in Memory of Professor Satō Yasumasa], edited by Shinji Nakano, 141–66. Tokyo: Kasama Shoin, 2018.

Stuart, Clark. "King James's *Daemonlogie*: Witchcraft and Kingship." In *The Damned Art: Essays in the Literature of Witchcraft*, edited by Sydney Anglo. Routledge Library Editions: Witchcraft Volume 1, 156–81. London and New York: Routledge, 2011.

Tsutsui, Isao. *Ainugo chimei to Nippon rettō-jin ga kita michi* [Ainu Place Names and the Path Travelled by the People of the Japanese Isles]. Tokyo: Kawade Shobō Shinsha, 2017.

Wills, Garry. *Witches and Jesuits: Shakespeare's* Macbeth. New York and Oxford: Oxford University Press, 1995.

Yamaori, Tetsuo, and Norio Akasaka. *Hanyokubō no jidai e: Daishinsai no sanka o koete* [Towards an Age of Anti-Excess: Having Overcome the Calamity of a Great Earthquake]. Tokyo: Tokyo Kyōiku Kenkyūjo, 2011.

Yamashita, Yūsuke. *Chihō shōmetsu no wana: "Masuda Report" to jinkō genshō shakai no shōtai* [The Extinction of Provincial Communities as a Trap: The "Masuda Report" and the Truth about a Society Undergoing Depopulation]. Chikuma Shinsho 1100. Tokyo: Chikuma Shobō, 2014.

Yamashita, Yūsuke. *"Fukkō" ga ubau chīki no mirai: Higashi nihon daishinsai / genpatsu jiko no kenshō to Teigen* [The Future Erased by "Reconstruction Measures:" Examination of and Suggestions for the Great East Japan Earthquake and Nuclear Meltdown]. Tokyo: Iwanami Shoten, 2017.

Yamashita, Yūsuke, and Toshiyuki Kanai. *Chihō sōsei no shōtai: Naze chiiki seisaku wa shippai suru no ka* [The Truth about Regional Revitalization: Why Regional Policies Fail]. Chikuma shinsho 1150. Tokyo: Chikuma Shobō, 2015.

PART IV

Freedom

10. "Mountainish inhumanity": the politics of religion, refugees, and ego from *Sir Thomas More* to Donald Trump

Kristin M. S. Bezio

Sir Thomas More, a history play, focuses on the rise and fall of its titular character during the reign of Henry VIII, the now-notorious quasi-tyrant with six wives and three legitimate children whose sexual and political exploits have been the subject of popular culture from the 1590s to HBO's *The Tudors*. The principal subject of the play is Henry's main councilor, Thomas More, a man whose loyalty to his own conscience superseded his loyalty to his king or his king's religion.[1] The question of loyalty was particularly germane in Shakespeare's England, just as it is today in modern states whose primary leader insists upon constructing his or her own narrative of patriotism and national identity. For More, freedom of conscience led to execution, an outcome lamented by both the play and the characters within it. Those in modern dictatorships or war-torn nations face similar consequences, and frequently choose, instead, to migrate from their homes and seek refuge elsewhere.

While today we hear about immigrants seeking asylum from Syria or Central America (specifically, Mexico, Guatemala, Honduras, and El Salvador), in Shakespeare's England a sizeable portion of refugees seeking asylum in England were from the Netherlands, victims of the war between Catholic Spain and the Dutch States General. In Shakespeare's England, immigrants—their language, customs, and, most of all, religion—were viewed as an ideological, economic, and sociopolitical threat to England and English identity. Fears about secret Catholics abounded, and those who came, especially from nations where religious wars were frequent, were considered highly suspect by the citizenry and government alike.

In *Sir Thomas More*, we find depictions of anti-immigrant violence and fears, but we are also presented with a serious consideration of the true sources of those fears. In particular, *Sir Thomas More* highlights the relative *un*importance of religious beliefs to one's loyalty to England. Such an argument flew in the face of English governmental propaganda, and there is considerable doubt as to whether *Sir Thomas More* ever saw production on the Elizabethan stage due to its controversial content. The play is a snapshot of a moment of resistance that challenges its audience to question the truth of rumor and propaganda. It asks whether or not religious—ideological—beliefs should condemn a good person, and, finally, raises the very serious choice between loyalty to nation and loyalty to an overly ambitious and larger-than-life leader more interested in satisfying his personal whims and ego than in ethical rule.

THE HISTORY BEHIND *SIR THOMAS MORE*

I begin with the context in which the play *Sir Thomas More* was written, focusing in particular on the political and religious concerns which framed popular anti-immigrant sentiment at the close of the sixteenth century in England. We will start with a discussion of English anti-Catholicism and conclude with a comparison of sixteenth-century English anti-immigrant attitudes with those evinced in the twenty-first century in Europe and the United States before turning to the play itself.

English Anti-Catholicism

English anti-Catholicism began in the time in which *Sir Thomas More* is set, about 70 years before Shakespeare and his collaborators set quill to paper. The English Reformation was set in motion by an appeal by Henry VIII in 1527 to obtain an annulment of his marriage to the Spanish Catherine of Aragon as a consequence, he claimed, of their marriage having been cursed because first she had been his brother's wife. It took two years for Henry to leave the Catholic Church after the Pope's refusal to grant his request, and another five for Parliament to pass the 1534 Act of Supremacy naming Henry as the head of the Church of England. From that point onward, England found itself in increasingly hostile opposition to the Catholic Church and the nations that claimed Catholic allegiance, including France and Spain, with the notable exception of the years of Mary I's reign (1553–8).

Although Henry's eldest daughter—born of Catherine of Aragon—remained steadfastly Catholic, his younger surviving children (Edward VI, son of Jane Seymour, and Elizabeth I, daughter of Anne Boleyn) were both Protestant, and Elizabeth spent most of her reign in conflict with the papacy and the Catholic powers of France, Spain, and the Italian states. With Henry's death in 1547, the crown passed to Edward VI, who was both underage and physically prone to illness, and although he was a staunch Protestant his short reign was able only to lay the foundations for England's future Protestant identity.[2] When he died in 1553, his eldest sister, Mary, assumed the throne, returning England to Catholicism and taking the Spanish King Philip II as her husband.

Mary's reign was viewed by the Spanish and the papacy as God's will returning England to the Catholic fold, and while England itself appears to have been largely accepting of a return to Catholicism, London and the government were somewhat resistant.[3] Parliament, for example, refused to remove Mary as Head of the English Church, and the Protestant minority in England was highly vocal in its disapproval of Mary's religious policies.[4] In fact, we might source the beginnings of the immigrant wave of the late sixteenth century to the counter-migration of Protestants from England during Mary's reign, as they fled to the Netherlands, Germany, and Switzerland.[5]

Under Elizabeth, who was crowned in January 1559, the English government returned to Protestantism. Things came to a head in 1570 when Pope Pius V issued a declaration, entitled *Regnans in Excelsis*, which tacitly gave permission to Catholics to disobey or even assassinate Elizabeth.[6] From 1570 onwards, the Elizabethan government—having (understandably) taken the pope's bull rather personally—began a long war with the Catholic faith and its adherents, including those both at home and, especially, abroad.

The rest of Elizabeth's reign was fraught by Catholic and anti-Catholic plots, attempted assassinations, and paranoia over the presence of foreigners and foreign spies, setting the stage for a general atmosphere of anti-immigrant sentiment, even against those who hailed from ostensibly allied nations. Throughout Elizabeth's reign (and into the reigns of the early Stuarts), the atmosphere faced by Catholics (especially foreign Catholics) in England bears striking similarities to that faced in twenty-first-century Western nations by Muslims and Muslim immigrants.[7]

Anti-Immigrant Attitudes in the Sixteenth and Twenty-First Centuries

Throughout Elizabeth's reign, London saw a nearly constant stream of Dutch, French, and Flemish refugees fleeing Spanish Catholic persecution, and the 1590s, specifically, saw that number surge in response to increased incidents of plague on the Continent.[8] As Stephen Alford remarks, "On one level they were welcomed as fellow Protestants. On another, many Londoners were troubled by fears of competition, especially given that many of the émigrés brought skills in clothworking, metalworking, printing and brewing."[9] The arrival of these immigrants in England produced considerable consternation; many English in the middling and lower classes feared that the new arrivals—much as we see in twenty-first-century anti-immigrant rhetoric—would threaten their livelihoods due to "the advanced skills and techniques the aliens possessed."[10] In 1593, only a handful of years before the production of *Sir Thomas More*,

> a number of tracts threatening the alien population with violence were published in close succession. One of these tracts was pinned to the wall of the churchyard in the Dutch Church, warning the alien community to leave by July or apprentices would rise up against them and commit violence upon "the Flemish and strangers."[11]

Violence against immigrants—something all too common in the twenty-first century—was therefore a significant part of early modern London culture; however, it is important to note that in Shakespeare's England, the *government* neither promoted nor ratified the actions of the malcontent populace, with Parliament repeatedly refusing to sanction proposals for the restriction of immigrant lodging and work.

We see parallels to this situation in the twenty-first century, considering US and European involvement in Syria and the Middle East more broadly, a link which has historically enabled the free exchange of goods, capital, and the movement of people seeking Western education or experience abroad. However, recent years have produced increasing animosity toward individuals hailing from these nations on the part of both Western governments and their citizens, producing a rise in anti-Islamic violence since 2016 and anti-Asian violence during the COVID-19 pandemic.[12] In the modern UK, Prime Ministers Theresa May and Boris Johnson both spoke out against accepting "low-skilled" immigrants from the EU, and Donald Trump used fearmongering to encourage the US to refuse entry to a migrant caravan from Guatemala, Honduras, and El Salvador in 2018.[13]

As happened in the sixteenth century, with the arrival of the COVID-19 global pandemic in early 2020, many nations closed their borders and instituted travel bans under the rhetorical guise of stopping Others from bringing the virus to their shores. In particular, US President Trump repeatedly insisted upon using the term "Chinese virus" (or, less often, "Wuhan virus" or "kung flu") in order to explicitly otherize the disease and foist blame upon immigrants and foreign nationals.[14] Similar tactics were used in Shakespeare's day with reference to plague, a disease whose outbreaks were associated with "an escalation in attacks on social minorities, including clerics, beggars, persons suffering from leprosy, *and foreigners* [emphasis added]."[15] Specifically, the English attributed surges in plague with the Middle East:

> Throughout the early modern era, the European imagination of plague's origin was being constantly replenished by news of plague from the port cities of the eastern Mediterranean, which led to durable associations between plague and the Ottomans … On the one hand, the European imagination dissociated itself from plague by

projecting the locus of the disease somewhere outside; on the other, it fashioned the Ottoman empire as a plague-exporter, against which Europe had to protect itself.[16]

Thus, we find significant parallels between twenty-first- and sixteenth-century beliefs about the importation of disease, concerns about religious and social corruption, and fears of economic depression associated explicitly with the arrival of migrant populations.

THE PLAY: *SIR THOMAS MORE*

The date of *Sir Thomas More* is the source of significant scholarly controversy.[17] I place *Sir Thomas More* circa 1597, following primary author Anthony Munday's return from the Spanish Netherlands. It was written primarily—or so scholars believe—by two men, Henry Chettle and Munday, with additional contributions from William Shakespeare, Thomas Dekker, and Thomas Heywood, and with edits and cuts made by the government's Master of the Revels, Edmund Tilney. As such, *Sir Thomas More* cannot fully be considered the work of any one of its authors and must be understood to reflect the different ideological views of the six men who took part in its composition.

Sir Edmund Tilney, a government official whose job was to authorize and censor plays for public and courtly consumption, made cuts to and comments about the play, directing the authors to alter the script. Whether it was ever successfully produced in its own era is not known. But regardless of whether *Sir Thomas More* saw the stage in 1597 or even in the decade or so following, the play's manuscript nevertheless gives us considerable insight into the perspectives of the men who lived and worked on London's South Bank, one of several locales in London that served as home to Dutch immigrants fleeing religious persecution.[18] As Christian M. Billings notes, the theaters by necessity had ties to the cloth-producing guilds as well as to clothiers, particularly—as in *Sir Thomas More*—when the plays called for nationally specific costumes.[19] Several of the playwrights themselves had also spent time in the Netherlands, either in military or intelligence service.

It is important to note the difference in the origins of the immigrants in *Sir Thomas More* and those most often encountered on the streets of 1590s London. Those living in London in the 1580s and 1590s were predominantly Dutch, Flemish, and French fleeing religious persecution by Catholics. However, the immigrants in *Sir Thomas More* are Lombards from northern Italy, a nation predominantly associated with Catholicism. English anti-Catholic sentiment therefore needs to be factored into the play's depiction of foreigners, or "strangers." The immigrants targeted by violence in *Sir Thomas More* are Catholic, and while in Elizabethan England Protestant refugees were positively viewed by the government, Catholic immigrants were not only abused, but also considered an active threat to the crown. This distinction is important, as anti-Catholic sentiment creates a veneer of permissibility for violence against the Lombards in *Sir Thomas More*. Yet the play itself turns against this religiously motivated persecution, yielding an odd sense that there is something more behind the play's vitriolic characterization of its foreign characters.

Evil May Day and Anti-Immigrant Sentiment in the Play

Despite (or perhaps because of) the familiarity of the play's collaborative authors with London's international population, the play begins with a scene that foregrounds and even excuses (to a degree) anti-immigrant violence. The scene specifically recreates the events of Evil May Day (May 1, 1517) when anti-immigrant riots took place in London. The Evil May Day riots included more than 1,000 citizens who gathered in St. Martin's-le-Grand Church, a Liberty district technically on the outskirts of the city.[20] Although London proper was under a curfew in anticipation of anti-immigrant violence, the Liberties were under no such restriction.[21]

According to sixteenth-century accounts, the historical Thomas More (Under-Sheriff) rode into the Liberty, despite lacking the legal authority, and attempted to dissuade the rioters. When they refused, he ordered his men to forcibly disperse the crowd. As Derek Wilson observes, "Within minutes, More and his escort were forced to make a hasty, ignominious retreat."[22] From there, the rioters "went on a rampage," attacking "the houses and business premises of foreign merchants and artisans," growing in numbers to more than 2,000 participants by the end of the day, or about 2 percent of the city's population.[23] It took the intervention of both the Duke of Norfolk and the Earl of Surrey leading armed retainers into the city streets to bring order.[24] The leaders of the riots were executed for treason, a horrific end, despite no lives having been lost.[25] Although the remaining participants and More (who had failed to curtail the violence) were ultimately pardoned by Henry VIII, the events created enough of a cultural memory of anti-immigrant violence that similar riots did not occur again until 1580.

The account of Sebastian Giustinian, Venetian Ambassador to England, provides the likeliest explanation of the ultimate cause of the riots. Although Henry's policies were welcoming toward immigrants and encouraged transnational mercantilism—which some historians blame for fomenting the bitterness of London artisans—it was "a sermon given at the preacher's cross in the precincts of St Mary Spitalfields" which struck the match:

> The speaker abused the strangers in the town, as well as their manners and customs, alleging that they not only deprived the English of their industry and the profits that

arose from it, but dishonoured their dwellings by taking their wives and daughters … Protected by his "cloth" from prosecution in the civil courts, the preacher (probably Dr Bell, the parish vicar) could stand back and let the slander do its insidious work.[26]

Similar rhetoric appears in the twenty-first century in the mouths of conservative evangelicals, such as James Dobson of Focus on the Family, who wrote of immigrant detainees being held in functional internment facilities:

What I've told you is only a glimpse of what is occurring on the nation's border. I don't know what it will take to change the circumstances. I can only report that without an overhaul of the law and the allocation of resources, millions of illegal immigrants will continue flooding to this great land from around the world. Many of them have no marketable skills. They are illiterate and unhealthy. Some are violent criminals. Their numbers will soon overwhelm the culture as we have known it, and it could bankrupt the nation.[27]

What we find, then, is that some 500 years before our time, the rhetoric of conservatism was leveled by religious leaders against immigrants as people who stole jobs and income and spread lifestyles which went against English honor—a rhetoric which finds echoes today in claims that immigrants are "un-American" and Mexican immigrants are "rapists," as well as in the United Kingdom's referendum to leave the European Union.

In *Sir Thomas More*, the details of Evil May Day are altered to foreground More's diplomatic skill rather than ineptitude. The first scene begins with a series of confrontations between foreigners—Francis de Barde and Cavaler, both Lombards—and English citizens—Doll Williamson, her husband (Williamson), and Sherwin—observed by Lincoln and George Betts. In the first, Barde tells Doll that "Thou art my prize, and I plead purchase of thee" (1.2–3), in other words, he wants to buy her sexual favors, despite her being married to Williamson.[28] The line summons the accusation from Bell's sermon—"taking their wives"—and also indicates that Barde has neither manners nor respect, treating Doll like a common prostitute. This is immediately followed by Williamson in pursuit of Cavaler, who has stolen two pigeons Williamson purchased for dinner:

CAVALER I say thou shalt not have them.
WILLIAMSON I bought them in Cheapside, and paid my money for them.
SHERWIN He did, sir, indeed, and you offer him wrong, both to take them from him and not restore him his money neither.
CAVALER If he paid for them, let it suffice that I possess them. (1.16–24)

If Sherwin is telling the truth (we have no reason to doubt him), then Cavaler has simply stolen the birds from Williamson. Thus, the play begins with evidence of abuses committed against good English citizens by foreign immigrants.

These actions cause Lincoln, at the center of the riots to come, to proclaim that "It is hard when Englishmen's patience must be thus jetted on by strangers, and they dare not to revenge their own wrongs" (1.26–9). His complaint is not that foreigners are arriving in the city and earning wealth and position, but that they are *stealing* it, and those who are native to London are forced to put up with the theft. Furthermore, Barde claims that his crimes can go unpunished because he is protected by the king's desire to maintain diplomatic ties with Lombardy. He mocks them, saying, "What art thou that talkest of revenge? My Lord Ambassador shall once more make your Mayor have a check if he punish thee not for this saucy presumption" (1.41–4), a claim which Williamson confirms, saying that he had in fact been arrested and sent "to Newgate one day, because, against my will, I took the wall of a stranger" (1.46–7).[29] When the two depart, Doll laments that "I am ashamed that free-born Englishmen, having beaten strangers within their own bounds, should thus be braved and abused by them at home" (1.80–3). Her complaint—that Englishmen won a victory in Lombardy only to be victimized back in England by Lombards—is one that has familiar echoes of twenty-first-century anti-Islamic rhetoric. Yet what is important here is that the English citizens' anger against Barde and Cavaler seems presented as justified in the play by the two Lombards' criminal actions.

In response to the injustice, Lincoln posts a bill on the door of the church (something the historical Lincoln also did) which reads:

> *For so it is that aliens and strangers eat the bread from the fatherless children, and take the living from all the artificers, and the intercourse from all merchants, whereby poverty is so much increased that every man bewaileth the misery of other; for craftsmen be brought to beggary, and merchants to neediness. Wherefore, the premises considered, the redress must be of the commons knit and united to one part. And as the hurt and damage grieveth all men, so must all men set to their willing power for remedy, and not suffer the said aliens in their wealth, and the natural-born men of this region to come to confusion.* (1.123–34)

Put simply, the complaint argues that immigrants have taken orphans' food, taken the jobs of artisans and merchants, and caused a general economic depression. It then exhorts its readers to rise up lest they starve to death while foreigners prosper and grow rich. The theme is familiar, if presented somewhat differently in the twenty-first century. Lincoln's bill might as well suggest that illegal immigrants are stealing citizens' jobs and using up social security and welfare, taking Americans' tax dollars and becoming "welfare queens" while Americans fall into poverty. The refrain is similar in countries across Europe with strong anti-immigrant sentiment.

Anti-Violence and More's Empathy

Thus far, the play seems only to confirm the validity of such feelings and to be exhorting its audience to do the same. It is likely because of this that the entire opening scene was censored by Tilney, who warned the company to cut the entire first scene "at your own perils":

> *Leave out the insurrection wholly and the cause thereof, and begin with Sir Thomas More at the Mayor's sessions, with a report afterwards of his good service done being Sheriff of London upon a mutiny against the Lombards – only by a short report, and not otherwise, at your own perils. E. Tilney* (0.1–6)

What is clear, whether or not the playwrights intended it, is that the Office of Revels *believed* that the scene tacitly justified anti-immigrant violence, and Tilney refused to permit it on stage, most likely out of fear that it might result in actual violence, although his notes make it unclear whether the concern was about violence explicitly against (Protestant) immigrants or just unrest and riot more generally.

Tilney's edits throughout the play also attempt to reinforce an anti-Catholic rather than generalized anti-foreign sentiment. At several points, the lines in the manuscript suggest that Cavaler is a Frenchman rather than a Lombard (for instance, 3.44), and Tilney occasionally corrects "Frenchman" to "Lombard" (as at 3.53) and even "stranger" to "Lombard" (as at 3.49) in order to maintain the specificity of problematic foreigners being associated with Catholicism.[30] Tilney similarly cuts most references to civil insurrection, such as a Messenger's report that "the City is in an uproar, and the Mayor / Is threatened if he come out of his house" (3.74–5).

Yet despite Tilney's objections, the insurrection is what enables More—who, although the hero of the play, doesn't *do* much until Scene 6, when he puts down the rebellion in a dramatic alteration of the historical facts (in the portion of the play entirely written by Shakespeare)—to rise to heroic status. More uses language—not force—to subdue the riot:

> **MORE** Grant them removed, and grant that this your noise
>　　Hath chid down all the majesty of England.
>　　Imagine that you see the wretched strangers,
>　　Their babies at their backs, with their poor luggage,
>　　Plodding to th' ports and coasts for transportation,
>　　And that you sit as kings in your desires,
>　　Authority quite silenced by your brawl,
>　　And you in ruff of your opinions clothed:
>　　What had you got? I'll tell you: you had taught
>　　How insolence and strong hand should prevail,
>　　How order should be quelled. And by this pattern
>　　Not one of you should live an aged man;
>　　For other ruffians, as their fancies wrought,
>　　With selfsame hand, self reasons, and self right,
>　　Would shark on you, and men, like ravenous fishes,
>　　Would feed on one another. (6.83–98)

More uses an argument which must have appealed enormously to Tilney, who clearly believes that even a staged revolt might cause a real riot. Yet More's speech here specifically appeals to empathy and emotion; he summons images of refugees bearing children and few possessions being driven from their country, essentially accusing the rioters of bullying when he says, "You had taught / How insolence and strong hand should prevail." He reminds them that although they might not share a nation of origin, they are not so different, as they could very well suffer the same fate if their violence is permitted to succeed.[31]

We therefore see that Tilney failed to understand (or did not care) that the playwrights' purpose in including the early scenes in which Barde and Cavaler abuse Williamson and Doll was to suggest that the actions of a few *do not justify* wholesale bigotry. In fact, More explicitly points out the increasingly global nature of the early modern world and the possibility that one day the rioters, too, may find themselves refugees (as did, for instance, many of

Elizabeth's Privy Council, including Francis Walsingham and William Cecil, her principal secretaries, during Mary's reign):

> **MORE** Go you to France or Flanders,
>   To any German province, Spain or Portugal,
>   Nay, anywhere that not adheres to England:
>   Why, you must needs be strangers. Would you be pleased
>   To find a nation of such barbarous temper
>   That, breaking out in hideous violence,
>   Would not afford you an abode on earth,
>   Whet their detested knives against your throats,
>   Spurn you like dogs, and like as if that God
>   Owed not nor made not you, nor that the elements
>   Were not all appropriate to your comforts
>   But chartered unto them? What would you think
>   To be thus used? This is the strangers' case,
>   And this your mountainish inhumanity. (6.143–56)

In this speech, More invites the rioters to travel abroad themselves and imagine how they might feel if faced with the inability to find food or shelter because the inhabitants of that nation treated them as they now were treating immigrants within their own city, terming such actions "mountainish inhumanity."

More's speeches are successful in dissuading Lincoln and his followers from rebellion, and they agree to "be ruled by you, Master More" (6.6.159–60). Because of this success, More is promoted by the king to the Privy Council, rising from commoner to courtier, and, shortly thereafter, to the position of Lord High Chancellor. The extent of More's reward confirms to the audience—and to us—that More's view, and *not* Lincoln's, is the correct one. By setting up More's successful empathetic argument in this scene, Shakespeare specifically attempts to appeal to audience members who might share Lincoln's anti-immigrant sentiment, only to turn on them with an appeal, which Lincoln himself accepts, to the contrary.

More's Conscience and the King's Ego

When More is named Lord High Chancellor, we are less than halfway through the play. It falls to the remainder of the text to demonstrate the failure of empathy in the face of dictatorial ego, a particularly dangerous suggestion for Shakespeare, Munday, and company to have made, given that the possessor of said ego (Henry VIII) was the father of the current queen.[32] The conflict between More and the king—although Henry never actually appears on stage—is one of conscience and religion.

The playwrights do not actually show us the circumstances which led to Henry's divorce from Catherine of Aragon and his proposal to Anne Boleyn

(Elizabeth's mother); those events happen "behind the curtain," leading to the final scenes in the play.[33] During a meeting of the Privy Council discussing Henry's potential alliance to France, Sir Thomas Palmer enters with a set of unnamed documents and presents them to the Council for ratification: "My lords, his majesty hath sent by me / These articles enclosed, first to be viewed, / And then to be subscribed to" (10.68–70). John Jowett notes that these are the articles of the Oath of Succession, which required subscription "to bear faith, truth, and obedience alonely to the king's majesty, and to his heirs of his body of his most dear and entirely beloved lawful wife Queen Anne."[34] To subscribe to these articles required Henry's Privy Council to accept Anne as his lawful wife; to do so required them to reject the authority of the pope and accept Henry not only as king, but also head of the Church of England.

What is deeply interesting is that the play, which should, by rights, be valorizing the Church of England and the Tudor line, seems to support More's decision to reject Henry's authority. Both More and the Bishop of Rochester refuse to subscribe to the oath, because, More says, "Our conscience first shall parley with our laws" (10.73). The invocation of "conscience" in Shakespeare's day was far more complicated than in the twenty-first century. Although conscience did have the meaning that we still use of "the internal acknowledgement or recognition of the moral quality of one's motives and actions; the sense of right and wrong as regards things for which one is responsible," according to the *Oxford English Dictionary* (c. 1255), it also contained a complex cultural valence which included toleration for Catholicism.[35] Specifically, the idea of "freedom of conscience," according to John Bossy, was "the free decision of the mode of existence of one's household" based on a "distinction in the order of society between what was the Queen's and what was one's own."[36] Under Elizabeth, a subset of Catholics, called Appellants, pleaded with the queen to permit them "liberty of conscience," by which they meant the "separation of the temporal and spiritual spheres" that "placed the individual at the conjunction of both and allowed for the development of individual conscience."[37] In other words, the Appellants wanted what amounted to a (very early) separation of church and state that would permit them to be both loyal citizens of England *and* Catholic, something Elizabethan law strictly forbade.

For *Sir Thomas More* to explicitly summon the word "conscience" was to engage both senses of the word, particularly because More himself, in context, is seeking to uphold a Catholic viewpoint against the Tudor founder of the Church of England. In the scene, Rochester refuses to take the oath and is arrested, while More instead asks for "time to bethink me of this task" (10.86). While he considers, he says, "I do resign mine office / Into my sovereign's hands" (10.87–8). Thus, although More might disagree with Henry, he does not seek to actively oppose the king, remaining loyal to his monarch even as he has a conflict of conscience. Interestingly, Tilney cuts most of this scene, as well, suggesting that the Master of Revels was unwilling to authorize a section of the play in which Rochester and More are both valorized for resisting the will of their monarch.

Henry, however, is unwilling to accept that More might have a legitimate objection, not unlike US president Donald Trump suggesting that US state governors need to "treat [him] right" in order to receive aid in treating COVID-19.[38] The play ends with More and Rochester both being executed for their refusal to obey Henry's dictates, and both are depicted in the play as martyrs rather than traitors. As he is led to his death, Rochester proclaims that "In this breast / there lives a soul that aims at higher things / Than temporary pleasing earthly kings" (12.2–4). More, speaking to his wife, says that

> **MORE** the King, of his high grace,
> Seeing my faithful service to his state,
> Intends to send me to the King of Heaven
> For a rich present; where my soul shall prove
> A true rememberer of his majesty. (13.85–9)

The tenor of this speech is meant both to reassure his wife that he will go to Heaven—because of his faith—and as a sardonic comment upon Henry's motivations. Of course the king has no intention of transforming More into a martyr (although the historical Thomas More is, in fact, a sainted martyr) or of aiding him in achieving Heaven; rather, Henry (offstage) acts out of ego, removing the two members of his council who attempt to thwart his will. This catering to the leader's whims—not unfamiliar to twenty-first-century citizens—as being above the good of commonwealth or citizenry remains central to the final scenes of the play as a warning to both present and future monarchs against allowing ego to trump empathy.

The play ends with More's death, as More proclaims that he will "satisfy the King even with my blood" (13.179). Given the anti-Catholic context in which Munday, Shakespeare, and their collaborators were writing, it is remarkable that More remains a hero (and a Catholic one, at that), a fact reinforced across multiple levels of society, with other members of the court, More's family, and even the Warders claiming that "the poor will bury him in tears. / I never heard a man since I was born / So generally bewailed of everyone" (14.12–14). Even the Lieutenant of the Tower, who says to More that "God and his blessed angels be about ye!" (17.26), and the Hangman, who begs his forgiveness, regret More's death. Once the execution has been accomplished, Surrey proclaims that "A very worthy gentleman / Seals error with his blood" (17.125–6), concluding the play with an ambiguous line which could be read as referring either to the end of More's error (in following Catholicism) or to Henry's error in having More executed.

The conclusion of the play is deeply unsatisfying to an audience who might wish for clearer lines between right and wrong. It was, perhaps, equally unsatisfying to Tilney, which may explain its lack of performance in 1597 (if at all), as the play quite firmly refuses to grant justification to the government or Henry for More's death. As such, the play presents a potential argument for freedom of conscience alongside its emphasis on toleration of immigration; these things, not surprisingly, are linked by the person of More. More's willingness to accept those who are unlike him—the Lombards—is echoed by the play's own refusal to condemn More himself for not agreeing with Henry, even as he is willing to follow the king's laws.

CONCLUSION

In Shakespeare's England, the play's message would translate to a plea to the English government for increased toleration of freedom of conscience—Catholicism—and the continued support of immigrant populations. Both things, unsurprisingly, are deeply tied to the burgeoning sense that the world was actually a great deal smaller than most early moderns had previously thought. By 1597, when *Sir Thomas More* was being written, England was engaging in global trade, with an outpost in what is now North Carolina and trading ports and partners in North Africa, the Middle East, Russia, Turkey, and beyond. London itself was a rich mélange of diverse peoples, with immigrants from France, the Netherlands, Italy, Portugal, and Africa across all classes and callings. In the aftermath of the Reformation, nations throughout Europe were beginning to experiment with religious toleration (even as early as the 1530s), and *Sir Thomas More*'s playwrights seem to hint that perhaps they wished England would do the same.

Ultimately, it is worth noting, the immigrants to London in Shakespeare's day and those who seek refuge in the US and Europe in the twenty-first century are not the primary threat to the economic and social stability of the nations to which they travel. In sixteenth-century London,

> alien craft expertise greatly contributed to England's expanding economy, introducing to London the production of commodities as such lace, and the economically important New Draperies. Flemish weavers brought the knowledge of how to create these desirable fabrics that allowed England to better compete in international markets.[39]

In addition, London included "French merchants, Dutch craftsmen, Italians who kept seedy bowling alleys, a handful of Africans, foreign teachers and printers, refugee doctors … rich, poor or middling."[40] Similarly, in the twenty-first century, we have considerable evidence that our economy and our scientific and technological progress benefit from the work, service, and diversity of immigrant populations. As the world grew more interconnected, England grew more and more powerful, becoming a global empire thanks to its willingness to engage in trade and toleration across multiple continents. It is worth noting that while England did have positive relations with its Islamic neighbors and a treaty with the Ottoman Empire, it was not above enslaving or abusing indigenous peoples across the world. However, for its time, England's willingness to engage in cross-cultural conversations (rather than persecution, as was the case with the Spanish Inquisition) made it, for a while, the most powerful nation in the Western world.

When we read *Sir Thomas More* in the twenty-first century, we find alarming parallels to both the opening scene's anti-immigrant riots and the concluding scene's toxic egoism of King Henry, who would execute a loyal and beloved councilor for nothing more than ideological disagreement.[41] The play suggests that perhaps a significant mitigating factor to unchecked power might be the willingness of a leader to accept critique and advice from advisors (or, at least, not indiscriminately decapitate or fire them). We can take the lesson from *Sir Thomas More*, then, that ego and matters of cultural difference should matter less than our common humanity, whether in the face of economic downturn or disease, as we are all better off together than we ever could be apart.

NOTES

1. More was remembered in Shakespeare's time as an early humanist, the author of *Utopia*, and partial subject of Desiderius Erasmus's *Moriae Encomium*, translated to *The Praise of Folly*, but which also puns on More's name with a secondary meaning of "Praise of More." Despite his Catholicism, then, More was generally considered a positive role model.
2. Christopher Haigh, *English Reformations: Religion, Politics, and Society under the Tudors* (Oxford: Clarendon Press, 1993), 180.
3. Eamon Duffy, *Saints, Sacrilege & Sedition: Religion and Conflict in the Tudor Reformations*, paperback (2012 hardcover) (London: Bloomsbury, 2014).
4. Haigh, *English Reformations*, 235.
5. John Coffey, *Persecution and Toleration in Protestant England 1558–1689*, Studies in Modern History (Harlow: Longman, 2000), 80.
6. Stephen Alford, *The Watchers: A Secret History of the Reign of Elizabeth I* (New York: Bloomsbury, Inc., 2012), 45.
7. Kristin M. S. Bezio, "Muslims Are the New Jesuits: What We Can Learn about Leadership and Modern Islamophobia from Shakespeare's England," in *Leadership, Populism, and Resistance*, ed. Kristin M. S. Bezio and George R. Goethals, Jepson Studies in Leadership (Cheltenham, UK and Northampton, MA, USA: Edward Elgar, 2020), 30–45.
8. Beth Norris, "London Aliens," interactive resource (The Map of Early Modern London, 2016), Austin Friars, https://mapoflondon.uvic.ca/ALIE1.htm.

9. Stephen Alford, *London's Triumph: Merchant Adventurers and the Tudor City* (London: Penguin Random House UK, 2017), 16.
10. Norris, "London Aliens."
11. Norris, "London Aliens."
12. Kelly Weill, "Hate Crimes Spiked After Trump's Anti-Muslim Tweets, Study Finds," *The Daily Beast*, May 14, 2018, sec. us-news, https://www.thedailybeast.com/hate-crimes-spiked-after-trumps-anti-muslim-tweets-study-finds; Hyung-Jin Kim, "Fears of New Virus Trigger Anti-China Sentiment Worldwide," *PBS NewsHour*, February 2, 2020, sec. Health, https://www.pbs.org/newshour/health/fears-of-new-virus-trigger-anti-china-sentiment-worldwide.
13. Tom McTague, "Theresa May Unveils New UK Immigration System," POLITICO, October 1, 2018, https://www.politico.eu/article/theresa-may-unveils-new-uk-immigration-system/; "What Is the Migrant Caravan Heading to US?" *BBC News*, November 26, 2018, sec. Latin America & Caribbean, https://www.bbc.com/news/world-latin-america-45951782.
14. "Trump Defends Calling Coronavirus the 'Chinese Virus,'" *Aljazeera*, March 23, 2020, online edition, https://www.aljazeera.com/programmes/newsfeed/2020/03/trump-defends-calling-coronavirus-chinese-virus-200323102618665.html.
15. Anna Colet et al., "The Black Death and Its Consequences for the Jewish Community in Tàrrega: Lessons from History and Archaeology," in *Pandemic Disease in the Medieval World: Rethinking the Black Death*, ed. Monica H. Green, The Medieval Globe 1 (Kalamazoo: ARC Medieval Press, 2015), 64.
16. Nükhet Varlik, "New Science and Old Sources: Why the Ottoman Experience of Plague Matters," in *Pandemic Disease in the Medieval World: Rethinking the Black Death*, ed. Monica H. Green, The Medieval Globe 1 (Kalamazoo: ARC Medieval Press, 2015), 204.
17. William B. Long, "The Occasion of the *Book of Sir Thomas More*," in *Shakespeare and Sir Thomas More: Essays on the Play and Its Shakespearian Interest*, ed. T. H. Howard-Hill (Cambridge: Cambridge University Press, 1989), 45–56; David Womersley, "Shakespeare and Anthony Munday," in *Literary Milieux: Essays in Text and Context Presented to Howard Erskine-Hill*, ed. David Womersley and Richard McCabe (Dover: University of Delaware Press, 2008), 77; M. St. Clare Byrne, "Anthony Munday and His Books," *The Library* 1, no. 1 (1921), 249; Thomas Merriam, "The Misunderstanding of Munday as Author of *Sir Thomas More*," *The Review of English Studies* 51, no. 204 (2000): 544; Vittorio Gabrieli and Giorgio Melchiori, "Introduction," in *Sir Thomas More*, The Revels Plays (Manchester: Manchester University Press, 2002), 12; G. B. Harrison, "The Date of Sir Thomas More," *The Review of English Studies* 1, no. 3 (1925): 339; Charles R. Forker and Joseph Candido, "Wit, Wisdom, and Theatricality in *The Book of Sir Thomas More*," *Shakespeare Studies* 13 (1980): 85.
18. Norris, "London Aliens."
19. Christian M. Billing, "Forms of Fashion: Material Fabrics, National Characteristics, and the Dramaturgy of Difference on the Early Modern English Stage," in *Transnational Mobilities in Early Modern Theater*, ed. Robert Henke and Eric Nicholson, reprint (2014) (Abingdon: Routledge, 2016), 145.
20. The Liberties of London were peripheral districts outside of the jurisdiction of the Common Council of London and were exempt from certain laws and restrictions. Playhouses, gaming houses, brothels, and other places of entertainment were also located in the Liberties to avoid legal restrictions.
21. Derek Wilson, "Evil May Day 1517," *History Today* 69, no. 6 (June 2017): 67.

22. Wilson, "Evil May Day 1517," 67.

23. Wilson, "Evil May Day 1517," 67.

24. Wilson, "Evil May Day 1517," 67.

25. Wilson, "Evil May Day 1517," 67.

26. Wilson, "Evil May Day 1517," 71.

27. Quoted in Brandon Massey, "James Dobson's Anti-Immigrant Rhetoric Is Dangerous," *Sojourners*, July 3, 2019, https://sojo.net/articles/james-dobsons-anti -immigrant-rhetoric-dangerous.

28. All citations from the play are taken from Anthony Munday and Henry Chettle, *Sir Thomas More*, ed. John Jowett, The Arden Shakespeare (London: Methuen, 2011).

29. "Taking the wall" meant that Williamson walked on the wall-side of the street, an act of social insult to someone of higher rank because of the open sewage often flowing down the center. That Williamson "took the wall against a stranger" meant that Williamson had walked up against the wall when passing a "stranger," or foreigner, who complained to the ambassador and had Williamson imprisoned.

30. Most French refugees in Elizabethan England were Huguenot Protestants, rather than Catholics, and the English government supported the Huguenot cause.

31. Shakespeare has a history—as in *Troilus and Cressida*, *Coriolanus* (see chapter 3), *2 Henry VI*, and *Richard III*—of characterizing the commons as ill-equipped to make political decisions. There may be some hint of this here, as well, although More specifies the value of "strangers" repeatedly.

32. This may be another reason why the play may never have made it to the stage.

33. What we do see in the play is the arrival of a document at the Privy Council requir-ing its affirmation. This document would not only affirm Anne Boleyn as queen, but also confirm the legality of Henry's divorce from Catherine of Aragon *and* his supremacy over the newly created Church of England. The play does not go into the details of any of these events.

34. John Jowett, "Introduction," in *Sir Thomas More*, ed. John Jowett, The Arden Shakespeare (London: Methuen, 2011), 273 (note).

35. "Conscience, n.," in *OED Online* (Oxford University Press), accessed April 2, 2020, http://www.oed.com/view/Entry/39460.

36. John Bossy, "The Character of Elizabethan Catholicism," *Past & Present*, no. 21 (April 1962): 41.

37. Sandra Jusdado, "The Appellant Priests and the Succession Issue," in *The Struggle for the Succession in Late Elizabethan England: Politics, Polemics and Cultural Representations*, ed. Jean-Christophe Mayer, Astraea Collection 11 (Montpellier: Université Paul-Valéry Montpellier, 2004), 212.

38. Michelle Goldberg, "Column: In an Act of Flagrant Corruption, Trump Is Playing Domestic Quid pro Quo with Governors," *chicagotribune.com*, March 30, 2020, sec. Opinion, https://www.chicagotribune.com/opinion/ct-nyt-opinion-trump -favors-governors-coronavirus-20200331-vd6ww33wejejfoqejnbxcnvsuy-story .html.

39. Norris, "London Aliens."

40. Alford, *London's Triumph*, 16.

41. The depiction of More in the play is, of course, one written through distinctly rose-colored glasses. More, like any ambitious political figure, is historically considered somewhat ethically ambiguous, and historians have not settled the question of his relative virtues.

REFERENCES

Alford, Stephen. *London's Triumph: Merchant Adventurers and the Tudor City.* London: Penguin Random House UK, 2017.

Alford, Stephen. *The Watchers: A Secret History of the Reign of Elizabeth I.* New York: Bloomsbury, Inc., 2012.

Bezio, Kristin M. S. "Muslims Are the New Jesuits: What We Can Learn about Leadership and Modern Islamophobia from Shakespeare's England." In *Leadership, Populism, and Resistance*, edited by Kristin M. S. Bezio and George R. Goethals, 30–45. Jepson Studies in Leadership. Cheltenham, UK and Northampton, MA, USA: Edward Elgar, 2020.

Billing, Christian M. "Forms of Fashion: Material Fabrics, National Characteristics, and the Dramaturgy of Difference on the Early Modern English Stage." In *Transnational Mobilities in Early Modern Theater*, edited by Robert Henke and Eric Nicholson, reprint (2014), 131–55. Abingdon: Routledge, 2016.

Bossy, John. "The Character of Elizabethan Catholicism." *Past & Present*, no. 21 (1962): 39–59.

Coffey, John. *Persecution and Toleration in Protestant England 1558–1689.* Studies in Modern History. Harlow: Longman, 2000.

Colet, Anna, Josep Xavier Muntané i Santiveri, Jordi Ruíz Ventura, Oriol Saula, M. Eulàlia Subirà de Galdàcano, and Clara Jáuregui. "The Black Death and Its Consequences for the Jewish Community in Tàrrega: Lessons from History and Archaeology." In *Pandemic Disease in the Medieval World: Rethinking the Black Death*, edited by Monica H. Green, 63–96. The Medieval Globe 1. Kalamazoo: ARC Medieval Press, 2015.

"Conscience, n." In *OED Online*. Oxford University Press. Accessed April 2, 2020. http://www.oed.com/view/Entry/39460.

Duffy, Eamon. *Saints, Sacrilege & Sedition: Religion and Conflict in the Tudor Reformations*, paperback (2012 hardcover). London: Bloomsbury, 2014.

Forker, Charles R., and Joseph Candido. "Wit, Wisdom, and Theatricality in *The Book of Sir Thomas More*." *Shakespeare Studies* 13 (1980): 85–104.

Gabrieli, Vittorio, and Giorgio Melchiori. "Introduction." In *Sir Thomas More*, 1–47. The Revels Plays. Manchester: Manchester University Press, 2002. https://books .google.com/books/about/Sir_Thomas_More.html?id=Ine1pY9eaRMC.

Goldberg, Michelle. "Column: In an Act of Flagrant Corruption, Trump Is Playing Domestic Quid pro Quo with Governors." *chicagotribune.com.* March 30, 2020, sec. Opinion. https://www.chicagotribune.com/opinion/ct-nyt-opinion-trump-favors -governors-coronavirus-20200331-vd6ww33wejejfoqejnbxcnvsuy-story.html.

Haigh, Christopher. *English Reformations: Religion, Politics, and Society Under the Tudors.* Oxford: Clarendon Press, 1993.

Harrison, G. B. "The Date of Sir Thomas More." *The Review of English Studies* 1, no. 3 (1925): 337–9.

Jowett, John. "Introduction." In *Sir Thomas More*, edited by John Jowett, 1–129. The Arden Shakespeare. London: Methuen, 2011.

Jusdado, Sandra. "The Appellant Priests and the Succession Issue." In *The Struggle for the Succession in Late Elizabethan England: Politics, Polemics and Cultural Representations*, edited by Jean-Christophe Mayer, 199–216. Astraea Collection 11. Montpellier: Université Paul-Valéry Montpellier, 2004.

Kim, Hyung-Jin. "Fears of New Virus Trigger Anti-China Sentiment Worldwide." *PBS NewsHour*, February 2, 2020, sec. Health. https://www.pbs.org/newshour/health/fears-of-new-virus-trigger-anti-china-sentiment-worldwide.

Long, William B. "The Occasion of the *Book of Sir Thomas More*." In *Shakespeare and Sir Thomas More: Essays on the Play and Its Shakespearian Interest*, edited by T. H. Howard-Hill, 45–56. Cambridge: Cambridge University Press, 1989.

Massey, Brandon. "James Dobson's Anti-Immigrant Rhetoric Is Dangerous." *Sojourners*, July 3, 2019. https://sojo.net/articles/james-dobsons-anti-immigrant-rhetoric-dangerous.

McTague, Tom. "Theresa May Unveils New UK Immigration System." POLITICO, October 1, 2018. https://www.politico.eu/article/theresa-may-unveils-new-uk-immigration-system/.

Merriam, Thomas. "The Misunderstanding of Munday as Author of *Sir Thomas More*." *The Review of English Studies* 51, no. 204 (2000): 540–81.

Munday, Anthony, and Henry Chettle. *Sir Thomas More*. Edited by John Jowett. The Arden Shakespeare. London: Methuen, 2011.

Norris, Beth. "London Aliens." Interactive resource. The Map of Early Modern London, 2016. Austin Friars. https://mapoflondon.uvic.ca/ALIE1.htm.

St. Clare Byrne, M. "Anthony Munday and His Books." *The Library* 1, no. 1 (1921): 225–56.

"Trump Defends Calling Coronavirus the 'Chinese Virus.'" *Aljazeera*, March 23, 2020, online edition. https://www.aljazeera.com/programmes/newsfeed/2020/03/trump-defends-calling-coronavirus-chinese-virus-200323102618665.html.

Varlik, Nükhet. "New Science and Old Sources: Why the Ottoman Experience of Plague Matters." In *Pandemic Disease in the Medieval World: Rethinking the Black Death*, edited by Monica H. Green, 193–227. The Medieval Globe 1. Kalamazoo: ARC Medieval Press, 2015.

Weill, Kelly. "Hate Crimes Spiked After Trump's Anti-Muslim Tweets, Study Finds." *The Daily Beast*, May 14, 2018, sec. us-news. https://www.thedailybeast.com/hate-crimes-spiked-after-trumps-anti-muslim-tweets-study-finds.

"What Is the Migrant Caravan Heading to US?" *BBC News*, November 26, 2018, sec. Latin America & Caribbean. https://www.bbc.com/news/world-latin-america-45951782.

Wilson, Derek. "Evil May Day 1517." *History Today* 69, no. 6 (June 2017): 66–71.

Womersley, David. "Shakespeare and Anthony Munday." In *Literary Milieux: Essays in Text and Context Presented to Howard Erskine-Hill*, edited by David Womersley and Richard McCabe, 72–90. Dover: University of Delaware Press, 2008.

11. *Twelfth Night* and gender fluidity

Maria Carrig

Contemporary discourse of gender self-fashioning resonates in surprising ways in Shakespeare's romantic comedies of cross-dressing and deception, none more so than *Twelfth Night*, one of five plays featuring a cross-dressed heroine.[1] Shakespeare's comedy of disguise, misplaced attraction, revelry, and folly has provided a performance space for many eras to test cultural norms regarding gender and sexuality. Students today are surprised and delighted by the contemporary feel of a play written over 400 years ago, with its resourceful gender-switching heroine and confusion of hetero- and homoerotic attachments. Still, can a story that ends with heterosexual marriages and the abandonment of role-play have anything to teach us about ourselves and our times? I believe the answer is a qualified "yes" and that *Twelfth Night* proves more daring in its dramatization of the unruliness of love and the importance of breaking out of the limits of our gendered expectations than many twentieth-century treatments of the story.

Near the beginning of *Twelfth Night*, the heroine, Viola, asks some sailors who have saved her from drowning and deposited her on land, "What country, friends, is this?" (1.2.1).[2] The question is typical for a Renaissance play, allowing the actors to announce the setting of the action, for the platform stage would have been without scenery or backdrop. But it also alerts the audience that this will be a play of discoveries and surprises, hopes, and new beginnings, the stuff of which Shakespeare's romantic comedies are made. The question's wondering tone further hints that people as well as places will not be what they seem. When Viola proceeds to adopt a male disguise, identity becomes as fluid and unstable as the sea from which she has emerged. In Illyria, Viola will love and be loved by both a woman and a man, nimbly adopting a man's behavior while maintaining what she calls a woman's truth of heart (2.4.106). In its plot and dialogue, *Twelfth Night* raises questions as to what it means to be male and female, speaking with remarkable clarity to twenty-first-century culture's evolving spectrum of sexual and gender identity.

Modern audiences of *Twelfth Night* do not find it difficult to relate to Viola's disorientation. Our contemporary cultural landscape, like the country in which Viola finds herself, presents exhilarating new vistas for the exploration of the self. This freedom has emerged after decades of LGBTQ+ activism, the legalization of same-sex marriage, and the increasing availability of hormonal and surgical technologies through which to realign biological sex with one's gender identity. It is now commonplace to assert that gender does not originate in a person's biological or assigned sex, but that it is rather a set of attitudes and behaviors, a performance mandated by social and ideological norms that can be resisted and subverted. A new vocabulary expresses a broad spectrum of possible gender and sexual identities. Terms such as *gender-fluid*, *genderqueer*, and *nonbinary* suggest that one can choose how to express one's gender, or whether to identify with a gender at all.[3] Standard works of literary criticism contribute to this discourse, recommending that gender itself should be consigned to the dustbin of history, along with patriarchy, monarchy, and compulsory heterosexuality.[4] Yet considerable anxiety underlies such possibilities, both for the individual and for a society in upheaval. Even in the relatively safe space of college campuses, students juggle the possibilities of reinventing themselves with their anxiety about fitting in, wondering who they are as they prepare themselves to assume roles as workers and citizens in the wider society.

The question of what we might call relevance was not unfamiliar to Shakespeare himself. For the plot of *Twelfth Night*, Shakespeare drew, as he often did, on storylines popular since ancient times, and for this he was accused by his contemporary Ben Jonson of dredging up "mouldy tale[s]."[5] Yet he reinvented these stories by making his characters reflective and self-aware: they and their audience know they are not simply fictional characters, but performers on a stage, in a time when the profession of actor had existed for only a few decades.[6] Dissatisfied, full of desire and ambition, they become fluid—free to choose, at least for a time, their identities, in short, to perform, sometimes even to step outside and comment on their own narratives.

The story of *Twelfth Night* goes as follows: twins Viola and Sebastian are shipwrecked, each landing separately in the country of Illyria and believing the other to be drowned. Viola disguises herself as a boy, Cesario, and, while serving as page to Duke Orsino, becomes part of a romantic triangle: she falls in love with Orsino, while he pines for the Lady Olivia, who is herself in mourning for her dead brother. Acting as courtly messenger to Olivia on behalf of Orsino, Viola-Cesario becomes the object of Olivia's desire. The comedy of misplaced attraction is complicated by mistaken identity when Sebastian also appears on the scene, creating an escalating series of errors leading to a denouement in which the twins are reunited, Viola marries Orsino, and Olivia finds herself with Sebastian (whom she had married thinking he was Cesario). These entanglements alternate with scenes of the drunken revels taking place in Olivia's house, where the puritanical steward Malvolio is tricked into believing Olivia is in love with him and indulges in his own form of "cross-dressing," famously putting on yellow stockings and crossed garters in order to woo Olivia.

It has long been noted that *Twelfth Night* undermines the heterosexual order of things.[7] The heroine, Viola, seems unquestionably female and heterosexual, never wavering in her devotion to Orsino. At the same time, by adopting male disguise, she introduces an ongoing tension regarding her gender and sexuality that affects the characters with whom she interacts, a tension she sometimes bewails ("Disguise, I see thou art a wickedness" (2.2.27)) and other times accepts ("I am not what I am" (3.1.139)). Stephen Orgel observes that Viola initially plans to disguise herself as "an eunuch" in Orsino's court, "for I can sing / And speak to him in many sorts of music" (1.2.53–5). Her choice of the name Cesario, Orgel suggests, calls up the concept of castration (the Latin past participle *caesus* means "cut") and the related figure of the castrato, a man who "can sing both high and low."[8] As neither man nor woman—or in musical terms, both man and woman—the eunuch seems an ideal representation of Viola's gender fluidity.

Viola does not follow up on her initial plan to disguise herself as a eunuch, and her male disguise almost immediately creates difficulties. In the last scene of Act 1, Viola-Cesario, secretly in love with Orsino, must act as messenger to woo Olivia on Orsino's behalf. Cesario's eloquent love speeches and androgynous good looks succeed in making Olivia forget her mourning, but unfortunately not in the way Cesario intended. When she realizes Olivia has fallen in love with her, Viola-Cesario soliloquizes:

> **VIOLA** What will become of this? As I am man,
>   My state is desperate for my master's love;
>   As I am woman, now alas the day,
>   What thriftless sighs shall poor Olivia breathe?
>   O time, thou must untangle this, not I.
>   It is too hard a knot for me t'untie. (2.2.36–41)

The tangled knot of attractions cannot be "untied" by Viola because she herself, the man-woman, is the problem. She recognizes both Olivia's and her own desires are destined to be thwarted by her indeterminate gender. Their complementary predicament is further indicated by the fact that the names Viola and Olivia are virtual anagrams. Unmasking might solve Viola's dilemma, but would reveal the "thriftlessness," or futility, of Olivia's love. In this sense, her bald assertion that she is both man and woman discloses a deeper difficulty that *Twelfth Night* explores: the prohibition of homosexual love. If Olivia were to love Viola as a woman, or were Cesario to be loved by Orsino as a man, their states would indeed be desperate.[9]

These lines may have had a more bitter ring in Shakespeare's time, which enforced a heteronormativity far more profound than our own. Homosexuality was not recognized as a form of identity; however, homosexual acts, called *sodomy* (a term that encompassed same-sex and other non-normative sexual acts), could lead to a death sentence.[10] Looking forward to our own times, while civil rights are far more advanced, anti-LGBTQ violence remains a reality, and it was only in 2003 that the Supreme Court declared anti-sodomy laws unconstitutional. Viola's comments on her "desperate" state resonate with us, as well.

Looking at this monologue alone, one might dismiss Viola's identifying herself as both man and woman as mere wordplay. But the gendered ambiguity of sexual attraction emerges in each of the scenes involving intimacy with Viola-Cesario. Orsino, who has announced "the passion of my love" for Olivia in the opening scene and pursues it with violent declarations until the play's final scene, would seem a very pattern of cis-male desire. But since Orsino never actually interacts with Olivia until the final scene, Cesario becomes the surrogate and indirect object of his passion. Orsino makes this clear when he tasks Cesario with wooing Olivia as his "nuncio," or messenger, declaring, "It shall become thee well to act my woes" (1.4.26). Desiring Cesario to act out his own feelings, Orsino then proposes that Cesario will do this well because of his effeminate appearance: "For they shall yet belie thy happy years / That say thou art a man. Diana's lip / Is not more smooth and rubious; thy small pipe / Is as the maiden's organ, shrill and sound, / And all is semblative a woman's part" (1.4.30–4). Now, why does Orsino believe that someone who looks and sounds like a pretty young woman would be the best person to represent him? Orsino seems to be channeling either his own female side or his suppressed attraction to this young man. That attraction of course heightens romantic suspense for the audience, who knows of Viola's secret love and hopes the two will eventually be united as man and woman. But it also draws out a bittersweet acknowledgment of the homoerotic dimension of the romance. Orsino repeatedly calls Cesario "boy," a term that hints at a deeper affection and keeps the audience aware of the boy actor inhabiting Cesario's costume. Even Orsino's protestations to Cesario about gender difference undermine themselves. In Act 2, Scene 4, the two engage in an intimate conversation about the characteristics of men and women. While Orsino insists that men are bigger, stronger, and hungrier than women, he also aligns men with qualities conventionally associated with feminine weakness: "Our fancies are more giddy and unfirm, / More longing wavering, sooner lost and worn / Than women's are" (2.4.33–5).[11] The giddy Orsino seems as androgynous as Cesario.

During this scene, Orsino asks to hear a love song and tells Cesario, "Come hither, boy. If ever thou shalt love, / In the sweet pangs of it remember me" (2.4.15–16). While the Duke explicitly compares his current pangs of desire to

Cesario's future ones, listeners cannot help but notice that this seems a virtual request for Cesario's love. Orsino's words initiate a riddling dialogue:

> **DUKE** My life upon't, young though thou art, thine eye
>   Hath stayed upon some favor that it loves.
>   Hath it not, boy?
> **VIOLA** A little, by your favor.
> **DUKE** What kind of woman is't?
> **VIOLA** Of your complexion.
> **DUKE** She is not worth thee then. What years, i'faith?
> **VIOLA** About your years, my lord. (2.4.23–8)

Viola's secret—that she is speaking not of someone like the Duke, but of the Duke himself—is complicated by the fact that Orsino keeps referring to this someone as a woman. It is as if they are revolving on contrary gender wheels. When their discussion turns to male and female love in general, and Orsino insists that women's love is fundamentally different from men's, Viola responds in a way that threatens to reveal her identity:

> **VIOLA** Ay, but I know –
> **DUKE** What dost thou know?
> **VIOLA** Too well what love women to men may owe.
>   In faith, they are as true of heart as we.
>   My father had a daughter loved a man
>   As it might be perhaps, were I a woman,
>   I should your lordship.
> **DUKE** And what's her history?
> **VIOLA** A blank, my lord. She never told her love,
>   But let concealment, like a worm i'th'bud,
>   Feed on her damask cheek. She pined in thought;
>   And, with a green and yellow melancholy,
>   She sat like Patience on a monument,
>   Smiling at grief. Was not this love indeed? (2.4.103–15)

Viola here speaks of herself in the third person, and it is typical of Shakespeare to allow her to express the power of women's love and sorrow only in her role as a man, feelings made all the more poignant because they are not understood by Orsino. As a woman constrained to silence by her disguise, she imagines a melancholy fate for herself, like Patience, smiling amidst her tears. The deep feeling of these lines moves us even today, evoking not only the timeless misery of unfulfilled love, but also the more profound cruelty inflicted on the countless people whose love has been forbidden and whose stories, ignored by history, have been rendered "a blank." This iconic moment in *Twelfth Night* continues to resonate with contemporary audiences, from "don't ask, don't tell" to ongoing violence against transgender people.

Viola expresses these fears and the human tragedies that underlie them, but at the same time, she distances herself from the silent Patience and the melancholy lover she describes. She will not remain the archetypal silent woman but will be the means by which characters free themselves from the constraints that keep them from acknowledging who they are and who they really love. We see this power at work in her dialogues with Olivia. Although Olivia has dedicated herself to mourning for her dead father and brother, within moments of her encounter with Cesario she has removed her mourning veil. While rejecting Cesario's embassy of love from Orsino, Olivia is aroused by Cesario's physical presence, rhapsodizing to herself, "Methinks I feel this youth's perfections / With an invisible and subtle stealth / To creep in at mine eyes" (1.5.288–90). In their second dialogue, Olivia aggressively woos Cesario, who sidesteps her overtures:

> **OLIVIA** Stay –
> 　I prithee tell me what thou think'st of me.
> **VIOLA** That you do think you are not what you are.
> **OLIVIA** If I think so, I think the same of you.
> **VIOLA** Then think you right: I am not what I am. (3.1.135–9)

In this riddling dialogue, they seem to be arguing about their relative social status: Viola-Cesario asserting that Olivia is stooping below her rank ("you do think you are not what you are"), while Olivia counters that Cesario is more a gentleman than servant ("I think the same of you"). But the exchange refers more subtly to Olivia's sexuality. What Olivia thinks she is—in love with a man—is *not* what she is—in love with a woman. Olivia expresses a lesbian attraction, though she does not fully know this herself.[12] While lesbianism would have been a buried reference in Shakespeare's time, contemporary performances have the power to bring these hints to the surface. Of course, the witty play on gender indeterminacy would have been especially pronounced on the Elizabethan stage, because the female characters were played by boy actors. When Viola says "I am not what I am," a sixteenth-century audience would have been aware of the fact that the "real" woman, Viola, was a male actor. The underlying joke would have been that two male actors were playing two females; neither actor was "what I am," but either way, they were engaging in same-sex flirtation.

In an influential essay, Catherine Belsey argues that *Twelfth Night* does not simply draw attention to the fact that gender can be performed; more radically, it dramatizes the artificiality of the two-sex model, "disrupting sexual difference, calling in question that set of relations between terms which proposes as inevitable an antithesis between masculine and feminine, men and women."[13] The play's undermining of the male-female binary reveals a curious parallel between the Renaissance and the postmodern age. Physiological theories of the human body in the sixteenth century, following the ancient writings of Galen, propounded a "one-sex" model: a woman's genitalia were seen as simply the inverse of a man's, having failed to emerge from the body because of a lack of heat.[14] This concept bears some resemblance to modern theories questioning the sexual binary, from examples of intersex individuals to the beliefs of transgender people that their identity does not correspond to their birth or "assigned" sex.

If *Twelfth Night*'s first four acts have thus opened up the possibilities of sexual experimentation and gender fluidity, Act 5 may seem to close those off, as the twins Viola and Sebastian appear together on stage, and the romantic mistakes are resolved in heterosexual marriages, aligning the social with the natural order. In the final scene, after Olivia has met Sebastian and dragged him to the altar, he reveals that he is Viola-Cesario's twin in a piece of wordplay: "So comes it, lady, you have been mistook; ... / You would have been contracted to a maid, / Nor are you therein, by my life, deceived. / You are betrothed both to a maid and man" (5.1.257–9). Sebastian is himself the "maid" (that is, a virgin) as well as man. But, he is still indistinguishable from Viola—Antonio has just said, "An apple cleft in two is not more twin / Than these two creatures" (5.1.218–20). Thus, Sebastian's words imply that Olivia has married a man and a woman; like Orsino and Viola in earlier scenes, he describes himself as androgynous, making Olivia, perhaps, pan-sexual. Shakespeare could not, of course, explicitly endorse same-sex marriage. Rather, the final scene is emotionally moving in expressing that the universal joy of union and reunion, of love shared, dissolves gender distinctions.

From this perspective, modern productions are generally less gender-fluid than those of Shakespeare's era, for the role of Viola is almost always played by a woman, thus strengthening the audience's visual sense that Viola is "really" female, rather than a boy playing a woman playing a man.[15] It is interesting to look at how *Twelfth Night* has been adapted both on the modern stage and in Hollywood cinema, as an index of current attitudes to norms of gender and sexuality. The play's ability to speak to young people's concerns about sex roles and status was demonstrated by the popularity of the 2006 film *She's the Man*, which turned the play into a high school comedy.[16] The film built on the success of movies like *Mean Girls* (Paramount, 2004) and *10 Things I Hate About You* (Touchstone Pictures, 1999, itself an adaptation of *The Taming of the Shrew*). These high school comedies appealed to female audiences, with their tales of an unconventional or outcast heroine who wins the popular guy and achieves social and romantic success.

In *She's the Man*, soccer-playing Viola disguises herself as her brother, Sebastian, in order to play on the team at his prep school. There she falls for her roommate, Duke, at the same time becoming the object of more than one girl's affections. Various hijinks ensue before Viola helps the team win the championship game, reveals her true gender, and is united with Duke. The film is feminist in its insistence on equal status on the playing field and makes some attempt to highlight the performed character of gender roles. Much of its humor has to do with the disguised Viola (played by a charmingly youthful Amanda Bynes) trying to mimic men's walks and crude sexual banter, while the hypermasculine Duke (Channing Tatum, frequently shirtless) turns out to be a "sensitive man," criticizing sexism and betraying a fear of spiders. Yet the story squeamishly avoids *Twelfth Night*'s homoeroticism. For example, the character of Antonio, whose passionate loyalty to Sebastian in the play goes well beyond the bounds of friendship—"I do adore thee so," he says, "That danger shall seem sport" (2.1.43–4)—is replaced in *She's the Man* with an ex-girlfriend of Sebastian's, who appears at key moments and mistakes Viola for her brother. The central relationship between Viola and Duke features only two moments of homoerotic bonding. The pair hug while jumping onto a bed to avoid an escaped pet tarantula, and, at the denouement, Viola, still in male disguise, says "I love you" to Duke; both moments are treated with intense discomfort. When Duke realizes Viola is female, he says, "From now on, everything would be a lot easier if you stayed a girl." The film's resolution returns Viola to her conventional gender role, and the couple is last seen being introduced to an admiring crowd at a debutante ball, Viola's long hair and close-cut dress emphasizing her femininity. In a publicity interview for the movie, Amanda Bynes said of her cross-dressing role, "It was fun because I felt like it was freeing and I got to be someone else." Years later, however, she admitted, "When the movie came out and I saw it, I went into a deep depression for four–six months because I didn't like how I looked when I was a boy."[17] Bynes's confession of her anxiety poignantly expresses the burden of gendered stereotypes; even in a film that supposedly critiqued sexism, even in male disguise, she felt she had to police her physical appearance.

She's the Man thus effectively eliminates the ambiguity and openness of *Twelfth Night*'s ending and takes fewer risks in its representation of the performance of gender. Indeed, at the end both Viola and Sebastian expose their bodies as proof of their sex (Viola shows her breasts, Sebastian drops his pants). In the play, by contrast, Sebastian's appearance on stage at the same time as Viola leads to a revelation of her true identity, but as discussed above this exposure is couched in gender-fluid terms. Orsino, seeing the two together for the first time, says, "One face, one voice, one habit, and two persons: / A natural perspective, that is and is not" (5.1.212–13). While acknowledging they are two people, he nevertheless describes them as one, an optical illusion created by a "perspective" or distorting mirror. This "both/and" language continues as the scene progresses. Sebastian looks at the disguised Viola and asks,

"Do I stand there?" (5.1.222). Viola tells him she can confirm her identity as female only by changing clothes:

> **VIOLA** If nothing lets [*hinders*] to make us happy both
> But this my masculine usurped attire,
> Do not embrace me till each circumstance
> Of place, time, fortune do cohere and jump
> That I am Viola – which to confirm
> I'll bring you to a captain in this town,
> Where lie my maiden weeds. (5.1.245–51)

The emphasis on clothing as indicator of gender and the indeterminacy of sexual identity under the clothes extend to the union of Viola and Orsino as well. Duke Orsino asks to see Viola "in thy woman's weeds" (5.1.269), but the two exit with Viola still dressed in male costume as Orsino declares, "Cesario, come – / For so you shall be while you are a man; / But when in other habits you are seen, / Orsino's mistress and his fancy's queen" (5.1.380–1). Orsino's "fancy"—a punning word referring to his love, but also to his tastes or "fantasy"—seems as fluid as Viola-Cesario's costume and gender.[18]

Twelfth Night thus seems more contemporary in its openness to what might be called "queer" identity than the somewhat dated gender dynamics of *She's the Man*. One sees the same conservatism in *Shakespeare in Love*, a film successful not just with teenagers but also with the general public and the Motion Picture Academy, which awarded it Best Picture in 1999 (along with six other awards, including Best Actress for Gwyneth Paltrow). In *Shakespeare in Love*, handsome Will Shakespeare falls in love with the unattainable aristocrat Viola de Lesseps, who meanwhile has disguised herself as a boy, "Thomas Kent," in order to be an actor in Will's company. The complications that ensue do not, however, involve any real sense of gender ambiguity. As Viola, Gwyneth Paltrow radiates femininity, her fair skin and golden hair glowing. Though she spends a significant part of the action in male disguise, Will quickly learns that "Thomas" is really a woman after a brief and seemingly same-sex kiss. Thus, viewers have no room to question Will's sexuality or the nature of sexual attraction in general. In fact, the film is remarkable for its lack of homoerotic humor, given that it features several cross-dressed actors. Most of the plot focuses on parallels between the course of Will's and Viola's love and the writing and rehearsing of what will become *Romeo and Juliet*. The movie is so "straight" that Viola even ends up playing Juliet, rather than Romeo, the part Thomas Kent was assigned.

Delightful as *Shakespeare in Love* is, it offers mostly Hollywood-style maxims about "true love." Interestingly, the conflict of the second half of the play has to do with a wager, presided over by Queen Elizabeth (Judi Dench, who herself played Viola some 30 years earlier), as to whether theater can portray the truth of love. The Queen has dismissed theater with the remark, "Playwrights teach us nothing about love. They make it pretty, they make it comical, or they make it lust."[19] At the film's climax, after Viola, playing Juliet, is "outed" as a woman on the Globe stage, Queen Elizabeth reveals herself to have been watching the performance and saves the day, declaring the actress is really a boy. Saying "I know something of a woman in a man's profession," the Queen pronounces that *Romeo and Juliet*—the quintessential heterosexual romance—has won the wager and "declared the very truth and nature of love."[20]

In contrast to the relative conservatism of these popular film adaptations, the play's stage history reflects the great changes in gender norms of the late twentieth and early twenty-first centuries. Beginning in the 1970s, several important productions expressed a post-Stonewall resistance to compulsory heterosexuality, focusing on the play's homoeroticism and "world turned upside-down" revels.[21] Since then, women have been performing many of the classic male roles from Shakespeare's repertoire: Harriet Walter played Brutus, Henry IV, and Prospero in three all-female productions (2012–16), while the Stratford Shakespeare Festival in Ontario staged *The Tempest* and *Julius Caesar* in 2018 with women playing Prospero, Brutus, Cassius, and Antony. Glenda Jackson took on the role of King Lear on Broadway in 2019, and Kathryn Hunter played a female Timon in Theatre for a New Audience's 2020 production in Brooklyn. Such reclaiming of roles traditionally played by men can be seen as an extension of decades of feminist critical attention to the patriarchal character of political, familial, and social relations in Shakespeare's plays. But these performances also speak to the shaking up of sexual identity in our own gender-fluid era. Shakespeare's heterosexual romances, for example, are being played by same-sex actors. In 2019 Skyler Cooper, a trans man, played Othello at California's Livermore Shakespeare Festival (a part he had acted as a female role in a 2005 Impact Theatre production). The opening up of roles to actors of different genders came full circle, in a way, in Tim Carroll's "original practices" production of *Twelfth Night* in 2002 (filmed in 2012), in which all the parts were played by males.[22]

Such casting choices form part of theater's social and political function both to mirror and challenge its audience's values. As Federico García Lorca once remarked, theater is "an open tribunal where the people can introduce old and mistaken mores as evidence, and can use living examples to explain eternal norms of the human heart."[23] When asked about the greatest changes in Shakespeare performance during the past decade, artistic directors repeatedly refer to contemporary relevance and inclusivity, particularly with regard to gender. Janet Alexander Griffin, artistic producer at the Folger Shakespeare Library, says, "Over the last decade, with relatively constant communication, it's much more about producing a conversation than about producing a 'show'

... [W]e increasingly must examine how our theater engages with the broader and louder cultural discourse of the 2010s."[24] Griffin implies that old plays must address contemporary issues, not simply in casting, but also in stimulating self-reflection and discussion.

Twelfth Night speaks to the modern theatrical spirit in an additional way: not through the central lovers we have been discussing, but in the below-stairs revelers Sir Toby Belch, Sir Andrew Aguecheek, and Feste the Clown. As their names attest, they function as caricatures who wear like a costume the ideas they represent: Sir Toby drinks and belches; Sir Andrew is skinny, clumsy, and awkward; and Feste entertains. Their scenes of joking, singing, and game playing—in short, having fun—lie outside the conventions of romantic comedy and open up connections to other kinds of contemporary performance beyond traditional theater. Cosplay (short for "costume play"), for example, is a contemporary form of theatricality that mirrors both the festive revelry and the spectacle of cross-dressing that characterize the two plots of *Twelfth Night*. In cosplay (an outgrowth of the history of fandom), a fan dresses up as a favorite TV, film, cartoon, or video game character and interacts with other fans, usually at a fan convention, in a playful atmosphere. This may or may not involve cross-dressing (or "crossplay"). Though they perform their roles, cosplayers don't enact scripted stories. They are somewhere between actors and revelers. Nevertheless, like actors, they use impersonation to expand their sense of who they can be and to call attention to the spectrum of possibilities between performance and reality. Abby Kirby, a cosplayer and scholar of media studies, describes the appeal of cosplay gatherings:

> If you were to walk into one of these spaces, you would be overwhelmed by the sheer number of people who are disguising who they are. You might not even recognize your friend ... Cosplay teaches you that your identity is fluid, and that slapping labels on people isn't necessary. It makes us aware that we are wearing a costume in our everyday lives. That a cosplayer can wear three different costumes in one weekend can provide a liberation. I don't have to be the same person today as I am tomorrow.[25]

Further, since cosplay often involves impersonating an animated character (or even a non-human one), it has the potential to take the performer outside the gender binary. Animated figures are playful, almost blank spaces; consciously artificial, they can't simply be compared to living subjects. Cosplay is not, then, like drag, which dramatizes and parodies gender roles. Rather, it is a "pure spectacle" not attached to any statement of gender identity.[26] While it would be oversimplifying to equate the performativity associated with cosplay with that of the characters in *Twelfth Night*, the two forms of theater share a common spirit.

Twelfth Night thus has proven remarkably versatile in its capacity to absorb the shifting waters of cultural norms. Fluidity seems an apt term, as well, to describe not only the gender but the moral progress of the play's characters. Water represents their mortality and grief: "She is drowned already, sir, with salt water, though I seem to drown her remembrance again with more," Sebastian says of his sister (2.1.28–9). Water evokes passion—"O spirit of love," says Orsino, "thy capacity / Receiveth as the sea" (1.1.10–11)—as well as pleasure, as Sir Toby Belch memorably reminds Malvolio: "Dost thou think because thou art virtuous there shall be no more cakes and ale?" (2.3.112–13). Maria links it to sexual prowess: "Bring your hand to the buttery bar," she says to Sir Andrew, suggestively drawing his hand toward her, "and let it drink"; while Olivia compares fluidity to wit: "Go to," she says to Feste, when she thinks he has been unfunny, "you're a dry fool" (1.5.37). In a sense, while it could be said to represent life itself, water also stands for the malleability of human identity: "I am for all waters," says Feste, meaning he can play any role, but also hinting that he finds pleasure in all "humors" (humors were fluids, such as blood and bile, that were believed to determine an individual's personality). As a sort of Chorus for *Twelfth Night*, he observes, comments and entertains, tells jokes and sings (even participating, vindictively, in the practical joke against the "dry" Malvolio). His wit and his music serve to sum up the complexity of human beings' humorous, fluid identities. No one, Feste remarks, is singular: "for give the dry fool drink, then is the fool not dry; bid the dishonest man mend himself – if he mend, he is no longer dishonest, if he cannot, let the botcher mend him. Anything that's mended is but patched: virtue that transgresses is but patched with sin, and sin that amends is but patched with virtue" (1.5.38–45). Our identities are a patchwork, a complex tapestry of virtue and vice, stasis, and change. The Fool affirms that the ability to "mend" or transform ourselves—our moral fluidity—constitutes an essential part of our humanity.

Yet the Fool is fundamentally an outsider who does not share in the rewards of love. His own gender and sexual desires are not acknowledged, and at play's end he remains alone, a universal figure, perhaps, of nonconformity. The Fool poignantly closes *Twelfth Night*, traditionally considered "the happiest and most golden comedy of love," with a melancholy song that guides us back to reality.[27] The first two verses (which Shakespeare may or may not have composed) are:

> **FOOL** When that I was and a little tiny boy,
>   With hey, ho, the wind and the rain,
>   A foolish thing was but a toy,
>   For the rain it raineth every day.

> But when I came to man's estate,
> With hey, ho, the wind and the rain,
> 'Gainst knaves and thieves men shut their gate,
> For the rain it raineth every day. (5.1.382–9)

The song looks back at the play's action like the memories of childhood, when "a foolish thing was but a toy": you could experiment, be a "fool," without serious consequences. But in the adult world, "men shut their gate" against lawbreakers. In the theater, anything is possible, but plays end and the fluidity of human potential solidifies into the reality of the world outside. In the theater, love might transcend all boundaries. In the real world of the sixteenth century, homosexuality was misunderstood, sodomy was illegal, and sumptuary laws dictated what clothing people were allowed to wear. For the twenty-first century, gender fluidity can still seem to some like merely a form of temporary revelry; in the face of the harsh dictates of economic anxiety, a shrinking job market, and political backlash against social change there may be little room for a serious consideration of one's assigned identity. Yet it is this very tension between the world inside and outside the theater—the play's "natural perspective, that is and is not"—which gives *Twelfth Night* its continuing power. Looked at one way, we exit the playhouse and shut the gate to the stage. But like the characters suspended on stage in their costumes, poised between potential identities, we take some of their fluid humanity with us.

NOTES

1. The female-to-male transvestite characters are Julia in *Two Gentlemen of Verona*, Portia in *The Merchant of Venice*, Rosalind in *As You Like It*, Viola in *Twelfth Night*, and Imogen in *Cymbeline*. Since women did not perform in the professional theater, male actors played the female roles, making cross-dressing a fundamental element of the stage. However, Shakespeare did not feature male-to-female cross-dressing in his plotlines, with the exception of Falstaff dressing as the Old Woman of Brainford in *The Merry Wives of Windsor*, a disguise notable for its disastrous results.
2. William Shakespeare, *Twelfth Night*, ed. Keir Elam, Arden Shakespeare, 3rd ser. (London: Methuen, 2008). References in the text to act, scene, and line numbers are to this edition.
3. There are over 50 terms in the current LGBTQ+ glossary, including words that relate to both sexuality and gender, such as *gender-fluid* ("not identifying with a single fixed gender ... having or expressing a fluid or unfixed gender identity"); *genderqueer* ("refers to individuals who identify as a combination of man and woman, neither man nor woman, or both man and woman, or someone who rejects commonly held ideas of static gender identities"); *nonbinary* ("not exclusively masculine or feminine—outside the gender binary"); and *gender nonconforming* ("not being defined by society's conventional definitions of gender"). See "PFLAG (Federation of Parents and Friends of Lesbians and Gays), National

Glossary of Terms," last modified July 2019, accessed January 12, 2020, https://www.pflag.org/glossary.

4.   For an excellent overview of sex- and gender-oriented approaches to Shakespeare, see Melissa E. Sanchez, *Shakespeare and Queer Theory*, The Arden Shakespeare (London and New York: Bloomsbury, 2019).

5.   "No doubt some mouldy tale, / Like Pericles, and stale / As the shrieve's crusts, and nasty as his fish / ... May keep up the play club," in Ben Jonson, "Ode to Himself," lines 21–6, in *Plays and Poems* (London: G. Routledge, 1895).

6.   The first custom-built professional theater, constructed in 1576 and known as The Theatre, was the site of performances by Shakespeare's company, the Lord Chamberlain's Men.

7.   See, for example, Catherine Belsey, "Disrupting Sexual Difference: Meaning and Gender in the Comedies," in *Alternative Shakespeares*, ed. John Drakakis (London and New York: Methuen, 1985), 170–94, discussed below. Belsey's essay, and others that followed in the next decade, critiqued the claims of critics such as C. L. Barber, who had argued, "The most fundamental distinction the play brings home to us is the difference between men and women ... Just as the saturnalian reversal of social roles need not threaten the social structure, but can serve instead to consolidate it, so a temporary, playful reversal of sexual roles can renew the meaning of the normal relation," in C. L. Barber, *Shakespeare's Festive Comedy: A Study of Dramatic Form and Its Relation to Social Custom* (New York: Princeton University Press, 1963), 6.

8.   Stephen Orgel, *Impersonations: The Performance of Gender in Shakespeare's England* (Cambridge and New York: Cambridge University Press, 1996), 53–4.

9.   As Orgel discusses, while erotic representations of same-sex desire were common in Renaissance art, and frequently hinted at in theater, this did not mean people could indulge openly in homosexual behaviors without risk. Same-sex love "becomes visible in Elizabethan society ... when it intersects with some other behavior that is recognized as dangerous and anti-social" (Orgel, *Impersonations*, 40).

10. The first civil law against sodomy, or "buggery," was passed in 1533.

11. "There is no woman's sides / Can bide the beating of so strong a passion / As love doth give my heart; no woman's heart / So big to hold so much ... But mine is all as hungry as the sea, / And can digest as much" (2.4.93–101).

12. See Jami Ake, "Glimpsing a 'Lesbian' Poetics in *Twelfth Night*," *Studies in English Literature 1500–1900* 43, no. 2 (Spring 2003): 375–94.

13. Belsey, "Disrupting Sexual Difference," 171.

14. The one-sex model was explored by Thomas Laqueur in *Making Sex: Body and Gender from the Greeks to Freud* (Cambridge, MA: Harvard University Press, 1990), especially chaps. 2 and 3.

15. As Clifford Leech noted many years ago, "Because on our [modern] stage the transvestism is single and not double, the effect has not the specially troubling character that emerges when a boy playing a girl becomes emotionally involved with a boy playing a girl disguised as a boy: with that complexity we reach a point where sexual distinctions begin to dissolve," in Clifford Leech, *Twelfth Night and Shakespearian Comedy* (Toronto: University of Toronto Press, 1965), 50. Leech's concern that gender fluidity is "troubling" seems dated, but his point is apt.

16. Andy Fickman, dir., *She's the Man* (DreamWorks Pictures, 2006), DVD, 105 min.

17. Kara Harshbarger, "Interview with Amanda Bynes and Channing Tatum," ifilm video, 5:23, posted to YouTube September 30, 2007, https://www.youtube.com/

watch?v=hrRstEUjT7o. Abby Schreiber, "Break the Internet: Amanda, Please," *Paper*, November 26, 2018, https://www.papermag.com/amanda-bynes-break-the -internet-2621549455.html?rebelltitem=40#rebelltitem40.

18. The way Viola's sexual indeterminacy is maintained beyond the final exits can be contrasted to that of the heroine in "Of Apolonius and Silla," a source upon which Shakespeare drew. In this novella, the cross-dressed heroine, Silla (Viola), reveals her identity to Julina (Olivia) when she is accused of impregnating Julina: "And here with all loosyng his garments doune to his stomacke, [Silla] shewed Iulina his breastes and pretie teates ... saiyng: Loe Madame, behold here the partie whom you haue challenged to bee the father of your child; see I am a woman." Silla's breasts constitute the proof of biological sex beneath the costume, discussed in Barnabe Riche, "Of Apolonius and Silla," in *Riche His Farewell to Militarie Profession ...* (London: Robart Walley, 1583), Ann Arbor, MI: Text Creation Partnership, 2011, https://quod.lib.umich.edu/e/eebo/A68653.0001.001/1:4.2?rgn =div2;view=fulltext.

19. John Madden, dir., *Shakespeare in Love* (Miramax, 1998), DVD, 123 min.
20. Madden, dir., *Shakespeare in Love*.
21. See Keir Elam's discussion in the Introduction to *Twelfth Night*, Arden Shakespeare, 3rd ser. (London: Methuen, 2008), 111–17.
22. See Elam's discussion of this production, which featured complex portrayals of Olivia (Mark Rylance), Viola (Eddie Redmayne), and Maria (Paul Chahidi) with no trace of camp (Elam, Introduction to *Twelfth Night*, 113–15).
23. Federico García Lorca, *Deep Song*, quoted in Christopher Maurer, "Poetry," in *A Companion to Federico García Lorca*, ed. Federico Bonaddio (London: Boydell and Brewer, 2007), 34.
24. Ben Lauer, "We Asked 5 Artistic Directors: How Did Making Shakespeare Change in the 2010s?" in *Shakespeare & Beyond* (blog), on the *Folger Shakespeare Library* website, December 13, 2019, https://shakespeareandbeyond.folger.edu/ 2019/12/13/making-shakespeare-2010s/?utm_source=wordfly&utm_medium= email&utm_campaign=ShakespearePlus27Dec2019&utm_content=version_A& promo=11671/.
25. Abby Kirby, in conversation with the author, January 28, 2020.
26. Joel Gn, "Queer Simulation: The Practice, Performance and Pleasure of Cosplay," *Continuum: Journal of Media and Cultural Studies* 25, no. 4 (August 2011): 583. Cosplay's cultural significance is made evident by the appearance of sewing patterns for cosplay in stores like Joann Fabrics and its being featured in episodes of the mainstream TV show *The Big Bang Theory*.
27. Leslie Hotson, *The First Night of* Twelfth Night (New York: The Macmillan Company, 1954), 35.

REFERENCES

Ake, Jami. "Glimpsing a 'Lesbian' Poetics in *Twelfth Night*." *Studies in English Literature 1500–1900* 43, no. 2 (Spring 2003): 375–94.

Barber, C. L. *Shakespeare's Festive Comedy: A Study of Dramatic Form and Its Relation to Social Custom*. New York: Princeton University Press, 1963.

Belsey, Catherine. "Disrupting Sexual Difference: Meaning and Gender in the Comedies." In *Alternative Shakespeares*, edited by John Drakakis, 170–94. London and New York: Methuen, 1985.

Elam, Keir. Introduction to *Twelfth Night*, by William Shakespeare, 1–153. Edited by Keir Elam. Arden Shakespeare, 3rd ser. London: Methuen, 2008.

Fickman, Andy, dir. *She's the Man*. DreamWorks Pictures, 2006. DVD, 105 min.

Gn, Joel. "Queer Simulation: The Practice, Performance and Pleasure of Cosplay." *Continuum: Journal of Media and Cultural Studies* 25, no. 4 (August 2011): 583–93.

Harshbarger, Kara. "Interview with Amanda Bynes and Channing Tatum." ifilm video, 5:23. Posted to YouTube September 30, 2007. https://www.youtube.com/watch?v=hrRstEUjT7o.

Hotson, Leslie. *The First Night of* Twelfth Night. New York: The Macmillan Company, 1954.

Jonson, Ben. "Ode to Himself." *Plays and Poems*. London: G. Routledge, 1895.

Laqueur, Thomas. *Making Sex: Body and Gender from the Greeks to Freud*. Cambridge, MA: Harvard University Press, 1990.

Lauer, Ben. "We Asked 5 Artistic Directors: How Did Making Shakespeare Change in the 2010s?" in *Shakespeare & Beyond* (blog), the website of *Folger Shakespeare Library*. https://shakespeareandbeyond.folger.edu/2019/12/13/making-shakespeare -2010s/?utm_source=wordfly&utm_medium=email&utm_campaign=Shak espearePlus27Dec2019&utm_content=version_A&promo=11671/.

Leech, Clifford. *Twelfth Night and Shakespearian Comedy*. Toronto: University of Toronto Press, 1965.

Madden, John, dir. *Shakespeare in Love*. Miramax, 1998. DVD, 123 min.

Maurer, Christopher. "Poetry." In *A Companion to Federico García Lorca*, edited by Federico Bonaddio, 15–38. London: Boydell and Brewer, 2007.

Orgel, Stephen. *Impersonations: The Performance of Gender in Shakespeare's England*. Cambridge and New York: Cambridge University Press, 1996.

PFLAG (Federation of Parents and Friends of Lesbians and Gays). National Glossary of Terms. Updated July 2019. https://www.pflag.org/glossary.

Riche, Barnabe. "Of Apolonius and Silla." In *Riche His Farewell to Militarie Profession* … . London: Robart Walley, 1583. Ann Arbor, MI: Text Creation Partnership, 2011. https://quod.lib.umich.edu/e/eebo/A68653.0001.001/1:4.2?rgn=div2;view=fulltext.

Sanchez, Melissa E. *Shakespeare and Queer Theory*. The Arden Shakespeare. London and New York: Bloomsbury, 2019.

Schreiber, Abby. "Break the Internet: Amanda, Please." *Paper*, November 26, 2018. https://www.papermag.com/amanda-bynes-break-the-internet-2621549455.html ?rebelltitem=40#rebelltitem40.

Shakespeare, William. *Twelfth Night*. Edited by Keir Elam. Arden Shakespeare, 3rd ser. London: Methuen, 2008.

Shakespeare, William. *Twelfth Night*. Directed by Tim Carroll. Shakespeare's Globe, 2012. DVD, 176 min.

12. Shakespeare in other tongues: translation and adaptation into Yoruba and Hausa in text, film, and stage productions in Nigeria

Kayode Gboyega Kofoworola

One of the common ways in which Shakespeare's universal appeal is manifested is through the desire to translate, adapt, and perform his works in languages and cultural contexts quite distant from the English original. It is through distinctly local languages and cultures that his works and their ethos can be made available to readerships and audiences around the world. African adaptations of Shakespeare's plays have been done for over three centuries. According to Rebekah Bale, two of Shakespeare's plays, *Richard II* and *Hamlet*, were performed in English around Sierra Leone as far back as 1607, though Edward Wilson-Lee thinks the 1607 performance location actually was near northwest Madagascar.[1] Thereafter, Africans began to translate Shakespeare's works into their own languages. An early example includes an Arabic translation of *Othello* and its performance in Egypt in 1884. But the most important achievement in this history of translations is no doubt the works of Solomon Plaatje, who was the first African to translate Shakespeare's works into an African vernacular (Setswana) in the early twentieth century.

Sol Plaatje translated six of Shakespeare's plays into Setswana, his mother tongue. Four of the plays, *Mashoabi-shoabi* (*The Merchant of Venice*), *Dintshontsho-ncho tsa bo-Juliuse Kesara* (*Julius Caesar*), *Diphosho-Phosho* (*The Comedy of Errors*) and *Matsepa-tsapa a Lefeala* (*Much Ado about Nothing*), were titled in Setswana, while the remaining two, *Othello* and *Romeo and Juliet*, even though translated, retained their English titles. Of these six titles only *Diphosho-Phosho* (1930) and *Dintshontsho-ncho tsa bo-Juliuse Kesara* (1937) were ever published. Why the other texts were never published remains a mystery.

In the middle of the twentieth century, Julius Nyerere, the first president of the republic of Tanzania, translated Shakespeare's *Merchant of Venice* (*Mabepari wa venisi*) and *Julius Caesar* (*Juliasi Kaizari*) into Swahili.[2] Bale suggests that Nyerere's translation contributed to a nationalistic narrative that insisted on the Africanization of Western literature through translations in order to make it culturally relevant in a postcolonial state.[3]

At this time, Western literature was considered an agent of colonialism, and Africanizing Western texts involved adapting them to African settings, producing them in African languages, and having African characters to which the audience could easily relate, while still retaining the universal themes that these works were thought to express. Southern and Eastern Africa thus became the epicenters for the translation of Shakespeare's work into vernacular languages in Africa. The languages into which Shakespeare has been translated and adapted include isiZulu, isiXhosa, Setswana, Sesotho, and Afrikaans.

The translation and adaptation of the works of Shakespeare in West Africa were initially believed to have begun in 1964 when Thomas Decker translated *Julius Caesar* into Krio, an effort that not only widely promoted the language, but also showed that vernacular West African languages could also engage with the complexities of a Shakespearean text. However, it has since emerged that the first, but little-known, translation of any of Shakespeare's work in West Africa is E. T. Johnson's *Iwe ere (Play) Ti Julius Caesar ti Shakespeare kọ ti a yipada si Ede Yoruba lati ọwọ alufa E.T. Johnson (Ọga Agba Ile-Iwe New High Class School, Eko, Nigeria)*, a translation of *Julius Caesar* into Yoruba believed to have been published in 1931. There is no other translation known to have been published during this period of colonial presence because very few Africans were exposed to Western education, which included the teaching of the works of Shakespeare. The period after 1960, when most African countries began to achieve independence, saw a re-awakening of interest in Shakespeare's work, and, consequently, in the desire to share and make it available to a wider readership and audience through translations and performances. Also, rather than engaging in literal translations of Shakespeare, these post-independence translations and adaptations sought to project the cultures of the continent onto Shakespeare's plays in order to underscore parallels indicating that the problems of power, morality, and leadership were not uniquely African, but were universal problems that predated the present. Since language is a vehicle for conveying culture, the post-independence publication of Shakespeare's works in African vernacular languages was thus an attempt to link the plays' universal realities to the unique cultural contexts of an African audience.

Shakespeare as iconic writer, playwright, and poet has been a frequent subject in the Nigerian literary landscape from postcolonial times to the present. Indeed, while the introduction of Shakespeare into the Nigerian education curriculum is a result of colonization by the British, the continued interest in the writings of Shakespeare, especially in the last 60 years after Nigeria's independence, has been due to the uniqueness of Shakespeare's approach to basic life issues and controversies. Some of the universal themes which he incorporates in his writing include the influence of the supernatural in man's daily affairs, as exemplified by the witches in *Macbeth* and omens in *Julius Caesar*; the complexity of human relationships in *The Winter's Tale*; and the dangers of human ambition, which are manifested in the struggle for power as presented in *Macbeth* and *Julius Caesar*. This universality has led to a resurgence in attempts by Nigerian writers to claim Shakespeare, as many other nations have attempted to do, specifically in order to inspire hope in a people despairing of being ruled by despots.

There is a plethora of adaptations of Shakespeare's work into Nigerian settings. Examples include Femi Osofisan's adaptations of Shakespeare's play *Hamlet* as *Wesoo, Hamlet! Or The Resurrection of Hamlet* and *The Merchant of Venice* as *Love's Unlike Lading: A Comedy From Shakespeare*, and Ahmed Yerima, who adapted *Othello* as *Otaelo*. However, these late-twentieth-century adaptations were all in English.

Even though English is the official language and language of education in Nigeria, it is also true that Nigeria's three major vernacular languages— Yoruba (spoken largely in the southwest), Hausa (spoken largely in the north), and Igbo (spoken largely in the southeast)—remain significantly important for trade, commerce, and communication. Each of these languages is regionally relevant, and speakers of these languages have constituted a majority of the national leadership in the political sphere, because Nigeria operates as a democratic plurality where population size is a factor in determining who is elected to public office. While there are many adaptations of Shakespeare's writings to Nigerian settings, the number of his plays adapted for performance or translated into Nigerian local languages is very few indeed. Among the many Nigerian languages (over 450), Shakespeare's plays have been translated or adapted into only Yoruba and Hausa, hence the focus of this chapter on translations and adaptations of Shakespeare into these two languages.

Incidentally, unlike the Igbo language, both Hausa and Yoruba are also regional languages spoken widely within the West African subregion. Outside of Nigeria, Yoruba is largely spoken in countries such as Benin, Ivory Coast, and Togo, while Hausa is largely spoken in countries such as the Niger Republic, Ghana, Sudan, Ivory Coast, Cameroon, Benin, and Chad. It is estimated that there are about 30–40 million Yoruba speakers worldwide. Aside from West Africa, where an estimated 20–28 million speakers live, Yoruba is also spoken in places as far-flung as Brazil, Cuba, Grenada, Trinidad, and the United States. On the other hand, there are about 75 million Hausa speakers across the African continent, of which about 61 million live in Nigeria. It is thus significant that these two languages combined have close to 80 million speakers within Nigeria alone. Considering that the current population estimates put Nigeria's population at about 200 million, it follows that speakers of both languages constitute around 50 percent of the population.

While the Yorubas' exposure to Western education ensured that they spoke and wrote English and thus were exposed to the British colonial curriculum, which encompassed the English poets (including the works of Shakespeare), the Hausas of Northern Nigeria were less receptive to Western education in the early colonial years, because the north had a largely Muslim population that considered Western education antithetical to their religion and culture. It is without question generally agreed that the Yorubas of southwest Nigeria are the most colonially educated and Westernized tribe or ethnic group in West Africa. Indeed, as mentioned above, the earliest known translation of Shakespeare was in Yoruba in the early twentieth century (E. T. Johnson's *Iwe ere (Play) Ti Julius Caesar ti Shakespeare ḳọ ti a yipada si Ede Yoruba*). It is not far-fetched to claim that these geopolitical facts affected the reception, translation, and adaptation of Shakespeare's work. Even though Alamin Mazrui has suggested that in the colonial period "some Shakespeare plays also exist in Hausa, Swahili and Zulu," he never provides any evidence of this, especially of such Hausa translations.[4]

Wale Ogunyemi's *Aare Akogun* (1969), which means *war chief*, similar to today's army defense chief, is an adaptation of *Macbeth* and is the very first known major translation into Yoruba of a Shakespearean play specifically for the purposes of performance. Written in collaboration with Dexter Lyndersay, a unique feature of the staging of this translation by the School of Drama Acting Company, which first took place in the Arts Theater of the University of Ibadan, was its embrace of the totality of African theatre—music, dance, dialogue—to explore the myth, history, and cosmology of the Yoruba. In so doing, this mid-twentieth-century production became an often-unacknowledged inspiration and progenitor for later adaptations, such as *Itan Oginintin*. *Aare Akogun* has been described as "a Nigerian Tragedy of the Supernatural based on Shakespeare's *Macbeth*," which hardly matches the original in grandeur of conception but emerges as an interesting experiment in Yoruba/English dialogue.[5]

Olalekan Balogun's contention is that Yoruba efforts to adapt Shakespeare through the lens of Yoruba epistemology and its aesthetic principles constitute an attempt at "writing forward" because they address their own societies rather than challenge the Shakespeare canon by "writing back" (a term which "designates a set of adaptations that challenge the cultural capital that Shakespeare privileges").[6] He argues that it is this approach to adapting Shakespeare which explains the cultural and social significance of adaptations in the Yoruba language. This chapter will develop this idea through its examination of Shakespeare adaptations by Wole Oguntokun, Abiola Sobo, and Mahmoon Baba-Ahmed, three Nigerian playwrights who (in spite of the general societal perception about the difficulty of engaging the works of Shakespeare) have dared to compel Shakespeare into their native tongues in the second decade of the twenty-first century. Wole Oguntokun directed *Itan Oginintin* (*The Winter's Tale*), which was performed in Yoruba at the Globe Theatre in 2012. Abiola Sobo's *In iRedu* is a film adaptation of a scene from Shakespeare's *Macbeth* backdropped by Yoruba culture and traditions, but performed in English. Mahmoon Baba-Ahmed is the first known writer to have translated Shakespeare's *Romeo and Juliet*, *Julius Caesar*, and *Macbeth* into Hausa.

ITAN OGININTIN

The Winter's Tale is the story of friendship between Leontes, King of Sicilia, and Polixenes, King of Bohemia. Polixenes pays Leontes a visit, but refuses Leontes's request to stay longer. He relents at Hermione's persuasion. This makes Leontes accuse her of having an affair with Polixenes, and Leontes then orders Camillo to poison Polixenes. Instead, Camillo and Polixenes flee. Leontes throws his wife in prison and orders Antigonus to abandon Hermione's new baby in a desolate place, even though the oracle of Delphi confirms that Hermione and Polixenes are innocent of Leontes's accusation of infidelity. Antigonus abandons the baby (Perdita) on the Bohemian coast, where she is found and raised by a shepherd. Sixteen years later, Florizel, Polixenes's son, falls in love with Perdita, to Polixenes's dismay. Florizel and Perdita, under cover, escape to Sicilia and are well received by a repentant Leontes, who is still in mourning over the deaths of his wife and son and the abandonment of his daughter. The shepherd narrates how Perdita was found, and Leontes realizes she is his daughter. The entire company, rejoicing, retires to the home of Paulina, Hermione's friend, to view a newly finished statue of Hermione, which, to everyone's amazement, comes to life. The play ends with the engagement of Camillo and Paulina and the whole company celebrating the miracles.

The challenges of translation and adaptation can be concisely exemplified by considering the translation of the title *The Winter's Tale* as *Itan Oginintin* (winter tales); this is because the definite article *the* is not available in Yoruba language usage. There is also no winter as such in Nigeria; however, the nearest example of what may resemble winter is what is translated as "*Oginintin*," a cold surge in the atmosphere which occurs especially during the rainy season and produces an approximation of winter conditions (without, of course, the snow typically seen in Northern Europe). Winter is usually understood in other parts of the world as a season, a part of the universal cycle of seasons; however, *Oginintin* is a by-product of a seasonal weather change. The need to find and utilize equivalents to what existed in Shakespeare's Europe is one of the central challenges faced by scriptwriter Tade Ipadeola and director Wole Oguntokun in their adaptation of *The Winter's Tale*. This is important for understanding the context of this translative approach.

The Winter's Tale in Yoruba (*Itan Oginintin*), staged at the iconic Stratford-upon-Avon stage, begins with a dance performance designed to introduce the audience to the story. Some of the significant changes to the original Shakespeare version are the use of a female narrator who introduces the setting of the story as Oyo (Sicily) and Ire (Bohemia), and the main characters who, instead of kings, are gods. Thus, Polixenes becomes Ogun, Leontes becomes Sango, and Hermione becomes Oya, in consonance with Yoruba mythology. In Yoruba mythology, Sango is the god of thunder, Ogun is the god of iron, and Oya is the goddess of thunder, lightning, tornadoes, winds, rainstorms, and hurricanes; she is the sister-wife of Sango, to whom she delegates some of her powers. Oya's binary nature as both single and married is cleverly exploited by the director of *Itan Oginintin* to allow for the possibility of her infidelity with Ogun, which Sango suspects. In giving godlike qualities to the main characters in *The Winter's Tale*, Tade Ipadeola and Wole Oguntokun have foregrounded a central aspect of the Yorubas' apprehension of life, which emphasizes that both the here and now and the hereafter are mutually symbiotic.

Ipadeola and Oguntokun adopt an older form of the Yoruba language, which is no longer in common use, in order to illustrate the importance of this symbiosis and to convey essential Yoruba values, which they believe modern Yoruba culture, diluted as it is, is unable to convey. In other words, for the translators, the preservation of aspects of the Yoruba culture, such as songs, proverbs, music, dance, festivals, and traditions, is closely linked to the preservation of the original language. Julie Sanders rightly suggests that the challenge for a performance of *Itan Oginintin* lies in its use of this archaic version of Yoruba, rarely deployed in everyday conversation but which Yoruba scholars agree provides the tonal fluidity required to execute a translation of a difficult playwright such as Shakespeare.[7]

Itan Oginintin cannot be considered a translation in the strictest sense, but, rather, it is the metamorphosis of a play grounded in English culture into one deeply embedded in Yoruba culture, thereby making the original play accessible to a wider African audience. A very adept Yoruba speaker would probably notice the unusual tonal inflections in the use of the words on stage. Indeed, a Yoruba speaker who dwells in the city would likely recognize that the Yoruba spoken in the performance is not standard Yoruba. For instance, the Old Shepherd's son (the Clown), in his conversation with Ikoko, uses the phrase '*eri e*' ("your head") which is still commonly used among the Yoruba speakers of Ilorin (who, it is believed, had migrated from Oyo centuries ago during the Oyo civil war, but had largely married the Fulani to produce a Yoruba sub-culture), while today's Yoruba speaker would say '*ori re*' ("your head"). The translators probably chose *eri* because in today's Yoruba *ori* refers to the physical head; however, *eri*, as used in early versions of Yoruba, is a term that encompasses both the physical and mystical connotations of a head as a seat, not just of intellect but also of destiny for the individual.

In performance, a very strong attempt has been made to show the versatility of the Yoruba language in accommodating and embracing other languages. So the character Igba ("Time," played by Motunrayo Oribiyi) in her narration uses the phrase *gbogbo duniya* ("the whole world") instead of the phrase *gbogbo agbaye* ("the whole universe"). The second phrase speaks not just to the physical world, like the first phrase does. However, what makes the usage of the first phrase significant is the idea that the material earth becomes the play-space of gods who mingle with humans as "men." It is not particularly clear at what point the word *duniya* entered the Yoruba language. It is believed to be an Arabic word, which might be an indication of early Yoruba language contact with Arabs. Also, as in the tradition of the Greek and Roman chorus, this adaptation includes a single female narrator who appears throughout the play, telling the story in a series of songs and chants. This is significant because in Yoruba culture women were generally prohibited from taking such lead roles in a performance involving men.

In an emphatic attempt to convey Yoruba culture on stage, *Itan Oginintin*'s directors introduce what Mark Hudson, in his review of the performance, refers to as "wonderful visual moments, such as the appearance—for reasons I couldn't quite fathom—of a pair of swaying, bending dancers dressed in tube-like constructions 12 feet high."[8] However, to someone conversant with the Yoruba culture, the tube-like constructions represent *Egungun* masquerades that indicate the presence of the ancestors in the festivity or ritual being carried out. The *Egungun* is thus a physical manifestation of the ancestors' spirits, who visit their people to celebrate with and bless them. However, *Egunguns* could also visit to warn and bring retribution to wrongdoers in the community who refuse to repent. The appearance of *Egunguns* is usually accompanied by drumming, dancing, singing, pomp, and pageantry. In this adaptation, we see them appear at the beginning of the performance and at the end; their first appearance serves celebratory purposes, and the second serves to condemn the evil done by Leontes.

The basic elements of the original story of Shakespeare's *The Winter's Tale* have to do with the perpetual tensions between universal binaries. Examples of these binaries include the oppositions between good and evil, hate and love, rich and poor, royalty and commoner, etc. Some of these basic tensions are retained in the *Itan Oginintin* version, where examples include the contestation between the poor (Autolycus) and the rich (the Old Shepherd), and between the kings/gods, Leonates/Sango and Polixenes/Ogun. It is not inconceivable that, in an attempt to accentuate these binaries in *Itan Oginintin* as performed at the Globe Theatre, the entrance of the actors on stage begins with intense drumming and singing before an opening introduction of the story in a wonderful Yoruba tonal stretch that thrusts the audience *in medias res* with the banishment of the so-called illegitimate child, Perdita (Oluola, played by Oluwatoyin Alli-Hakeem). The celebratory dimension at both the beginning and the end of the performance speaks to how integral singing and dancing is to the cultural identity and worldview of the Yoruba in the explication of life's binaries, where life begins with celebration and ends with the same.

In introducing the main protagonists Leonates/Sango and Polixenes/Ogun, Igba (Time) eulogizes them through their *orikis* (praise names) in order to establish their significance to the social, political, and cosmic environment and to distinguish their temperaments, characters, and intuitive dispositions. Ogun opens the narrative with a display of his skills and agility as he rejoices at the end of a great hunt. This may be an indirect allusion to the scene in Shakespeare's original in which a bear mauls Autolycus after he deposits Perdita on the coast of Bohemia. Since, of course, there are no bears within the eco-landscape into which the story is transported, this adaptation substitutes the bear with the successful hunt of a deer, carried center stage and, after much rejoicing dance, backstage. The approach here is an attempt to show that in Yoruba culture, anyone able to hunt an animal with a deer's agility must be celebrated, not just because the hunter contributes to the food stability of the community, but because it "is a site of cultural signification for which the table is just a starting point."[9]

Autolycus, a rogue in *The Winter's Tale*, is recast in *Itan Oginintin* as Ikoko, a trickster like Esu in Yoruba cultural mythology.[10] Perhaps a masterstroke of this adaptation is to make the character female, a rogue with a relatively likable character who defrauds unsuspecting individuals across Iree (Bohemia). She lies and cheats, all the while luring and baiting her victims via interspersed singing and dancing, thus generating a festive spirit befitting of a Shakespearean comedy. Most trickster figures in Yoruba culture are men pretending to be women; in *Itan Oginintin*, this convention is deconstructed, thus demolishing masculinity or femininity as biologically based and perhaps challenging traditional patriarchal claims about masculinity.

As indicated above, the plot sequence of the original text is slightly amended in *Itan Oginintin*. The story in *Itan Oginintin* begins with intense drumming and dancing that indicates boat movements, with the dancers holding paddles. The miming of paddling in the dance indicates the riverine nature of the setting of the story and is designed to suggest the commencement of a journey. Agbomabiwon (Antigonus) alights from the boat with the baby Oluola (Perdita) wrapped in swaddling clothes. While still contemplating whether or not to carry out his duties, he is murdered by a bandit (Shakespeare's version says he was eaten by a bear), and his body is dragged into the underbrush, leaving both baby and bag (box) unattended.

The bundle of joy—baby Oluola (Perdita), so named by Agbomabiwon (Antigonus)—is discovered by an itinerant, old, but rich, shepherd who carries the baby in his arms and surmises that the child must be the product of an illicit relationship, hence the abandonment. The shepherd's son arrives and jokes about what the abandoned bag contains. The son (who is a clown) and father argue about who should open the bag to view its contents. The son eventually chooses to obey his father but insists he needs to urinate on the bag before doing so. Eventually, the bag is opened, and both are amazed at what it contains: jewels and a note written by Paulina that reveals the baby's name, high birth, and unfortunate fate.

Some of the key departures from the original tale are found in the suggestion by the clown that he would need to neutralize (with urine) whatever negative powers might be associated with the bag before opening it to see what it contained. This generates laughter from the audience, but is also intended to provoke discussion about the superstitious beliefs of the Yoruba. The communicative capacity of *Itan Oginintin* lies in its excision of large portions of conversations from the original tale, replacing them with songs containing proverbial statements that convey specific cultural messages and which initiate the audience into the Yoruba worldview. This is because proverbs and songs are a strategy for resolving conflict in Yoruba society.[11]

It is instructive that at certain points in the performance members of the audience are brought on stage and involved in the singing and dancing. This probably speaks to the participatory nature of performance within Yoruba culture, in which there is no demarcation between actors and audience. This reflects the Yoruba belief in the fluidity of human existence, as there are no boundaries between the spirit and physical worlds, and they co-exist in an unending cyclical continuum.[12]

Without doubt, *Itan Oginintin* is not and was never intended to be a line-by-line translation of *The Winter's Tale*; instead, it is an interpretation of the play in light of Yoruba mythology, ethos, and worldview. Olalekan Balogun, in attempting to provide an understanding of the significance to be attached to the transformation of Time in *The Winter's Tale* into a female narrator (Igba), argues that the character is an *orisa* (spirit) who tells a story "with a mixture of chant, poetry and music."[13] *Orisas* are significant in Yoruba culture and Yoruba religious belief because it is believed that they can interact directly with human beings to influence human affairs and communicate messages from the spirit world. By employing this narrator, *Itan Oginintin* discards the linear sense of time so germane to *The Winter's Tale* for a "non-linear, disjunctive narrative structure [that] reflects a Yoruba conception of time, in which the past is linked to the future through the present."[14]

Everything ends the way it begins in *Itan Oginintin*, reflecting the Yoruba emphasis on the cyclical continuum of human life. Little Oluola (baby

Perdita), sent to be destroyed as a result of being rejected by her father, returns as a full-grown woman ready to be married and warmly accepted, and thus reintegrated into the royal family. The re-imagining of the scene in *The Winter's Tale* in which Oya's (Hermione's) statue comes back to life is altered by the producers. In *Itan Oginintin*, Oya comes back to life only briefly for her daughter's, rather than her husband's, sake and returns to being a statue while her husband rejoices at her return. This re-imagining reflects the Yoruba belief that the living and the dead are in constant conversation even when it is not physically obvious. Explaining that his approach contradicted the ending in the original translated manuscript produced by Tade Ipadeola, as well as in *The Winter's Tale* itself, Oguntokun provides a rationale: "I directed she should first come to life and then become a statue once more, seeing that in many of our stories, there are always just deserts."[15] While *The Winter's Tale* concludes with forgiveness and reconciliation, *Itan Oginintin* ends with regrets and teaches Sango (Leontes) that unpardonable behaviors have lasting consequences.

IN IREDU

Shakespeare's *Macbeth* has been adapted in many ways to suit different times, age groups, and cultures, performed in both the original language and in translation. *Macbeth* is generally studied in literature classes in Africa because it reflects and refracts contemporary African tragedies of leadership. It provides insight into what propels people toward seeking power, and how power, after it is obtained, not only corrupts them, but brings them to destruction as they break every rule to retain it.

Abiola Sobo's *In iRedu* is the first Nigerian film effort at adapting Shakespeare's *Macbeth*. The challenge of this production lies in its very brevity (12 minutes). The film, which is an adaptation of Act 1, Scene 3 where Macbeth meets the witches, is a unique Nigerian take on this play that attempts to explore the role of the supernatural in access to power and public office, an issue of great concern to a Nigerian audience, especially considering the nation's history of coups (both bloody and bloodless) and its fumbling democratic experimentations. The role of the supernatural in accessing power is of particular interest to a Nigerian audience because *In iRedu* excavates the dynamics of human interaction with the supernatural, which often gives the individual a false sense of invincibility in the pursuit of human desire and ambition.

Even though the story is in English, it is deeply ensconced in Yoruba culture through its language, costumes, and ideology. The film is set in a fictional African country (although obviously meant to represent Nigeria) with four main tribes. The character Ogagun (Deyemi Okanlawon) is a general from the western region who meets with the witches (Adenike Ayeni, Kemi 'Lala' Akindoju, Ijeoma Grace Agu) in iRedu to find what the future entails for him. The film was one of the finalists in the second edition of the Afrinolly Short Film Festival.

In iRedu, even though overshadowed by the presence of the Yoruba general Ogagun, is actually designed to tell the story of tribal tensions in Nigeria. It places the Yoruba tribe at the forefront of an alliance of the tribes. While the most important aspect of Shakespeare's *Macbeth* is the narrative arc that traces its protagonist's actions, in *In iRedu* the story is built around the setting. This translative strategy is captivating, because while Shakespeare's play places its significance on the person of the main character, Macbeth, in *In iRedu* the emphasis is on the place. Amongst the Yoruba of Southwest Nigeria, a person is only as significant, important, or even worthy of honor as their place of origin, or what is generally referred to as their hometown. Thus, it is not just a coincidence that iRedu, the fictional town in the western region, becomes the center of action in this short film after which it is named. It is not clear whether it is the capital of just the western region or of the whole fictional country. However, it could be safely assumed that iRedu replaces Glamis in this adaptation. Thus, just as Macbeth is from Scotland, Ogagun is from iRedu. The word *iRedu* seems to be a place name coined specifically for the setting of the film, as no such word seems to exist in Yoruba.

A major detour in the adaptation of *Macbeth* to *In iRedu* is the adoption of a narrator who continuously interrupts the story with his gripping and heart-wrenching poetic narration. The narrator of *In iRedu* describes an era of African existence that he claims has never been documented and tells a tale of military incursions, of a great war general, three witches, prophecies, and betrayal. The setting of the film, the narrator says, is a different era, a time when Africa was called the Dark Continent, or better yet, "the black continent," referring probably to traditional Western constructions of Africa and its people as somehow mysterious and dangerous.

The film contains four powerful tribes: the northern Hues ruled by the Sultans, the southern Gates led by the Obis, the eastern Shoe ruled by the Igwes and the western Bars ruled by the Obas. For decades these tribes lived in peace, but with the appearance of the Ogbayas, the Obas' special guards led by Ogagun Ajagun (Macbeth), a great war general from the west, the alliance was broken. The Ogbayas laid siege to the northern and eastern territories, destroying the lands in the name of Oba Ijaobi (King Duncan), much in the same way Macbeth battles against the armies of the Thane of Cawdor and the King of Norway. After capturing the key town of Enugu, Ogagun is secretly summoned by the three heinous witches of iRedu; they foretell his rise as the new Oba, as well as his demise and betrayal by Boladeji (Banquo), his second-in-command. Ogagun takes matters into his own hands and begins his play for the throne and eventually the entire region. The film thus mirrors the present-day contentions for power between the Yoruba of the southwest (Obas), the Igbos of the southeast (Igwes), the Hausas of the northwest (Sultans), and the peoples of the south (Obis), which have been a bane of Nigeria's political existence. As an adaptation, *In iRedu* conveys how difficult it is to transpose *Macbeth* into a cultural setting as complex as that of the Yorubas, in spite of the general universality of the themes broached in Shakespeare's play.

While in *Macbeth* the witches meet up with the protagonist, in *In iRedu* Ogagun purposefully goes to meet the witches to divine his future. In the film, moreover, Ogagun kills each of the witches with the sword of Hekate. It is significant that this sword is named after the Greek goddess Hecate, who in ancient Greek religion and mythology is variously associated with magic, witchcraft, ghosts, and necromancy and is usually depicted in triple form. In the original play, the witches endure to the end, but in Abiola Sobo's *In iRedu*, the director enables Ogagun to use the Hekate sword to execute the witches. This is because in Yoruba culture witches are not placated but killed when they engage in evil, which includes manipulations of a person's destiny to bring them to a destructive end. In Yoruba culture, it is often believed that witches are ruthless. They are subject to their gods and would incur utter destruction if they dare carry out their own will as the witches in *Macbeth* had done. Consequently, it is not surprising that the filmmakers allow Ogagun to become the instrument for the gods to exact judgment on the witches. This approach is in line with present-day reality in Nigeria, where the law forbids witchcraft and makes it punishable by a jail term.[16]

Due to the brevity of the film, however, it is not difficult to understand why, unlike in *Macbeth* where Macbeth is depicted as acquiescing to the witches, Ogagun kills them to bring about resolution and to contradict the divination concerning him. Overall, *In iRedu* is a gripping metaphoric account of the formation of a nation and the emergence of its leadership, as well as of how individual ambitions intersect in momentous historical periods.

JARMAI ZIZA (JULIUS CAESAR) AND *MAKAU (MACBETH)*

From the sixteenth to the nineteenth centuries, the area known today as Northern Nigeria witnessed many wars, from the campaigns of Queen Amina, the jihadist wars, and, of course, present-day insurgencies. There is therefore a fascination borne out of apprehension with the place of wars and warriors within the region. Baba-Ahmed's reflections on this may have influenced his choice of *Macbeth* and *Julius Caesar* for translation into Hausa. Only two writers from Northern Nigeria, Ibrahim Yaro Yahaya and Mahmoon Baba-Ahmed, are known to have translated Shakespeare's plays into Hausa.[17]

This section of the chapter is interested in Baba-Ahmed's translative process in *Makau* and *Jarmai Ziza*, two of his three Shakespearean texts in translation available to the public.

There are no known critical works on the translations of Shakespeare's writings into Hausa by Mahmoon Baba-Ahmed. However, from a careful examination of the translations themselves, as well as from the words of the author in several interviews, we are able to gain some insight into his translative process. In an interview with Ibraheem Hamza Muhammad of the *Daily Trust Newspaper* published on December 29, 2013, Baba-Ahmed briefly attempts to outline his engagement with translation into Hausa, especially his translation of Shakespeare's plays. To the question of how he became an author, he answers:

> It is for the interest of improving the Hausa Literature. I had also written many books
> in Hausa and some were direct translations of the famous works of the English Man
> William Shakespeare as *Macbeth, Julius Caesar* and *Romeo and Juliet.* Macbeth in
> Hausa I called Makau, all the characters in the book were given local names. Julius
> Caesar was Jarmai Ziza. Jarmai in Hausa means a brave warrior, and Ziza means
> a beautiful girl. All these attributes is why I have all these names. Makau is Macbeth,
> Duncan who was the King of Scotland is Dannau, Danco [Banquo] is Dankau. This
> is to guide any reader to understand when compared with the original book.[18]

It is hard to understand the idea of *Jarmai* (brave warrior) and *Ziza* (beautiful girl) being used together, as the name suggests, since at no time are we told that the main character is female. Indeed, ordinarily it would seem awkward to combine *Jarmai* with *Ziza* as a translation for *Julius Caesar*; however, there might be a cultural sub-text to this nomenclature. The name might not be unconnected to Baba-Ahmed's familiarity with the legend of Queen Amina of Zazzau, a warrior queen who lived in the mid-sixteenth century and ruled for about 30 years at a time when the society was male dominated. Indeed, like Julius Caesar, she was considered an individual with great supernatural powers. She is believed to have maintained power through sorcery and divination. In fact, it was said that she chose not to marry and killed off every lover the morning after consorting with them. How Queen Amina died is shrouded in mystery. While some accounts indicate she might have died by enemy hand in battle, other accounts indicate she might have been assassinated by one of her own soldiers who loathed the idea of fighting for a woman. Either way, the legend of her fighting prowess has outlived her in a society that is even more patriarchal than it was in her time.

Mahmoon Baba-Ahmed's coinage of the character's name is unique in the sense that there are no direct word correlations, only appropriations of the names from English to Hausa, though he also attempts to maintain a semblance of tonal fidelity to ensure that readers (especially native Hausa speakers) who have read the English version would easily recognize the close similarities in the Hausa version. Since neither of the words *Julius* nor *Caesar* exists in Hausa, Mahmoon Baba-Ahmed's ingenuity in translating the title of Shakespeare's *Julius Caesar* as *Jarmai Ziza* is quite significant, because it amounts to an approximation of *Julius Caesar* in such a way that the connection to the original text might still be made by readers of English with some competence in the Hausa language. Consequently, the characters Baba-Ahmed adopts for his translations of both *Julius Caesar* and *Macbeth* are phonetically renamed. Perhaps it might be safe to say that the translated text was specifically more targeted at bilingual readers of Shakespeare, even though the collateral advantage is that native speakers of Hausa might have the privilege of an encounter with Shakespeare's work in their own language.

Mahmoon Baba-Ahmed's text makes a point not just to provide a cast of characters, but also to ensure that the cast of characters in the original English version is placed next to the Hausa names in order to facilitate a quick grasp of how characters have been renamed, which is especially helpful for those who have read the English version. *Jarmai Ziza* (*Julius Caesar*) makes use of 33 characters. Baba-Ahmed eliminates many of the minor characters, such as Cato and the generic senators, citizens, guards, attendants, and so forth. Instead of categorizing the characters as Shakespeare has done— for instance, Shakespeare lists Marcus Brutus, Cassius, Casca, Trebonius, Ligarius, Decius Brutus, Metellus Cimber, and Cinna as conspirators against Caesar—Mahmoon Baba-Ahmed provides, in the opening scene, a long preamble to the dialogue which follows. In it, he explains that on a Friday on the fourteenth of the lunar month, a gathering of Ruma (Rome) citizens celebrating Ziza's (Julius Caesar's) triumphant return from war was broken up by Mahari (Marallus) and Fantami (Flavius), two elected officials who were still loyal to Badaru (Pompey), whom Ziza (Julius Caesar) had defeated in battle. They tried to persuade the citizens of their foolishness for preferring Ziza over Badaru and encouraged them to take down the banners on which they had put his name and stop marching in his honor, in order to send a message to Caesar that all was not well in the republic. It is instructive that this preamble situates the setting of the opening scene on a Friday, which many Hausa Muslim people of Northern Nigeria consider to be a holy day.

Whereas in *Macbeth* Shakespeare provides a general description of his characters' identities in the *dramatis personae*, in *Makau* Baba-Ahmed does not. Indeed, perhaps to show the differences between the Hausa emir's court system and the Scottish court in Shakespeare's play, Baba-Ahmed's *Makau* does not accommodate the over 40 members of the cast of characters in the original version; instead, he reduces the cast to about 25 members. Shakespeare's cast has Hecate and the three witches as one character column, but Baba-Ahmed separates them and gives names to each witch, since, in Hausa communities, a witch, or *maye*, is always named. Thus, the witches in *Makau* are not anonymous as they are in Shakespeare's *Macbeth*. Moreover, while in *Macbeth* the witches are supposed to be on errands for Hecate, in Hausa culture a witch is not necessarily associated with evil, but is simply someone with exceptional abilities. Baba-Ahmed's approach to showcase the personality of these witches is perhaps a product of this cultural context.

The challenge in finding equivalent words in Hausa to words in Shakespeare's work can be highlighted by the difficulty Baba-Ahmed had in determining the difference between a soothsayer and a doctor. In English, these two terms are distinct. In both texts, Baba-Ahmed referred to these characters (the Doctor from *Macbeth* and the Soothsayer in *Julius Caesar*) as *Boka*. In traditional Hausa culture, a boka is a traditional healer or medicine man who is responsible for curing physical as well as spiritual diseases. In addition, bokas function as diviners. It is to them that warriors and commoners alike go in order to establish what the future holds. In addition, they possess the capacity for sorcery, which they use to protect their clients by harming their clients' enemies.

The translation of a Western text with its underlying Christian influence into Hausa language, which has largely functioned for several hundred years under Islamic influence, is challenging. It would then seem that these translations attempt to affirm existing cultural practices of the Hausa, such as the place of royalty and loyalty, in the face of a globalizing world that is increasingly Westernized and contemptuous of other people's cultures and ways of life.

CONVERGENCES/DIVERGENCES

In all the three versions of *Macbeth*, *Makau*—Hausa (text), *Aare Akogun*—English and Yoruba (text and performance), and *In iRedu*—Yoruba (film), the character of Macbeth is approached quite differently. Since there is no direct correlation to the name Macbeth in Hausa, Mahmoon Baba-Ahmed elects to "corrupt" the name to Makau; Ogunyemi and Abiola Sobo, on the other hand, take a different approach by electing to name the character of Macbeth based on his profession as a warrior. In the Yoruba language, different dialects often referred to a warrior in different ways. For Ogunyemi, the idea of war features prominently in the naming of Macbeth, so he uses the term *Aare Akogun*, while Abiola Sobo uses the term *Ogagun*, which basically means the same thing (except, of course, for the linguistic difference that guarantees a measure of tonality and musicality, especially when presented on stage). Also, in his adaptation, Abiola Sobo avoids the use of the prefix "*Aare*" which means "chief"; Abiola Sobo could just as well have written Macbeth as *Oga Ogun* ("*Oga*" means "boss") but chooses to match the prefix with the main word to create a single word, which evokes a more powerful image than *Aare Akogun*.

CONCLUSION

Since 2013, when the second burst of translations and adaptations of Shakespeare's plays in Nigeria ended, there has been a chilling lull in efforts to translate Shakespeare into other tongues in Nigeria. Manipulating an original text to convey its message through a different medium in such a way that it resonates both with those conversant with the original text as well as with an audience unfamiliar with Shakespeare requires a lot of skill. For some years now, because of the perceived difficulty, interest has dwindled in the writings of Shakespeare, especially within the school system. This has been worsened by the increasing desire to Africanize the curriculum to include more African writers. Consequently, any effort at translating or adapting Shakespeare as has been done in *Itan Oginintin*, *In iRedu*, *Jarmai Ziza*, and *Makau* must be highly applauded.

NOTES

1. Rebekah Bale, "Shakespeare in Africa," paper presented at the NEH Summer Institute: Shakespeare from the Globe to the Global, Prince Mohammad bin Fahd University, Dhahran, Saudi Arabia, June 5, 2015; Edward Wilson-Lee, *Shakespeare in Swahililand: Adventures with the Ever-Living Poet* (London: HarperCollins, 2016).
2. Linda Mhando, "Comparative African Experiences: Prolific Philosophers," in *The Scholar Between Thought and Experience*, ed. Parviz Morewedge (New York: Global Academic Publishing, 2001), 307.
3. Bale, "Shakespeare in Africa."
4. Alamin M. Mazrui, *English in Africa: After the Cold War* (Clevedon: Multilingual Matters, 2004), 61.
5. Dapo Adelugba, "After the Civil War: Drama," in *European-Language Writing in Sub-Saharan Africa*, vol. 2, ed. Albert S. Gérard (Amsterdam: John Benjamin's Publishing Company, 1986), 772.
6. Olalekan Is'haq Balogun, "Orisa-Shakespeare: A Study of Shakespeare Adaptations Inspired by the Yoruba Tradition," PhD diss. (Victoria University of Wellington, 2017), 1.
7. Julie Sanders, "Creative Exploitation and Talking Back," in *Shakespeare Beyond English: A Global Experiment*, ed. Susan Bennett and Christie Carson (Cambridge: Cambridge University Press, 2013).
8. Mark Hudson, "Globe to Globe: The Winter's Tale, Shakespeare's Globe," theartsdesk.com, May 27, 2012.
9. In traditional Yoruba society, hunters were the elite. The society depended on them not just for food but also for security and intelligence. See Kayode Ayobami Adeduntan, "Texts and Contexts of Yoruba Hunter's Narrative Performance," PhD diss. (University of Ibadan, Ibadan, Nigeria, 2009), 1–2.
10. Esu, often written as Eshu, Elegba, or Legba, is a trickster god identified with the Yoruba people in Nigeria. See Britannica, "Eshu," accessed September 2, 2020, https://www.britannica.com/topic/Eshu.

11. James Bọdé Agbájé, "Proverbs: A Strategy for Resolving Conflict in Yorùbá Society," *Journal of African Cultural Studies* 15, no. 2 (December 2002), 237.
12. Wole Soyinka has captured this understanding clearly in his discussion of the fourth stage of human existence. He proposes that life, death, and rebirth are three stages of existence, but not the most important; the most important for him is the fourth stage, which is the stage of transition between the three mentioned stages. See Wole Soyinka, *Myth Literature and the African World* (Cambridge: Cambridge University Press, 1976).
13. Balogun, "Orisa-Shakespeare," 84.
14. Balogun, "Orisa-Shakespeare," 84.
15. Wole Oguntokun, "Yoruba Winter's Tale at William Shakespeare's Globe Theatre," *Vanguard*, June 21, 2012.
16. Section 210 of the Criminal Code, Cap C38 of the Laws of the Federal Republic of Nigeria.
17. Ibrahim Yaro Yahaya's translation of *Twelfth Night*, titled *Daren Sha Biyu*, was published in 1971. See Ibrahim Yaro Yahaya, *Daren Sha Biyu* (Zaria: Northern Nigerian Publishing Company, 1971).
18. Ibraheem Hamza Muhammad, interview with Mahmoon Baba-Ahmed, *Daily Trust Newspaper*, December 29, 2013.

REFERENCES

Adeduntan, Kayode Ayobami. "Texts and Contexts of Yoruba Hunter's Narrative Performance." PhD dissertation, University of Ibadan, Ibadan, Nigeria, 2009.
Adelugba, Dapo. "After the Civil War: Drama." In *European-Language Writing in Sub-Saharan Africa*, volume 2, edited by Albert S. Gérard, 770–80. Amsterdam: John Benjamin's Publishing Company, 1986.
Agbájé, James Bọdé. "Proverbs: A Strategy for Resolving Conflict in Yorùbá Society." *Journal of African Cultural Studies* 15, no. 2 (December 2002): 237–43. https://www.jstor.org/stable/3181419.
Baba-Ahmed, Mahmoon. *Jarmai Ziza Fassarar littafin Julius Caesar na Williams Shakespear*. Kaduna: Garkuwa Publications, 2012.
Baba-Ahmed, Mahmoon. *Makau Fassarar littafin Macbeth na Williams Shakespear*. Kaduna: Garkuwa Publications, 2009.
Bale, Rebekah. "Shakespeare in Africa." Paper presented at the NEH Summer Institute: Shakespeare from the Globe to the Global, Prince Mohammad bin Fahd University, Dhahran, Saudi Arabia, June 5, 2015.
Balogun, Olalekan Is'haq. "Orisa-Shakespeare: A Study of Shakespeare Adaptations Inspired by the Yoruba Tradition." PhD dissertation, Victoria University of Wellington, 2017.
Britannica. "Eshu." Accessed September 2, 2020. https://www.britannica.com/topic/Eshu.
Hudson, Mark. "Globe to Globe: The Winter's Tale, Shakespeare's Globe." theartsdesk.com, May 27, 2012.
Ipadeola, Tade. "Itan Oginintin." Unpublished playscript, 2012.
Johnson, E. T. *Iwe ere (Play) Ti Julius Caesar ti Shakespeare kọ ti a yipada si Ede Yoruba lati ọwọ alufa, ọga agba ile-iwe New High Class School, Eko, Nigeria*. Lagos: Tika-Tore Press, 193? [year of publication unknown].

Mazrui, Alamin M. *English in Africa: After the Cold War*. Clevedon: Multilingual Matters, 2004.

Mhando, Linda. "Comparative African Experiences: Prolific Philosophers." In *The Scholar Between Thought and Experience: A Biographical Festschrift in Honor of Ali A. Mazrui*, edited by Parviz Morewedge, 303–26. New York: Global Academic Publishing, 2001.

Oguntokun, Wole. "Yoruba Winter's Tale at William Shakespeare's Globe Theatre." *Vanguard*, June 21, 2012.

Ogunyemi, Wale. *Aare Akogun*. Lagos: Nigeria Magazine, 1969.

Osofisan, Femi. *Love's Unlike Lading: A Comedy From Shakespeare*. Ile-Ife: Ife Performance Circle, 2007.

Osofisan, Femi. *Wesoo, Hamlet! Or The Resurrection of Hamlet*. Lagos: Concept Publications Ltd, 2012.

Sanders, Julie. "Creative Exploitation and Talking Back." In *Shakespeare Beyond English: A Global Experiment*, edited by Susan Bennett and Christie Carson, 241–50. Cambridge: Cambridge University Press, 2013. doi:10.1017/CBO9781139629119 .040.

Shakespeare, William. *Julius Caesar*. In *The Complete Works of William Shakespeare*, 361–77. Glasgow: The Gresham Publishing Company, 2001.

Shakespeare, William. *Macbeth*. In *The Complete Works of William Shakespeare*, 521–36. Glasgow: The Gresham Publishing Company, 2001.

Shakespeare, William. *The Winter's Tale*. In *The Complete Works of William Shakespeare*, 641–61. Glasgow: The Gresham Publishing Company, 2001.

Sobo, Abiola. *In iRedu*. NU Independent Pictures in association with Blacreek Pictures, 2013. YouTube video, 15:20 min. https://www.youtube.com/watch?v= -enQeP_VVsg.

Soyinka, Wole. *Myth Literature and the African World*. Cambridge: Cambridge University Press, 1976.

Wilson-Lee, Edward. *Shakespeare in Swahililand: Adventures with the Ever-Living Poet*. London: HarperCollins, 2016.

Yahaya, Ibrahim Yaro. *Daren Sha Biyu*. Zaria: Northern Nigerian Publishing Company, 1971.

Yerima, Ahmed. *Otaelo*. Ibadan: Kraft Books, 2000.

Epilogue: *The Art of the De'ill*

Raphael Seligmann

---

1. A PERFECT CONVERSATION

From NSA intercepts, 2014, redacted.

S███:   I would like you to do us a favor, though.

M███████:   At your service, Sir. Eternally.

S███:   Key Performance Indicators topside are trending the wrong way: war down, democracy up, hunger down, life expectancy up, and global connectedness starting to form a universal human identity. I need you to help me turn things around.

M███████:   But you're fine if you just wait a bit. Greenhouse gas emissions higher every year, four degrees of warming by the end of the century. Droughts, wildfires, ocean acidification, coastal flooding, mass migration, civil unrest, martial law, novel pandemics, and prehistoric diseases from thawing permafrost will solve your problems for you.

S███:   Not waiting. First of all, I'm an immediate-gratification kind of guy. Second, I don't trust the topsiders not to adapt. They're already talking about terraforming and hydro-engineering, floating cities, drought-resistant hybrids, and an Arctic breadbasket. Third, climate change is too impersonal for my taste. What's my motto?

M███████:   "Our greatest resource is our people." Words to live by.

S███:   I want to put a human face on their calamity. As you know, I'm a Great-Man-theory kind of guy. You said it yourself: violent change in civil institutions must be achieved by a great prince acting alone. So, about that favor I mentioned. I need you to design me a leader who can shatter all these institutions, compacts, doctrines, and dreams that retard the march of chaos across the globe. Since you get that people are both rational and prone to evil, you will equip him with such qualities that once I place him topside he'll acquire a mass following of unshakeable devotion who will readily discard principles they once held dear and restraints they formerly respected in order to further his destructive mission, not knowing or caring that he acts only to satisfy his own appetites. And mine.

M: But you know how I hate chaos and corruption. Why would I help you grow the evils I want to curb?

S: You've been doing exactly that for the past 500 years. Surely you know your reputation topside. And don't tell me they all miss the point about ends and means. You've been wearing my jersey ever since you startled peddling that "cruelty well used" and "necessary evil" junk. Everyone but you smells the pitch in your pitch. Hell, they call me Old Nick after *you*. So don't go all *non serviam*-y on me.

M: Alright. I've got no place else to go.

S: Good. You'll present your design to the Board of Tartarustees. If we like it, we'll fast-track it for delivery topside. Put away the ink pen. Here's a Kindle Fire loaded with SulfurPoint. It makes slides as dull as PowerPoint, and it's just as frustrating to use, plus you can add smells for emphasis—burning flesh, sulfur, plague breath. Keeps the Board in their comfort zone.

M: Is it connected to the Infernet?

S: Hell no. Do you think I'd trust you not to leak?

M: Come on! There hasn't been a leak from down here since 1320. Besides, I'd never get anything proprietary through the Firewall.

S: Basta, Nicco! Here's a copy of The Manual. I want you to refer to it religiously. In it you'll find every type of folly and vice to include, as well as every human virtue to avoid.

2. TED TALK

Slides and excerpt from audio transcript: source uncertain. Date uncertain, likely 2014.

Fortunately, The Manual contains some promising raw material. We have a partial model in King Richard III—the "troubler of the poor world's peace." However, as this slide shows, Richard's qualities are necessary but not sufficient for our strategy.

Let's go down the list. First and foremost, Richard tramples norms of behavior. His come-on to Lady Anne is revealing. He does not deny her assertion that he "knows no laws of God nor of man." What's more, he revels in his

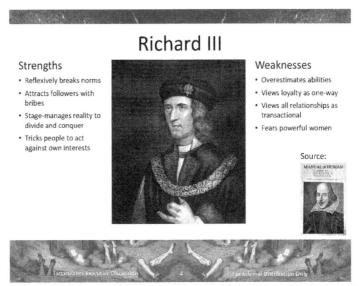

Note: images in the PowerPoint slides of Richard III, Henry V, and the sufferers in Hell (Gustave Doré graphic) are licensed to the author from Shutterstock.com.

Figure 13.1　Machiavelli TED Talk slide 1

transgressions, crowing, "Was ever woman in this humour wooed? / Was ever woman in this humour won?" Note that celebrating innovation is as important topside as it is down here.

Next, he has a knack for finding men willing to assist in his most transgressive enterprises, from violating sanctuary to murder. With these men, a simple quid pro quo usually stifles any lingering moral qualms. And when a wholesale approach to influence building is needed, Richard creates fictions that exploit the crowd's hopes and fears. For instance, after the rival princes have been killed, imprisoned, or delegitimized, he and his accomplices stage a scene of patriotic pleading and pious reluctance designed to win the acceptance of the London populace. Richard's most characteristic form of reality doctoring, however, is the false conspiracy. Time after time, he hides his own plots using baseless, yet minimally plausible, claims of other parties' perfidy. I counted eleven instances of this tactic in The Manual's account, each one successful.

Through such means, Richard gets people to act against their own interest, often with fatal consequences. As old Queen Margaret warns Queen Elizabeth: "Thou whet'st a knife to kill thy self." I mentioned the wooing of Lady Anne. Another instance is the fate of the Lord Chamberlain, Hastings. Despite having just seen three fellow courtiers executed on trumped-up charges, Hastings ostentatiously displays his loyalty to Richard when wiser men keep their heads down. This gives Richard the opportunity to seize on Hastings's one moment of hesitation and make public support of killing him a required demonstration of everyone else's loyalty. In terms of our project, you can see the value of knowing how to simultaneously leverage individual vulnerability and stoke collective bloodlust.

Let's take stock for a minute. Obviously, Richard achieved a lot with these qualities. In Queen Elizabeth's words, he turned England into a slaughter-house. And clearly, his heart was in the right place, as Margaret understood when she called him "that foul defacer of God's handiwork" and "hell's black intelligencer." We can take Richard at his own word in his promise to lead his troops "if not to heaven, then hand in hand to hell." Yet good intentions are not enough, even if the road to us is paved with them. Peace was soon restored, a result far short of Elizabeth's vision: "I see, as in a map, the end of all."

Moving on to the debit side, I propose four reasons why Richard's success was not sustainable. First, he overestimates his power to bend circumstances to his will: "My counsel is my shield … The King's name is a tower of strength," etc. This common enough foible causes him to dispense with planning and strategy—creating confusion, yes, but not the universal kind we seek. Second, he views loyalty as something owed to him, but otherwise without value. This renders his power brittle, as expressed by one of his enemies: "He hath no friends but what are friends for fear, / Which in his dearest need will fly from him." A third, related weakness is his purely transactional view of all human relationships, which only works when you have something others want and the ability to deliver it. Otherwise, you end up absurdly attempting to trade notional kingdoms for real horses.

The fourth reason is a bit less obvious: a fear of powerful women. Misogyny is found in the toolbox of most leaders, useful for instance in rousing insecure men to violence. But with Richard it is personal and self-defeating. Able to feign patriotism and even religious devotion, he cannot hide his loathing of women. With no way to enlist them on his side, Richard must instead spend energy trying to contain and defame them. Just how serious a blind spot he has regarding women is seen when he presses Elizabeth to make her daughter his bride using an argument sure to win over any mother: having killed her sons, he can make amends by impregnating her daughter. Not surprisingly, the queen rushes off to make a marriage deal with Richard's nemesis.

So, we're off to a promising start, but need to tweak the prototype before we can achieve transformational results. Fortunately, The Manual shows us another ruler whose strengths we can leverage and whose weaknesses we can avoid.

Never mind that students of The Manual often think of Henry as the "good" ruler and Richard the "bad" one. The two are much closer than you'd think.

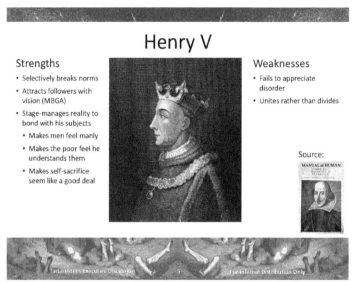

Note: images in the PowerPoint slides of Richard III, Henry V, and the sufferers in Hell (Gustave Doré graphic) are licensed to the author from Shutterstock.com.

Figure 13.2   Machiavelli TED Talk slide 2

Henry's chief qualities overlap with and improve on Richard's. Consider their relations to norms of conduct. Where Richard reflexively delights in outrageousness ("I am determined to prove a villain"), Henry uses it selectively to strengthen his position. To demoralize the French, he poses as a remorseless, atheistic war criminal and later slaughters prisoners in flagrant violation of chivalry, bringing about both a truce and an advantageous marriage. If you look past the distasteful words "truce" and "marriage," it's apparent that controlled norm breaking changes the status quo better than across-the-board villainy.

Next, consider how both men attract their followers. While Richard appeals mainly to "discontented gentlemen" with promises of individual preferment and score settling, Henry captivates a diverse cohort of men with visions of glory. Both rulers exploit a similar dynamic of wish fulfillment, but with Henry it surpasses the transactional and becomes a matter of national pride: making Britain great again. With respect to our objectives, that's a decisive improvement in reach and sustainability.

Compared to Richard, Henry deploys illusion-making techniques in a more sophisticated, comprehensive way. Whereas Richard launches short-term schemes to make himself seem more virtuous to whomever he's with at the moment, Henry spends years living as a wastrel in order to establish a convincing narrative of moral growth and awakened responsibility. Not only do Henry's fictions serve his image-making strategy, they also serve as force multipliers, binding his subjects *en masse* to his success. Richard's signature trick is to frighten and divide with illusions of hidden treachery; Henry's is to reassure and unify with illusions of commonality. One classic Henry illusion is using words and gestures to project his vigor and wholeness onto aging, broken, or tired bodies, a symbolic testosterone boost. Another is to erase the often-huge differences of social status between himself and the troops, conjuring the fantasy of a classless meritocracy: "We few, we happy few, we band of brothers."

Now here's the thing: follow Henry and you're almost as likely to end up discarded or dead as if you had followed Richard. Once Falstaff is no longer useful to provide an air of *dis*respectability, Henry rejects him with gratuitous cruelty. In Henry's foreign policy, following his father's advice, he makes war to distract his subjects, not to protect them. The main difference between Richard's victims and Henry's is that the former curse the author of their fate while the latter bless him. Right after claiming that Henry's rejection was the cause of Falstaff's death, his friend Nim says, "The King is a good king, but it must be as it may." Upon being arrested, the conspirators Scrope, Cambridge, and Gray seem to compete with one another in publicly thanking the king for their punishment. For his part, Henry does not miss the opportunity to frame their death sentence as not only just, but patriotic. This is the practical effect of the shift from transaction to ideology I just mentioned. When the subjects, without irony, cry, "God for Harry! England and Saint George!" self-abasement and self-sacrifice become status symbols.

Of course, Henry has his flaws. He acts uninterested in the disorder his qualities could unleash. The last words spoken by him in The Manual are "May our oaths well kept and prosp'rous be." Read that flabby paean to complacency in light of The Manual's first description of Henry and grieve for the potential left unfulfilled: "Then should the warlike Harry, like himself, /Assume the port of Mars, and at his heels, / Leashed in like hounds, should famine, sword, and fire / Crouch for employment."

So, judging things by their results—which I've long said is all that matters—Richard vs. Henry comes out a wash: peace and unity win out both times. A twofold tale of missed opportunities. Richard of Gloucester got the better of his adversaries up until the end, but the end was preordained because he never bothered to found a Gloucester-*ism* that others could live within and use to justify their sacrifices. Meanwhile, Henry V built a following so devoted that they'd lay down their lives for his territorial aims rebranded as the nation's destiny, but he never bothered to channel that zeal into anything more than inspirational myths of common purpose.

"All is vanity," agreeth our CEO and the Other Guy. Is that the point? No, Gentlefiends of the Board, the transitory nature of chaos is *not* our take-away. The Manual points to a clear path forward.

Here's a thought experiment. Imagine, in a single person, the troublemaking brilliance of a Richard combined with the visionary mass appeal of a Henry. Or to put it more precisely, what would happen if we took Richard's ability to stir up momentary individual resentment and added Henry's ability to stir up long-term tribal feeling?

This new creature would stir up *long-term tribal resentment*.

For now, we'll call our prototype creature the Stable Genius. *Stable* not because of any inward constancy or composure—far from necessary qualities—but because of the way he'll institutionalize strife as a constant of future existence. And *genius* not because of any superior cognitive aptitude or imagination, but because of his unique ability to exploit fissures among his fellow humans.

Now let's look at just how much transformation—*damage* from the topside perspective—our Stable Genius might cause. The bullet list on the slide shows some of the characteristics the Genius, and by extension, the nation under his influence would possess.

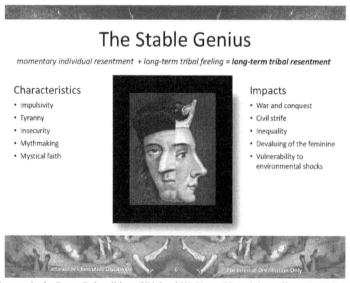

Note: images in the PowerPoint slides of Richard III, Henry V, and the sufferers in Hell (Gustave Doré graphic) are licensed to the author from Shutterstock.com.

Figure 13.3   Machiavelli TED Talk slide 3

Impulsivity—The Genius casts Richard-like "me-first" misbehaviors as Henry-like "nation-first" acts of collective self-preservation. Following his lead, instances of thoughtless grasping and lashing out can always be excused, whether in interpersonal relations or national foreign policy. Best of all, these behaviors create self-perpetuating, escalating cycles of grievance demanding retribution.

Tyranny—Driven by an impulse to divide and conquer, the Genius incites divisions within the nation à la Richard, then, à la Henry, promotes his faction's agenda as the will of the people. This process is nation building in reverse: a deliberate fostering of tribalism. Tribes have membership requirements that inspire constant policing, so anxiety about purity and subversion leads to segregation, harsh punishment, and the suspension of liberties. Cycles of resentment occur as tyranny becomes the go-to expedient of the formerly oppressed once the tables are turned.

It's important not to assume that a trait must be avoided just because it proved counterproductive to a ruler in The Manual. As long as the negative effects of that trait can be offset by the positive effects of a trait from the other ruler, the first trait can be useful in the Genius. For instance, Richard's one-way notion of loyalty cost him many of his closest followers, but lack of reciprocity stops being a problem under the Henrician premise that the leader embodies the will of the people.

Insecurity—Insecure himself, the Genius defensively instills insecurity in his followers. The identification of leader with nation helps accelerate and institutionalize this insecurity. If loyalty to the Genius is a measure of love of the homeland, the political and psychological risks of opposing him rise sharply, along with anxiety about whether one can ever show sufficient devotion. This insecurity is a useful deterrent against followers' ambitions when reinforced by regular public humiliations and punishments over perceived disloyalty.

Mythmaking and **Mystical Faith**—The Genius, shielded by tribal bonds and induced insecurities, eventually folds every one of his characteristics into the myth of his specialness. This applies even to highly unproductive Ricardian traits like misogyny. For the Genius, mistreating women serves the myth as a sign of his strength, useful for impressing young men and other authoritarian leaders. For his followers, misogyny helps them cover up their insecurities while displaying their allegiance to the Genius.

Once the myth of the Genius takes hold, the supporting illusions harden into accepted truths. Imaginary threats and exaggerated triumphs become much harder to debunk—especially when buttressed by spectacles of power, such as official investigations of predecessors and rivals, forced testimonials from leading scientists, or the use of law enforcement to incite and then crush unrest.

Before long, some followers discern the workings of providence in the Genius's deeds. This is tremendously helpful to our cause because their faith widens the gap between adherents and skeptics and attaches apocalyptic stakes to every dispute.

The bullets on the slide outline what these characteristics might do to the nation and the world. Leaders adopt the Genius's tactics and reflexes as their own. Some rise to absolute power, remaking their nations' values in the image of the Genius. Wars break out as international alliances crumble under nation-firstism, and impulsive adventures replace grand strategy. Inequality grows as the strong dispossess the weak, breeding mass migration, mass incarceration, and mass revolt. Humane priorities and modes of policymaking that can be labeled feminine (most anything that's not zero-sum) are discontinued or left untried. Mythmaking and mystical faith prevent effective response to natural disaster and climate change, further increasing inequality and conflict. In this environment, a small disturbance, such as an infectious disease, could wreak outsize havoc.

In short, the Stable Genius project promises immediate return on investment and steadily increasing snareholder value for a long time to come. With that, I'm ready to take your questions.

3.   INTO PRODUCTION

Fragment from NSA intercept, May 2015, redacted.

S█████:   Alecto, call Speer in Design.
Feminine PDA voice: Calling Speer in Design.
S█████:   How are you coming along on the escalator? We're going to need it topside next month for the launch. Don't hold back. Think of what your last boss would have wanted and then go bigger.
A████ S█████:   ██
████████████
S█████:   Good, make it so. Alecto, call Vladimir.

NOTES

1.   A Perfect Conversation

At your service, Sir. Eternally: The intercept's mysterious M can be tentatively identified as the living spirit of Niccolò Machiavelli (1469–1527), historian, playwright, and Florentine bureaucrat. Machiavelli is best known as the author of *The Prince*, a manual intended to help newly installed rulers win friends and influence people. M's answer to his boss's summons may provide some hints as to the identity of the boss, S, the location of the encounter, and the relationship between the two figures. Focusing on M's use of the word *eternally*, analysts suspect the response may be tongue-in-cheek, alluding to Machiavelli's posthumous reputation as a follower of Satan. M may even be ruefully signaling that he knows this reputation gave rise to the image of a demonic mischief-maker called the Machiavell—the role S seems to have tapped him to play. Machiavelli's bad reputation and the resulting caricatures arose from his seemingly uncritical endorsement of cruel and duplicitous tactics and from the absence of recognizable Christian morality in his advice on getting and keeping power. However, keen-eyed readers have long suspected hidden ironies undercut that advice, prompting readings of his works as cryptic arguments for justice and limited government. The intercepts transcribed here unfortunately fail to settle the debate.

War down: https://slides.ourworldindata.org/war-and-violence/#/6

Democracy up: https://ourworldindata.org/democracy

Hunger down: https://ourworldindata.org/famines

Life expectancy up: https://ourworldindata.org/life-expectancy

Global connectedness starting to form a universal human identity: Khanna, *Connectography*, xvi, 383

Four degrees of warming: www.climateactiontracker.org

They're already talking about terraforming: Khanna, *Connectography* 255–6

Great-Man-theory kind of guy: The Great Man theory is a framework for understanding history, which holds that individuals of exceptional will or charisma shape the world more than impersonal factors such as social movements, natural phenomena, or technological change. The idea was first articulated shortly after the Napoleonic wars, though its individualistic outlook is implicit in the earliest legends of hero liberators, lawgivers, and empire builders. No surprise that S espouses the Great Man theory, considering the many theological and literary portrayals of his own influence. In *Paradise Lost*, for instance, the prospect of Great Manhood is a salve for Satan's wounded pride: after being expelled from heaven, he looks forward to a second act as ruler of "more than half" the earth "as Man ere long, and this new World shall know" (Milton, *Paradise Lost*, Book IV, lines 112–13).

Violent change in civil institutions must be achieved by a great prince acting alone: Machiavelli, *The Prince*, 132; see also De Grazia, *Machiavelli in Hell*, 235.

But you know I hate chaos and corruption: Here M seems to play off the views of the historical Machiavelli against the nihilism of the Machiavel figure. See De Grazia, *Machiavelli in Hell*, 271, on a strain of moralism running through Machiavelli's writings: "He rails against personal ambition, greed, envy, ingratitude, and their outcome—civil division, weakness, war, defeat, loss of freedom and the common good, in short, a world out of joint." But in the intercept, is M really taking a stand for good government, or is he just trying to get out of an assignment he doesn't want to do? As critic Erica Benner writes in *The Guardian*, March 3, 2017, "Machiavelli's writings speak in different voices at different times."

Since you get that people are both rational and prone to evil: See De Grazia, *Machiavelli in Hell*, 268: "All men know that they should put the common good above the private good ... But they are not so inclined."

The point about ends and means: Machiavelli never said the ends justify the means, but he comes close with lines like "It is a sound maxim that reprehensible actions may be justified by their effects" (*Discourses*, I.9). He qualifies such remarks in various ways and often palms them off as the perspective of "the many." Such rhetorical dodges did not deter critics from tying him to the view that results are the only things that matter.

That "cruelty well used" and "necessary evil" junk: See De Grazia, *Machiavelli in Hell*, 305–6, 296.

So don't go all non serviam-*y on me*: In Roman Catholic lore, the phrase *non serviam* (Latin for "I will not serve") is attributed to Satan as he declares his rebellion against God. By attaching the phrase to M, S shows he too has a sly sense of humor.

Board of Tartarustees: In the classical tradition, Tartarus is the lowest point in the world. It is where the defeated Titans were imprisoned. In some Christian commentaries, it is the pit into which the fallen angels who followed Satan were thrown.

Every type of folly and vice ... every human virtue: Analysts have determined that The Manual is the works of William Shakespeare. S's recommendation of it is in sync with his endorsement of the Great Man theory and aligns him with hero-worshipping critics like Harold Bloom, who wrote that "Shakespeare will go on explaining us, in part because he invented us" (Bloom, *Shakespeare: The Invention of the Human*, xviii).

2.   TED Talk

Unless otherwise indicated, all references in this section are to *William Shakespeare: The Complete Works*, ed. Stanley Wells and Gary Taylor (Oxford: Oxford University Press, 1988). *R3* is *Richard III*, *2H4* is *2 Henry IV*, and *H5* is *Henry V*.

Troubler of the poor world's peace. (*R3* 1.3.218)
Knows no laws of God nor of man. (*R3* 1.2.70)

Was ever woman in this humour wooed? / Was ever woman in this humour won? (*R3* 1.2.215–16)

He and his accomplices stage a scene of patriotic pleading and pious reluctance. (*R3* 3.7) When the citizens of London seem unenthusiastic about accepting Richard Gloucester as their king, he pretends that he doesn't want to rule and wants only to spend his days in pious meditation. This trick of reverse psychology has the desired effect, stimulating the crowd's appetite to see him crowned.

I counted eleven instances of this tactic: (1) "Prophecy" about Clarence blamed on Lady Gray (*R3* 1.1.38–40). (2) "Lies well seeled with weighty arguments" to King Edward against Clarence (*R3* 1.1.147–8). (3) Claims to Anne he was provoked by Queen Margaret to kill Prince Edward (*R3* 1.2.97). (4) Accuses Elizabeth of persecuting Clarence (*R3* 1.3.78–82). (5) Blames Queen Elizabeth for stirring Edward against Clarence (*R3* 1.3.130–1). (6) Blames "guilty kindred of the Queen" for Clarence being killed (*R3* 2.1.93–137). (7) Has Rivers, Gray, and Vaughn arrested for conspiracy (*R3* 2.4). (8) Accuses Queen Elizabeth and Jane Shore of bewitching him (*R3* 3.4.60–1). (9) Stages an insurrection to justify beheading Hastings, then claims overzealous supporters killed him (*R3* 3.5.14–22). (10) Delegitimizes the young princes (*R3* 3.5.71–3). (11) Pretends to be afraid of the Lord Mayor and citizens ("He fears, my lord, you mean no good to him") (*R3* 3.7.87).

Thou whet'st a knife to kill thy self. (*R3* 1.3.242)

Foul defacer of God's handiwork. (*R3* 4.1.51)

Hell's black intelligencer. (*R3* 4.1.71)

If not to heaven, then hand in hand to hell. (*R3* 5.6.42–3)

I see, as in a map, the end of all. (*R3* 2.4.53)

My counsel is my shield ... The King's name is a tower of strength. (*R3* 4.3.56, 5.3.12)

He hath no friends but what are friends for fear, / Which in his dearest need will fly from him. (*R3* 5.2.20–1)

Otherwise, you end up absurdly attempting to trade notional kingdoms for real horses. (*R3* 5.7.7, 5.7.13)

Just how serious a blind spot he has regarding women. (*R3* 4.4.242–361)

I am determined to prove a villain. (*R3* 1.1.30)

To demoralize the French, he poses as a remorseless, atheistic war criminal: As in Henry's threats to the governor of Harfleur: "What is't to me, when you yourselves are cause, / If your pure maidens fall into the hand / Of hot and forcing violation?" (*H5* 3.3.19–21)

While Richard appeals mainly to "discontented gentlemen." (*R3* 4.2.37)

A matter of national pride, making Britain great again: Perhaps that last phrase is the otherwise baffling "MBGA" in M's slide. Henry is pointedly advised by his counselors that he needs to replenish England's prestige by winning a victory over France as great as the English win at Crècy sixty years earlier (*H5* 1.2).

A symbolic testosterone boost: In a remarkable gesture, Henry takes a cloak from a feeble old officer to make the man feel the cold more keenly and thus feel more alive (*H5* 4.1). In his St. Crispin's day speech, Henry explicitly tells his troops that other men will "hold their manhoods cheap" compared to them (H5 4.3.66).

We few, we happy few, we band of brothers. (*H5* 4.3.60) Henry knows his scenario of a classless brotherhood-in-arms is a fiction. After the battle of Agincourt, when he calls out the casualties on the English side, he reads off the names of four knights and adds, "None else of name" (*H5* 4.8.105). So much for all the soldiers being remembered "to the ending of the world," as Henry promised before the battle (*H5* 4.3.59).

In Henry's foreign policy, following his father's advice: See Henry IV's advice to Prince Harry: "Be it thy course to busy giddy minds / With foreign quarrels" (*2H4* 4.3.342–3)

The King is a good king, but it must be as it may. (*H5* 2.1.20)

God for Harry! England and Saint George. (*H5* 3.1.34)

May our oaths well kept and prosp'rous be. (*H5* 5.2.369)

Then should the warlike Harry ... /Crouch for employment. (*H5* Prologue 5–8)

So, judging things by their results. (Machiavelli, *The Prince*, p. 132.)

3.   Into Production

Alecto, call Speer in Design: Analysts suggest that S uses a knock-off of Amazon's personal data assistant Alexa. In Greek mythology, Alecto was one of the three Furies sent by the gods to punish mortals. Speer is possibly the living spirit of Hitler's architect Albert Speer (1905–81), who was largely responsible for the distinctive look of Nazi buildings and urban design.

REFERENCES

Benner, Erica. "Have We Got Machiavelli All Wrong?" *The Guardian*, March 3, 2017. https://www.theguardian.com/books/2017/mar/03/have-we-got-machiavelli -all-wrong.

Bloom, Harold. *Shakespeare: The Invention of the Human*. New York: Penguin Putnam, 1998.

De Grazia, Sebastian. *Machiavelli in Hell*. New York: Vintage Books, 1989.

Khanna, Parag. *Connectography*. London: Weidenfeld & Nicholson, 2016.

Machiavelli, Niccolò. *The Prince*. Translated by Luigi Ricci. Revised by E. R. P. Vincent. New York: New American Library, 1952.

Machiavelli, Niccolò. *The Discourses*. Edited by Bernard Crick. Translated by Leslie J. Walker. London: Penguin Books, 1983.

Milton, John. *Paradise Lost*. Edited by Northrop Frye. New York: Holt, Rinehart and Winston, 1951.

Shakespeare, William. *William Shakespeare: The Complete Works*. Edited by Stanley Wells and Gary Taylor. Oxford: Oxford University Press, 1988.

POST-SCRIPT

An Interview between the editors and "M" over FiendBook Messenger, July 27, 2020.

[July 27, 2020 at 00:00:01 AM] Kristin Bezio:
Thank you so much, M, for agreeing to meet with us. We've stumbled upon an extraordinary transcript from back in 2014 which seems to suggest your involvement in a very deep state conspiracy behind our current political crisis in leadership. Before getting into the details of the transcript, we'd like to ask you about your background, especially your expertise in leadership. What makes you an authority?

[July 27, 2020 at 00:06:34 AM] Unknown:
I thought that we agreed not to talk about that! Finito! We're done here!

[July 27, 2020 at 00:07:21 AM] Unknown:
Alright, alright. What've I got to lose? What makes me an authority? Let's see. First of all, longevity. Most political consultants last a campaign or two. But me, as the Rolling Stones sang about my boss, "I've been around for a long, long year." Given that, and my future prospects, I take the long view. Second, reading, a whole lot of reading. Mostly the classics: ancient historians and philosophers. Third, observation. I've gotten up close and personal with a lot of statesmen, brigands, statesman-brigands. Finally, hands-on experience with the workings of government, from leading troops to being trussed up like a turkey and dropped repeatedly from a great height.

[July 27, 2020 at 00:09:05 AM] Kristin Bezio:
Fair enough, I suppose. In the transcript, the mysterious S seems to be a fan of Great Man theory. Your experience suggests that you've had some contact with so-called "Great Men" over the years. What is your opinion?

[July 27, 2020 at 00:09:50 AM] Unknown:
My opinion is my opinion doesn't matter. Every one of my employers imagines he's the Great Man bending the world to his will. My job is, one, to make him think he can overpower Dame Fortune, the world's true ruler, and, two, to help him convince his subjects that he can. Giving him that boost of confidence

while giving his subjects that dose of awe clears space for the boss to do what he wants to do. How that shakes out—well, it depends.

[July 27, 2020 at 00:11:23 AM] Anthony Russell:
Hmm. You describe yourself as a political consultant and you go by M. Are you Manafort??? Which brings me to another question: Do you think a leader's (or a state's) greatness is about unleashing or governing chaos?

[July 27, 2020 at 00:12:37 AM] Unknown:
Manu fortis = strong hand? Not my style, son. I'm more of a strong will, fortis mente, fellow. We can debate the nature of greatness for longer than your remaining time on earth, which I can check on if you'd like. :-) For this interview, I'd just say that unleashing chaos is a good strategy for regime change; governing chaos is good for regime preservation. Which you choose depends on where your investments lie.

[July 27, 2020 at 00:13:01 AM] Anthony Russell:
Your answer seems to presuppose "chaos" as the starting point—or default—that all leaders must confront. Is that true? Do "the people" they lead or manipulate, or both, naturally tend towards disorder?

[July 27, 2020 at 00:15:12 AM] Unknown:
Since transitioning to my present role, I've learned a lot about cosmic starting and ending points. May write about that one of these millennia. If I can just get beyond the procrastination, a hazard of my present condition. So no spoilers today, sorry. In previous books, I've written that chaos in a nation is a result of human vice. The people are easily corrupted, and that tendency is exploited by rival politicians or awakened by the leader's own vices.

[July 27, 2020 at 00:16:25 AM] Anthony Russell:
What's with the priority given these days by leaders across the world to their hyper-masculinity?

[July 27, 2020 at 00:16:48 AM] Unknown:
Judging from the news that reaches me downside (as we call it), I'd say it's what an ex-doctor I work with calls compensation. I don't mean some kind of personal issues with "small hands." A moment ago, I mentioned vice corrupting the people. Well, I've often said the antidote is virtù, a kind of energy and audacity associated with the young and directed toward the common good. The leaders I see trumpeting their manhood on terravision tend to be lazy, vice-ridden old men trying to compensate for their shortcomings by passing off a blustering, quarrelsome, sexist manner as signs of virtù.

[July 27, 2020 at 00:18:00 AM] Kristin Bezio:
About that term, "sexist" …

[July 27, 2020 at 00:18:04 AM] Unknown:
Before you go "gotcha!" I'll admit I once wrote a very nasty fantasy sequence about ambitious, virtù-driven young men sexually violating Dame Fortune. What can I say? It was a rougher time. I've learned a lot since then. Please don't stop reading me because of that, topsiders, or there'll be no one to write for but

[July 27, 2020 at 00:25:58 AM] Anthony Russell:
M?

[July 27, 2020 at 00:26:13 AM] Anthony Russell:
M?

[July 27, 2020 at 00:27:42 AM] Unknown:
Still here.

[July 27, 2020 at 00:27:51 AM] Anthony Russell:
Four years into the reign of the Stable Genius, what can we topsiders hope will save us from S's plan for endless chaos?

[July 27, 2020 at 00:28:34 AM] Unknown:
You'd better hope I gave S bad advice.

[July 27, 2020 at 00:29:36 AM] Anthony Russell:
So the fate of the world depends on whether you were being ironic about creating the perfect bad leader?

[July 27, 2020 at 00:30:15 AM] Kristin Bezio:
Ironic? Wait a minute! M! Are you? Is it possible that you're actually The Niccolò Machiavelli? The Italian Renaissance political philosopher?

[Connection terminated July 27, 2020 at 00:30:59 AM. A wisp of sulfurous smoke rises from the interviewers' smartphones.]

Index